THE YALE LIBRARY OF MILITARY HISTORY

SPARTA'S SECOND ATTIC WAR

The Grand Strategy of Classical Sparta, 446–418 B.C.

Paul A. Rahe

Yale UNIVERSITY PRESS

New Haven and London

Published with assistance from the Kingsley Trust Association Publication Fund
established by the Scroll and Key Society of Yale College.

Yale University Press books may be purchased in quantity for educational, business,
or promotional use. For information, please e-mail sales.press@yale.edu (U.S. office) or
sales@yaleup.co.uk (U.K. office).

Maps by Bill Nelson.

Set in Minion Roman and Trajan Pro types by Integrated Publishing Solutions.
Printed in the United States of America.

Library of Congress Control Number: 2019953866
ISBN 978-0-300-24262-1 (hardcover : alk. paper)

A catalogue record for this book is available from the British Library.

This paper meets the requirements of ANSI/NISO Z39.48-1992 (Permanence of Paper).

10 9 8 7 6 5 4 3 2 1

Antonia M. Rahe

Treaties are like young girls and roses; they last as long as they last.

CHARLES DE GAULLE

Contents

Maps

Introduction

An Enduring Strategic Rivalry

IT is much easier to initiate a war than to end one. Even when an attempt to do the latter seems, to the unsuspecting glance, to be an unqualified success, it frequently lays the foundations for a renewal of conflict. The origins of the Second Punic War, of the War of the Spanish Succession, and of the Second World War can be found in the armistices and treaties of peace that ended the First Punic War, the War of the League of Augsburg, and the First World War.

In analyzing the first of these examples, the Greek historian Polybius articulated a principle that applies with equal force to all three. "Statesmen," he warned,

> must take heed lest the aims of those breaking off hostilities . . . escape their notice. Above all else, they must ascertain whether those coming to terms have yielded to circumstances or are broken in spirit. In this fashion, they can be constantly on guard against the former, who are apt to be lying in wait for a favorable opportunity, and they may trust in the latter as subjects and true friends and readily call upon them for whatever services occasions demand.

As Polybius implies, if the conditions that initially gave rise to a strategic rivalry persist, that rivalry is almost certain to revive, and a renewal of war may well be the consequence.[1]

Sparta's second Attic war allows us to test Polybius' claim. The peace treaty that brought her first Attic war to an end settled nothing. That contest had had its roots in the fear inspired at Lacedaemon by the dramatic growth in Athenian power, and the treaty did nothing to reduce that power, prevent its further growth, assuage Lacedaemon's fears, or alter the strategic assessment that had induced the Spartans to contemplate and plan an attack and the Athenians to anticipate such an assault and launch a preventive war.

Of course, had the war in question come to a conclusion with the decisive defeat of either hegemonic power and with its elimination as a threat, there would not have been a second Attic war. But, in 446 B.C., it ended, instead, with an attempt at restoring something like the status quo ante—back before the antagonism first developed when the two powers had operated more or less amicably within different spheres. In consequence, though Athens had lost the war, she was not broken in spirit; and she did not suffer a great diminution in power.

By the same token, had Persia's Great King Artaxerxes staged a massive invasion of Hellas at this time on the model of the invasion mounted by his father Xerxes in 481, the two main Greek powers might well have worked again in tandem, and the peace between them would almost certainly have endured—at least for a time. But three years before, in 449, the King of Kings had accepted the terms that the Athenians had once dictated to his father; and, to all appearances, Persia had withdrawn from the scene, leaving that empire's former antagonists warily eyeing one another.

In the circumstances, there was much for statesmen, would-be statesmen, and ordinary citizens to ponder. Was the struggle with Persia genuinely over? Was the contest setting Sparta and her allies against Athens and hers really finished? Or were the two agreements bringing combat to an end—the Peace of Callias and the Thirty Years' Peace—no more than truces? Could there ever be a lasting settlement with Persia? Could trust and goodwill be reestablished between the two principal Greek powers? Or, in the absence of a common threat, was there no foundation for their cooperation? And if this was the case, was Sparta's victory in 446 a freak accident or an indication of her enduring strategic superiority?

These were the questions asked at the time, and there were more—for Athens was supreme at sea and Sparta on land, and it was exceedingly difficult, if not impossible, for either city to project power on the element dominated by the other. In time, everyone wondered, were war to break out again, which of the two would have the greater leverage? In extremis, would the weaker party look to Achaemenid Persia for aid? And would the Great King intervene?

There were a great many other questions asked as well. For each of the cities within the two coalitions had her own history and her own peculiar concerns; and the same can be said for the communities which had been neutral during Sparta's first Attic war. Moreover, most of the Greeks who lived in these divers cities and were possessed of a voice in the public assemblies that governed these tiny republics were extremely narrow in their outlook; and, within their particular *póleis*, they were a quarrelsome lot. In the best of circumstances, they were inclined to calculate solely with regard to their own community's parochial interests. In the worst of circumstances, they would turn on one another, and each of the factions that emerged would be tempted to seek support abroad.

In *The Spartan Regime*, which was intended to serve as a prelude to a series on the evolution of Lacedaemonian foreign policy, I analyzed the character of the Spartan polity, traced its origins, and described the grand strategy that the Lacedaemonians first articulated in the mid-sixth century—before the Persians burst on the scene—for the defense of that polity and the way of life associated with it. In the early chapters of the first volume in the series—*The Grand Strategy of Classical Sparta: The Persian Challenge*—I restated the conclusions reached in that prelude and explored in detail the manner in which the Spartans gradually adjusted that strategy to fit the new and unexpected challenge that suddenly loomed on the horizon when the Mede first appeared. Then, in the last four chapters of the work, I described the fashion in which they organized and managed the alliance with which they confronted and defeated the invader bearing down on Hellas.

In that volume's sequel, *Sparta's First Attic War*, I traced the manner in which the victorious Hellenes gradually and awkwardly worked out a postwar settlement that seemed to suit all concerned, and I paid particular attention, as in its predecessor, to neglected aspects of the story—above all, to the grand strategy pursued by the Lacedaemonians in this period, to the logic underpinning it, to the principal challenge to which it was exposed, and the adjustments that had to be made; but also to the noiseless revolution that took place at Athens in these years and to the implications of this change of regime for the rearticulation of Athens' traditional grand strategy. Then, I considered the fragility of the postwar settlement; I traced its collapse and the manner in which Sparta and Athens came into conflict; and I described the war they fought and the peace they forged.

In this volume, I briefly review Sparta's first Attic war with an eye to exploring two salient themes: the geopolitical logic it disclosed, and the profound
impact it had on the postwar preoccupations, fears, and expectations of those
who had participated in it. Then, I revisit the forging of the Thirty Years' Peace,
assess its prospects, and consider the process by which it collapsed and Athens
and Sparta clashed a second time. Thereafter, I investigate their aims in this
new war and the character of the military strategy adopted by each, and I examine the actual fighting; the reasons why the hopes and expectations of both
sides proved erroneous; the manner in which, in response to deadlock, each
city with some success adjusted her military strategy; and the fashion in which
mutual exhaustion eventually gave rise to another fragile, ultimately unworkable treaty of peace. And, finally, I explore the manner in which—despite the
pretense, vigorously maintained on both sides, that Athens and Sparta were
at peace and on friendly terms—the war continued and very nearly produced
a decisive victory for the enemies of Lacedaemon.

If I bring this volume to a close with the battle of Mantineia in 418, some
sixty years after Mardonius' defeat in the battle of Plataea, and not in 404—
when Athens was forced to surrender, give up her fleet, and tear down her
walls—it is because I believe that, from the perspective of the Spartans, their
victory at Mantineia on this particular occasion marked the end of an epoch
and paved the way for a radical shift in their grand strategy.

The series, of which this volume forms the third part, is meant to throw
light not only on ancient Sparta; her first great adversary, Achaemenid Persia;
and her initial chief ally and subsequent adversary, Athens. It is also intended
as an invitation to reenvisage Greek history from a Spartan perspective, and I
hope as well that these volumes will turn out to be a contribution to the study
of politics, diplomacy, and war as such. As I have argued elsewhere and try in
this volume and in its predecessors to demonstrate by way of my narrative,
one cannot hope to understand the diplomatic and martial interaction of polities if one focuses narrowly on their struggle for power. Every polity seeks to
preserve itself, to be sure; and in this crucial sense all polities really are akin.
But there are also, I argue, moral imperatives peculiar to particular regimes;
and, if one's aim is to understand, these cannot be dismissed and ostentatiously
swept aside or simply ignored on specious "methodological" grounds. Indeed,
if one abstracts entirely from regime imperatives—if one treats Sparta, Persia,

Corinth, Argos, Athens, and the like simply as "state actors," equivalent and interchangeable, in the manner advocated by the proponents of Realpolitik— one will miss much of what is going on.

Wearing blinders of such a sort can, in fact, be quite dangerous, as I suggested in the preceding volumes. For, if policy makers were to operate in this fashion in analyzing politics among nations in their own time, they would all too often lack foresight—both with regard to the course likely to be taken by the country they serve and with regard to the paths likely to be followed by its rivals and allies. As I intimate time and again in this volume and in its predecessors, in contemplating foreign affairs and in thinking about diplomacy, intelligence, military strength, and that strength's economic foundations, one must always acknowledge the primacy of domestic policy. This is the deeper meaning of Clausewitz' famous assertion that "war is the continuation of policy by other means."

It was with Clausewitz' dictum and this complex of concerns in mind that Julian Stafford Corbett first revived the term "grand strategy," reconfigured it, and deployed it both in the lectures he delivered at the Royal Naval War College between 1904 and 1906 and in the so-called Green Pamphlet that he prepared as a handout for his students.[2] And it was from this broad perspective that J. F. C. Fuller wrote when he introduced the concept to the general public in 1923. As he put it,

> The first duty of the grand strategist is . . . to appreciate the commercial and financial position of his country; to discover what its resources and liabilities are. Secondly, he must understand the moral characteristics of his countrymen, their history, peculiarities, social customs and system of government, for all these quantities and qualities form the pillars of the military arch which it is his duty to construct.

To this end he added, the grand strategist must be "a student of the permanent characteristics and slowly changing institutions of the nation to which he belongs, and which he is called upon to secure against war and defeat. He must, in fact, be a learned historian and a far-seeing philosopher, as well as a skilful strategist and tactician."

With this in mind, Fuller drew a sharp distinction between strategy and grand strategy. The former is, he explained, "more particularly concerned with the movement of armed masses" while the latter, "including these movements, embraces the motive forces which lie behind them," whether they be "material" or "psychological." In short, "from the grand strategical point of view, it is just as important to realize the quality of the moral power of a nation, as the quantity of its man-power." The grand strategist must, then, concern himself with establishing throughout his own nation and its fighting services "a common thought—the will to win"—and he must at the same time ponder how to deprive his country's rivals of that same will. If he is to outline for his own nation "a plan of action," he must come to know "the powers of all foreign countries and their influence on his own." Only then will he "be in a position, grand tactically, to direct the forces at his disposal along the economic and military lines of least resistance leading towards the moral reserve of his antagonist," which consists chiefly, he observed, in the morale of that nation's "civil population." In consequence, Fuller insisted, "the grand strategist" cannot restrict his purview to matters merely military. He cannot succeed unless he is also "a politician and a diplomatist."[3]

Some would argue that, in the absence of modern military education and something like a general staff, there can be no grand strategy; and there can be no doubt that in recent times institutions of this sort have proved invaluable. But, if having a general staff really were a necessity, we would have to reject the obvious: that the great statesmen of the past—such as Cardinal de Richelieu, Louis XIV, and the first duke of Marlborough; the elder William Pitt and George Washington; Alexander Hamilton and John Quincy Adams; Napoleon Bonaparte and the duke of Wellington; Otto von Bismarck; the count of Cavour; and Woodrow Wilson—were all grand strategists. Moreover, as recent studies of the Roman, Byzantine, and Hapsburg empires strongly suggest, every political community of substance that manages to survive for an extended time is forced by the challenges it faces to work out—usually, by a process of trial and error—a grand strategy of sorts and to develop a strategic culture and an operational code compatible with that strategy.[4]

It is the burden of these volumes to show that in ancient Lacedaemon, Persia, Corinth, Athens, and Argos there were statesmen who approached the question of war and peace from a broad perspective of the very sort described by Fuller and that it is this that explains the consistency and coherence of these polities' conduct in the intercommunal arena. There is, I would suggest, nothing of lasting significance known by grand strategists today that figures such as Thucydides and the statesmen he most admired had not already ascertained.

*

When they alluded to Athens, Corinth, Megara, or Lacedaemon by name as a political community; and, strikingly, even when they spoke of one of these *póleis* as their fatherland [*patrís*], the ancient Greeks employed nouns feminine in gender, personifying the community as a woman to whom they were devoted—which is why I with some frequency use the feminine pronoun to refer to Sparta and other Greek cities here.

Sparta's Second Attic War

Prologue

A Sudden Reversal

What most men call peace, he held to be only a name. In truth, for everyone, there exists by nature at all times an undeclared war among cities.

PLATO

IN mid-summer 449, the Athenians were on top of the world. Apart from a brief span of time following their magnificent victory at Eurymedon two decades before, they had been at war with the Persians for half a century—and now, finally, the humiliating terms of peace that they had forced on Xerxes after that battle had been reaffirmed by the Achaemenid monarch's son and heir, Artaxerxes.

For the Athenians, this was an immense relief. In the interim after Artaxerxes' repudiation of the agreement his father had made, they had gone on the offensive, and they had even taken a stab at detaching Egypt from the Persian Empire. But that audacious enterprise had ended in tears five years before with their loss of something on the order of 230 triremes. For a city with a population of fifty to sixty thousand adult male citizens, this was a terrible blow. The galleys which the Athenians deployed were triple-banked shells, one hundred to one hundred thirty feet long and about fifteen to eighteen feet wide, and each was manned by a crew of 170 rowers and thirty or more officers, specialists, archers, and marines—a substantial proportion of them Athenian citizens.

Although, in Egypt in 454, they may have lost a third or more of their citizen body, the Athenians managed, by a heroic effort at Cypriot Salamis in 451, to reestablish their command of the sea. And in the aftermath, defeated on both land and sea, the Great King of Persia sued for peace. If the deal the two sides then negotiated was presented to the world as a solemn edict issued

1

as a command by that proud monarch, as it almost certainly was, it was of no significance to the Athenians. They cared far more about the substance than the form. Indeed, from their perspective, there were only two things that mattered: that the edict conceded Thrace, the Aegean, the Bosporus, the sea of Marmara, the Hellespont, and the western and much of the southern Anatolian coast to the Athenians and their allies; and that the arrangement worked out with the young Achaemenid monarch was apt to endure for the foreseeable future.

The settlement's likely longevity stemmed from its one undeniable virtue. It reflected the geopolitical realities. Painful experience had taught both sides that neither was capable of establishing and sustaining its dominion over the territory claimed and effectively controlled by the other.

Xerxes' royal son really was what he called himself: he was the King of Kings. There was none like him. The Achaemenid empire, which at its height encompassed three of the four great river-valley civilizations, controlled a greater proportion of the world's population and material resources than any dominion before or since. But defeat after defeat had shown that it nonetheless lacked the moral resources with which to regain the hegemony on the high seas exercised before 480 by Artaxerxes' father, grandfather, and great-uncle; and none of this Great King's successors ever again made more than a halting attempt at its recovery.

The Athenians were similarly situated. They, too, were supreme within their sphere. They ruled the vasty deep; and, with the help of their naval allies, they could land marines and project power from the sea almost anywhere along the coasts of Asia Minor and the Levant. This mattered enormously because, on terrain where Persia's cavalry could not be deployed to advantage, the archers and infantrymen of the Mede were no match for the hoplite phalanx of the Greeks with its wall of interlocking shields. But the manpower needed for seizing and keeping Cyprus, let alone Egypt, Syria, and the interior of Anatolia—this the Athenians and their allies lacked; and after 454 they never again tried to do anything of the sort.

Within Hellas at this time, the Athenians were also in a singularly advantageous position. The league that they had founded in 477 with the Samians, the Chians, and the various communities on Lesbos for the purpose of continuing the war against the Persians was not just intact. It had grown to include almost all of the islands of the Aegean and the Hellenic communities situated

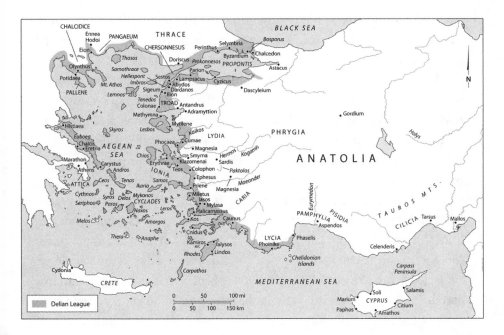

Map 1. Athens' Delian League, ca. 445

in Thrace, the Hellespont, the sea of Marmara, and the Bosporus as well as those scattered along the western shore and much of the southern coast of Anatolia. Over the course of three decades, moreover, this league had become for all intents and purposes an empire, functioning as a gigantic protection racket—with a handful of cities retaining their autonomy and contributing ships, and the rest making financial contributions [*phóros*] determined by the Athenians so that Athens could herself deploy an immense fleet to do their fighting for them.

There was, to be sure, one great hitch. Since 461, the Athenians had been at war, on a second front, with the Lacedaemonians and their allies—their erstwhile comrades and boon companions in the early stages of Hellas' epic struggle with Achaemenid Persia. Here, too, however, Athens was well positioned in the mid-summer of 449. At the outset of this conflict, there had been a bitter quarrel between Megara and Corinth and the former had withdrawn from what we now call the Peloponnesian League and had sought Athens' protection—a circumstance which conferred on the latter city an invaluable strategic advantage. If the Athenians fortified the passes leading from the

Corinthiad over Mount Geraneia into the Megarid and guarded them with sufficient vigilance, they could bottle up within the Peloponnesus the hoplite infantry and the other forces fielded by Sparta and her allies.

In the course of the struggle that followed the formation of this alliance, the Athenians had not only secured control of the Saronic Gulf by defeating the navies of Corinth and Aegina. They had actually forced the latter *pólis* into their alliance, and there is good reason to suppose that later, after seizing control of the Corinthian Gulf, they had imposed a blockade on the former with galleys operating with impunity on both sides of the Isthmus of Corinth—from Salamis and Aegina to the east and in the west from the Megarian port at Pegae, from the settlement they had established at Naupactus in 455, and from the little Corinthian colony Chalcis, which they had seized at the same time. Moreover, when challenged at Tanagra in Boeotia by a Peloponnesian army smuggled across the Corinthian Gulf, the Athenians had fought the Spartans and their allies to a standstill; and in the aftermath, although they had withdrawn from the battlefield and were technically the losers, they had turned an inconsequential tactical defeat into a strategic victory by returning to the region and subjugating Boeotia in its entirety.

Lacedaemon's Plight

If, in these years, the Athenians had a relatively free hand vis-à-vis Lacedaemon's allies, it was in part because the Spartans were preoccupied with grave difficulties at home and in their near abroad. Theirs was, in the best of circumstances, a delicate situation. The citizens of Lacedaemon were all gentlemen of a sort. They did not work with their hands. They did not themselves farm. They relied, instead, on the labor of a servile population called helots. This system of provision left the Spartiates—who constituted Lacedaemon's juridically defined ruling order—free to devote their lives to exercise, to military training, to athletic contests, to music and the dance, to horse racing, hunting, dining together, and other gentlemanly pursuits.[1]

The members of this ruling order lived a life of inordinate privilege, which made them the envy of Greece. But with privilege, at Sparta, came heavy responsibilities—and grave danger besides. The helots greatly outnumbered their masters—perhaps by a margin of seven to one, as the ancient literary evidence suggests; perhaps by a smaller ratio, as some modern scholars believe; but certainly by a lot. Those in Messenia—to the west across Mount Taygetus from the Eurotas Valley, where the Spartans resided—regarded themselves and were regarded by outsiders as a people in bondage, and from time to time they rose up in revolt. Even within the confines of what we today call Laconia, Aristotle reports, the helots lay in wait for a disaster to strike their masters.[2]

Lacedaemon's strength in the face of the helot threat derived in part from the discipline her hoplites displayed on the field of battle. As I have argued in detail elsewhere, the need to counter this threat went a long way toward explaining the Spartans' practice of infanticide; their provision to every citizen of an equal allotment of land and of servants to work it; the sumptuary laws they adopted; their sharing of slaves, horses, and hounds; their aversion to commerce; their intense piety; the subjection of their male offspring to an elaborate system of education and indoctrination; their use of music and poetry to instill a civic spirit; their practice of pedagogic pederasty; and their exclusion of foreigners and unwillingness to allow the young and impressionable to travel abroad—as well as the rigors and discipline to which they habitually subjected themselves and their constant preparation for war. This threat accounts as well for the articulation over time within Lacedaemon of a mixed regime graced with elaborate balances and checks. To sustain their dominion in Laconia and Messenia and to maintain the helots in bondage, the Spartans had to nourish within their own ranks courage, discipline, determination, solidarity, and communal devotion. And to this end, they had to eschew faction; foster among themselves the same opinions, passions, and interests; and employ (above all, in times of great strain) procedures—recognized as fair and just and thought of as sanctioned by the gods—by which to reach a stable political consensus consistent with the dictates of prudence.[3]

The strength that the Spartiates derived from this civic ethos was multiplied many times over by their ability to leverage the manpower of their neighbors—above all, the Corinthians and the Eleans as well as the Tegeans, Mantineians, and Orchomenians of Arcadia, and these communities' subject allies, not to mention the Phliasians, Sicyonians, Epidaurians, Troezeneans, and Hermioneans. This alliance system, which Lacedaemon had constructed within the Peloponnesus with painstaking care in the sixth century, was the bastion of her security.

This system was also, however, quite fragile. For the cities that Sparta

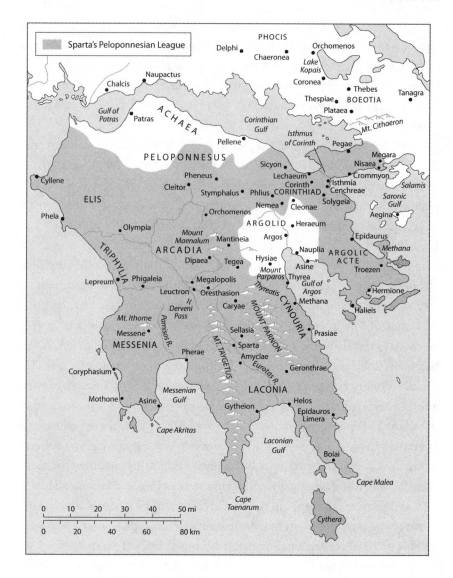

Map 2. Sparta's Peloponnesian League, ca. 445

commanded were genuine allies, not subjects. Moreover, like all the Hellenic
póleis, they possessed an agonistic culture likely to give rise to factional strife
and bitter disputes concerning public policy—and civic ambition could easily
set one or more of them at odds with their hegemon. To complicate matters
further, within the Peloponnesus there lay another powerful, populous *pólis*—
named Argos—which was profoundly hostile to Lacedaemon and eager to

recover from that city her lost province Cynouria. Year after year, the Argives watched and waited, hoping to lure away Sparta's allies, wrest from her the hegemony, liberate the Messenians, and regain Cynouria.

In later years, one Corinthian leader would sum up Sparta's strategic position elegantly by comparing her to a stream. "At their sources," he noted, "rivers are not great and they are easily forded, but the farther on they go, the greater they get—for other rivers empty into them and make the current stronger." So it is with the Spartans, he continued. "There, in the place where they emerge, they are alone; but as they continue and gather cities under their control, they become more numerous and harder to fight." The prudent general, he concluded, will seek battle with the Spartans in or near Lacedaemon where they are few in number and relatively weak.[4]

The Lacedaemonians understood the danger. They knew from the beginning what history would eventually disclose: that it took but a single major defeat in warfare on land to endanger the city's very survival. It was for this reason that, in and after 477, they grudgingly acquiesced in Athens' seizure of the leadership of the Hellenes at sea. They knew that, if the Persians were allowed to reconquer that element, Hellas would again be in peril. But there were at that time no more than eight thousand adult male Spartiates—not enough to reliably fulfill their responsibilities at and near home if, in substantial numbers, they were deployed in the Aegean and beyond. Moreover, the Spartans had good reason to suspect that the vaunted discipline of their compatriots was a hothouse flower not apt to survive the temptations on offer in the outside world. Pausanias son of Cleombrotus, the Agiad regent responsible for the Hellenic victory over the Persians at Plataea in 479, had disgraced himself the following year, when in command of the Hellenic forces at sea, by taking on Persian airs, brutally mistreating Lacedaemon's Ionian allies, and trafficking in a highly suspicious manner with the minions of the Great King. If they wanted their regime to survive, his fellows thought, they should leave the war at sea to the Athenians.[5]

In the three decades that followed, the situation of the Spartans became fraught. In around 494, in anticipation of Persia's first intervention in mainland Greece, the Lacedaemonians had settled matters close to home by means of a preventive war—in which they inflicted on Argos at Sepeia a crushing, demographically devastating defeat. In the aftermath they had put an end to that city's hegemony over the Argolic Acte, and they had liberated her subject communities within the Argeia itself. As was to be expected, a quarter century thereafter, when their population had bounced back and a new generation had appeared on the scene, the Argives reasserted themselves—initially, for the purpose of recovering what they had lost locally; and then with an eye to regaining Cynouria and challenging Lacedaemon's primacy within the Peloponnesus as a whole.

To this end, the Argives forged an alliance with Tegea, a city situated athwart the road leading from Laconia to the Argolid, which had unfulfilled ambitions of her own. The Tegeans were intent on uniting all of their neighbors within Arcadia in a league under their leadership. This the Lacedaemonians could not tolerate—for keeping this highland region divided and loyal was essential to their security. Strategically, Arcadia was the fulcrum of the Peloponnesus. It bordered on both Laconia and Messenia; the men who lived within this district were numerous and warlike; and the principal cart road leading around Mount Taygetus from the valley of the Eurotas in Laconia to that of the Pamisos in Messenia ran across south-central Arcadia—where, if the Arcadians were hostile, the Spartans' supply lines would be exceedingly vulnerable to attack.

We do not know precisely when and how the Argos-Tegea axis was formed. But there is every reason to suspect that Themistocles son of Neocles had something to do with it. This canny Athenian was the greatest man of the age. He—and he alone—had anticipated Xerxes' invasion of Greece. He had negotiated Athens' alliance with Sparta, and he bore much of the responsibility for the Hellenic victory at Salamis in 480. Then, following the Hellenic victories at Plataea and Mycale the following year, he had suddenly turned on the Lacedaemonians.

Up to a point, Themistocles had been on this latter occasion persuasive. When he urged that the Athenians defy the wishes of their Spartan allies and rebuild the walls of their town, that they fortify the Peiraeus and use it as their principal port, and that they make provision for the construction of twenty new triremes each year, they embraced his advice—and they may even have seen wisdom in his claim that the Peiraeus would prove to be "more useful to the Athenians than the city up-country" and good sense in his advice that, "if they were overpowered on land, they go down to the Peiraeus and withstand all of mankind with their ships." They were not a trusting lot. But when Themistocles later tried to convince his compatriots that Achaemenid Persia was no longer a grave threat, and when he argued that the dual hegemony of Athens at sea and Sparta on land championed by his younger contemporary Cimon son of Miltiades would ultimately prove to be unworkable and that Athens' reliance on the forbearance of the Lacedaemonians would leave her in a perilous position—beholden to a community apt in time to turn on her with a vengeance—he did not succeed.

After having failed in this attempt at suasion, Themistocles was subjected to a formal ostracism by his compatriots in or soon after 472. But he was not the sort to give up, and what he did do at this time earned him the enduring hatred of the Spartans. At the beginning of the ten-year term stipulated for his exile, Themistocles settled in Argos; and from there, we are told, he traveled extensively within the Peloponnesus. The fact that his journeying coincided in time with the formation of the Argive-Tegean axis can hardly have been fortuitous. The man dubbed Athens' Odysseus is not likely to have then been traveling in this particular region solely for his health and amusement.

Though he had lost the political struggle at Athens, Themistocles had numerous fervent admirers in that *pólis*, and they rallied in support of his Peloponnesian enterprise. Circa 469, when the Spartans found themselves forced to fight at Tegea a battle for their own survival against the Argive-Tegean coalition, the number of Athenian volunteers in the coalition army was sufficient to merit mention by Themistocles' great friend the poet Simonides. Had Athens as a political community not remained aloof, had she dispatched a proper army of three or four thousand hoplites to support the Argives and the Tegeans, the Lacedaemonians might not have fended off what was, in fact, for them an existential threat.

The setback which the Spartans inflicted at this time on the Argos-Tegea axis did not fully obviate the danger in which they found themselves. The Argives and the Tegeans were anything but broken in spirit; and, though chastened, neither of these two communities abandoned their joint enterprise. In the aftermath, with Tegean help, the Argives renewed their quest to reunite the Argeia, and the Tegeans continued their efforts to draw into alliance their fellow Arcadians. Moreover, both cities made dramatic progress in the wake of the fateful winter of 465/4—when a series of earthquakes struck Laconia, killed half of the Spartiates, and occasioned a general helot revolt that the Lacedaemonians, under their alert young Eurypontid king Archidamus son of Zeuxidamos, barely managed to contain.

This catastrophe notwithstanding, a much diminished Spartan army did manage to defeat Tegea and her Arcadian allies at Dipaea circa 464. Thereafter, however, the Tegeans continued to breathe defiance. Moreover, in this period, the Argives managed to conquer Mycenae and Tiryns and reunite the Argeia—and while this was going on, for nearly a decade, the Lacedaemonians had to devote the better part of their energies to besieging a host of doughty helot insurgents holed up on Mount Ithome in Messenia.

It was not until the mid-450s that the Spartans were willing and able to negotiate the withdrawal of these intrepid souls and found themselves able to give serious thought to threats elsewhere within the Peloponnesus. Well before this time, however, there had been a dramatic shift in public opinion at Athens occasioned by the Athenians' discovery that, shortly before being hobbled by the great helot rebellion, their Spartan allies had conspired against them.

In the wake of the battle of Eurymedon circa 469, when Xerxes agreed to a settlement and it briefly looked as if the Athenians had eliminated the Persian threat, the Spartans began to think of Athens, with her enormous fleet and the massive income she derived from the contributions pledged by her allies, as an emerging threat; and at this point, we have reason to suspect, they began to contemplate a preventive war. Then, in 465, an opportunity presented itself. The citizens of Thasos—infuriated by Athens' encroachment on that wealthy and powerful island's holdings in Thrace and persuaded that they no longer needed the protection afforded by her league—withdrew from Athens' anti-Persian alliance, lost a battle to her at sea, came under siege, and appealed to Lacedaemon for support. In response, the Spartans promised that in due course they would march into Attica.

Against an invasion of this sort—conducted, as it would have been, at harvest time in the late spring—the Athenians had no defense. There was no obstacle to hinder the Peloponnesians' entry into their territory. The smallholders of Attica who possessed the wherewithal to purchase the spear, sword, and shield needed for service in the hoplite phalanx were, as warriors, rank amateurs. They could not defeat so large and formidable an army; and the town of Athens, situated inland as it was, could not long withstand a siege.

On this particular occasion, however, the Athenians were fortunate. Thanks to the earthquake that took place in Laconia in the winter of 465/4 and to the general helot revolt which this catastrophe occasioned, the Spartans were unable to keep their promise to the Thasians.

In 462, when Thasos fell, the Athenians appear to have learned of Lacedaemon's pledge. Soon thereafter, they voted to ostracize Cimon; and Themistocles' admirers came to the fore and persuaded their compatriots to stage a diplomatic revolution. It was at this time that the Athenians renounced their association with Lacedaemon; forged an alliance with Megara and with the Medizers from Argos and Thessaly; built Long Walls to link the town of Megara with Nisaea, its port on the Saronic Gulf; fortified the passes over Mount Geraneia; and planted garrisons at Pegae on the Corinthian Gulf and elsewhere in the Megarid. It was also at this time that they launched a war against Corinth, Aegina, and Sparta's other Peloponnesian adherents. And soon thereafter, mindful that they might not always control the Megarid and the passes over Mount Geraneia and that their population had become much too large for the Peiraeus to suffice as a refuge, they set out to transform their own *pólis* into a virtual island impervious to invasion by land and, to this end, they began constructing Long Walls to link the town of Athens in the interior of Attica with the Peiraeus, the Athenians' fortified port on the Saronic Gulf.

Athens' new leaders regarded Themistocles' recent past as their prologue. They knew, as he had known, that the only way to eliminate the threat posed by Lacedaemon was to foment trouble for Sparta within the Peloponnesus, and they were haunted by what might have been achieved in the battles at Tegea and Dipaea had it not been for the policy of peaceful coexistence and cooperation foisted on Athens by Cimon. So, while the Spartans were preoccupied with the siege at Mount Ithome, they followed Themistocles' example and did what they could to bolster Argos, encourage Tegea, lure into rebellion Lacedaemon's remaining allies, and rally them against her. This they did with an eye to staging another hoplite battle deep within the Peloponnesus—to defeating Sparta in such a contest, to liberating her Messenian underlings, and leaving her isolated and weak in her Laconian redoubt. Their aim, then, in subduing Aegina and visiting punishment on Corinth and Lacedaemon's other maritime allies was to re-create the opportunity that Athens, under Cimon's leadership, had squandered in the period stretching from 469 to 464.[6]

Of course, after the debacle in Egypt and the massive losses in manpower incurred by the Athenians and their allies, the former found it necessary to put their ambitions on hold and to swallow their pride, recall Cimon, and charge him with negotiating a truce with the Lacedaemonians. It was their hope that the Spartans would be sufficiently fearful of the Persian resurgence that they would be willing to comply, and their expectations were met.

For the five-year respite that Cimon managed to secure, however, his compatriots were made to pay a hefty price. It left them in 451 blessedly free to focus their attention single-mindedly on the Mede and to devote their much-diminished manpower to the formidable task at hand. But they had to leave their Argive allies in the lurch, and this enabled the Spartans to force their ancient enemy to agree to a peace of thirty years' duration. Thereafter, with Argos neutered, the Lacedaemonians restored their position within Arcadia by intervening at Tegea, staging a coup, installing an oligarchy, and bringing that wayward, strategically placed community back into their alliance.[7]

The World Turned Upside Down

These setbacks notwithstanding, come high summer in 449, the Athenians were, as we have already observed, riding high—and they were intent on making the best of their good fortune. In celebration of their victory over the Persians, they solemnly dispatched twenty heralds, each over fifty years in age, to the various communities in Greece, summoning them to a conference focused on fulfilling the vows made by the various participants in the course of their common struggle with Persia and on providing for freedom of the seas and for Hellas' future defense.

The Athenians cannot have supposed that the Spartans and their Peloponnesian allies would accept an invitation to a conference over which the upstarts from Attica would preside. To do so would be to acknowledge Athens as the leader of the Hellenes. To refuse, however, would be to leave the disposition of the matters under consideration to the Athenians and to those, dependent on them, who responded to their call. The Lacedaemonians were in an awkward position. They had to choose between losing face and ceding the moral high ground—and in the event they chose the latter, condemning themselves to irrelevance in the world outside the Peloponnesus, and tacitly permitting Athens' maritime empire to acquire without challenge a new rationale and a new lease on life.

The Athenians' triumph was, however, short-lived. Three years thereafter, they found themselves suddenly and unexpectedly at the mercy of the Peloponnesians. Their troubles began in Boeotia. Late in 447, exiles seized the cities of Orchomenos and Chaeronea in that region's northwest, and the expedition that the Athenians sent under Tolmides son of Tolmaeus to crush this bold incursion was ambushed at Coronea near the southern shore of Lake Kopais while en route home. Many of the Athenians within this expeditionary force were killed outright. Others were taken hostage.

The following year, almost certainly while negotiations were taking place between the Athenians and the triumphant Boeotian rebels, the cities on the nearby island of Euboea concerted a revolt. Then, when the Athenians, under pressure, agreed to withdraw altogether from Boeotia and dispatched a force to reconquer the neighboring island that was their most prized possession, the Megarians rose up, massacred the Athenian garrison, and opened their gates to their Corinthian, Epidaurian, and Sicyonian neighbors.

By this time the five-year truce had lapsed, and the Spartans were quick to seize the opportunity that these successive rebellions afforded them. Soon after the Megarian revolt, Pleistoanax son of Pausanias led a Peloponnesian army into the Corinthiad, over Mount Geraneia, and through the Megarid into Attica—where he caught the Athenians unprepared and at a disadvantage with their forces divided, with at least one unit stranded and at risk outside Attica, and with the Euboeans still in revolt. From the Athenians, before leading his army back to the Peloponnesus, this Agiad king appears to have elicited a commitment not only to give up most of what he and his compatriots regarded as their ill-gotten gains, but also to withdraw from the Peloponnesus and the Megarid and agree to an extended truce.[8]

Part I

THE HATCH AND BROOD OF TIME

There is a history in all men's lives
Figuring the natures of the times deceased;
The which observed, a man may prophesy,
With a near aim, of the main chance of things
As yet not come to life, who in their seeds
And weak beginnings lie entreasurèd.
Such things become the hatch and brood of time.

WILLIAM SHAKESPEARE'S EARL OF WARWICK, *HENRY IV, PART TWO*

THE arrangement that the Athenians worked out with the Spartans late in the fall of 446 or the winter of 446/5 was no less well crafted than the so-called Peace of Callias that they had forged with Persia. It, too, reflected an enduring balance of power. It acknowledged the facts and left the Spartans and their allies supreme on land and the Athenians supreme at sea. In the aftermath, neither coalition was in a position to strike terror into the other. The Peloponnesus was once again a bastion of defense for Lacedaemon; and, although they had given up Megara, her ports on the Saronic and Corinthian Gulfs, and the passes over Mount Geraneia, the Athenians retained their maritime allies, their enormous fleet, and the Long Walls they had built in response to the prospect that the Peloponnesians might someday invade Attica by land. Those at Sparta with long memories and a capacity to imagine what the eastern Mediterranean would be like if Athens were to go under could take comfort in the fact that, for all of her faults, their erstwhile opponent could still be relied upon to keep the Persians at bay.

It was also promising that neither Sparta nor Athens nursed a grievance. Apart from Aegina and Naupactus and perhaps Molycreium to the north of the Corinthian Gulf and Chalcis to the west on the north shore of the Gulf of Patras, Athens relinquished everything that she had seized in the course of the war. None of her remaining acquisitions lay within Lacedaemon's natural sphere of influence; and, to head off possible objections on the part of the Spartans, she may even have agreed to honor the autonomy of their sometime allies the Aeginetans.

The terms of the agreement were in other ways sensible as well. There was not to be another Megara, for the treaty listed the allies of each of the two parties and specified that neither could accept into her confederacy a city allied with the other. It also allowed a measure of flexibility. Both parties were free to admit into their leagues communities hitherto neutral; and, although Athens was barred from once again entering into a formal alliance with Argos, she was free to have close and friendly relations with that formidable *pólis*. There was even provision for quarrels unforeseen in a clause stipulating that disputes be settled by arbitration.

The handiwork of the diplomats of Lacedaemon and Athens differed, however, from the accord worked out by Athens with Persia in two important particulars. It was not, as the latter appears to have been, an informal arrangement. It was a formal treaty, which both parties solemnly swore to honor; and its duration was not indefinite. Like the agreements forged in the past between those perennial Peloponnesian rivals Sparta and Argos, it had a specified term. At the end of thirty years, it would lapse. In short, it was not a putatively perpetual pact like the agreement founding the anti-Persian maritime alliance that we now call the Delian League. There was no pledge of friendship, and the accord was not, strictly speaking, a treaty of peace. It was a truce between once and future foes, albeit an extended truce; and it expressly advertised itself as a temporary expedient and as nothing more.[1]

The instrument recording the agreement reached by the Lacedaemonians and the Athenians reflected a brute fact. Both parties were exhausted. Although nearly twenty years had passed, the Lacedaemonians had not fully recovered from the demographic damage inflicted on them in and after the winter of 465/4 by the great earthquake and the helot revolt—and the Athenians still felt the cumulative impact of the dramatic losses they had suffered at Tanagra, in Egypt, at Coronea, and elsewhere. Those who forged the deal in 446 were persuaded that each of the two parties needed a generation in which to recover. Apart from those in the grips of Panhellenic nostalgia, no one imagined that the two would henceforth be on amicable terms and that the deadly rivalry between them had come to an end. For that to happen, there would have to be a full-scale revival of the Persian threat.

This may seem strange to us. When we sign a peace agreement, it is nearly always meant to last. Or, at least, that is the pretense. We piously presume that peace is the norm and war, an almost unthinkable, highly regrettable exception. Under the influence of Immanuel Kant, many in our number even dream that peace can be made perpetual.[2] We fight wars to end all wars and to make the world safe for democracy. These are the lies we tell ourselves.

The ancient Greeks did not anticipate our optimism in this particular. They told themselves and others no such uplifting tales. For moral guidance, they looked not to a god who had suffered crucifixion and died on their behalf; who had urged them to love their neighbors, turn the other cheek, and themselves take up the cross; and who came to be called the Prince of Peace. They looked, instead, to Homer, and from this poet—whom Plato rightly termed "the education of Hellas"—they learned to take war for granted, to thrill to prowess in battle, and to admire canniness in council. In consequence, ordinary Hellenes would have nodded their heads in approval of the opinion attributed by Plato to the lawgiver of Crete: "What most men call peace, he held to be only a name. In truth, for everyone, there exists by nature at all times an undeclared war among cities." And they were less inclined to mourn this fact than to embrace it with excitement and without regret.[3]

In the event, as we shall soon see, this particular cessation of hostilities was short-lived. It did not last even half of its thirty-year term. This should come as no surprise. For, however well-crafted the treaty may have been, one insuperable obstacle stood in the way of its success, distinguishing it sharply from the agreements reached with the Mede. Xerxes and Artaxerxes undoubtedly regretted Persia's inability to project power overseas, but repeated, decisive defeats at sea and on the land nearby had persuaded each in turn to eschew ambition, at least for the time being, and to put on hold the quest for universal empire dictated by the great god Ahura Mazda—and for their part, the Athenians, by this time a people of the sea, had grown wary of troop commitments ashore in Africa and Asia. The sharp distinction drawn by Polybius between powers that "have yielded to circumstances" and those that are "broken in spirit" is pertinent. Both parties to the conflict setting the Hellenes against the Persians were, in the requisite sense, "broken in spirit." Neither could any longer imagine continued war as a way forward to anything but senseless bloodshed, and neither could stomach that thought. By way of contrast, however, within Hellas Athens remained an unsatisfied—some would say, an insatiable—power. *In extremis,* she had, indeed, "yielded to circumstances"; and she could be expected "to lie in wait for a favorable opportunity" and to then again launch a war.[4]

Athens had once been an agricultural community intent first and foremost on the defense of her territory. But, thanks to her long war with Persia, this was no longer the case. She had become a city of salarymen. They built her temples. They constructed and repaired her triremes. They rowed in her galleys, guarded her port and walls, fought in her wars, administered her empire, served on her juries, prepared the agenda for her assemblies, and held her magistracies. These salarymen, who numbered more than 20,000, depended for their livelihood to a considerable degree on the *phóros* collected each year from the communities in Athens' empire that did not provide triremes; and these denizens of the Peiraeus, the town of Athens, and the villages nearby ruled the *pólis*—for the landless thetes who made up the majority of these salarymen were far more likely to turn out for the civic assemblies held in the town of Athens every ten days than were the country folk, who were busy tending their farms. The Long Walls that these salarymen had built to join the town of Athens with the Peiraeus were a reflection of their political community's transformation and reorientation. In a crisis, if not caught off guard, as they had been in 446, the Athenians would retreat behind their walls and sacrifice the farmland in Attica and the interests of the men who worked it while defending to the death their mastery over the sea and the empire that they had acquired and very much hoped to expand. This was something that everyone intuited.[5]

Of course, Athens might sidestep Peloponnesian entanglements for a time. But she was still governed by the spirit of ambition, innovation, audacity, and greed that had inspired her dramatic growth in power. If the Egyptian debacle had left the Athenians chastened, the splendid victory they had won on both land and sea at Cypriot Salamis had in considerable measure restored their confidence—and, thanks to the restraint foolishly exercised in the field by Lacedaemon's inexperienced young Agiad king, it was easy for them to suppose their defeat at the hands of the Peloponnesians what the ancient Greeks dismissed with disdain as a mere "theft of war."[6]

In 447 and 446, there had been a cascade of what appear to have been carefully coordinated rebellions—in Boeotia; then, on Euboea; and, finally, at Megara—and the Athenians had been outwitted, outmaneuvered, then faced with the prospect that they would be overwhelmed. This was undeniable. The Spartans had snatched from them an impressive victory, but they had not overpowered, defeated, and humiliated them on the field of battle. They had not demonstrated their moral, material superiority. They had not forced the Athenians to grovel, beg, and acknowledge their primacy—and for Pleistoanax' failure in this particular, many a Spartiate rightly feared, his compatriots would eventually have to pay an exceedingly heavy price.

CHAPTER 1

An Uneasy Truce

We have done nothing wondrous, nothing contrary to human ways, in accepting an empire given to us and in not yielding it up, having been conquered by the three greatest things—honor, fear, and advantage. Nor were we the first such, for it has always been the case that the weaker are subject to those more powerful.

THUCYDIDES' ATHENIANS

IN the years subsequent to their humiliation at the hands of the Spartans and their allies, the Athenians repeatedly demonstrated that they were anything but "broken in spirit." When opportunity outside the Peloponnesus presented itself, they did what everyone with any sense had reason to expect. They assiduously expanded Athens' influence and her domain.

As soon as they had achieved victory at Cypriot Salamis, the Athenians had begun establishing independent colonies and cleruchies—agricultural outposts manned by Athenian citizens—here, there, and everywhere within their dominion. In this period, according to Plutarch, Pericles son of Xanthippus dispatched one thousand of his compatriots to the Thracian Chersonnesus, another five hundred to Naxos, one hundred fifty to Andros, and one thousand to western Thrace "to reside alongside the Bisaltae."

Then, after recovering Euboea in 446, the Athenians expelled the Histiaeans, and they sent one or two thousand Athenians to take their place—while at Chalcis they once again seized the holdings of that city's wealthy Cavaliers [Hippobátai] and distributed them to Athenian cleruchs; and it was probably in these years that Athens dispatched a colony to Brea, which appears to have been situated on the Thermaic Gulf in what we now call the Chalcidice. The literary testimony concerning these developments is at least partially confirmed by the surviving *phóros* records, which strongly suggest that these seizures of land occasioned a sharp reduction in the contributions demanded from the communities within the Delian League to which the cleruchs had been conveyed.[1]

As Plutarch makes clear, Pericles and his compatriots established these cleruchies and colonies in part as a means of satisfying the material needs of the impoverished thetes and of the *zeugítai* smallholders on whom this land was conferred. But the city did so also for the same reason that the Persians had long done the like—for the purpose of establishing garrisons of a sort throughout her empire and of consolidating control within the territory she already possessed. To this end, she sought to make the most of her manpower. As the Attic orator Antiphon would later put it, her aim was "to turn all of the thetes into hoplites" by making them smallholders capable of supplying their own spears, swords, and shields. Over time, we are told, tens of thousands of Athenians profited from these efforts.[2]

Thurii

Athens did not restrict herself to territory already controlled by her league. The demographic damage inflicted on her in the battles at Tanagra in 458, in Egypt in 454, and at Coronea in 447 limited her ability in this period to send citizens further afield, but it did not stop her entirely. Her establishment of the colony of Thurii on the Gulf of Taranto in southernmost Italy on a site once occupied by Sybaris is a case in point.

Italy and Sicily lay outside the sphere of Athens' dominion, but not beyond the purview of Athenian statesmen. Themistocles had demonstrated a keen interest in the Greek-occupied southern Italian region that the Romans would call Magna Graecia. One of his daughters he had named Italia. The other he called Sybaris; and, at a moment in 480 when he was at odds with Athens' Hellenic League allies, he threatened that his compatriots, who had already evacuated from Attica, would jettison their confederates, sail west to the boot of Italy, and reestablish their city on the long-abandoned site of the ancient Ionian colony at Siris.[3]

Sybaris was another abandoned Greek city. Settlers from Achaea and Troezen are credited with her establishment in the late eighth century; and, like Siris, she had been highly prosperous in the late archaic period. In 510/9, however, roughly two centuries after her foundation, her neighbor Croton had defeated the Sybarites and seized the town; and, over the course of the

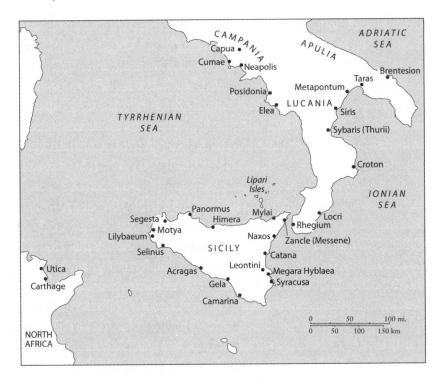

Map 3. Magna Graecia, Sicily, and Carthage

subsequent six decades, that community thwarted repeated attempts by Sybarite refugees and their offspring to reestablish their *pólis*. Finally, in 446, out of desperation, the offspring remaining issued to both Sparta and Athens an appeal for help and an invitation to share in the resettlement of Sybaris. The response this appeal elicited reflected the character and situation of the respondents. As always, the Lacedaemonians had their hands full at home and had no interest in a venture so far afield. And the Athenians, though depleted in numbers and stretched thin, leapt at the opportunity to gain a foothold in the west. They were always willing to help . . . themselves.

Shortly after the promulgation of what we now call the Thirty Years' Peace, the Athenians dispatched ten ships—loaded with prospective colonists, their gear, and their wives. These sailed under the leadership of Xenocritus and of Pericles' friend and sometime agent the soothsayer Lampon, who, as *oıkıstaí*— founders or oecists—were fully in charge. Or so they thought. For, upon arrival, the Athenians and their wives discovered to their dismay and fury that, although they outnumbered the native Sybarites and it was their presence that rendered the settlement defensible, they were nonetheless slated to be second-class citizens. They were barred from the rich land near the urban center, denied access to the most important magistracies, and insult was added to injury. For, in celebrating religious rites, the wives of the original Sybarites were to take precedence over those of the newcomers.

Before long, in predictable fashion, violence erupted between the two discrete populations. Some Sybarites were killed; others fled; and the son of Xanthippus and his compatriots soon faced a dilemma. If the project was to succeed, more men were needed than Athens could spare. And so the Athenians opted to make a virtue of necessity. In 444/3, they asserted once again their community's primacy within Hellas by generously issuing to all of their fellow Greeks an invitation to join them in founding on the territory of Sybaris a city entirely new—this one to be named Thurii.

Pericles, his minion Lampon, and Xenocritus went to considerable lengths to confer on the project a certain élan. According to Plato's student Heraclides Ponticus, the oecists recruited the famous sophist Protagoras of Abdera as the new city's lawgiver; and there is reason to suppose that they persuaded the renowned political theorist and city-planner Hippodamus of Miletus, who had laid out the streets of the Peiraeus in a series of orthogonal grids, to do the like at Thurii. The exiled Spartan notable Cleandridas is known to have joined the expedition and to have so distinguished himself in defense of the colony that, when he died there, a hero cult was established in his honor. The historian Herodotus of Halicarnassus is thought to have been a participant; and, perhaps at Pericles' urging, his wealthy friend the Syracusan exile Cephalus apparently also joined in, taking with him his young sons Polemarchus, Lysias, and Euthydemus.

These men were by no means alone. This time Athens' Panhellenic proposal met with success—for, within Greece, there was no shortage of men intent on bettering their lives. Athenian collaborators, exiled from communities in the Peloponnesus and central Greece that had been aligned with the Athenians in the 450s and early 440s, joined with adventurers of all sorts and with poor men from Arcadia and elsewhere in flocking to Athens' standard. It speaks volumes that there were tribes at Thurii named after Arcadia, Achaea, Elis, Boeotia, Doris, Ionia, Euboea, the Islanders, and the Delphic Amphictyony as well as Athens herself.[4] The Athenians were, of course, the largest single contingent, and they no doubt supposed that they would remain in charge. But this was by no means certain—for, as a venture, the foundation of a multi-ethnic city was risky, as Pericles' compatriots would eventually learn.[5] As a display of grandeur, however, such an enterprise was hard to top.

Aggrandizement of this sort was in no way ruled out by the agreement the Athenians had forged with Sparta. But it was nonetheless apt to render them a more formidable threat in the eyes of the Lacedaemonians and their allies—especially if, as seems likely, it was in these interwar years that Lampon, presumably on an embassy, visited Catana in Sicily and perhaps Naxos and Metapontum as well; that the general Diotimos son of Strombichos sailed, almost certainly with an Athenian fleet, into the bay of Naples at the request of the Greeks of Neapolis to institute a torch race in honor of the Siren Parthenope as demanded by the Delphic oracle; that a contingent of Athenians was then added to the citizen body of the Neapolitans; and that Athens negotiated with Rhegium at the tip of the Italian toe and with Leontini in Sicily the alliances known to have been renewed at their request in 433/2.[6]

Kinship evidently played an important role in Athenian calculations. Every one of these cities was an Ionian foundation. All owed their existence directly or indirectly to the colonizing activity of the Chalcidians of Euboea in the early archaic period; and, given their situation, they were all in need of protection. At this time, the Neapolitans may already have come under pressure from the Oscan peoples of the interior, and all six of these Ionian communities are apt to have regarded distant Athens as a counterweight to the one Hellenic power of consequence operating in their vicinity: Syracusa in eastern Sicily—a Dorian stronghold three centuries old, which just happens to have been founded by Corinth.[7]

The Middle Wall

By this time, the great war with Persia was for most Lacedaemonians an increasingly dim and distant memory. Fewer and fewer among the younger men gave much thought to the prospect that the King of Kings might once again mount a massive assault on Hellas. They were far more impressed, as human beings nearly always are, by their own recent experience—and by the damage done a short time before to Corinth and their other allies. They recognized the power of the impulse driving Athenian expansionism—it was present and palpable—and by the 440s those who feared first and foremost the growth in Athens' power had at Lacedaemon become both numerous and influential. The fact that, soon after the forging of the peace, Pleistoanax and his principal advisor, Cleandridas, were driven into exile tells the tale. It shows that, at Sparta, there were men in positions of authority—not few in number—who fiercely regretted Lacedaemon's failure in 446 to inflict on Athens a devastating and dispiriting defeat and put an end to her maritime hegemony once and for all. These men were apt to press for a renewal of war if and when favorable circumstances once again presented themselves.

This Pericles and his supporters understood only too well. They were aware of what had happened to the Agiad king and his counsellor, and they knew why—which explains their decision at this time to reinforce the system of defense linking the city of Athens with the sea. Of the original Long Walls, one ran directly from the fortifications surrounding Athens to its heavily fortified port at the Peiraeus, where it linked up with the circuit of walls that Themistocles had constructed on that town's landward side. The other extended from the town of Athens to the bay of Phalerum, which, though never fortified, had for generations served as Athens' principal port and may well have continued to play an ancillary role. This arrangement, as the Athenians eventually came to realize, left Athens vulnerable in one particular. By means of a surprise attack, an enterprising foe could land a commando force of hoplites and light-armed troops on the shore between Phalerum and the Peiraeus, and these soldiers could then seize control of one of the gates in the Long Walls and open the way for an army, situated in the countryside nearby, to march in, isolate the town of Athens from its port, and initiate a siege.

There were two ways to preclude this possibility. The Athenians could fortify the coastline from Phalerum to the Peiraeus, or they could construct a third wall, running directly to the Peiraeus, parallel with and close to the one that already followed that route. The latter option had this advantage. In a pinch, a force of modest size, even one composed of superannuated men and of ephebes roughly eighteen years in age, could far more easily guard and defend a five-mile-long walled corridor less than two hundred yards in width than an immense circuit more than three times as long, stretching from Athens to the Peiraeus, then from the Peiraeus to Phalerum, and finally from Phalerum back to Athens. And so, on the presumption that the Peloponnesians were apt at any time to return and that they might again catch the Athenians

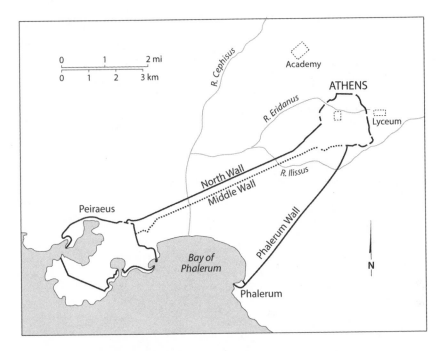

Map 4. Athens, the Peiraeus, and the Long Walls, ca. 440

off guard, as they had in 446, Pericles recommended building what came to be called the Middle Wall; and his compatriots voted to do so.[8]

That this was a sensible move soon became obvious. For not long after this decision was made, the Athenians were unexpectedly drawn into a quarrel between two of the cities within their alliance, which eventuated in an armed rebellion on the part of the more powerful of the two; and, as events unfolded, both the Persians and the Lacedaemonians toyed ominously with the possibility of intervening in that city's defense.

The Samian Revolt

Within the Delian League, the hegemon performed two distinct functions. The first of these was obvious and needs no commentary. With the help of the Chians, the Samians, the *póleis* on Lesbos, and the other cities that at one time or another supplied ships, the Athenians were charged with keeping the Persians at bay. The second function was ancillary and nowhere expressly stipulated. But it was, nonetheless, essential to solidarity within the alliance.

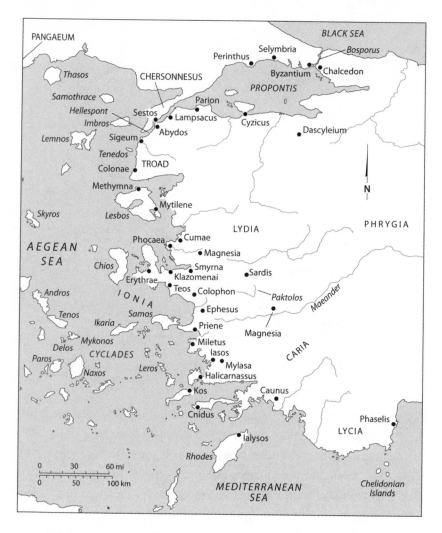

Map 5. The Revolt of Samos and Byzantium (detail on next page)

The Athenians were expected to protect the numerous small cities within their league from their larger neighbors. It is this tacit commitment that explains a provision within the constitution of the alliance, which came to be resented by its more powerful subordinate members, guaranteeing that none of these could ever mount a challenge from within to Athens' leadership. By stipulating that in the league synod every *pólis,* as such, be accorded an equal vote, this provision conferred formal authority on the multitude of communities most in need of Athens' protection and least likely to object to her plans.[9] The

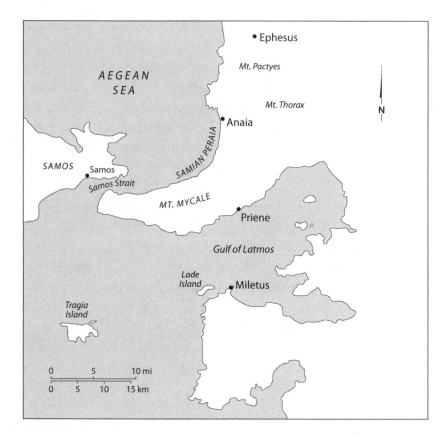

quarrel that erupted a few years after Sparta's victory late in the summer of 446 turned on the ambitions of a large city—persuaded that Athens was no longer capable of restraining her or reluctant to do so—and on her attempt to seize territory from a smaller one.

Priene, the smaller of the two cities, was an ancient Ionian *pólis*. Situated in Asia Minor some miles directly north of Miletus on a bay then located at the mouth of the river Maeander, she occupied a territory which lay adjacent to the southernmost part of the *peraía*—the extraterritorial domain on the mainland on the western slopes of Mount Pactyes, Mount Thorax, and Mount Mycale and along the coastal plain below—long claimed by Samos, an island polity located just off the Anatolian coast. For centuries the two had disputed ownership of these borderlands.[10]

In the late archaic period, Priene had been reduced to tributary status— initially, by the Mermnad kings of Lydia and, later, by their Persian successors.

But her citizens were not without spirit and spunk. Priene participated in the Ionian revolt in the 490s. She supplied twelve ships to the Ionian force marshaled at Lade near Miletus in 494; and at some point after the battle of Mycale she joined the Delian League, to which, we know, she faithfully contributed *phóros* on at least seven occasions in the late 450s and the 440s.[11]

Samos, which was also an ancient Ionian *pólis,* had long been a naval power of no small significance. She had never fallen prey to the Mermnads based at Sardis, and it was not until the reign of Darius that she fell under the sway of the Mede. She, too, had participated in the Ionian Revolt; she had dispatched sixty triremes to Lade in 494; and after the battle of Salamis fourteen years later, notables from the island took the lead in pressing Leotychidas, Sparta's reluctant Eurypontid king, to drive the Persians from Ionia. The Samians had been among the first in Ionia to join the Hellenic League. With the Chians and the islanders from Lesbos, they had subsequently played an especially prominent role in the foundation of the Delian League, and with the triremes that they provided they had distinguished themselves in that alliance's subsequent operations. In later years, for example, at Eurymedon and again in Egypt, the Samians had won renown, and in the league synod they were the first to suggest that the treasury be transferred to Athens.[12] To all appearances, the Samians were the most enthusiastic of Athens' allies, and they may have supposed that they could trade on this fact and that the Athenians would look the other way as they bullied the citizens of Priene.

This the Athenians might have done had the Milesians not come to Priene's defense. Miletus, which was also an ancient Ionian *pólis,* had a history even more distinguished than that of Samos. In the archaic period, she had fielded a large fleet, conducted an extensive commerce, and planted anywhere from thirty to ninety colonies in the Propontis and all around the Black Sea. Samos she had always regarded as a rival. The Milesians had successfully resisted Mermnad aggression. Alone among the Greek cities on the Anatolian mainland, they had maintained, by dint of a canny display of diplomacy, a measure of independence in the time of Cyrus and Cambyses. Moreover, in 499, it was Miletus that had spearheaded the Ionian revolt, and her citizens had reason to harbor resentment against the Samians. For at Lade five years thereafter, on signal, all but eleven of the Samian triremes had betrayed the rebellion, fled, and left their fellow Ionians to the mercy of the Mede. Moreover, in the aftermath, it was Miletus that had suffered the most. The city was sacked; many of her citizens were killed; and all but a few of the survivors were carted off to spend the rest of their lives at Ampe on the shores of the Persian Gulf.

When the Persians had finished pacifying Ionia, there were refugees who returned to Miletus, but they were few in number. It was not until after the battle of Mycale in 479 that a full-scale city was reestablished on the ancient site. The surviving refugees no doubt played a role, and of those deported a few may have found their way back from Ampe. But most appear to have come from the colonies to repopulate their ancient metropolis.

Miletus was in a weaker position than Samos. She is known have been among the *póleis* which in 454/3, in the wake of Athens' defeat in Egypt, paid the *phóros;* and it is unlikely that she ever supplied ships to the Delian League. The odds are also good that, in the aftermath of the settlement that the Athenians reached with Persia, she was required to dismantle a section of her city walls, for Athens appears to have demanded this of all the Greek cities scattered along the coasts of Asia Minor.[13] In coming to the defense of Priene, then, the Milesians were taking a considerable risk. It was perfectly possible— it was even likely—that the Samians would do what they, in fact, did: which was to dispatch an expeditionary force to attack Priene's ally.

It was in these circumstances—some five years after the ratification of the Thirty Years' Peace, late in the fall of 441 or in the winter of 441/40—that the Milesians and a faction on Samos eager for a change of regime sent an appeal to the hegemon of the Delian League. Pericles' chief rival Thucydides son of Melesias had been ostracized three or four years before, and the son of Xanthippus, who was elected general every year thereafter until his death, was now in effect unchallenged and more or less fully in charge. The fact that he moved with great dispatch says much about his understanding of the role that, in such circumstances, it was incumbent on Athens to play if the city was to keep her alliance intact.

First, the Athenian statesman had a decree passed calling on the Milesians and the Samians to stop the fighting and submit their dispute to Athens for arbitration. Then, when the latter refused, he set out for Samos with a fleet of forty triremes, seized the island, and set up a democracy. To guarantee the acquiescence of the notables, he took fifty boys and fifty men as hostages from among their number and had them conveyed to Athens' cleruchs on Lemnos for safekeeping. To bolster the new regime, he installed a garrison; and to

Figure 1. Bust of Pericles (Museo Pio-Clementino, Muses
Hall, Vatican City. Photographer: Jastrow. Published
under the following license issued by Jastrow [Marie-
Lan Nguyen]: "I, the copyright holder of this work,
release this work into the public domain. This applies
worldwide. In some countries this may not be legally
possible; if so I grant anyone the right to use this work
for any purpose, without conditions, unless such
conditions are required by law.")

cover the cost, he exacted from the Samians eighty talents (more than two
tons) of silver before heading home. Athens was not about to tolerate wars
between the members of her league.

As it turned out, Pericles had underestimated his opponents, and he had
blundered in not depriving the Samians of their fleet. The prominent families
that had ruled the island early in the archaic period and again for nearly forty

years after the battle of Mycale had been caught napping and had suffered a "theft of war." But they were no less enterprising and no less determined than the Athenians. Some of their members eluded capture, fled to Anatolia, and secured support from Pissouthnes son of Hystaspes—a great-grandson of Cyrus, grandson of Darius, nephew of Xerxes, and cousin of Artaxerxes who served as satrap in Sardis. Not long thereafter, under cover of darkness, this cohort of men crossed back over to the island from the mainland, bringing with them seven hundred mercenaries; and, with the cooperation of the most powerful of the notables who had remained on Samos, they overpowered the Athenian garrison, seized control, and restored oligarchic rule. Then, after recovering the hostages from Lemnos and handing over to Pissouthnes the Athenian garrison and its commanders, they began—apparently, with additional material support from the satrap—making preparations for a renewed assault on Miletus. It was, we must suspect, early in the summer that the Byzantines—inspired by the audacity of the Samians—joined the rebellion.

There is something quite odd about the conduct of the Samians at this juncture, and it is telling in more ways than one. They had reason, no doubt, for animus against the Milesians, but the latter posed no threat. It was about the Athenians that the oligarchs should have been thinking. Pericles and his compatriots were bound to send an armada to crush the rebellion, and it was vital that the Samians be ready to withstand the assault. The fact that the city's rulers concentrated on Miletus, instead, is an indication of the firm grip that fury, directed against their ancient foe, had on them. It is also a reminder of the degree to which—in an honorific, martial society shaped by an upbringing based first and foremost on Homer's *Iliad*—rage can warp strategic judgment.

The single-minded Samian focus on Miletus strongly suggests that the oligarchs on the island anticipated further help from abroad. Artaxerxes' cousin had supported the counter-coup they had mounted late in the spring or very early in the summer of 440, and he had presumably done so only after consulting the King of Kings via the Persian analogue to the Pony Express. Without this satrap's help, the oligarchs could not have raised a force of seven hundred mercenaries. Pissouthnes is said to have played a role in wresting from the Athenian cleruchs on Lemnos the hostages whom Pericles had quartered on the island, and he is said to have supplied the Samians with material support for the expedition against Miletus. He must also have raised their expectations that he could persuade the Great King to send the Phoenician fleet into the

Aegean to protect them from the Athenians—for they acted as if this was a done deal.[14]

Megabyzus' Revolt

Pissouthnes' meddling may have been payback for similar mischief on the part of the Athenians. If Ctesias—who would serve as a physician at the Persian court some forty years thereafter and pay close attention to the gossip he heard—is to be trusted at all, Artaxerxes had recently had to deal with a revolt on the part of one of his satraps; and there is reason to suspect that the Athenians may have lent this rebel semicovert aid of a sort similar to that at this time afforded the Samian oligarchs by Pissouthnes.

The satrap in question, Megabyzus son of Zopyrus, was a figure of no mean importance. His like-named grandfather had been one of the seven conspirators who had made Darius son of Hystaspes Great King in 522. His father had for Darius put down a fierce rebellion in Babylon. As a young man, this Megabyzus had accompanied Xerxes on the march into Greece, and he had served as one of his marshals. At some point, he had even married one of that Great King's daughters; and, in the aftermath of Xerxes' assassination, he had stood by his brother-in-law Artaxerxes, had divulged the nature of a plot against him, and had seen to it that the plotter's machinations were thwarted. He it was whom Artaxerxes had dispatched in the 450s to wrest Egypt from the Athenians.

According to Ctesias, sometime soon after fulfilling his mission, Megabyzus had managed to secure the surrender on terms of the rebel prince Inaros and of the six thousand Athenians in his immediate entourage by promising that the former's life would be spared and that the latter would be given safe conduct home. In the end, however, Megabyzus' promise was not honored. Artaxerxes' mother Amestris had been fond of Achaemenides (i.e., Achaemenes, the satrap of Egypt) and was enraged when he was killed by Inaros' forces. Five years after the capitulation—perhaps in 448 or 447—Artaxerxes finally gave way to the entreaties of his embittered mother and allowed her to execute the rebel leader and fifty of the Athenians. His honor besmirched, Megabyzus is said to have withdrawn from the court and to have returned, with the king's permission, to his satrapy in Syria, taking with him the remaining Athenians. It was from there that he reportedly launched a rebellion in which he inflicted severe defeats on two Persian armies before negotiating a reconciliation with Artaxerxes.

The story that Ctesias tells concerning Amestris, the fate of Inaros, and the role played in this drama by court intrigue is rife with error and confusion; and, although it may in some particulars be correct, it is, to say the least, open to question. That the rebellion took place, however, we need not doubt—for the generals said to have led the forces of the Great King against Megabyzus were Persian notables of high rank mentioned in no other surviving Greek document but instanced in the Babylonian tablets of the time; and the testimony of Herodotus confirms Ctesias' claim that Megabyzus' son Zopyrus subsequently ended up a refugee at Athens.

In his epitome of Ctesias' account, Photius nowhere states that Megabyzus owed his victories in Syria to a coordination of the heavy infantry of the Greeks with the cavalry of the Mede, but it is reasonable to suspect that this was the case. Hellenic soldiers of fortune were nothing new in the eastern Mediterranean. Like the neo-Assyrian kings, their Babylonian successors, and the Saite pharaohs of Egypt in earlier times, the satraps of western Asia normally employed Greek mercenaries as a supplement to the feudal levy of their provinces, which is what enabled Pissouthnes to be of use to the Samians.

Megabyzus had all that was required to effect this combination of arms and make what would later prove in the hands of Cyrus the Younger, Philip of Macedon, and Alexander the Great to be a signal advance in the art of war. The younger Cyrus may well have been the first to remark that the command of ten thousand Greeks would enable a man to wear the tiara of the Great King in his heart even if another man wore it on his head, but it is not likely that he was the first to recognize what such an infantry force could accomplish on the plains of Asia if its flanks were protected by first-rate cavalry. As the reconquest of Egypt demonstrated, the son of the elder Zopyrus had a genius for things military; and he had, in addition, a close familiarity with Greek practices stretching back by this time nearly thirty-five years and a keen awareness of the superiority that the hoplite infantrymen of Greece had demonstrated at Marathon, Plataea, Mycale, Eurymedon, and Cypriot Salamis. If there is any truth in the story Ctesias told about the Persian court, Megabyzus also had in his immediate entourage a cohort of experienced Athenian hoplites. Moreover, via his initiation of the diplomatic negotiations that followed the double-battle at Cypriot Salamis, he had forged ties with Athens, which controlled the seas through which mercenaries trained as hoplites could be transported from Arcadia and elsewhere in Hellas to Syria's distant shores. It is telling that his firstborn son, whom he named after his father Zopyrus, ended up at Athens; and it is hard to see how a satrap with the limited resources of his province could without support along these lines have defeated army after army fielded against him by the King of Kings.[15]

The Prospect of Persian Intervention

If the Athenians had provided Megabyzus with assistance in this fashion, it would not only help explain Pissouthnes' meddling. It would also throw light on Pericles' conduct in the war that followed. For he clearly feared that the Mede would do far more than Pissouthnes had up to this point done, and at every stage in the struggle he framed his strategy with an eye to this possibility. Early in the summer in 440, after the Athenians got wind that they were facing a full-scale revolt, they dispatched the son of Xanthippus and the other nine generals—the tragedian Sophocles among them—with a fleet of sixty ships to quell the uprising. Sixteen of these triremes Pericles and his colleagues detached from the main force. Some of these were sent—with the celebrity Sophocles on board—to summon assistance from Chios and the *póleis* on Lesbos and to encourage them to remain loyal. Others—no doubt, the fastest they had—made their way to Caria on the south shore of Anatolia on the lookout for the Phoenician fleet.

The forty-four triremes remaining under Pericles' command caught the rebel fleet off the coast of the little island of Tragia near Lade twelve miles south-southeast of Samos as the ships were making their way back from Miletus. The Samians had fielded fifty triremes and twenty troop transports. Though outnumbered, the Athenians emerged victorious. Soon thereafter, forty more triremes arrived from Athens and an additional twenty-five from Chios and Lesbos. The marines on board—in all likelihood, some forty per ship—they then landed on the island; and, in customary fashion, they walled in the city and conducted a blockade of the harbor by sea.

Before the blockade was fully in place, however, five Samian triremes had slipped past the enemy fleet and had headed south, then east along the southern coast of Anatolia to summon Phoenician help. And after the siege had begun, intelligence came in that an Achaemenid armada was on its way, and the son of Xanthippus set out in haste for Caunus on the border between Caria and Lycia with a fleet of sixty ships. Once again, however, he had underestimated the Samians. In his absence, under the leadership of the intrepid Eleatic philosopher Melissus son of Ithagenes, their hoplites and light-armed troops sallied forth and seized the unfortified camp of their adversaries. Then, the remainder of their fleet destroyed the squadron blockading the harbor, engaged and defeated the other triremes that attacked, and seized control of the sea so that they could bring in supplies.

Two weeks later, after the Persians had failed to make an appearance and Pericles and his fleet had returned, the Samians found themselves once again confined. Thereafter, additional reinforcements arrived—sixty more triremes from Athens and thirty more from Chios and Lesbos—and, if Ephorus is to be trusted, the Athenians eventually resorted to siege engines. Late in the spring or early in the summer of 439, after an eight-month siege the Samians opened negotiations; and, per the agreement reached, they were forced to raze their walls, give hostages, hand over their ships, fork over an immediate indemnity, and pledge to pay in installments the remaining expenses of the war—which, added together, had amounted to more than fourteen hundred talents in silver. The Byzantines reportedly surrendered on terms at about the same time.[16]

Because of the cordial relations that had so long existed between the Athenians and the Samians, both parties felt betrayed, and their conflict was especially bitter. The Athenians reportedly treated their captives as runaway slaves, tattooing them on the forehead with an image of the owl represented on their coins. The Samians are said to have retaliated in kind by tattooing the foreheads of the Athenians they seized with an image of a Samos craft [*sámaına naûs*]—a pot-bellied penteconter of Samian design, suited for carrying cargo and for locomotion both by oar and by sail. Duris of Samos, writing a century and a half after these events, claimed in the annals he composed concerning the history of his native city that Pericles and the Athenians took the trierarchs and marines they had captured to the marketplace in Miletus and had them bound to planks—presumably in the time-honored fashion, with iron collars about their necks and irons about their ankles and wrists—and there for ten full days left them exposed to the elements. Those who survived the ordeal were then reportedly taken down, and their heads the Athenians crushed. The corpses they then cast outside the city and left unburied.[17]

Ion of Chios, who was frequently in residence at Athens in these years, reports that Pericles was inordinately proud of his achievement. Where it had taken Agamemnon ten years to capture Troy, the Athenian boasted that he had overcome "the first and most powerful of the Ionians" in a mere eight months. In the funeral oration that he delivered in the wake of the war, however, the son of Xanthippus appears to have contained himself and to have focused the attention of his audience on the sacrifice made by their compatriots. Those who had died in battle he compared with the gods, remarking that he and his fellow Athenians provided evidence for the immortality of both by the honors they conferred on them and the offerings they made. It may well have been on this occasion that he famously remarked, "When a city has lost her young men, it is as if the year has been deprived of its spring."[18]

Portents

It would be hard to overstate the significance of the revolt of the Samians and the Byzantines. Putting it down required the expenditure of nearly forty tons of silver and the deployment of one hundred sixty triremes and up to thirty-six thousand eight hundred men. More than three decades thereafter, it was possible to imagine that the Samians had come exceedingly close to depriving the Athenians of their command of the sea. Although exaggerated, this judgment is not all that far from the truth. Had the Mytilenians, who contemplated rebellion at some point in these years, or the Chians boldly followed the Byzantines into rebellion, or had the Great King not balked and had Pissouthnes been able to make good on his promise that the Achaemenid fleet would intervene, Athens' empire might well have collapsed.[19]

The same might also have happened had the Peloponnesians once again invaded Attica and had the Corinthians intervened with their fleet on the side of the Samians, as they considered doing. At some point—almost certainly quite soon after the Samian exiles had returned to the island with the resources provided by Pissouthnes and had seized power and launched their revolt—the rebels appealed to Lacedaemon for aid. Although their intervention would have been an egregious breach of the terms of the Thirty Years' Peace and an act of flagrant impiety, the Spartans evidently voted to propose to their allies a renewal of the war with Athens, and they apparently would have launched an attack had the Corinthians, the only Peloponnesian community with a substantial fleet, not dug in their heels.[20]

Given the large number in attendance at meetings of the Spartan alliance and the human propensity for gossip, word must have gotten out quickly both regarding the matter discussed and the stances taken by the opposing parties.[21] Pericles and his compatriots can hardly have found the news reassuring. Like the punishment visited on Pleistoanax and Cleandridas, it was a powerful warning against a reliance on the truce negotiated in 446/5.

Moreover, if the Corinthians opposed war at this time, Pericles and his colleagues knew that it was not out of good will. In the war recently brought to an end, Corinth had suffered grievously, both on land and at sea; and the blockade that we have excellent reason to believe that the Athenians conducted is apt to have done Corinthian commerce and the well-being of Corinth's merchants and that of her citizens more generally untold harm. The historian Thucydides son of Olorus tells us that the Corinthians had contracted a "violent hatred" of the Athenians as a consequence of the latter's intervention in defense of Megara, and there is not the slightest reason to doubt that hatred's endurance.[22]

If, in 440, the Corinthians were averse to returning to war, it was because they, too, were exhausted and perhaps also because they had no desire to enter into a struggle at Lacedaemon's behest in which the burden and the risks would once again fall almost entirely on them. Public opinion at Corinth was nonetheless volatile. It would not take much at all to stir and stoke the ire of her citizens. When Thucydides tells us that the son of Xanthippus and a host of others at Athens judged that it was just a matter of time before the war would be renewed, we should take him at his word.[23]

Amphipolis

The effort required to crush the Samian revolt interrupted the expansion and consolidation of Athens' empire. But it did not measurably slow it down. In 437/6, just two years after Samos' surrender, Hagnon son of Nicias—a well-born, wealthy friend of Pericles who had been among his colleagues in the generalship at Samos three years before—led an expedition to Ennea Hodoi, a site in Thrace on the river Strymon upstream from Eion, where, in the days when Cimon son of Miltiades directed Athenian policy, Athens had made a spectacularly unsuccessful attempt to establish a settlement. There, not many miles from Drabeskos, where a host of his compatriots and their allies had been ambushed and massacred by the Edonians and the other Thracian tribes-men of the area in 464, he endeavored to found a colony, which he named Amphipolis in celebration of the fact that the mighty river flowed around the site selected on more than one side.[24]

Ennea Hodoi was, as the Athenians had long known, a location of no mean strategic significance. Nearby, on the lower Strymon, there was in abun-dance fir suited for the construction of triremes, and the site was close enough to command the mines of Mount Pangaeum to the northeast in the Daton valley. From it, one could also control and tax the commerce that ran up and down the river; and the circumstance could also be turned to advantage that it lay astride the great road—which the Romans would call the Via Egnatia—stretching from Epidamnus on the Adriatic coast of Illyria to Byzantium on the Bosporus. To mention none but these thoroughfares, however, would be to understate the commercial and military importance of Ennea Hodoi—for there, where Xerxes had bridged the Strymon more than forty years before, nine different roads converged, as its name indicates. He who ruled "Nine Roads" could not just monitor and regulate—he could, if he would, block—all traffic between eastern and western Thrace.[25]

Of course, none of this would have much mattered had it been impossible to construct a defensible settlement at Ennea Hodoi. There, however, near the narrows where the Strymon was most easily bridged—nestled in a great bend where the river flowed west, southwest, south, southeast, then back east before turning once again south—lay a natural acropolis, a cluster of hills visible from afar, towering some 460 feet above the Strymon, which one could with some effort turn into a sizable citadel by building a wall, generous in its pro-portions, below and around the elevated area.

To judge by the polygonal masonry that survives from this inner wall with its circuit of 1.3 miles, Hagnon did this right away. One could also then con-siderably expand the protected space by building two more walls—running, respectively, from the northeastern and northwestern corners of this citadel northwest toward the river—and then by adding in the north yet another wall, roughly parallel to the river, to link these two. And this was eventually done. One could increase this space even more by then extending these walls in a loop south of the inner circuit, as was certainly done at some point—at which time the outer circuit extended more than four miles in length and encom-

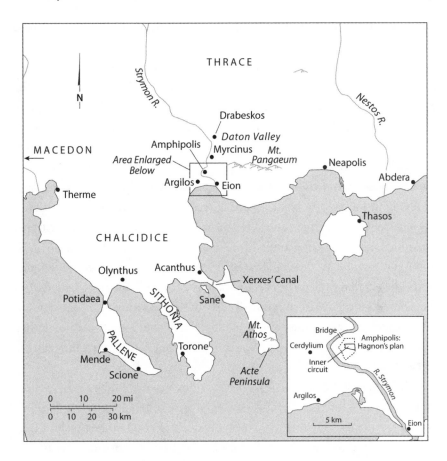

Map 6. The Chalcidice, the Strymon Valley, and Amphipolis

passed an area two-and-a-half times that enclosed by the enceinte Themistocles had hastily had thrown up around Athens in 479.

As reconstructed notionally, on the basis of the extensive archaeological remains, the two latter elements in the ultimate Amphipolitan system of defense were complementary. In tandem they jibed perfectly with Thucydides' description of Hagnon's master plan—which called for building the new city's walls in a great loop, beginning at one point quite near the river and ending at another—and there is every reason to believe that, in the first thirteen years that followed the foundation of Amphipolis, her citizens made considerable strides toward extending their fortifications to the north. Whether in these early years they also built walls to the south we do not know.[26]

Had Athens suffered at this time from overpopulation, Hagnon might have included none but his compatriots in the venture. Had this been possible, it certainly would have been advisable—for, in the long run, the city's loyalty to Athens was apt to be a function of her makeup. But this the new foundation's oecist could not achieve. Athens was even less able to afford the numbers required in 437 than she had been in the mid-460s. So, like the earlier attempt, the enterprise mounted on this occasion had to be a joint endeavor—this time involving just a handful from Athens alongside thousands from the cities in her alliance lying nearby. Quite a few of the colonists were erstwhile citizens of Argilos, a settlement founded by Andros on a site on the Aegean coast to the southwest just a few miles away. Even more of them, if we are to judge by the dialect that came to be predominant in the new settlement, hailed from the *póleis* said to have been founded early on by Euboeans from the cities of Chalcis and Eretria some twenty to fifty miles south-southwest of Ennea Hodoi on the peninsula shaped like a three-fingered hand that we now call the Chalcidice.[27]

Though, in some respects, Hagnon's venture resembled the abortive effort undertaken in Cimon's time, this new enterprise differed from it in two important particulars. First, at the outset, the oecist consulted the oracle at Delphi, which directed him to recover the bones of the Thracian king Rhesus, said in the *Iliad* to have been slain in a raid by Diomedes at Troy, and to return that hero's remains to his native land—which, to the best of his abilities Hagnon did. Then, having by this solemn act established the legitimacy of his claim to the territory, he drove the Edonians out of the lower Strymon valley altogether; and, as one would expect, his labors thereafter in founding Amphipolis were crowned with success.[28]

Later, in the summer of 436, Pericles mounted an expedition no less grand. From Athens—in all likelihood as a snub to the Persians for the support Pissouthnes had lent the Samian rebels—he conducted a fleet up through the Hellespont, the sea of Marmara, and the Bosporus deep into the Black Sea, which had hitherto been an Achaemenid lake. We know that he sailed along the north shore of Anatolia, displaying for all to see Athens' capacity to project power in distant parts, and intervening, where appropriate, to champion the

Map 7. The Propontis, the Bosporus, and the Black Sea

Greek cities of the coast against the barbarians of the interior and their Achaemenid overlords.

Here and there we get a glimpse of the details. At Sinope, for example, Pericles detached thirteen triremes and a force of hoplites under the command of a young general named Lamachus son of Xenophanes to assist the city's exiles in ousting the tyrant Timesilaus and his associates. In the aftermath, presumably at the invitation of these erstwhile exiles, he sent out from Athens six hundred settlers to bolster their cause and stiffen their resolve; and among these was divided the land and property owned by the tyrant and his friends. Further east, in all likelihood at this time, the city Amisos accepted a substantial contingent of Athenian colonists and was renamed Peiraeus; and the like was effected at Astacus at the northeastern end of the sea of Marmara. In every case, Panhellenism was a cover for Athens' advance—as it had been at Thurii, Neapolis, and Amphipolis. In every case, by doing good to their fellow Hellenes, the Athenians managed also to do well.

We are not told that the son of Xanthippus circumnavigated the Euxine, which would have been a real feat. But he may well have done so. There were

Greek settlements in Anatolia and on the coast of the Caucasus well to the east of Sinope and Amisos; there was no shortage of such settlements in Crimea and elsewhere on the Black Sea's northern and western shores; and there is reason to suspect that hitherto they may all have acknowledged the suzerainty of Achaemenid Persia and even paid tribute. Moreover, two years before, a new dynasty, under the leadership of a man named Spartocus, had seized control of the Bosporan kingdom, which was situated along the easternmost shores of Crimea and the narrow straits separating eastern Crimea from the mainland; and it may have been part of Pericles' purpose to lend support to the new rulers of this kingdom and negotiate an arrangement with them guaranteeing that they would continue shipping grain from the Cimmerian Bosporus to Athens—as, we know, they did.

There is no evidence that the cities of the Euxine were made to pay *phóros* to Athens in the late 430s or the early 420s, and with regard to this period we hear of no further Athenian interventions in the region. But, in the latter case, our ignorance may simply reflect the scarcity of evidence available to us. For there is every reason to believe that alliances were negotiated in the course of Pericles' voyage. A decade thereafter, in 425, when Athens was hard pressed for money, she would assess *phóros* in the Euxine—from more than forty cities— and the following year the Lamachus who had intervened at Sinope showed up with a small fleet to collect what these cities owed.[29]

Corinth's Grand Strategy Reconfigured

In 446, when Pleistoanax led the forces of the Spartan alliance back from Attica, the Corinthians are apt to have been even more furious than were the Spartiates who forced the Agiad king and his advisor Cleandridas into exile. They certainly had reason to be angry. During the First Attic War, the Athenians had done them real damage—both in battle and, we can be confident, commercially—and the Spartans had fallen short once again.

When the dust settled and the Thirty Years' Peace was ratified, however, the Corinthians seem to have taken a sober look at the situation and to have judged it something with which they could live. Corinth looked both east and west. She was situated at the crossroads between the Saronic and the Corinthian Gulf. She had harbors on both sides of the isthmus that separated these two bodies of water, and she presided over much of the trade that passed between the northeastern Mediterranean, on the one hand, and the Ionian Sea, the Adriatic, Italy, Sicily, Carthage, and the western Mediterranean, on the other. With her fleet, Corinth had once exercised influence in the east as well as the west. But her primary orientation had always been to the latter. To the east, she had but one colony—Potidaea at the entrance to Pallene, the western-most prong of what we now call the Chalcidice. To the west—near the mouth of the Corinthian Gulf, along the coast of the Ionian Sea and the Adriatic, and in Sicily—she had founded or cofounded a considerable number of settle-ments. In the east, Corinth had always faced rivals. Before Athens burst on the scene, there had been Aegina in the Saronic Gulf and, before Darius became Great King, Miletus, Samos, Chios, and Mytilene further east. Along the trade route stretching west, she had never known any rival—apart from her rene-gade colony Corcyra, which occupied a large and fertile island, shaped like a fish hook or a sickle, that was situated at the mouth of the Adriatic and ex-tended for something like forty miles along the forbidding, mountainous coast of ancient Epirus.[30]

In 446, when Corinth became party to the treaty of peace, she tacitly ac-cepted Athens' hegemony in the east. In 441, when she dug in her heels against Sparta's attempt to persuade her allies to renew the war with Athens, she had justified her position on the grounds that "each city has a right to punish her own allies."[31] This is, at least, the story that she later told, and this may well have been the standard to which she appealed in 441. On the face of it, this principle suited her interests well. If it required her acquiescence in Athens' domination of the Aegean, it also required Athens' acceptance of her predom-inance in the west. Or so she supposed.

The relations between a Greek metropolis and her colonies were not every-where the same. In some, if not most, cases, although the historical connection gave rise to sympathy, the ties were otherwise loose almost to the point of nonexistence. In other cases, relations were exceedingly tight. To the descen-dants of some, if not all, of the colonists they had dispatched to the Propontis and the Black Sea, the Milesians accorded a right to return to the mother city, take up residence, and assume citizenship there. In response, the pertinent colonies reciprocated by offering citizenship to refugees and others who im-migrated there from the metropolis.[32]

The Corinthians labored in another fashion to sustain a close connection with their colonies. Every year, without fail, they sent one or more officials—

called *epidēmiourgoí*—to Potidaea to share in the city's governance, and they are apt to have done the same with regard to nearly every *pólis* that they had founded in distant parts. If so, Corinth presided over an association of sorts—one centered chiefly on the Ionian Sea and the Adriatic and focused on the larger world to the west.[33]

As an instrument of empire or even self-defense, this association was defective in one, crucial particular. The largest, most prosperous, and most strategically important of Corinth's colonies in the region categorically refused to acknowledge the connection, treated her mother city with open contempt, and practiced a policy of proud and splendid isolation. The quarrel between Corinth and Corcyra went back to the archaic period. Its original grounds are hard to discern. But, for our purposes here, its origins are not germane. For what matters is this: in the second half of the fifth century, the island of Corcyra in the Adriatic was a power of consequence, equipped with hundred twenty triremes, the second largest fleet in Hellas. She sat astride the route that merchant ships and triremes almost invariably followed when they made their way from the Aegean and the Corinthian Gulf up the Balkan coast, then across the strait of Otranto to Italy, Sicily, and beyond. She profited enormously from their need for shelter, provision, and protection; and the antipathy which the metropolis and her colony evidenced for one another was real, palpable, enduring—and bitter in the extreme.[34]

Of course, little, if anything, of this was new. But what had long been an irritant had in the course of the fifth century become something far more serious. The war with Athens had been a tremendous shock to the Corinthians. Never before in their long history had they suffered severe defeats on the sea as well as on land. Never before had they been cut off in any serious way from commerce with the outside world. In the 450s, their expectations had been upended. Their situation had once seemed impregnable, but this had turned out to be an illusion. There had been a seismic shift in the geopolitical balance of power.

In the 450s, the Corcyraeans—with their large fleet—had been perfectly positioned to tip that balance back in Corinth's favor. But at no point in this period did they in any way come to the rescue of their metropolis. In circumstances such as these, the indifference and hostility of one's kin is more than an insult. It verges on injury.

In 446, though they had suffered grievously, the Corinthians were no more "broken in spirit" than their erstwhile opponent. After the negotiation of the long-term truce with Athens, they had one overriding aim—guaranteeing their own future security and prosperity. It was only natural that they should want to revise their grand strategy to fit the conditions at this point prevalent and that they should set out to resituate themselves in such a fashion that the Athenians could not repeat what they had done in the 450s. To this end, it was, of course, vital that Megara be firmly anchored to the Spartan alliance. But this was not sufficient. The Corinthians also had to strengthen their position in the Corinthian Gulf, the Ionian Sea, and the Adriatic. If Corinth was once again to be secure, if she was not to be a pawn in the rivalry between Athens and Sparta, she would have to reassert herself, build up her fleet, and by diplomacy or war regain control of her lifeline to the west.[35]

In the mid-450s, the Athenians with Pericles as their general had operated in tandem with the Acarnanians. There is every reason to suppose that they remained thereafter on intimate terms. In 455, the Athenians had taken responsibility for the Messenian refugees, who had recently withdrawn under truce from their stronghold on Mount Ithome, and they had settled them near Acarnania at Naupactus—right next to the narrowest point in the Corinthian Gulf, where its northern and southern shores were separated by a mile and a bridge now spans the divide. We know that Athens remained the patron of this community; she almost certainly retained control of Molycreium and Chalcis further to the west; and it was a foregone conclusion that, when the great war was renewed, she would once again station a fleet at this strategic choke point (later known as Lepanto) to monitor and, when expedient, prevent traffic from entering and exiting the Corinthian Gulf.[36]

Next to no one supposed the Thirty Years' Peace anything more than a truce. When the day arrived in which the war was renewed, it was vital that the Corinthians be ready. It was essential that they have command of the requisite resources. They had to be able to keep a firm hold on Megara and bar the Athenians from Pegae on the Corinthian Gulf, and it was essential that they oust Athens' clients from Naupactus and recover their colonies Molycreium just north of the Corinthian Gulf and Chalcis on the Gulf of Patras. In addition, they had to prevent the Athenians from renewing the alliance they had forged in the 450s with Achaea on the opposite shore, and they needed to force the Acarnanians to foreswear their ties with the Athenians. Put simply, it was crucial that the Corinthian Gulf and the Gulf of Patras once again become a

Map 8. The Ionian Sea, the Adriatic, and the Entrance to the Corinthian Gulf

Corinthian lake—and, to this end, the Corinthians had to rally their colonies in the west and turn what had been a loose association into a proper military alliance.

By 435, they had made some headway. Chalcis they appear to have regained, and the same may have been true for Molycreium nearby. On some of their former colonies in the Ionian Sea, the Corinthians could also now certainly rely. There was, however, one fact that seriously complicated their efforts. A number of the colonies claimed by Corinth were joint foundations. Leucas may have been one such, and Anactorium was another. Apollonia was a third, and there was, as we shall soon see, a fourth. At a time in the late seventh century when the Corinthians and the Corcyraeans were on good terms, they had cooperated in the foundation of most if not all, of these *póleis*. Later—at some point well before 465, almost certainly in the immediate aftermath of the battles of Salamis and Plataea—a dispute concerning responsibility for the foundation of Leucas had arisen between the two; and Themistocles, who had been asked to arbitrate, had awarded Corcyra an indemnity in silver of twenty talents (more than half a ton), and he had declared the colony a joint foundation. By 435, however, Leucas was firmly in the Corinthian camp, and the same can be said for Apollonia.[37]

We do not know how this was achieved, and we do not know when. Nor, alas, do we know when war broke out between the Acarnanians and an important Corinthian colony in their vicinity. Its strategic significance, however, we can surmise. We are told that the Acarnanians and their Amphilochian neighbors, who lived along the Ionian Sea immediately to the north of the Corinthian Gulf, had quarreled with their Ambraciot neighbors, who lived along the coast still further north. The dispute concerned Amphilochian Argos—which the Amphilochians and the Ambraciots had once shared. We are told that the Acarnanians and Amphilochians sought Athenian help and that Phormio son of Asopius, who was among the Athenian generals tasked with crushing the Samian revolt, was dispatched from Athens with thirty triremes to help the Amphilochians recover the city. We have reason to suspect that, at this time, his thirty ships managed to defeat a force of fifty triremes fielded by the Ambraciots and their allies in the region, and we are told that, as a result of the support that he provided to the Acarnanians in their time of need, they came to be firmly allied with the Athenians.[38] At the western end of the Corinthian Gulf and along the shores of the Ionian Sea, the Athenians and the Corinthians were both asserting themselves, and they surely both knew that there could be a clash. In the event, it was not long in coming.

CHAPTER 2

Pericles' Calculated Risk

One must turn Thucydides over line by line and read the thinking hidden behind what he says [*Hintergedanken*] with as much discernment as his actual words: there are few thinkers who are so rich in thoughts left unexpressed [*hintergedankenreiche*].

FRIEDRICH NIETZSCHE

THUCYDIDES son of Olorus was a fully grown man at the time that the Athenians and the Corinthians once again came to blows, and it is in describing the immediate background of their clash that his narrative of the great war between the Athenians and the Peloponnesians begins in earnest. With regard to his account of "the deeds done by those active in the war," the historian denies that he thought it proper to write on the basis of chance reports or his own transient impressions. Regarding the deeds "which I witnessed and those I learned about from others," he asserts, "I checked out each insofar as was possible with scrupulous exactitude [*akríbeia*]," adding that "these investigations required a great deal of labor because those present at particular events were at odds with one another as a consequence of favoritism or a failure of memory."[1]

What we know from other sources suggests that, in striving for accuracy, Thucydides was as good as his word. On rare occasions, of course, he falls short of the *akríbeia* he advertises, and he tells us considerably less about domestic politics at Athens and about Persia, Lacedaemon, Argos, Corinth, Thebes, Megara, Mantineia, Tegea, Elis, Syracusa, and other, less important Hellenic cities than we would like to know. But his description of the events of the late 430s and thereafter is highly accurate and chronologically precise. Except, then, where there is excellent reason to think him in error, in the remainder of this volume, I will treat his account as fact.[2]

With regard to the speeches that adorn his narrative, Thucydides takes a different tack. He begins by acknowledging that both he and his informants "found it difficult to remember or otherwise preserve [*diamnēmoneûsai*] with precise accuracy [*akríbeia*] that which was said," and he admits that to some degree he was forced to rely on his own impressions. Then, in explaining the procedure he followed in his book, he advances a cryptic—and some would say, a self-contradictory—claim: "When, in my judgment, each of those speaking most fully expressed what was demanded by the situation then at hand [*perì tôn aieì paróntōn tà déonta*], this I had him say, sticking as closely as possible to the overall gist [*xumpásē gnómē*] of what was actually said."

In reporting what was said at the time, Thucydides was highly selective, as all historians are; and for the most part he ignored idle chatter, inane comments, and other inconsequential utterances, as all historians try to do. On occasion, however, he may have done something that modern historians scrupulously avoid: he may have exercised something verging on poetic license. His aim was to relate the arguments of importance that were articulated at the time; and, as is evident from the literary character of the speeches that he provides us with, he did so generally in dense prose, to a considerable degree in words of his own choosing, arranging the material with an eye both to its dramatic impact and to the light, he believed, contemporary commentary (when accurate, when in error, and also when deliberately deceptive) could cast on the thinking and argumentation that informed and illuminated the deeds of men. Where he had no idea what was actually said, he may for dramatic purposes or for the purpose of illumination have supplied what was, he thought, apt to have been uttered because appropriate to the occasion. Where he had a pretty good idea of what was said, however, he simply selected out the argumentation that he thought especially revealing or otherwise apt. If the arguments made by different men on opposed sides at different gatherings sometimes seem to respond to one another, it is not, as some suppose, because the speeches in Thucydides are a species of historical fiction. It is because the historian thought these particular arguments, when and where they were in fact articulated, especially apt and worthy of being highlighted and because he took delight in their juxtaposition.[3]

It is incumbent on the modern historian to keep this in mind when he draws on such material. In what follows, with regard to speeches that Thucydides is likely to have heard himself or to have heard a great deal about, I will presume that his summaries are indicative of what he took to be the more telling of the arguments actually made.

There is one additional matter of vital importance for understanding our primary source for this period. Its author greatly admired foresight. Some men, he knew, needed no instruction in this regard. Themistocles achieved what he achieved "by his own native intelligence, without the help of study before or after." If, "in a future as yet obscure he could in a preeminent fashion foresee both better and worse" even "when there was little time to take thought," it was solely because of "the power of his nature." Such was Thucydides' conviction.

Most men, he knew, were not so blessed. But among these, he believed, there were some who possessed a capacity to profit not only from study but also from reflecting on their own experience and from weighing that of others. It was for these men that Thucydides composed his book. The great war between the Peloponnesians and the Athenians he considered a revealing event of world-historical importance. In a justly famous passage, which helps explain the immense effort he put into achieving *akríbeía,* the historian tells us that he composed his account of the war not as "a contest piece to be heard straightaway" but as "a possession for all times." He was aware that the absence within his book of "the mythic" or "fabulous [*tò muthôdes*]" would render it "less delightful [*aterpésteron*]" to some than the work of Homer and Herodotus. But he did not care. It would, he confesses, satisfy his purpose if his work were "judged useful by those who want to observe clearly the events which happened in the past and which in accord with the character of the human predicament [*katà tò anthrópinon*] will again come to pass hereafter in quite similar ways." In short, Thucydides saw himself as a political scientist intent on discerning patterns and as an educator of use to prospective statesmen.[4]

Despite or, rather, because of his didactic purpose, Thucydides eschewed pedantry. He took to heart the principle of rhetoric later voiced by Theophrastus:

> It is not necessary to speak at length and with precision on everything, but some things should be left also for the listener—to be understood and sorted out by himself—so that, in coming to understand that which has been left by you for him, he will become not just your listener but also your witness, and a witness quite well disposed as well. For he will think himself a man of understanding because you have afforded him an occasion for showing his capacity for understanding. By the same token, whoever tells his listener everything accuses him of being mindless.[5]

No one appreciated this dimension of Thucydides' achievement more fully than did Thomas Hobbes, who shared the Athenian historian's predilections and judged it "the principal and proper work of history . . . to instruct and enable men, by the knowledge of actions past, to bear themselves prudently in the present and providently toward the future." In the preface to the translation of Thucydides' account of the war that he published in 1628, the English philosopher singled out the Greek historian as "the most politic historiographer that ever writ," explaining his judgment in the following way:

> [Thucydides] filleth his narrations with that choice of matter, and ordereth them with that judgment, and with such perspicuity and efficacy expresseth himself, that, as Plutarch saith, he maketh his auditor a spectator. For he setteth his reader in the assemblies of the people and in the senate, at their debating; in the streets, at their seditions; and in the field, at their battles. So that look how much a man of understanding might have added to his experience, if he had then lived a beholder of their proceedings, and familiar with the men and business of the time: so much almost may he profit now, by attentive reading of the same here written. He may from the narrations draw out lessons to himself, and of himself be able to trace the drifts and counsels of the actors to their seat.[6]

What Thucydides did not do, however, was to openly tell his readers what to think. As Hobbes would later put it, "Digressions for instruction's cause, and other such open conveyances of precepts, (which is the philosopher's part), he never useth; as having so clearly set before men's eyes the ways and events of good and evil counsels, that the narration itself doth secretly instruct the reader, and more effectually than can possibly be done by precept."[7]

Hobbes was by no means the last to make this observation. Jean-Jacques Rousseau described Thucydides as "the true model of a historian," adding as an explanation: "He reports the facts without subjecting them to judgment, but he omits not one of the circumstances appropriate for inducing us to judge them ourselves. He places everything he recounts before the eyes of his reader. Far from interposing himself between the events and his readers, he shies away and conceals himself. One no longer believes that one reads; one believes that one sees."[8] One must, Friedrich Nietzsche would later add, "turn Thucydides over line by line and read the thinking hidden behind what he says [*Hintergedanken*] with as much discernment as his actual words: there are few thinkers who are so rich in thoughts left unexpressed [*hintergedankenreiche*]."[9]

Put bluntly, if these supremely intelligent readers are correct, Thucydides is less interested in instructing his audience in what to suppose about particular developments than in inducing its members to think strategically and in teaching them how to go about it. If he is as sparing in spelling out his own analysis of events as he is generous and precise in detailing those events, it is because he is eager that his readers learn to figure things out for themselves. His goal is to educate citizens and statesmen, not to train automatons, and so he leaves his readers with a host of puzzles on which to ruminate.

In trying to make sense of what happened in and after the late 430s, our task must then be, in part, to do for ourselves what Thucydides leaves it for us to do—which is, to elucidate what he left unsaid. To this end, we must pull together the fragments of information that Thucydides provides; we must add to that information from the other surviving sources; and we must "draw out lessons" for ourselves and "trace the drifts and counsels of the actors to their seats." Most, if not all, of the time we will find ourselves discovering what he had recognized at the outset.

Push Comes to Shove

In 436 or early 435, the Corinthians found themselves confronted with a fateful opportunity. Civil strife, the bane of nearly all of the Greek cities, had erupted at Epidamnus. This *pólis* was a populous settlement of ample wealth and considerable strategic importance. She was situated on an easily defended peninsula, six miles in length, named Dyrrachium (which is occupied today by Durrazzo, the capital of modern Albania). This placed her conveniently near the silver mines of Illyria at the western end of the great road that led across the Balkans to Amphipolis and on to Byzantium. In Roman and Frankish times, and surely in earlier epochs as well, her harbor served as the chief jumping-off point for the voyage across the strait of Otranto from the Balkans to Italy and Sicily. For those in a tremendous hurry, there were shorter routes further south. But on such a voyage one could not take advantage of the prevailing winds, which sweep down the Adriatic, and one would risk encountering high seas at that body of water's mouth, where contrary winds and conflicting currents clash and storms generated by the Acroceraunian mountains, which run along the coast of Epirus, frequently disturb the vasty deep.[10]

According to Thucydides, the democratic faction, which controlled Epidamnus, found itself besieged at this time by exiled Epidamnian oligarchs and their allies among the Illyrians of the interior. For help in mediating the dispute, these democrats turned to their mother city Corcyra, which appears to have been a sister democracy; and in keeping with the well-thought-out policy of isolationism that had kept them out of the Persian Wars and the First Attic War, the Corcyraeans spurned their colonists' appeal. In desperation, the Epidamnian democrats then sent an embassy to the oracle at Delphi, hoping that it would sanction an appeal on their part to Corinth, which, as it happens, was at this time an oligarchy. Centuries before—when, for a time, relations with Corcyra had been everything that they were supposed to be—the Corinthians had, in accordance with their custom, appointed an oecist to lead colonists drawn from among the citizens of Corcyra to the place picked out for the establishment of Epidamnus on the Illyrian shore. This provided the Epidamnian democrats with the requisite excuse. The oracle, when asked and perhaps supplied with an inducement, opined that their city was, in fact, a Corinthian colony; and, with an eye to their own security needs, the Corinthians leapt at the opportunity they were then afforded.[11]

With little delay, the Corinthians dispatched colonists drawn from among their citizens and those of their allies to join with the Epidamnian democrats in refounding the city, knowing full well that, in doing so, they might become embroiled with Corcyra, as they had on occasion in the past. The Corcyraeans had already had Leucas and Apollonia wrested from their grasp. They would certainly not welcome yet another intervention on Corinth's part in their immediate neighborhood.

In this regard, the fears of the Corinthians were fully realized. The Corcyraeans responded by accepting an appeal for support from the exiled Epidamnian oligarchs and their Illyrian allies and by initiating a siege of the city by both land and sea. The Corinthians then began to equip a relief force, and to this end they drew material support from nearly all of their Peloponnesian allies—apart, that is, from Sicyon, Sparta, and the landlocked cities and towns of Arcadia.[12]

At this point the Corcyraeans blinked. They sent an embassy to Sparta and Sicyon, and, with the encouragement and support of these two cities they approached the Corinthians, demanding at first that the latter abandon Epidamnus as no concern of theirs, and then suggesting that, if this was unacceptable, the dispute be arbitrated by the oracle at Delphi or by one or more of the cities in the Peloponnesus as agreed upon by both parties. Thucydides does not tell us what the Corcyraeans intended, but it is nonetheless clear. In suggesting that the dispute be arbitrated by powers allied with Corinth or by an oracle that had already sanctioned Corinth's intervention at Epidamnus, the Corcyraeans were offering to surrender their claim if the Corinthians were willing to allow them to save face. In the process, however, they warned the Corinthians that, if they had to do so, they would seek help elsewhere. When the Corinthians replied that no such discussions could take place until and unless the siege was lifted, the Corcyraeans offered them a series of alternatives: that they would withdraw their forces if the Corinthians were willing to do the same, that the struggle could continue while arbitration was under way, or that there could be an armistice and arbitration.[13]

Thucydides does not explain why the Spartans and the Sicyonians sent ambassadors to support the Corcyraean appeal, but this, too, is easy to discern. The authorities in both *póleis* recognized that, if the Corcyraeans were driven to seek help from the Athenians and succeeded in securing it, their own communities might eventually become embroiled in the dispute; and in the circumstances, at a time when Athens was not in any obvious way especially vulnerable, this they very much wanted to avoid. When the Corinthians resolutely refused to let the Corcyraeans gracefully back down, at least some of the ephors and *gérontes* at Lacedaemon must have thought the situation alarming.

The conduct of the Corinthians is, in part, explicable in terms of bitterness and ire. The Corcyraeans had been a thorn in their side off and on for nearly two centuries. This was certainly a part of the story, as Thucydides makes clear. More important than resentment, however, was a strategic consideration, which he leaves to us to discover for ourselves: if the Corinthians annihilated the Corcyraean fleet and seized the island, especially if they managed to secure Epidamnus in the bargain, they would have in hand the resources necessary to confine or eliminate the Messenians at Naupactus and to reestablish their own hegemony in the Corinthian Gulf, the Ionian Sea, and the Adriatic along the coastal trade route linking the Balkans with Italy and Sicily. It was a real gamble, but—given what the Corinthians had evidently been through during the war with Athens—the risk was well worth taking. Or so it must have seemed at the time.

Had the fleet dispatched by Corinth and her allies in 435 defeated the Corcyraeans just off Cape Leukimne in the southernmost part of the channel separating Corcyra from Epirus on the mainland, the former probably would have won the game. But they lost that battle. In the aftermath, Epidamnus fell to the Corcyraeans and their allies; and when the Corinthians responded by mounting a supreme effort to build a great armada capable of reversing the decision at Cape Leukimne, the Corcyraeans made good on the threat issued by the embassy that they had sent to Corinth. They turned to Athens, and the Athenians were drawn in.

The latter had no real interest in the quarrel. They owed Corcyra nothing, and they did not much care for the Corcyraeans. No one did. As Thucydides' early readers did not have to be told, in 481, these islanders had promised to send sixty triremes to support the Hellenes against the Persians; and, in the summer of 480, when this force was desperately needed, it did not appear.[14]

The Athenians were, nonetheless, alert—and, when faced with the facts, they winced. They could not stand idly by while the city fielding the third largest fleet in Hellas conquered the city fielding its second largest fleet—not, at least, if they were given an opportunity to prevent this conquest from taking place. Corinth's bold venture threatened the naval balance of power and did so in a manner that the sovereign of the sea simply could not ignore. To such a possibility, the Athenians, who depended for their nourishment on grain imported by sea from Crimea, could not be indifferent. And so, at first, they waited, watched, and prepared for the worst by conserving their forces. In or soon after 434—when trouble erupted at Thurii, when the Athenian element in the colony's population lost control, and the *pólis* approached Delphi with an eye to seeking divine sanction for her desire to renounce Athens' status as her mother city—they did not intervene. They had other, more pressing concerns nearer to home.[15]

If there was to be a clash with Corinth, it was to the advantage of the Athenians that responsibility for the conflict be pinned on the Corinthians alone—for this might obviate a general war, and it would certainly produce strains within the Spartan alliance. The son of Xanthippus handled the situation deftly in a manner worthy of comparison with the skill displayed more than two millennia thereafter by Otto von Bismarck. When the Corcyraean delegation arrived and the Corinthians sent an embassy as well, both addressed the Athenian assembly. After hearing them, the Athenians voted to reject the Corcyraeans' request for a full-scale, all-purpose *summachía*, requiring that the two parties have the same enemies and friends and committing Athens to an out-and-out war with Corinth in breach of the Thirty Years' Peace. The next morning, after sleeping on the matter, they met again to reconsider their decision. This time—at Pericles' urging, so Plutarch reports—they voted instead to form with the Corcyraeans an *epimachía,* a purely defensive alliance aimed solely (or so it seemed) at deterring Corinthian aggression.[16] The Athenians had no desire to be the initiator of a general war with the Spartan alliance. They were not spoiling for a fight. Their sole purpose was to defend the territorial integrity of Corcyra. This, Thucydides invites us to infer, they wanted to broadcast to both friend and foe.

When it became clear that the Corinthians had not been deterred and that a battle was in the offing and the Corcyraeans invoked the alliance and asked for Athenian aid, Pericles saw to it that his compatriots dispatched only ten ships. These he put under the command of a *próxenos* of the Spartans at Athens, who just happened to be a son of his old rival Cimon. Tellingly, the man bore the name Lacedaemonius, and he and his colleagues were told to enter the battle if and only if the Corcyraeans were on the verge of defeat. It was, it appears, only as an afterthought some three weeks later that the Athenians successfully pressed Pericles to send to Corcyra twenty additional ships to reinforce the original ten, and this time as well the commanders dispatched appear to have been critics of Pericles known to have been friendly to the Lacedaemonians.[17] Here again, Thucydides induces us to conclude, the Athenians ostentatiously signaled their reluctance, and he allows us to speculate that they would not have regretted it had a clash of the Corinthians and Corcyraeans greatly reduced the naval power of both.

Had the Corcyraeans proven victorious without Athenian help in the battle that took place in 433 near the Sybota Isles at the southern entrance to the channel separating Corcyra from Epirus on the mainland, the diplomatic crisis looming on the horizon might well have been averted. But it took Athenian intervention to save them, and this left the Corinthians not only frustrated and furious but, we can infer, desperate as well. In the years following their defeat off Cape Leukimne, they had gone all out. At that battle, they had fielded anywhere from thirty to thirty-eight triremes, and they had lost fifteen of these. Two years later, they had turned the surviving triremes into ninety, and they had persuaded their Ambraciot colonists to increase their contingent by a similar ratio. Then, with a fleet of one hundred fifty triremes deployed on the high seas just off the Sybota Isles east of the southern tip of Corcyra, Corinth and her allies had proved superior. They had destroyed, disabled, or seized seventy of the one hundred ten triremes deployed by the Corcyraeans while losing only thirty themselves. They had captured more than a thousand mariners and no doubt killed many, many more. In the end, however, thanks to the intervention of the ten Athenian triremes and the appearance on the horizon of the twenty sent as reinforcements, they had suffered what, for perfectly understandable reasons, they bitterly regarded as "a theft of war."[18]

Being denied their prize at the mouth of the Adriatic was a painful blow, and it was rendered doubly painful by the fact that, on that fateful day near the Sybota Isles, the conquest of Corcyra had been within Corinth's grasp. There was, however, more at stake for the Corinthians that day than an assertion of their superiority and the subjugation of a renegade colony. For more than a decade, they had patiently pursued the new grand strategy—aimed at shoring up their regime and at preserving their independence and their way of life—which they had carefully articulated in the wake of their earlier war with Athens. In the summer of 433, they had very nearly achieved its goal. They had very nearly established their mastery over the seas to their west. They had tasted success. Then, they had been handed a strategic defeat; and, contrary to their calculations, their worst nightmare had come true. Thanks to their decision to turn the squabble over Epidamnus into an attempt to conquer Corcyra, Athens was no longer just an alarming presence in the seas the Corinthians considered their own. She was now predominant therein. In such a result no power of consequence could acquiesce.

The Road to War

To add insult to injury, the Athenians then took precautions in the wake of the clash in a manner certain to add to the fury of the Corinthians. Potidaea on Pallene in what we now call the Chalcidice was the only Corinthian colony of any significance in the Delian League. Her citizens may have caused Athens trouble in the past. The Potidaeans were, we know, a manly lot. In the wake of the battle of Salamis, Herodotus reports, they had rebelled against Persia, survived a siege initiated by Artabazus son of Pharnaces, and managed to convey three hundred hoplites to Plataea in time to battle the Mede. Their complete absence from what we possess of the *phóros* lists for the period stretching from 454 through 446 suggests something else of interest which Thucydides did not

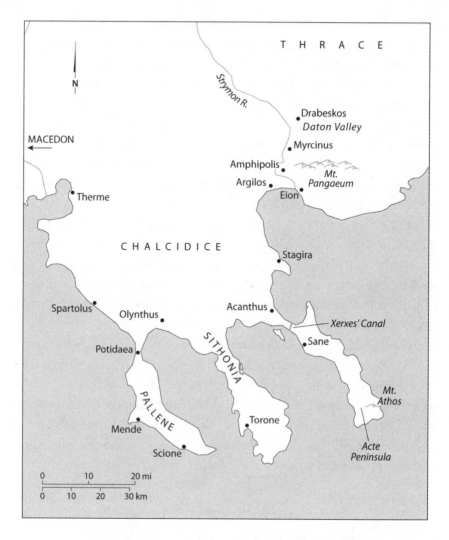

Map 9. Potidaea, Spartolus, and Olynthus in the Chalcidice

think it essential that we know: that, when Athens and Corinth came to blows, the Potidaeans may have withdrawn from the Delian League, and that their return was a consequence of the Thirty Years' Peace.[19] It was with an eye to the likelihood that Corinth would call on her colony again for support and that these spirited men would once again assert their independence that, in the fall of 433, the Athenians instructed the Potidaeans to raze the section of their walls which faced south down the Pallene peninsula and demanded that they hand over hostages, dismiss the *epidēmiourgoí* sent by Corinth to participate in the governance of their *pólis,* and refuse to accept *epidēmiourgoí* dispatched in the future.

Once again, however, as in the case of Samos, the Athenians were tardy in sending a fleet with marines to enforce their commands, and they were overconfident—for the flotilla which they finally dispatched was insufficient. As Thucydides makes clear, the Potidaeans had cleverly played for time. They had sent an embassy to Athens to appeal the decision made; and we learn from the epigraphical record that, in the spring of 432, they had paid the *phóros* in a timely fashion as they appear to have done in every year since 445. In the meantime, however, as Thucydides informs us, they had secretly sought support from Corinth and from "the authorities [*tà télē*]" at Lacedaemon. The Corinthians had then sworn to come to their aid; and from, we must suspect, the "little assembly" consisting of the ephors, the *gérontes,* and the two kings or their regents at Sparta, they had received a promise, no doubt elicited by the Corinthians, that, if the Athenians attacked Potidaea, the Lacedaemonians would invade Attica.

Come early June, when the thirty triremes dispatched by Athens to western Thrace finally arrived, the Potidaeans were in open revolt, and they had secured local support. For some time, the Athenians had been at odds with Perdiccas son of Alexander, who is thought to have fought his way to the Macedonian throne at some point in the first seventeen years following his father's death circa 452. Like his father before him, Perdiccas found Athens' involvement in the Thraceward region alarming, and he was especially unhappy about the recent establishment of the Athenian colony Amphipolis on the Strymon athwart the crossroads called Ennea Hodoi. Even more recently, moreover, the Athenians had lent aid to a rival claimant to the Macedonian throne. Now Perdiccas seized the opportunity to take revenge and reduce Athens' influence in the region. To Potidaea he promised support. The Bottiaeans nearby and the Chalcidians more generally he persuaded to rebel; and he encouraged the latter to withdraw from the host of small, indefensible towns scattered throughout Sithonia and the area situated directly to its north in which they had hitherto resided and join the contingent of Chalcidians, once led by Kritoboulos of Torone, to whom Xerxes' marshal Artabazus had given Olynthus almost half a century before.

Located about two miles above the Gulf of Torone north and east of Poti-daea, Olynthus sat atop a fortified bluff, which overlooks on all sides a sizable district rich in fertile farmland. In response to the doubling of the city's pop-ulation, her citizens, who had hitherto resided on the southern of the two hills constituting this bluff, cleared a flat space atop its northern counterpart and laid out a grid on the model pioneered by Hippodamus. Then they divided the available land into equal allotments and assigned to each of the newcomers one of these. From this time onward, as the Athenians discovered to their dismay, the Chalcidians concentrated at Olynthus were a force to be reckoned with.

The Corinthians exercised a measure of restraint. Instead of formally de-claring war and conveying to western Thrace a force of triremes and a proper army made up of their own citizens, they engaged in a quasi-covert action by hiring mercenaries and providing support to those of their citizens who were willing to fight as volunteers. In consequence, forty days after the Potidaean revolt, Aristeus, son of the Adeimantus who had led the Corinthian contin-gent at Salamis, arrived in the Thraceward region, bringing with him a force of sixteen hundred hoplites and four hundred light-armed troops to stiffen the resistance. Some months thereafter, probably in October, a battle was fought, which the new and larger force sent in the interim from Athens managed to win—and the siege of Potidaea commenced.[20]

Athens' assault on the autonomy of the Potidaeans and on the ties that bound Corinth's colony to her metropolis were not, however, the matters that most disturbed the Corinthians. We are not told outright that alarm was added to fury and despair when the citizens of Corinth learned that, in the aftermath of the battle at the Sybota Isles, the Athenians had passed a series of decrees, tantamount to an embargo, barring the Megarians both from trading in the markets at Athens and in her empire and from entering the ports be-longing to the cities in the Delian League.[21] But we are given the information requisite for sorting out the timing of this development and for judging its significance.[22]

On the face of it, the so-called Megarian Decrees were occasioned by two developments: first, a minor territorial dispute and a charge of impiety, which pitted the Athenians against their Megarian neighbors, who were purportedly farming land along their border with Attica which was sacred to Demeter and Persephone; and, second, the fact that the city of Megara had begun giving refuge to slaves that had run away from Athens (which was a decidedly hostile

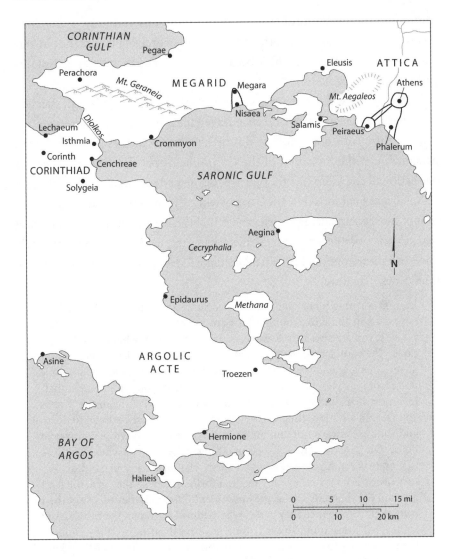

Map 10. The Saronic Gulf

act). But Athens' leaders almost certainly had another, more narrowly strategic motive for proposing the decrees as well. Of the members of the Spartan
alliance quite closely tied to Corinth that were nestled along the Saronic Gulf
within Athens' immediate vicinity, four cities—Epidaurus, Hermione, Troezen,
and Megara—had sent ships to join the Corinthian fleet that had fought off
Cape Leukimne. We do not know whether in the interim, between that battle
and Corinth's second clash with Corcyra, the Athenians had issued a word of

warning to these *póleis*. All that we can say with any certainty is this: that, according to Thucydides' report, only one of them opted to ignore the obvious danger and to send ships to the Sybota Isles as well, and that it was against this city that Athens passed the Megarian Decrees.[23]

It was in the wake of these developments that the Corinthians dispatched an embassy to Lacedaemon and encouraged the Megarians and others among Sparta's allies with grievances to do the like. It was in these circumstances, presumably at the invitation of the Corinthians, that the Aeginetans sent a delegation to complain that they were being denied the autonomy which, they claimed, was guaranteed by their treaty with Athens. And it was on the occasion of this general airing of grievances that the Corinthians are said to have issued a memorable warning, characterizing the Lacedaemonians and their once and future opponents. "The Athenians," they reportedly observed, "are innovators." They are

> keen in forming plans, and quick to accomplish in deed what they have contrived in thought. You Spartans are intent on saving what you now possess; you are always indecisive, and you leave even what is needed undone. They are daring beyond their strength, they are risk-takers against all judgment, and in the midst of terrors they remain of good hope—while you accomplish less than is in your power, mistrust your judgment in matters most firm, and think not how to release yourselves from the terrors you face. In addition, they are unhesitant where you are inclined to delay, and they are always out and about in the larger world while you stay at home. For they think to acquire something by being away while you think that by proceeding abroad you will harm what lies ready to hand. In victory over the enemy, they sally farthest forth; in defeat, they give the least ground. For their city's sake, they use their bodies as if they were not their own; their intelligence they dedicate to political action on her behalf. And if they fail to accomplish what they have resolved to do, they suppose themselves deprived of that which is their own—while what they have accomplished and have now acquired they judge to be little in comparison with what they will do in the time to come. If they trip up in an endeavor, they are soon full of hope with regard to yet another goal. For they alone possess something at the moment at which they come to hope for it: so swiftly do they contrive to attempt what has been resolved. And on all these things they exert themselves in toil and danger through all the days of their lives, enjoying least of all what they already possess because they are ever intent on further acquisition. They look on a holiday as nothing but an opportunity to do what needs doing, and they regard peace and quiet free from political business as a greater misfortune than a laborious want of leisure. So that, if someone were to sum them up by saying that

they are by nature capable neither of being at rest [*echein hēsuchían*] nor
of allowing other human beings to be so, he would speak the truth.

To this analysis, the Corinthians are said to have added an ominous threat:
that, if the Spartans failed to come to their defense, they would themselves do
what the Corcyraeans had done. They would look elsewhere for help—and
they would take other members of the Spartan alliance with them.

It is not entirely clear where the Corinthians were threatening to turn.
There were, in fact, two possibilities, and it is not plausible to suppose that
either would have conferred on them the naval hegemony that they had quite
recently with such vigor sought. In the Peloponnesus, there was Argos, the
only power mentioned by the scholiast who glossed this passage. Abroad,
there was Athens. Argos lacked the wherewithal to aid Corinth in this fashion,
and Athens was not about to sponsor the emergence of another naval power
of real consequence. Either way, however, the Corinthians would have disbur-
dened themselves of Sparta, and this was surely the point.[24]

The suffering inflicted on the Corinthians during the First Attic War derived from their close relationship with Lacedaemon. When Athens accepted
Megara into alliance in 461, she did not do so out of any particular solicitude
for the welfare of the Megarians. The two neighboring cities had long been at
odds. Nor was she acting out of hostility to Corinth as such. The two cities had
long had cordial relations. Her immediate aim was to guarantee her own security by bottling up the Spartans and their Peloponnesian allies within the
Peloponnesus. Her larger purpose at that time was to disrupt and dismantle
the Spartan alliance.

If Corinth abandoned Sparta for Argos or Athens, she would not regain
thereby the standing she had once possessed, but she would gain this: no one
with the ability to cause her trouble would have any particular interest in in-
terfering with the commerce that was the source of her prosperity. Her willingness to contemplate this prospect was a sign of her desperation.

Of course, the Corinthians were not especially eager to be confined to the
status of a wealthy, commercial backwater. For this reason, they pressed the
Spartans, and they pressed them hard. The Athenians had made their task of
persuasion considerably easier when they passed the Megarian Decrees. The
Corinthians and the Megarians were not the only members of the Spartan
alliance that found the embargo alarming. When the Athenians passed these
decrees, they touched a nerve also at Lacedaemon, as we shall soon see.

Pericles' Gamble

On the face of it, the conduct of Athens would appear to be consistent with the hypothesis that the son of Xanthippus, who was firmly in control of the direction of policy, had come to see the wisdom of the grand strategy pursued in the late 470s and most of the 460s by his erstwhile rival Cimon.[25] As we have seen, when the Corcyraeans appeared before the assembly at Athens, the Athenians at first rejected their pleas. Only after sleeping on the matter did they agree to make an alliance with Corcyra, and then they stipulated that it be a defensive alliance only. Moreover, when they sent a fleet to support the Corcyraeans, it was, as we have also seen, a tiny flotilla, of ten ships only, commanded by the *próxenos* of the Spartans at Athens, a son of Cimon who tellingly bore the name Lacedaemonius. His instructions were to enter the battle only if the Corcyraeans were on the verge of defeat, and it appears to have been only upon reflection that the Athenians dispatched twenty additional ships to reinforce Lacedaemonius' ten; and they, too, were commanded by men favorable to peaceful coexistence with Sparta. All of this was intended as a signal to the Lacedaemonians that the Athenians had no desire for war. All of it was aimed at pinning responsibility for the battle to come, and for the troubles that might follow, on Corinth and Corinth alone. This we can infer.

In the aftermath of the battle off the Sybota Isles, the Athenians followed the same course. They could argue, and argue they did, that nothing that they had done involved a breach of the Thirty Years' Peace. That agreement specified that neutral powers, such as Corcyra, could be accepted into either alliance. Nowhere did it stipulate that the hegemon of a league could not bar from her markets and harbors and those of her allies a member of the opposing league, as Athens had done in the case of Megara. Technically, the Athenians had not broken the treaty. In any case, they quite rightly insisted, even if they had, there was provision within the instrument itself for the peaceful settlement of disputes. They were supposed to be submitted to arbitration, and the Athenians signaled their readiness to do so. Everything that the Athenians said seemed to be aimed at getting the Lacedaemonians to pull back from the brink. This, too, we can conclude.[26]

It need not, however, have been Pericles' intention that, in Greece, a dual hegemony be sustained on the model advocated by Cimon son of Miltiades in the wake of the Persian Wars. Athenian conduct admits of another, quite different interpretation; and this interpretation jibes far better with the passage of the Megarian Decrees and with Pericles' fierce resistance to their repeal.[27] To make sense of this possibility, we must situate the son of Xanthippus within a foreign policy tradition.

There were, as we have seen, two such traditions at Athens. One derived from Themistocles; the other, from Cimon; and it is clear that, early in his career, Pericles had been an adherent of the former.[28] There is no good reason to suppose that he ever changed his mind. That, in the wake of the debacle in Egypt, he reversed course, arranged for Cimon's recall, and supported him in negotiating a five-year truce with Sparta; and that in 446, when the Boeotians and the cities on the island of Euboea revolted, when the Megarians rebelled and massacred the city's Athenian garrison, and the Spartans with their Peloponnesian allies marched into Attica, Pericles negotiated the Thirty Years' Peace—these developments tell us an enormous amount about the straits in which the Athenians found themselves on these two occasions, and they testify to the great man's flexibility as a statesman and to his willingness to yield to circumstances. They say nothing, however, that would prove a change in overall attitude on his part with regard to Lacedaemon. That Pericles had learned that it is unwise to fight a two-front war is perfectly clear. That he was prepared to compromise in the face of a strategic defeat is also evident. But that he had come to think of Athens as a saturated, satisfied power is not.

There are only two statesman whom Thucydides praises at length. As we have had occasion to note, he admired Themistocles' "native intelligence" and thought him "worthy of greater admiration than anyone else." He marveled that, "without the help of study before or after, he was at once the best judge in matters, admitting of little deliberation, which require settlement on the spot, and the best predictor of things to come across the broadest expanse." Of Pericles, he wrote in similar, but by no means identical terms:

> When the war broke out, in this . . . he appears to have foreknown the city's power. He lived on thereafter for two years and six months; and, when he died, his foreknowledge with regard to the war [*pronoía . . . es tòn polémon*] became still more evident. For he told them that they would win through [*periésesthai*] if they remained at rest [*hēsucházontas*] and looked after the fleet and if, during the war, they made no attempt to extend their dominion and refrained from placing the city at risk.[29]

If we compare the two passages, we can infer from Thucydides' silence what we would in any case be inclined to suspect after examining the conduct of policy in Athens from 461 on—that the *pronoía* possessed by the son of Xanthippus was less a matter of "native intelligence" than something acquired from experience. If Pericles told the Athenians that they would "win through" if and only if they restrained themselves, maintained their fleet, avoided unnecessary risk, and put off all ventures aimed solely at increasing their empire, it was because he had been among Athens' leaders when, in the midst of their first war with the Peloponnesians, they had persuaded their compatriots to dispatch a great armada to Egypt on an ill-fated mission to help wrest the Nile valley from Persian control and because he had learned something about the dangers associated with overreaching from having to cope with the fallout from that catastrophic campaign.

From these two passages, we can also draw another inference. For it is difficult to believe that Thucydides would have praised these two men so extravagantly for their foresight had they held radically different opinions regarding the dangers faced by Athens and the overall strategy she should follow.[30] If, moreover, we are to judge Pericles' attitude from what he said to the Athenians in the three speeches that Thucydides records, he continued throughout his life to think as Themistocles had. He urged them to be cautious, to be sure, and he specifically warned against an untimely attempt at expansion. But he evidently thought that an increase in the empire might properly follow upon a victory over Sparta. This, in fact, he clearly favored. He told the Athenians that they were masters of the sea, and he held up before them an image of glory and grandeur. Pericles' Athens was, by his own admission, a tyrant *pólis*—the unwanted mistress of a great empire—but this did not bother him in the slightest. "We inspire wonder now," he exulted, "and we shall in the future. We have need neither for the panegyrics of a Homer nor for the praises of anyone to whose conjecture of events the truth will do harm. For we have forced every sea and every land to give access to our daring; and we have in all places established everlasting memorials of evils [inflicted on enemies] and of good [done to friends]."

Furthermore, in the last speech that he delivered to the Athenians before his death, Pericles encouraged them to dream of a universal dominion over the sea, extending well beyond the bounds of the empire they currently held; and at this time, he exhorted them:

> Remember that this city has the greatest name among all mankind because she has never yielded to adversity, but has spent more lives in war and has endured severer hardships than any other city. She has held the

greatest power known to men up to our time, and the memory of her
power will be laid up forever for those who come after. Even if we now
have to yield (since all things that grow also decay), the memory shall
remain that, of all the Greeks, we held sway over the greatest number of
Hellenes; that we stood against our foes, both when they were united and
when each was alone, in the greatest wars; and that we inhabited a city
wealthier and greater than all.

"The splendor of the present," he concluded, "is the glory of the future laid up
as a memory for all time. Take possession of both, zealously choosing honor
for the future and avoiding disgrace in the present." Such is not the outlook
that one would be inclined to encourage in the citizenry of what one regarded
as a saturated power.[31]

Pericles' deeds matched his words. It was in his heyday that Athens sent
colonies to Thurii on the boot of Italy, to Brea in western Thrace, and to Amphipolis on the Strymon. It was almost certainly on his watch that the Athenians negotiated alliances with Rhegium in Italy and Leontini in Sicily and
that Diotimos son of Strombichides sailed with an Athenian fleet into the
western Mediterranean, intervened at Neapolis in Campania, and settled a
contingent of his compatriots there. Moreover, it was Pericles himself who led
an armada north and east to sail about the Black Sea, to display to citizen and
to foreigner alike the greatness of Athenian arms, and to settle Athenians at
Sinope, Amisos, and Astacus. All of this he oversaw or accomplished himself—
not before, but after negotiating the Thirty Years' Peace.[32]

Pericles and his compatriots were aware that the Spartans had promised
help to the Thasians in 465 at the time of their rebellion, and he had reason to
suppose that they would have made good on that promise had it not been for
the great earthquake and the helot revolt the following winter. Any wishful
thinking that his fellow Athenians may have engaged in after 446/5 and the
commencement of the peace was shattered five years later, at the time that
Samos in the Aegean and Byzantium at the entrance to the Bosporus revolted
from the Delian League, when the Spartans called a meeting of their allies and
tried to persuade Corinth and the others that they should invade Attica and
send a fleet to aid Athens' rebellious allies.

The evidence suggests a certain consistent inconsistency on the part of the
Spartans. They were, in a word, ambivalent. They were timid and hesitant. They
were appreciative of the fact that it was the Athenians who kept the Persians
at bay. But, as Thucydides contends, they were also profoundly uncomfortable

with the growth that had taken place in Athenian power; and whenever the Persian threat appeared to have receded and the Athenians were in deep distress, they had been—and surely in the future would again be—sorely tempted to take advantage.

Thucydides was almost certainly at Athens when the Corcyraeans came to that city seeking help, and he knew his compatriots. We should believe him when he reports that the Corcyraeans argued on this occasion that conflict with Sparta was nigh and when he adds that they told the Athenians, "You are anxiously scanning the horizon that you may be in readiness for the outbreak of the war that is all but upon you." We should believe him when he confirms that, in depicting his compatriots, the Corcyraeans were right and then tells us that the Athenians regarded "the coming of war with the Peloponnesians" as "merely a question of time." After all, in the circumstances, had they thought otherwise, it would have been decidedly odd. "It was clear before that Sparta was conspiring against us," Pericles told his compatriots on the eve of the war. "It is even clearer now." Dionysius of Halicarnassus was surely right when he argued that Sparta's first Attic war and her second constituted a single conflict.[33]

In judging Athens' conduct in these years, we have to be open to the probability that, like Thucydides himself and Themistocles before him, Pericles and a majority of his compatriots believed that peaceful coexistence with Sparta could be no more than a temporary expedient and that they, therefore, looked on the Thirty Years' Peace as an interlude and regarded a renewal of the war with Sparta as inevitable. This, in turn, suggests that the son of Xanthippus was himself intent, as anyone of keen intelligence so circumstanced would have been, on staging the war's renewal at a time when the terms on which it would be fought would be highly favorable to a decisive victory on Athens' part. In short, we have to be open to the possibility that Pericles was in the fullest sense of the word Themistocles' heir—that his ultimate goal was Sparta's demise; that his immediate aim was the dismemberment of her alliance; that, from 446 on, he and those who shared his outlook had been "lying in wait for a favorable opportunity"; and that, in the mid- to late 430s, the means he adopted for achieving these aims were indirect and quite circumspect.[34]

Everything that Pericles did in these years was aimed at strengthening Athens while depriving the Spartans of any genuinely plausible justification for going to war. This much is clear. But, by the same token, everything he did appears also to have been calculated with an eye to enraging the Corinthians.

For both purposes, the *epimachía* with Corcyra and Athens' display of reluctance in the battle off the Sybota Isles could not have been more finely calibrated. Technically, neither the defensive alliance nor Athens' fulfillment of its terms was a breach of the Thirty Years' Peace. Moreover, it could plausibly be argued, as the Corcyraeans did argue, that the Athenians had no alternative. The Corinthians were behaving recklessly, and the Spartans knew it. This is why, early in the crisis, they had sent an embassy to Corinth supporting acceptance of the Corcyraean offer of arbitration. The Athenians were surely aware of the Spartans' misgivings—the Corcyraeans will not have kept these a secret—and by now Pericles understood the Corinthians. Given their bitter experience in the previous war, one could bank on the fact that their loss in the battle off the Sybota Isles would inspire in them recklessness and fury—especially if, at the same time, one skillfully raised the Megarian question.

This was a sore subject for both Corinth and Sparta. Athens' occupation of Megara in the period stretching from 461 to 446 had been a disaster for the former and a humiliation for the latter. The decrees passed in 433/2 were, moreover, quite brilliantly designed. Though technically not a breach of the Thirty Years' Peace, they put the Megarians in a terrible bind.

In the fifth century, Megara was a populous, quite prosperous city located on a tiny territory. Though the Megarid was no larger than one hundred eighty square miles and no more than a quarter of this was arable, the *pólis* situated thereon was able, at the time of the Persians Wars, to field an army of three thousand hoplites at a time when Athens, with a territory nearly six times as large, could put in the field no more than ten thousand such heavy infantrymen.[35] That the population of the Megarid at this time exceeded its carrying capacity, that Megara's citizens then derived a considerable portion of their income from industry and trade, and that she was a major importer of grain is a given. It was a catastrophe for such a *pólis*—especially, for a community as commercial as fifth-century Megara must have been—to have her citizens cut off from all the harbors and markets on their principal trading route.

These decrees were no doubt an irritant in one other particular. For, like Athens' ban on Corinth's dispatch of *epidēmiourgoí* to Potidaea, they promised to obstruct the ties, of profound sentimental and some practical importance, linking Megara with her colonies; and they may in part have been intended to prevent her from stirring up trouble for Athens within the latter's dominion.[36]

The measures directed at Megara served also to heighten the anxiety of the Corinthians. They reinforced their sense that they were beleaguered and stoked their forebodings that an especially ugly and painful episode in their recent history was about to repeat itself. Above all, they caused the citizens of Corinth to fear that, if the Spartans stood idly by while the Megarians faced deprivation and possibly, in the long run, a shortage of food as well,[37] the latter would once again bolt from the Spartan alliance and join that of the Athenians, taking with them the strategically vital port at Pegae on the Corinthian Gulf, which could accommodate a much larger fleet than the little harbor at Naupactus and facilitate a renewed blockade.

Thucydides does not tell us this outright, but he does invite us to put the pieces together, to puzzle over them, and reach such a judgment. It is, we must conclude, inconceivable that Pericles had no notion of what he was doing when he induced the Athenian assembly to pass the Megarian Decrees. He had, after all, been warned. In the speech which they delivered at Athens in 434 before the battle of Sybota and the passage of these decrees, the Corinthians had pointedly alluded to Athens' previous occupation of the Megarid.

Pericles' gambit worked. The Spartans were trapped. Although here also Thucydides does not tell us as much outright, it is easy to see that arbitration was not for the Lacedaemonians a viable option. They cannot have failed to recognize that, under the terms of the treaty, they would in all likelihood lose, and the Corinthians would not be placated. In the circumstances, therefore, the Spartans were faced, as they knew only too well, with two choices alone—neither palatable. They could stand idly by while the Corinthians in fury bolted from their alliance; sidled up to the Argives, the Athenians, or both; and sought to lure away their other allies. Or this exceptionally pious people could go to war, knowing in their heart of hearts, especially when setbacks caused them to pause and ponder, that, in doing so, they had incurred the wrath of the gods by breaking their oaths.[38]

The Final Steps

As in the past, there were those at Sparta who welcomed the prospect of such a war, and on this occasion they had such strong support from the Corinthians that they had little trouble in persuading the Lacedaemonian assembly to vote that the Athenians had contravened the terms of the Thirty Years' Peace. Thucydides—who tells us repeatedly that fear, inspired by the growth in Athenian power, compelled the Spartans to go to war—clarifies his claim by adding that it was when the Athenians began to encroach upon the Spartan alliance that the Lacedaemonians finally found themselves fully faced with this necessity.[39] As Thucydides expects us to note, it was not the autonomy of Aegina nor the liberty of the Potidaeans nor even the Megarian Decrees that the ephor Sthenelaidas harped on when he pressed for war and put the question to the Spartan assembly. It was the integrity of Sparta's Peloponnesian alliance.

There were others at Lacedaemon who were, nonetheless, appalled at the prospect of war, as one would expect. Among them was Archidamus, Sparta's Eurypontid king. Tellingly, he did not in any way defend Athens' conduct. Nor did he suggest that his compatriots should leave well enough alone. It is doubtful that he thought anything of the kind. But, even if he did so, he certainly knew better than to suppose that, in the circumstances, such an argument would have purchase—and so he argued simply that Sparta and her allies were unready for the species of war they were apt to encounter.

Archidamus was a man of experience who had been king for nearly forty years, and he had had decades in which to size up Pericles and his compatriots. His grandfather Leotychidas had commanded the maritime forces of the Hellenic League at the battle of Mycale in 479, and Pericles' father Xanthippus had led the Athenian contingent. It was almost certainly at that time that the *xenía*—guest-friendship—governing relations between their offspring was formed, and it was this connection that had put the Eurypontid king in a privileged position from which to observe his counterpart and ruminate on the grand strategy the man had persuaded the Athenians to adopt.

Archidamus was among the few at Lacedaemon who correctly assessed the geopolitical transformation that Pericles and his compatriots had carried out. He knew that this time Athens was fully ready for a military confrontation with the Peloponnesians; that she would not quickly fold; that the Long Walls, now in all respects complete, rendered her impervious to invasion by land; and that Sparta and her allies, because they lacked the wherewithal with which to fund the enormous fleet required for Athens' defeat, had no obvious and easy path to victory. The war they were contemplating might, he predicted, last a generation or more. To win, he contended, the Peloponnesians would need money in abundance; and this, he intimated, they could not secure unless they had support from the Great King. Above all, Archidamus argued, they needed time in which to make the proper preparations. And so, for now, he counseled delay; and, to this end, he urged that his compatriots request an arbitration of the disputes outstanding.

Thucydides introduces the Eurypontid king as a man "experienced in many wars," who was "reputed to be both intelligent [*xunetós*] and moderate [*sóphrōn*]"; and, by way of the oration that he reports, he shows us the grounds for the man's reputation. But, in describing the decision for war at this time as a matter of necessity and in singling out as crucial Athens' encroachment on the Spartan alliance, he indicates that, of the two who discoursed before the Lacedaemonians on this fateful occasion, it was Sthenelaidas—spare in speech and no doubt grave in countenance—who had the better appreciation for what was required by the situation at hand.[40]

The son of Xanthippus was cunning. In certain circumstances, he recognized, policy can be a continuation of war by other means. By 432, he had the Spartans precisely where he wanted them. If they chose not to go to war, their alliance would come apart and there would very likely be once again an opening, an opportunity for the formation within the Peloponnesus of a counter-alliance of the sort that Themistocles had forged and exploited in the early 460s. If, however, the Lacedaemonians opted for war, they would only demonstrate to all and sundry their fecklessness. In time, when their morale faltered and they began to think their failures a sign of divine displeasure, they would grow weary of war, sue for peace, and secure it on less than fully favorable terms. Then, the Corinthians would in all likelihood bolt, as they had threatened to do; others would follow them out of the Spartan alliance; and the same sort of opening would present itself to the Athenians. The key to understanding what Pericles had in mind is this: that—in what promised to be a war pitting a power supreme on land against a power that had fully mastered the sea—he had a strategy, first, for avoiding defeat and, then, for achieving a genuine victory; and he knew full well that the Spartans had none.[41]

After ignoring the Athenian appeal for arbitration and voting that Athens had broken the treaty, the Spartans did what they could to bolster their own morale and that of their allies. To begin with, they turned to the oracle at Delphi, seeking divine sanction for what would otherwise have been regarded as an obvious and egregious breach on their part of the oaths they had taken when they ratified the peace; and, from Pythian Apollo, they secured an ambiguous, cryptic oracle that they easily could and, in fact, did interpret as a firm endorsement of the course they had in mind. Then, after a conclave of the Spartan alliance had endorsed going to war, while they and their allies were making preparations for an invasion of Attica, the Lacedaemonians sent envoys to Athens to formally register complaints. Their aim was not just to obtain for themselves the greatest possible excuse for going to war, as Thucydides suggests.[42] They also sought to assert their supremacy and to test the Athenians' resolve, undermine their morale, and encourage rebellion within their dominion, as he allows us to see.

The first set of envoys commanded the Athenians "to expel those accursed by the goddess." This demand was directed against Pericles and others at Athens who were descended from magistrates responsible, in the late seventh century, for executing supporters of the would-be tyrant Cylon who had sought refuge as suppliants at altars on the acropolis. It presupposed what nearly everyone in Hellas believed: that a community which failed to drive out those guilty of pollution would itself incur divine wrath.

The Athenians responded in kind. First, they reminded the Lacedaemonians of the manner in which, just over thirty-five years before, death had been dealt out in an impious manner both to helot suppliants at the temple of Poseidon at Taenarum and to the renegade Agiad regent Pausanias son of Cleombrotus at the temple of Athena Chalkiokis on the Spartan acropolis. Then, they demanded that the Spartans "expel those accursed" as a consequence of these unholy deeds. If, as seems tolerably likely, Archidamus was himself, in his capacity as a member of Lacedaemon's *gerousía* and "little assembly," among those complicit in the deliberate starvation of Pausanias or the slaughter of the helot suppliants, the Athenian retort would have had considerable bite.

Of course, neither of these demands was apt to have much in the way of an immediate impact on those to whom they were directed. But, in time, if things did not go well in the war for one side or the other, they would be recalled to mind; and doubts would be raised as to whether the defeats inflicted on the city in distress were not the work of the gods.[43]

The second Spartan embassy eschewed religious injunctions, but it, too, issued a peremptory and insulting command, demanding that the Athenians lift the siege at Potidaea and allow Aegina autonomy; and the third and last such embassy dropped all particular demands and announced to the Athenians, "The Lacedaemonians are willing for there to be peace if you allow all of the Hellenes to be autonomous."[44]

The demands made by the second set of Spartan ambassadors with regard to Potidaea and Aegina reflect the complaints made by the Corinthians and the Aeginetans at the original assembly in Lacedaemon and clearly had a propagandistic purpose, as was even more emphatically the case with the more general demand issued by the third set of envoys. There was no way that the Athenians could honor any of these demands without in effect abandoning their hegemony, and the Spartans knew it. What the latter wanted when they directed their delegation to issue these demands was a pretext for war. What they sought was a rallying cry that would unite their allies and, they hoped, inspire rebellion throughout the Aegean. Mindful that Lacedaemon had a long and distinguished history as the scourge of tyranny, the Corinthians, at the meeting of the Spartan alliance, had repeatedly branded Athens as "a tyrant *pólis*." The war against this tyrant would be fought, as the Persian Wars had been, for the freedom of the Greeks. Or so its proponents, who thought this goal indistinguishable from Athens' demise, repeatedly proclaimed.[45]

There was, however, more to these exchanges than propaganda. For we are told by Plutarch that Archidamus was still active behind the scenes, attempting to head off war; and according to Thucydides, on the occasion of the second embassy, Lacedaemon's ambassadors made it "exceedingly clear that there would be no war if the Athenians repealed" or suspended the Megarian Decrees.[46]

The statement of this set of ambassadors concerning Athens' policy with regard to Megara suggests something that Thucydides does not spell out: a genuine desire on their part to avoid a clash and a conviction that, if Athens lifted the embargo, they could persuade their compatriots to back off. According to Plutarch, when the Athenians responded that they were barred by law from even considering their repeal, one of the Lacedaemonian envoys told them that it would be sufficient if they turned to the wall the stone on which the decrees were inscribed—something that they had apparently done as a dodge when similarly trapped in the past.[47]

This effort on the part of Sparta's emissaries suggests yet another conclusion that Thucydides does not draw: that sobriety had set in and that the misgivings initially voiced by Archidamus were by this time more widely entertained at Lacedaemon than before. There is no reason to suppose that the Spartans were invested in the slightest in Corinth's imperial project in the west. Early on, as Thucydides allows us to see, they had tried to head off her clash with Corcyra. They were surely aware that, in coming to Corcyra's defense and in not going on the offensive, the Athenians had defended her interests while carefully sidestepping a breach of the peace, and the envoys they sent to Athens made no mention of the matter.[48] Nor is there any ground for presuming that a majority at Lacedaemon cared about the fate of the Potidaeans and the Aeginetans as such. The Spartans—and, for that matter, their Corinthian allies—had renounced all such concerns when they ratified the Thirty Years' Peace.

Of course, in a general way, the Lacedaemonians were made nervous by the growth in Athenian power, as Thucydides claims; and, if Athens were in dire straits, they would certainly be tempted to take advantage, as they had repeatedly demonstrated in the past. But, in 432/1, Athens was not in any obvious trouble, and there were some at Lacedaemon, led by a Eurypontid king experienced in war and blessed with high repute, who doubted that, in the circumstances, their countrymen and their allies were likely to win a quick and easy victory; who feared that they might leave this war to their children; and who were still doing everything within their power to persuade their compatriots and their allies to seek a peaceful resolution of their dispute with Athens.

The Spartans' decision for war had been prompted by Corinth's threat that she would otherwise withdraw from the alliance and take others with her. But we can be confident that the Lacedaemonians did not relish being bullied, especially by one of their own allies. Moreover, for good reason, many at Lacedaemon were suspicious of the absolution thought to have been offered by the Delphic oracle and entertained a lingering suspicion that, in rejecting Athens' offer of arbitration, they were the ones breaching the agreement and breaking their vows.[49] The envoys who suggested that it was still possible to preserve the peace took it for granted, as should we, that their compatriots were once again of two minds.

There was, however, an obstacle that seemed to these ambassadors insuperable. The decrees that the Athenians had passed with regard to the Megarians verged on an act of war. Violence was not involved, to be sure, and they were not—at least technically—a breach of the Thirty Years' Peace. But, as we have seen, they put the Megarians in an impossible situation. Had the Lace-daemonians been in the throes of a helot revolt, had they been embroiled at this time in wars with their neighbors close to home, as they had been in the past, they might not have cared all that much. But these conditions no longer pertained. The Spartans were blessedly free from strife at home and from con-flict in their near abroad—and a failure to come to Megara's defense would almost certainly have eventuated in her leaving the alliance, as she had in 461.

Politics is generational. The memory of catastrophes fades with the pas-sage of time. Recent events, however—especially, events universally experi-enced as a calamity—have a way of impressing themselves on the minds not only of those who live through them but also of those within the generation which grows up in their shadow. The prospect that these events might be re-peated concentrates the minds of such men wonderfully.

The intercommunal order is governed by necessity, not by law. It mat-tered, of course, that there was no provision within the Thirty Years' Peace guaranteeing the members of the two alliances access to markets and harbors abroad, but such technicalities can never be dispositive. The Spartans could not hold their alliance together if they failed to come to Megara's defense, and they knew it. Corinth was, even more emphatically than Megara, a commer-cial city. If the Lacedaemonians were to successfully call her bluff and recon-cile her to the fact that they were not about to go to war in defense of her imperial venture in the west, they would first have to demonstrate that they could—and, if need be, would—defend their allies' freedom to truck, barter, and exchange one thing for another in distant parts. Intercommunal trade may not have been a strategic necessity for most of the cities in the Pelopon-nesus, but it was for Corinth and apparently for Megara as well.

Pericles was, however, adamant. He was not about to let the Spartans off the hook; and so he insisted on the letter of the law and responded with an obvious nonstarter. He offered to arrange a repeal of the Megarian Decrees if and only if the Lacedaemonians gave up with regard to Athens and her allies the practice, essential to their security, of regulating and restricting foreign access to Laconia. In the debate that followed, he repeatedly told his compa-triots that they had no alternative but to stand their ground and refuse repeal, for arbitration was the only honorable way out. He knew that, under the terms of the Thirty Years' Peace, the restrictions directed at Megara would be vindicated. He was also confident that the Spartans, anticipating this result, would refuse his offer. And he firmly believed that, if there was war, Athens would emerge victorious.

In the speech he delivered at Athens on this occasion, the son of Xanthippus did not tell the truth, the whole truth, and nothing but the truth. Politicians almost never do. He did not, for example, unveil the complex logic underpinning his canny handling of the Corcyraean request for an alliance, of the battle off the Sybota Isles, and of the difficulties that Athens had had with Potidaea and Megara. He posed, instead, as an innocent defender of Athens' interests and as a faithful, even pious, adherent of the terms to which Athens and Sparta had subscribed when they agreed to the Thirty Years' Peace. He indicted the Lacedaemonians for making demands incompatible with that treaty, and he harped on their refusal to submit disputed questions to arbitration.

In addressing his compatriots, Pericles was no more forthcoming with regard to the war to come. He described neither the manner in which he planned to conduct the war nor what he hoped to achieve. In passing, he even drew attention to his reticence. He acknowledged to his compatriots that he had "many reasons to be hopeful . . . *other than those*" he had outlined in his speech, and he promised that "these would be disclosed in another oration *as events required.*" Where he might have outlined the strategy he intended to pursue and where he might have told his fellow Athenians what he expected them to do, he stressed, instead, what they should not do; and, when he promised them that they would "win through," he deliberately employed a verb— *periésesthai*—which was ambiguous. Those listening could easily presume that he had pledged that they would somehow "prevail," which is no doubt what most of them assumed. Or they could suppose that he had merely promised that they would "survive." If Pericles did not explain to his compatriots that, if they did in fact survive, they would soon thereafter be in a position to prevail, it was because he had something to hide. To divulge this information in public at this time, before an audience numbering more than ten thousand, would be, he knew, to risk revealing to Athens' foe the particulars of a strategy that would rely as much on canny diplomacy and subversion as it would on outright war. Mindful of the necessity for discretion, Pericles spoke in general terms and said no more than the immediate situation demanded.[50]

In the speech he gave, Pericles began by justifying a rejection of Sparta's demands, arguing that to give way in any particular would be to invite further demands and to court slavery. The Megarian Decrees he cannily played down. They might well be "a trifle," he confessed. "But this trifle encompasses your steadfastness of purpose and constitutes a trial of your resolve as a whole."

Then, Pericles turned to the war to come. To counter Athens, he observed, the Spartans and their allies would have to take to the sea. This they would find it hard to do. In the pertinent nautical experience and expertise they were notably lacking, and such things could not be acquired quickly or easily. Even more to the point, they were without the requisite capital. Theirs, moreover, was not a proper hegemony. It was an association of disparate peoples with different and opposed interests, incapable of vigorous action and apt to succumb to paralysis. In addition, the great majority of those whom the Lacedaemonians would summon were farmers, dependent on the cultivation of the soil. They might be good for service in person on a single campaign, but they could not afford an extended absence from home.

Athens was, he insisted, more than ready. She had the ships, the men, the experience, the expertise, and the funds. Even if the Peloponnesians raided the treasuries at Olympia and Delphi, they would not be able to lure away with a promise of higher pay those who rowed in the Athenian fleet. To begin with, many of these were citizens of Athens; and the hirelings hailed from Athens' dominion and had no desire to be banished forever from the cities they called home.

There were only two things, in Pericles' estimation, that the Athenians had to do. They had to be willing to take refuge behind the Long Walls and give up for the nonce their houses in the country and their land. If they did so, there was nothing that the Peloponnesians could do of any real significance against them—while, if they marched out and fought in their defense, they would not just lose. Their defeat and the loss of life would encourage uprisings within their domain. The Athenians also had to be exceedingly vigilant in guarding their city and the sea.

There was, the son of Xanthippus added, one further matter of tremendous importance: the Athenians had to vigorously resist the temptation to try to add to their dominion while at war, and they had to refrain from that to which they thrilled: the willful courting of risk. He knew the predilections of his compatriots. He had witnessed the catastrophes attendant on the failure of their ventures in Egypt and Boeotia, and he had firmly resisted proposals that his compatriots involve themselves in Egypt again. "I fear," he bluntly told them, "your own blunders far more than the contrivances of our opponents."[51]

In the winter months that followed, while the Peloponnesians organized themselves for an invasion of Attica, the Athenians made their own preparations. The odds are good that they had begun in a preliminary fashion taking precautions shortly after they voted to make an *epimachía* with the Corcyraeans. It was quite likely at this time or in the immediate aftermath of their clash with the Corinthians at the battle off the Sybota Isles that they suspended their expenditure of funds for the construction of the Propylaea at the entrance to the acropolis, voted to consolidate in the sanctuaries on that high hill under the newly created Treasurers of the Other Gods at least some of the funds hitherto lodged in the temples scattered throughout the countryside of Attica, and acted to set the city's finances in order by drawing on the reserves held in the treasury of the Delian League. Three thousand talents of silver (well over eighty-five tons) were shifted to the treasury of Athena on the acropolis. Subsequently, the remaining funds were to be used to liquidate the city's debts to Athena and to the other gods, and what was left was employed to repair the community's dockyards and walls.[52]

Now, with war approaching, they took the next step. In these winter months, those with flocks of sheep and herds of cattle may have begun moving them across the water to Euboea and the islands nearby, and those who resided in the countryside may have begun gathering and organizing the valuables that they would want to have with them when they sought refuge in the city. The more astute in their number will also have begun moving to storage places in Athens and the Peiraeus the wheat and barley stowed in the granaries near their farms. When word came that the Peloponnesians were on the move, the country folk of Attica, even at this time a majority of the Athenians, brought with them everything that they could load on carts—including the window frames and the doors of their abodes—and they ruefully left behind their homes, their burial grounds, their villages, their cult sites, and the country life.[53]

In his eagerness to take advantage of the situation, to drive a wedge between Lacedaemon and her allies, and to force the Spartans to choose between alienating Corinth, on the one hand, and breaking their oaths and initiating a war they could not win, on the other, Pericles had stood firm. He knew that there would be a war sooner or later, and he understood the fault lines within the enemy coalition. The ultimate outcome he could foresee, and its achievement would not take all that long. Of this he was confident. For, like Themistocles—Athens' Odysseus—Pericles was a mastermind of war who had left nothing to chance. Or so he supposed.

CHAPTER 3

A Tug of War

To fight and conquer in all your battles is not supreme excellence; supreme excellence consists in breaking the enemy's resistance without fighting.

SUN TZŪ

THUCYDIDES admired Themistocles above all other statesmen, and Pericles he held in high esteem. Moreover, as we have seen, he shared the strategic vision articulated by these two Athenians; and he agreed with Pericles that Athens had the resources and the strength to "win through" in her struggle with Lacedaemon and the latter's Peloponnesian allies. To Pericles, he persisted in attributing "*pronoía* with regard to the war"—even after the great man's expectations had come to naught. In writing the history of the war initiated by that formidable statesman, Thucydides had as his principal aim to discover and explain to his own satisfaction how and why things went so badly amiss.

In the war as such, everything of real importance initially worked out pretty much as Pericles had expected. Of course, he may not have anticipated the surprise attack that the Thebans launched on Plataea at the very beginning of the spring in 431. But while the conquest of that city would be regrettable, would strengthen the hand of Thebes within Boeotia, and make it considerably easier for her to lend assistance to the Peloponnesians while the latter were in Attica, Plataea's demise—when viewed in light of the conflict Pericles had in mind—was strategically of little importance. Thanks to the Long Walls, Athens was not going to be defeated on land.[1]

At the time, however, almost everyone else supposed the opposite. Almost everyone presumed either that the Athenians would quickly give in or that there would be a hoplite battle and that Athens would suffer defeat both on the field and in the war. They all knew about the Long Walls, of course. Those alert to their significance generally supposed that the Athenians might hold out for a year or two or three. But next to no one imagined that year after year they would hunker down behind Athens' fortifications and stoically absorb the damage that the Peloponnesians would inflict. So Thucydides tells us, and his testimony makes perfect sense. Never in the history of the Hellenic mainland had the citizens of a self-governing *pólis* of any consequence fought a war in which they refused battle and cowered behind their walls while Greek invaders with impunity repeatedly ravaged their land. Within the great republics of classical Hellas, pusillanimous conduct of this sort verged on the unthinkable.[2] For this, there was a reason—one fundamental to the character and ethos of the ancient Greek *pólis.*

If the communes of medieval and early modern Europe rarely, if ever, put an army of citizens in the field, it was because they were profoundly bourgeois in character. Their citizens were artisans, skilled craftsmen, laborers, merchants, bankers, and the like. Where the *città* in which these *cittadini* had their homes possessed a *contado,* a country district under its control, the farmers who tilled the land in that district—the *contadini*—were subjects denied political rights.

The *póleis* of ancient Greece were, by way of contrast, agrarian in character. For them, the *contado* was, as Machiavelli once observed with regard to Rome, the *città.* These ancient communities were associations of farmers. They were martial in character, and the hoplite phalanx was their foundation. It enabled ordinary citizens—well-to-do gentry and smallholders alike—to defend their families, their land, and their liberty; and its efficacy in battle gave them the confidence that they could refuse to knuckle under and actually govern themselves.

In many Greek cities, artisans, bankers, merchants, and other landless men were excluded from the civic assembly. Everywhere—except, tellingly, to some degree at Corinth—artisans and the like were regarded with suspicion and contempt. Men who secured their livelihood in this fashion were not worthy of trust. Their wealth and their skills were mobile. If the *pólis* succumbed, they could move on. Lacklands had next to no stake in the community's defense.[3]

Fifth-century Athens was peculiar—and not just or even primarily because in that *pólis* artisans, merchants, and other landless men were full citizens. In 480 and again in 479, the Athenians had done the unthinkable. In the face of the Persian invasion, they had evacuated the countryside. They had abandoned their urban center and its port, and they had taken to the sea. This was a revolutionary act. What was inconceivable elsewhere the Athenians had actually done—not once but two years in a row—and to very good effect.

Moreover, in the aftermath of the Hellenic victories at Salamis and Plataea, the statesman who had persuaded his compatriots to withdraw from Attica saw not only to the rebuilding of the walls of its urban center. He also convinced his compatriots to fortify with even greater care their new port at the Peiraeus, and he oversaw the program of construction himself. At the time, as we have seen, he argued that the Peiraeus would be "more useful to the Athenians than the city up-country." This man, Thucydides tells us, who "in a future as yet obscure could in a preeminent fashion foresee both better and worse," urged his compatriots "to go down" to the Peiraeus "if they were overpowered on land and withstand all of mankind with their ships," and he did so not once or even twice but "over and over and over again."[4]

In the intervening years, as we have also had occasion to note, Themistocles' successors took his exhortations to heart; and, mindful of Athens' demographic growth, they made further prudent preparations for such an eventuality. His rival Cimon, who was no one's fool, laid the foundations for what came to be called the Long Walls; those who opposed Cimon's policy of accommodation with Lacedaemon built them; and then, upon reflection, as we have seen, Pericles persuaded his compatriots to add the Middle Wall. Well before 431, the town of Athens and the port of Peiraeus had become from a military perspective, as Pericles himself made clear, a virtual island—a single, impregnable fortress protected by land and blessed with easy access to the sea—where a substantial proportion of the political community's population found employment either as entrepreneurs engaged in manufacturing and trade or as salarymen rowing in the city's fleet, serving in magistracies and on her juries, or working in her dockyards and on her construction projects.[5]

Archidamus' Maneuvers

Sparta's Eurypontid king was among the few Lacedaemonians with a keen appreciation of what the Athenians had achieved and were now apt to do, and in the assembly at Sparta he had not minced his words. But he had lost the argument and, with Pleistoanax in exile and the latter's son Pausanias a minor, he was the only proper king available to lead the forces of the Spartan alliance. In consequence, in the spring of 431, he found himself responsible for conducting a campaign he thought foolhardy in the extreme. It says much about the qualities that earned him so sterling a reputation that he did so with considerable skill and acumen to the best of his abilities.

Archidamus' experience in armed conflict had equipped him with an excellent understanding of the role played in wartime by the human imagination. When he spoke in the Spartan assembly in opposition to going to war right away and in favor of taking two or three years to prepare, he had emphasized that the prospect that one is going to be seriously harmed is often psychologically more devastating than the experience of actually suffering such harm. The Athenians, he contended, would be more apt to submit if over time they saw serious preparations under way, if they were made to hear arguments indicative of the horrors to come, and if they possessed land as yet unravaged and had occasion to take counsel concerning the preservation of present goods as yet unspoiled. "Their land," he told his countrymen, "you should think of as nothing other than a hostage in your hands, of value in proportion to the quality of its cultivation. It you should spare for as long as you can, and you should not drive its owners into desperation and render them less easy to manage."[6]

In 431, Archidamus was not in a position to act as he had urged. He feared the worst—that what his compatriots were attempting would ignominiously fail and "bring on the Peloponnesus shame and the sense of perplexity and desperation that one feels when one is wholly at a loss." But he was a patriot and a good soldier, and he did what he could. At the Isthmus of Corinth, he mustered a levy consisting of two-thirds of the soldiers of each of the cities within the Spartan alliance. Plutarch tells us that his army numbered sixty thousand. Most scholars think this figure impossibly high—which would perhaps be true if Plutarch had none but hoplites in mind. In the circumstances, however, it is perfectly possible—and even likely—that the Peloponnesians brought along a host of light-armed troops to help lay waste the land.[7]

His own doubts about the enterprise Archidamus suppressed. He told the men under his command what the situation demanded and what they needed to hear. He acknowledged that there were those who thought it certain that the Athenians would refuse to meet them in the field. But he did not report that this was his own considered opinion. Instead, he foisted on them what he took to be a salutary lie, as able political leaders are wont to do. "We are not proceeding against a city incapable of defending itself," he said.

> We are proceeding against one exceedingly well-equipped in every respect. So it is very much incumbent on us to expect that they will join battle and that, if they have not already come forth prior to our arrival, they will do so when they see us in their land wasting and ruining their farms. For fury falls upon those who see themselves with their own eyes suffering in the present moment something to which they are unaccustomed. And those least inclined to engage in calculation are then most apt to be driven into action by anger. The Athenians, more than others, are so inclined—for they think themselves worthy to rule others and are more accustomed to ravage the land of their neighbors than to see their own treated in such a fashion.

It was a good speech. It was intelligent, it suited the occasion, and its author knew perfectly well that it was apt to be wrong.[8]

In consequence, Archidamus dragged his feet and delayed the ravaging for as long as he could. He loitered at the isthmus. From there, he sent a herald to Athens and waited for his return. When the herald came back empty-handed, the Eurypontid king marched on Oenoe, a walled town on Athens' Boeotian border, coveted by the Thebans, which the Athenians used as a fortress in wartime; and there he tarried, preparing for an assault while those Athenians who had been dilatory carted their valuables into the city. His soldiers were understandably angry, but Thucydides intimates that there may have been method to what they regarded as mad or worse. "It is said," he reports, "that he held back, hoping that the Athenians, while their land was still unharmed, would shrink back from seeing it ravaged and give way a little." It was also no doubt supposed that Archidamus was eager to please Sparta's Theban allies, as he surely was.

It was not until after the assault on Oenoe had failed that Archidamus broke camp and finally entered Attica. Roughly eighty days had passed since the Theban surprise attack on Plataea. It was, from an ancient Greek perspective, midsummer—which is to say, late May or, perhaps, early June. The grain was ripe, and the Peloponnesians could live in some measure off the land. They ravaged the Thriasian plain and paused outside Eleusis, where in 446 Pleistoanax had stopped and then turned back. If Archidamus dawdled there, it was no doubt because he hoped for an overture from Athens similar to the one that had brought peace fifteen years before. When no messenger appeared, the Eurypontid king moved on to Acharnae, the largest and one of the most prosperous of Athens' demes and one which, if Thucydides' text is correct, supplied to the city a disproportionate number of hoplites. There, Archidamus reportedly hoped, the spectacle, visible from Athens' walls, of a Peloponnesian camp situated on rich farmland barely seven miles from the city would so infuriate the Athenians that they would take the field.[9]

But this was not to be—for Archidamus was up against the son of Xanthippus. The Athenians were in an uproar, as the Eurypontid king had anticipated. According to Thucydides, who is apt to have been present, nearly everyone, especially among the young men and the Acharnians, was eager for a fight. Groups of men gathered in knots in the streets, and Pericles became an object of anger. But he was imperturbable—all was taking place as he had foreseen—and he refused entreaties to call a special meeting of the assembly. He may even have persuaded the Council of 500 that, in the emergency, it would be wise to delay the one meeting that the Athenian political calendar dictated be held in this stretch of time. In the meantime, he saw to the defense of the walls and did what he could to make life difficult for the invaders.[10]

There was almost no precedent for the policy pursued by Pericles. It was counterintuitive; and there were ambitious demagogues of keen intellect and genuine talent, such as Cleon son of Cleaenetus, who were quick to seize on the fury of their compatriots as an occasion for denouncing as cowardice Pericles' refusal to defend the city's farmland. Had the great man not been so firmly ensconced at the helm, Archidamus would probably have had a battle on his hands. Had this occurred, the Peloponnesians would almost certainly have overwhelmed the Athenians, and Lacedaemon would have quickly won the war.

But Xanthippus' proud son commanded respect, and Athens held firm. In time, Archidamus and the Peloponnesians worked their way northeast through the gap between Mount Parnes and Mount Pentelicon, ravaging the countryside as they proceeded; and, when they ran short of provisions, they withdrew from Attica via Oropus and returned to the Peloponnesus across the southern reaches of Boeotia. We do not know how long the Peloponnesians were active in Attica, laying waste the land, but, given the time that Archidamus had spent at the isthmus and at Oenoe, it cannot have exceeded by much three weeks, if that.[11]

Archidamus had hoped that the Peloponnesian invasion would lure the

Map 11. Attica, Southern Boeotia, and the Eastern Megarid

Athenians onto the field of battle, but he had not expected it to do so. He did, however, entertain another expectation. He had lived a long time. He had been in office for more than two decades when his compatriots fought the Athenians at Tanagra; and he was aware that, at that time, there had been men at Athens so bitterly opposed to the construction of the Long Walls and to the policy these fortifications embodied that they were willing to betray the city. He knew that his ravaging would inflict losses on the propertied classes— on the exceedingly wealthy *pentakosiomédimnoi,* on the *hippeîs* who rode in Athens' cavalry, and on the *zeugítai* smallholders who served in the ranks as hoplites—while leaving the landless thetes who rowed in the fleet entirely unharmed; and he hoped thereby to set the landed and the lacklands against one another and "introduce division [*stásis*] into the public counsels" at Athens. So we are told by Thucydides.[12]

A year later, in 430, with this last end in mind, Archidamus and the Peloponnesians returned to Attica—this time in earnest, for there was no longer any reason to hope that the threat of ravaging would itself be sufficient to force the Athenians to fight. This time, there was no dawdling, no delay. This time, the enemy army remained on Athens' territory for a full forty days. They covered as broad an expanse as was possible. They tarried in the Paralia just above Cape Sunium, laying waste the territory, as yet untouched, which faced the Peloponnesus, then that opposite the islands of Euboea and Andros—and they did as much damage as they could. Naturally, all of this weighed heavily on the Athenians. But once again Pericles managed to restrain his compatriots, and they did not put an army in the field.[13]

Over the following three years, the Peloponnesians invaded Attica two more times—in 428 under the leadership of Archidamus and the following year, after the Eurypontid king was incapacitated or had died, under Pleistoanax' younger brother Cleomenes, who was regent for the exiled Agiad king's young son and heir Pausanias.[14] On each occasion they laid waste the land of the Athenians but to no real purpose. Archidamus' original psychological insight was proven correct. Once the initial damage was done, the Athenians adjusted to the new situation; and although they regarded the subsequent incursions as a great irritant and even as a painful blow, they did not consider them a catastrophe that they could not withstand.

What Thucydides does not adequately convey—in part because he had no standard of comparison by which to bring home to his readers what had taken place—is that the damage which ancient invaders could do over a month or even six weeks in ravaging a large territory was quite limited. The enemy could appropriate or burn cereal crops left behind in granaries. If the grain in the fields was ripe, they could within a limited expanse laboriously harvest and consume it. With effort, they could also torch some fields. But, even at harvest time, wheat and barley are generally too green to be easily combustible; and, in all seasons, olive trees are fire-resistant. Short of being uprooted, they are almost impossible to destroy; and, though vines can be cut, they grow back quickly.

Attica was immense, encompassing nearly one thousand square miles.

Scholars estimate that it contained two hundred thousand acres of farmland, five to ten million olive trees, and even more vines. Each year, the Peloponnesians' window of opportunity was short. In the best of circumstances, the territory that they could cover was limited; the work involved was tedious and exhausting; and, for the soldiers supplied by Lacedaemon's allies, there was a price—for the weeks they spent in Attica got in the way of their completion of tasks required on their farms back home.[15] In this particular case, moreover, their enterprise was made considerably more difficult by something the Athenians had learned the hard way in the course of their earlier wars.

In 454, the Athenian general Myronides had suffered an unexpected setback in Thessaly when he led an expeditionary force to the outskirts of Pharsalus to punish those who had turned coat at the battle of Tanagra and to put Athens' friend Orestes son of Echecratides back in charge. On this occasion, the Athenians had had no trouble in commanding the field. But they were unable to storm the town; and, when they dispersed to forage for provisions, to loot, and ravage the rich farmland in the vicinity of Pharsalus, the renowned horsemen of that city sallied forth and cut them down. In consequence, while there, Myronides' men found themselves for the most part confined to a fortified camp; and, when they ran short of provisions, they were forced to decamp and depart with their mission unfulfilled.

By the time of Archidamus' first invasion the Athenians were prepared, to the best of their abilities, to do to his soldiers what the Pharsalians had done to them twenty-three years before.[16] To this end—almost certainly, when they began building the third of their Long Walls and settled on the strategy for defending the Athenians that Pericles would pursue in 431—they had made provision by way of subsidies for a corps of one thousand cavalrymen and two hundred horse-archers. Especially when reinforced by the cavalry of Athens' Thessalian allies, as we know it was in 431, this mobile strike force was capable of harrying any Peloponnesians who left the confines of their camp to gather provisions and ravage the land.

To some degree, Archidamus was able to deploy horsemen from Boeotia, Locris, and Phocis to provide cover for the Peloponnesians foraging for food and laying waste the countryside; and those Athenians who later argued that, had the Peloponnesians lacked cavalrymen, they would not have bothered to invade at all had a case. Otherwise, had the Boeotians not proved exceedingly useful and had it not been in the interest of the Lacedaemonians to appease the Thebans, it would be hard to explain why, in 429, Archidamus chose to give the Athenians a reprieve in Attica and waste an entire campaigning season on what was, from Sparta's perspective, a strategic distraction by conducting his army into Boeotia to help initiate a siege at Plataea.

Even, however, with the help of the Boeotians and their Phocian and Locrian neighbors, Archidamus' ravagers faced difficulties. It is almost certain that the cavalry force fielded by the Athenians was more numerous than that which the Boeotians supplied to the Peloponnesians. We are told that they were successful in providing protection to the land in the plain near their base in the city, and we can presume that they elsewhere restricted the range within which the interlopers could operate.[17]

Over time, as one would expect, the Peloponnesians grew weary of this charade. The expedition against Plataea must have been particularly burdensome. It began in late May or early June 429, when Archidamus first approached that city. His task was somewhat awkward. As he was well aware, when threatened, the Plataeans would charge the Lacedaemonians with injustice and impiety, referring back to the oaths taken by the Hellenes half a century before at the instigation of Pausanias son of Cleombrotus when that young Spartan regent had returned their land to the Plataeans in the immediate aftermath of his victory in the battle of Plataea and had called upon the allies to pledge that they would respect the city's autonomy and rally to her defense against anyone who tried to enslave her.

To answer this charge required a measure of sophistry, and Archidamus rose to the challenge. The Persian Wars had been fought, he noted, in defense of the freedom of the Greeks; and the same rationale applied to the war now being conducted against the Athenians. To support the Athenians was, therefore, a breach of the spirit that had governed the solemnities by means of which the Plataeans had regained their fatherland. It was impossible to square with the oaths taken at that time. Archidamus therefore invited the Plataeans to join once again in liberating the Hellenes. This was, he implied, their duty as much in 429 as it had been fifty years before. Mindful of the precise terms of the oaths taken in 479, however, he was willing to offer the Plataeans two alternatives: they could retain their homeland in peace if they agreed to abandon their alliance with Athens and for the rest of the war practice "*hēsuchía*" by remaining "at rest"; or they could evacuate their *pólis* on the understanding that their homes and land would be restored to them intact after the war.

When the Athenians, whom the Plataeans consulted, urged them to keep faith with their allies and promised to come to their aid to the best of their ability and when the Plataeans in turn rejected Archidamus' overtures, he called on the gods to witness the justice of his cause as he initiated a siege.[18]

The task at hand required on the part of Lacedaemon's allies immense labor over seventy days under the relentless gaze of their Spartan commanders. This effort was aimed, initially. at building a siege mound against the wall of Plataea; then, when that enterprise failed, at breaking through that wall with siege engines; and finally at burning the town in its entirety. All of this was tried, but to no avail; and the circumvallation of the Boeotian *pólis*, which followed, was not complete until late September.[19]

The following year—when, in late August, Archidamus summoned Sparta's allies for a second invasion of Attica with an eye to dramatically ratcheting up the pressure on the Athenians—they were so slow in responding that he was forced to call the whole thing off. At this season, Thucydides tells us, the Peloponnesians were busy with their own harvest—presumably, that of their grapes and olives—and by this time they were, in any case, heartily "sick of campaigning" and quite possibly annoyed at the Lacedaemonians, who seem not to have joined them in the labors required at Plataea the previous summer. Pericles' predictions and Archidamus' worst fears were close to being realized: the farmers of the Spartan alliance lacked the stamina for service abroad year after year in what seemed an endless war of attrition; and, given Athens' staying power, the conflict now threatened to "bring on the Peloponnesus shame and the sense of perplexity and desperation that one feels when one is wholly at a loss."[20]

Pericles' Response

Pericles' response to the Peloponnesian invasion was methodical. In 431, when Archidamus led his army out of Attica, he and his compatriots turned their minds from Athens' defense to the mounting of an offensive. They had already dispatched embassies to Zacynthus, Cephallenia, Acarnania, and Corcyra with an eye to rendering the already existing friendships more firm and to making it less difficult for them to circumnavigate the Peloponnesus and bring pressure to bear on the enemy. Now, Thucydides tells us, they established garrisons—often, we must suspect, naval in character—in the places on the land and near the sea that, they thought, they needed to guard throughout the war. It is a virtual certainty that they took special care with the Bosporus and the Hellespont—for it was through these narrow bodies of water and the sea of Marmara in between that the grain ships, which fed the Athenians and a host of other Greeks, made their way from Crimea and other places on the Black Sea. Moreover, a decree passed by the Athenian assembly five years thereafter mentions officials called the "Guardians of the Hellespont [*Hellespontophúlakes*]," situated at Byzantium, who were charged with monitoring and regulating shipping within the region and had it within their power to restrict the import of grain by particular cities.

It was probably also at the very beginning of the war that the Athenians built a small fort on the promontory of Budorum on Salamis near Nisaea and stationed three triremes there to impose a blockade and prevent, insofar as this was possible, ships from entering or leaving Megara's port on the Saronic Gulf. We are also told that the Athenians set aside a special fund of one thousand talents of silver (well over twenty-eight tons) to be used in an emergency, only if the city itself was in danger of attack, and made it a capital crime to tap into these funds in any other circumstances. To the same purpose, each year they were to hold in reserve a fleet of one hundred triremes, the best available that year, with their trierarchs.[21]

Already, while the Peloponnesians were still at Acharnae, the Athenians had dispatched one hundred triremes, carrying one thousand hoplites and four hundred archers, on a journey around the Peloponnesus—where, with the help of fifty triremes sent from Corcyra and infantrymen dispatched from Naupactus and perhaps Zacynthus, this fleet made its way along the coast, pausing from time to time to descend on cultivated country districts for the purpose of pillaging and ravaging. We are not given an exhaustive account of these attacks, but Diodorus mentions raids on the Argolic Acte—where Epidaurus, Troezen, and Hermione were to be found—and the burning of houses and farm buildings (including granaries, no doubt); and Thucydides offers a couple of examples, which nicely illustrate Athens' *modus operandi*.

On the southwestern coast of the Akritas peninsula, the westernmost of the three great promontories that thrust southward into the Mediterranean from the Peloponnesus, the historian tells us, the allies paused to attack Mothone, a town of the *períoikoi* where there was no garrison and the fortifications were weak. They would probably have seized and sacked the place had it

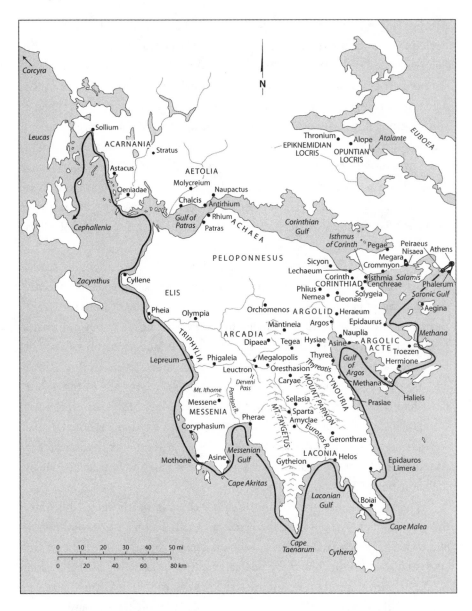

Map 12. Pericles Circumnavigates the Peloponnesus

not been for an enterprising Spartan named Brasidas son of Tellis, who had
been assigned to guard the district and who earned praise from his compatriots by rushing into the town with one hundred hoplites and securing it while
the Athenians and those with them were busy laying waste the countryside

nearby. To the north, the allied fleet later paid a similar sudden and unexpected visit to the district of Pheia in Pisatis near Elis on the west coast of the
Peloponnesus, where those on board ravaged the farmland for two days and
defeated an elite force of three hundred men who had come south from the
vale of Elis along the Peneios and from the Pisatan districts nearby. When a
squall came up, we are told, the fleet loaded up most of the ravagers, pulled
out, rounded Cape Icthys, and sailed into the protected harbor at the town of
Pheia where they rendezvoused with a group of Messenian ravagers from
Naupactus who, after being left stranded on shore, had marched from their
original landing place and seized the town. Theirs was, however, a hit-and-run
operation. For, by the time that the main army of the Eleans appeared, the fleet
and the forces it carried had moved on.[22]

Further north, near Acarnania, Thucydides adds, the Athenians seized
the closely held little Corinthian colony at Sollium and handed it over to the
Acarnanians of Palaira, and they stormed Astacus, liberated it from the tyrant
Evarchus, and added it to their own confederacy. Then, they put out to sea
once again, doubled back, and paid a visit to the four *póleis* on the isle of
Cephallenia, which occupies a strategic location opposite the Gulf of Patras
and, beyond it, the mouth of the Corinthian Gulf. In 435, one of these four
cities had contributed four ships to the fleet that fought for Corinth against
Corcyra at Cape Leukimne. In 433, however, her citizens had absented themselves from the clash off the Sybota Isles; and, at the outbreak of the war, the
Athenians had sent an embassy seeking the allegiance of all four *póleis,* which
they now pledged.[23]

While Archidamus was still in Attica, a second set of triremes—this time,
thirty in number—set out from the Peiraeus to cruise along the coast of Locris
and protect Euboea. The soldiers on board seized Thronium on the Locrian
coast and took hostages, and they defeated a host of Locrians further east at
Alope. Toward the end of the summer, the Athenians built a fortified post on
the island of Atalante, just off the Locrian coast, and there they apparently left
two triremes to intercept the pirates operating from Opuntian Locris, who
were intent on looting Euboea.[24]

It was probably also at this time that the son of Xanthippus, pointing to
Aegina, exhorted his fellow Athenians to "remove the pus from the eye of the
Peiraeus." To this entreaty, his compatriots, who had long been hostile to the
Aeginetans, appear to have responded with enthusiasm. They coveted the is-

land on which these men lived. It was, they noticed, close to the Peloponnesus. It could be put to military use, and its owners they charged with bringing on the war. For this the Aeginetans would have to pay, and pay they did. For, after the departure of the Peloponnesians from Attica, at some point not long before the solar eclipse of 3 August 431, the Athenians expelled these islanders from their ancestral homeland; and the Spartans, mindful of the aid that this people had afforded them in 465/4 at the time of the great helot revolt, relocated many of these refugees nearby at Thyrea in Cynouria. In their place, on Aegina, the Athenians settled a colony of their compatriots; and from there, we have reason to suspect, they not only staged raids against Sparta's allies along the nearby Peloponnesian coast. They also monitored and interfered with traffic coming in and out of Cenchreae, Corinth's chief port on the Saronic Gulf.[25]

Toward autumn, Pericles in person led the entire levy of Athenians as well as the metics enrolled—more than thirteen thousand hoplites in all—along with a host of light-armed troops into the Megarid. There they were joined by the *epibátai* and perhaps also the oarsmen from the hundred ships returning from their circumnavigation of the Peloponnesus; and this great horde then systematically ravaged the better part of Megara's farmland. This in ritual fashion, either with their cavalry or with all of their forces, the Athenians would do for the next seven years twice annually—at the time of the Megarian grain harvest, shortly after the Peloponnesians had withdrawn from Attica, and again on the cusp of fall, when the Megarians sowed their winter wheat. This was done, we are told, in compliance with a degree proposed by a close associate of Pericles in the wake of the Megarians' murder of an Athenian herald.[26]

The following year, while Archidamus and the members of the Spartan alliance were busy ravaging the Paralia, Pericles and his colleagues Hagnon and Cleopompus son of Cleinias led out a second expedition against the Peloponnesus. Once again, the Athenians dispatched one hundred triremes. Once again, Athens' allies—this time, the Chians and the cities on Lesbos—sent a contingent of fifty triremes to join them. On this occasion, however, the Athenians carried with them a much larger contingent of hoplites—four thousand in all—and, with the help of superannuated triremes reconditioned for use as horse transports, they also conveyed three hundred cavalrymen and their mounts. In numbers, this was as sizable an expedition as any that the Athenians would mount in the course of the war. They needed such a force because

Pericles hoped to storm and expected to conquer Epidaurus, Corinth's immediate neighbor to the south. At his direction, the Athenians mounted a full-
scale assault on the place, but to no avail. Whether he intended merely to sack
the *pólis,* to garrison the place and use it as a base from which to wreak havoc
within the Corinthiad to the north, to employ it as a bargaining chip with
which to entice Argos into the war, or any combination of the three—this, alas,
we are not told. But it is worth mentioning that, a decade later, the Argives
coveted Epidaurus, and it was taken for granted that Corinth's security would
be imperiled if an enemy controlled that city. With regard to the campaign led
by Pericles, all that we can say is that, in the end, the Athenians had to settle
for ravaging Epidaurus' territory and that of her neighbors Troezen, Hermione, and Halieis; and that later, while cruising along the Laconian coast, they
put in at Prasiae, a town of Lacedaemon's *períoikoi,* laid waste its territory, and
sacked the place.[27]

Eventually, the son of Xanthippus returned to Athens; and, soon thereafter, Hagnon and Cleopompus conducted this expeditionary force on a forty-
day foray to western Thrace with an eye to battling the rebellious Chalcidians
and to deploying *mēchanaí*—scaling ladders, battering rams, and the like—
against Potidaea, which was still in revolt. This enterprise came to nothing,
however. Potidaea, which occupied the narrow isthmus linking the Pallene
peninsula to the south-southeast with western Thrace, was well-placed for defense, well-fortified, and virtually impregnable, as Xerxes' marshal Artabazus
had learned half a century before. It was not until the winter of 430/29, when
the Potidaeans had been reduced by the siege to cannibalism, that they came
to terms and marched out of their city with little but the clothes on their backs,
leaving it to be colonized by the Athenians. The effort mounted by the Athenians against the Bottiaeans at Spartolus early the following summer ended in
defeat when the Chalcidian rebels quartered at Olynthus rallied to their neighbors' defense and the two peoples made a skillful use of their cavalry and peltasts against Athens' hoplites.[28]

At some point in the winter of 430/29, not long before the Corinthian
colony's surrender, Phormio son of Asopius—who had in the previous decade
been a commander both at Samos and in Acarnania and who had hitherto
played a prominent role in the siege—was recalled from Potidaea and dispatched with a force of twenty triremes around the Peloponnesus. He established himself in the small, fortified harbor at Naupactus, and it was probably

at this time that he managed to recapture the little Corinthian colony of Chalcis, which was located a few miles to the west on the north shore of the Gulf of Patras, and restore it to Athenian control. From Naupactus and perhaps also Chalcis, Phormio kept watch with an eye to preventing anyone from journeying by sea in or out of Corinth and the Corinthian Gulf more generally.[29]

Athens' efforts in these two years make sense from a variety of perspectives. The great expeditions dispatched while Archidamus and his troops were in Attica were no doubt intended to bolster Athenian morale, to show the Peloponnesians that the Athenians were unfazed, and to bring home to the latter the damage that a power in command of the sea can inflict on those who live along the shore. These expeditions may even have been aimed, as Diodorus claims, at inducing the Peloponnesians to withdraw from Attica and return home to defend their possessions.[30] The Athenians were also concerned with the recovery of Potidaea and the defense of the subject cities within their realm. Especially at the outset, it was far more important that they demonstrate the fecklessness of Lacedaemon's strategy than that they achieve major gains themselves. Pericles in these first few months was nothing if not cautious. But it is, nonetheless, a mistake to suppose, as many scholars do, that the great man's strategy was purely defensive.[31]

Thucydides tells us two things that ought to give us pause. On the one hand, he proudly reports that, at the very beginning of the war, he foresaw that it was going to be a great war, and he indicates what he has in mind when he intimates that it put in the shade Homer's Trojan War and Herodotus' Persian Wars. On the other hand, Thucydides leaves many of his modern readers with the impression that Pericles, to whom he attributes "*pronoía* with regard to the war," thought that the conflict would end quickly with a return to the *status quo ante* and with Lacedaemon's acceptance of Athens' maritime hegemony.[32] How, we should ask, could Thucydides attribute "foreknowledge with regard to the war" to a man who failed to appreciate what he himself grasped from the very start: that it would be a genuinely great war and not a minor skirmish quickly brought to a conclusion? To make sense of Thucydides' claims, we must suppose that there was more to Athenian strategy than immediately met the eye, that Pericles was intent on achieving something other than peaceful coexistence with the Lacedaemonians, and that Thucydides knew as much.

It is, of course, true that, on the eve of the war, the Athenian statesman had urged on his compatriots an unwonted *hēsuchía*: they were, he urged, to "remain at rest." They were to look after the fleet, to refrain from adding to their empire, and to avoid placing the city at risk. But, as Thucydides and the others in the assembly surely understood, Pericles' brief comments had to be interpreted with reference to Athens' recent past. What he had in mind when he argued for self-restraint was the Athenians' propensity for aimless expansion and risky ventures in places such as Egypt and Boeotia. It is with this in mind that he told his compatriots on the first occasion when he discussed the military posture they should assume during the war, "I fear your own blunders far more than the contrivances of our opponents." He did not mean that they should not seek strategic gains vis-à-vis Sparta and her Peloponnesian allies. He meant that they should focus single-mindedly on such gains and avoid dangerous distractions of the sort that had done them so much damage in the past—and these gains, as some scholars have noted, he pursued with vigor.[33]

Before the war, Pericles had sanctioned Phormio's renewal of Athens' alliance with the Acarnanians, and he had played the Corinthians and Corcyraeans off against one another. In this fashion, he prevented the former from reasserting their hegemony in the Corinthian Gulf, the Ionian Sea, and the Adriatic; and he turned the latter into dependents of Athens.

Now that the war had begun, he was doing everything within his power to force the Megarians to abandon their allegiance to Lacedaemon, align with Athens, and block the Peloponnesian League's annual invasions of Attica. He had cut them off from trade to the east; he had imposed on them a blockade; and twice a year he had the Athenians lay waste their land. In effect, he offered them a choice between an adherence to Athens and destitution, if not starvation.[34]

He had also tried to storm Epidaurus; he was putting pressure on Troezen, Hermione, and Halieis to switch sides, as the Athenians had in the 460s; and he had sent a fleet to reopen the route around the Peloponnesus, to acquire Cephallenia as an ally, to shore up relations with Acarnania, and to make it possible for Athens to initiate again a blockade against Corinth and in other ways consolidate what she had gained in the Corinthian Gulf, the Ionian Sea, and the Adriatic.

The first few years of the Archidamian War recall to mind the initial years of Athens' earlier struggle against the Peloponnesians.[35] The geopolitical imperatives were the same, and so were the means employed. Once again the Athenians were doing everything in their power to make life intolerable for

Sparta's maritime allies and to demonstrate that Lacedaemon was useless to them in their time of need. The only difference was that this time the Athenians were intent on avoiding distractions. Adding Corcyra, Zacynthus, Cephallenia, Epidaurus, Troezen, Hermione, Halieis, Achaea, and, above all, Megara and Corinth to the Athenian alliance would be well worth the effort and the risk. Imperial expansion on a grand scale further afield and the acquisition of a land empire in Hellas to the north of Attica—ventures of this sort would not only be a waste of resources. They might well imperil the city. But if the Athenians could bring pressure to bear on Lacedaemon's allies in the Peloponnesus and on Corinth's allies in the Ionian Sea, the former's alliance might come apart at the seams. It had done so in the late 470s and early 460s. To judge by the threats broadcast by the Corinthians in 432, it would do so again if the Lacedaemonians grew weary of the war and made peace on humiliating terms that fell far short of the ambitious goals announced in their propaganda.[36] If and when that day came and they saw an opening, the Argives—bound though they might be by a thirty years' truce with Sparta not slated to end until 421—would in all likelihood reenter the fray; and then the opportunity that Athens had squandered at Cimon's behest in the early 460s, when Argos and Tegea had squared off against Lacedaemon, would present itself once again. Such was the strategic vision of the son of Xanthippus, and it presupposed that the Peloponnesian War would, indeed, be what Thucydides thought it would be: an epic struggle between antagonists of the first rank, dwarfing in its magnitude—if not also in its length and the attendant suffering—Homer's war and that of Herodotus as well.

The War at Sea

It is not clear that anyone in the Peloponnesus had a full appreciation of the scale and scope of Pericles' strategic aims. But the principal actors did recognize that they were under threat. Thanks to the Megarian Decrees, the Lacedaemonians were aware that—in certain, crucial respects—their alliance was itself under attack; and the Corinthians rightly anticipated that the Athenians would once again exploit their maritime hegemony in the Saronic Gulf and their base at Naupactus in the Corinthian Gulf to shut down the trade that was the source of Corinth's legendary wealth. Moreover, possessed as they were of Long Walls of their own, they knew from the outset that the war would not be won or lost in Attica, as a majority of the Spartans initially supposed. It would, they realized, be decided at sea.

When—at the meeting of the Spartan alliance held in 432 subsequent to the vote in the Spartan assembly that the Athenians had breached the terms of the Thirty Years' Peace—the Corinthians sought to rally the delegates present behind a decision for war, they said next to nothing about pillaging and not one word about an infantry clash. Instead, they harped on the Peloponnesians' access to the moneys at Olympia and Delphi and on their ability to build a navy capable of wresting control of the sea from the Athenians. And they also insisted on the need for them to gain in the interim a mastery of the requisite nautical skills and on the willingness of Athens' subject allies to revolt if they thought that they could recover their freedom. If, the following year, their colony Syracusa and the other Dorian *póleis* in Sicily and Italy offered Lacedaemon their support, it was no doubt the work of the Corinthians; and they were surely the instigators when the Spartans directed their adherents in the west to build two hundred ships so that the coalition could field a fleet of five hundred triremes.[37]

At the beginning of the war, the Peloponnesians were well provided with galleys. Corinth and her allies had deployed one hundred fifty triremes in the battle off the Sybota Isles in August 433. They had destroyed, disabled, or captured seventy Corcyraean ships. They had lost thirty of their own: most of them Megarian and Ambraciot galleys posted on the right wing, where—early in the battle—they were routed by the Corcyraeans. In the interim, in preparing for war, the Peloponnesians had presumably more than made up that loss.

Sparta's allies were not yet a match for the Athenians in the Aegean. They were inferior in nautical science, as Pericles had observed. At the battle off the Sybota Isles, neither side had displayed a capacity for maneuver. Neither had employed the *diékplous* to shear off the oars of a rival trireme and leave it incapacitated, and the *anastróphē* seems not to have been a part of the repertoire of either fleet. Nor had there been a resort on either side to the *kúklos* or the *períplous*. Instead, both had loaded their triremes with hoplites, archers, and javelin throwers; and—by way of sidling up to one another, lashing the ships together, and boarding the triremes of their opponents—the two had fought a land battle at sea.[38] Their lack of skill notwithstanding, the Peloponnesians could nonetheless hope by means of numerical superiority to hold their own in the theater—distant from Athens and quite hard to reach—constituted by the Corinthian Gulf and the western waters more generally.

The Peloponnesians did not challenge the fleet of one hundred triremes that the Athenians sent to circumnavigate their peninsula in the summer of 431. But in the winter, after it had returned to Athens, the Corinthians dispatched forty triremes with fifteen hundred hoplites to restore Evarchus to his position as tyrant of Astacus. After doing so, they attempted to capture a number of places along the Acarnanian coast; they ravaged a district on Cephallenia; and they lost some men to a surprise attack launched by the inhabitants. The following summer, the Lacedaemonians joined the fray. While the Athenians busied themselves in the Aegean—in the Argolic Acte, along the coast of Laconia, and at Potidaea—the Spartans dispatched with their navarch Cnemus a fleet of one hundred triremes—supplied, no doubt, largely by Corinth and her colonies—and with a thousand Lacedaemonian hoplites this armada descended on Zacynthus, ravaged the countryside, and tried to force the Zacynthians to submit.[39]

The summer thereafter, Cnemus returned to the region with a more ambitious enterprise in hand. The Corinthian colonists in Ambracia and their barbarian neighbors the Chaonians, who lived to the north, had joined together for the purpose of conquering Acarnania and detaching that district from its alliance with Athens; and Perdiccas had agreed to send one thousand Macedonians. At the Ambraciots' request, the Spartans promised to provision a fleet and send one thousand hoplites. If the Acarnanians were attacked on land and by sea at the same time, the Ambraciots believed, those on the coast would be unable to come to the support of those in the interior, and both would fall. Moreover, they told themselves and others, if Acarnania fell, Zacynthus and Cephallenia would soon follow, and Naupactus might be seized as well. As the mention of Naupactus suggests, there was a geopolitical logic underpinning the original Corinthian expedition and the two Peloponnesian efforts that followed.[40]

It was not easy for a fleet of triremes based in the Aegean to circumnavigate the Peloponnesus. The "round boats" or "bathtubs" favored by merchants on some routes had this disadvantage: they depended on the wind. When the sea was becalmed, they were mired in place; and, though they could tack to some degree, when the breeze blew from an unfavorable quarter, they could not, given the state of naval technology at the time, sail all that close to the wind. They had certain compensating advantages, however. They could carry ample supplies of food, water, and other provisions; they offered travelers and the comparatively small number of crew members they required space in which to stretch out and sleep; and they could weather high seas.

Triremes did not depend on the wind. When the sea was becalmed, the crew took to the oars; and when the wind blew from the wrong quarter, they could row the galley wherever they wished. But they suffered at the same time from a variety of disadvantages. Their crews were numerous, and their need for food, water, and other provisions was considerable. But the space available for stores was quite limited, and they offered their crews nowhere to sleep. They had to stop frequently to replenish their supplies of fresh water and for the cooking of meals,[41] and their crews needed to spend the night ashore.

Unfortunately, along the long Laconian coast stretching south from the plain of Thyrea to Cape Malea, there were very few harbors and landing places; and the towns that did exist were inhabited by Lacedaemonian *períoikoi* none too friendly to the Athenians and their allies. Once they rounded Cape Malea, moreover, these triremes would face another challenge. In the open sea to the south of Capes Malea, Taenarum, and Akritas, contrary currents clash; there is no shelter from the high wind; and the seas can be extremely rough. In such circumstances, triremes, which have an exceedingly shallow draft, are hard to handle; and the waves tend to splash in over the sides.[42]

Tolmides son of Tolmaeus no doubt found stopping places when he pioneered this route with an Athenian fleet in 456. We know, for example, that he found at least temporary shelter at Cythera—an island, hitherto under Lacedaemonian control, located off Cape Malea—and we are told that he persuaded the Zacynthians and Cephallenians to side with the Athenians. He and his successors on this route clearly learned to cope with high seas. But it must always have been rough going; and the fact that Zacynthus, Cephallenia, and Acarnania provided the Athenians with resting places near the end of this difficult voyage was no small matter. At the outset of the war, when the Athenians dispatched envoys to these three places and to Corcyra, they did so, Thucydides tells us, because they believed that, if these communities were "firm in their friendship, they could themselves envelop the Peloponnesus in war." Later, when the Ambraciots sought support from the Lacedaemonians, they told them that, if they could take Zacynthus, Cephallenia, and Acarnania away from the Athenians, the latter would be "unable to circumnavigate the Peloponnesus as they had in the past."[43]

It was out of character for the Spartans to undertake the enterprises that Cnemus charted in the summers of 430 and 429. Thanks to the helot threat, they were homebodies not apt to be out and about, and the sea was not their element. To make such attempts required an audacity in short supply at Lacedaemon. There was, however, one Spartiate known to have possessed the qualities required; and, as it happens, he assumed office as eponymous ephor in September 431. His name was Brasidas son of Tellis. He would later display strategic vision; and, as we have seen, he had already distinguished himself as a tactician by fending off a host of Athenian interlopers at Mothone earlier that summer. The fact that he held high office at the time that Cnemus was first dispatched and that he reappears in midsummer 429 as one of three "councillors" sent from home to stiffen the navarch's resolution suggests that, like Archidamus, he shared the Corinthians' understanding of what it would take to win the war and that, alongside the Agiad king, he may have been the driving force behind Sparta's decision to take to the sea.[44]

Apart from sending a fleet in 431 to circumnavigate the Peloponnesus and confirm the support of Athens' allies in the west, the Athenians had not committed much in the way of resources to the region. In 431, the Cephallenians had fended off the Corinthians without Athenian help. In 430, the Zacynthians had weathered the Peloponnesian invasion in a similar fashion. In 429, the Athenians dispatched a flotilla charged, among other things, with putting an end to these attacks. One might think the twenty triremes commanded by Phormio at Naupactus insufficient. As it turned out, however, they were all that was required.

Not long after Phormio's arrival, triremes from Leucas, Anactorium, and Ambracia rendezvoused at Leucas while the Corinthians, the Sicyonians, the Megarians, and other communities with ports on the Corinthian Gulf equipped a fleet. In the meantime, Cnemus departed, either from Patras in Achaea or Cyllene in Elis, with a handful of transports, carrying a thousand Peloponnesian hoplites. Without attracting the notice of Phormio's flotilla, he slipped out of or past the Gulf of Patras and made his way northward along the Acarnanian coast to Leucas—where he was joined by hoplites from Ambracia, Leucas, and Anactorium as well as ample barbarian forces dispatched from Chaonia, Thesprotia, Molossia, Orestis, Atintania, and Parauaea to the north.

Perdiccas' forces and the fleet from the Corinthian Gulf were considerably less prompt in coming. Everyone else was ready and no doubt eager to get on with it. So Cnemus decided to march. The triremes from Ambracia, Leucas, and Anactorium descended on the Acarnanian coast while his army proceeded from the eastern end of the Ambraciot Gulf down the valley that runs through the contested territory of Amphilochian Argos to the Acarnanian capital at Stratus. Along the way, they sacked the unfortified village of Limnaea and, from there, they headed straight for Stratus—persuaded that the town's capture would bring resistance to an end.

Cnemus' strategy had its intended effect. The Acarnanians sought help from Phormio, who sent a message back that he could not leave Naupactus unprotected when a fleet was about to set out from Corinth. Those living along the Acarnanian coast remained at home intent on defending their property against the amphibious forces deployed against them, and the Acarnanians of Stratus were left to their own devices—and devise they did. While the forces commanded by Cnemus marched forward in three separate divisions, generally but not always in sight of one another, the Stratians set an ambush. Cnemus planned to conduct his army in an orderly fashion to the outskirts of the town—with the Leucadian and Anactorian hoplites on the right, the Peloponnesian and Ambraciot hoplites on the left, and the barbarian horde in the center. There, he hoped to camp, to open negotiations, and storm the city if persuasion failed. But he did not get the opportunity. Instead, the Chaonians and the other barbarians gave way to impulse and surged forward, hoping to take the town themselves by assault; and the Acarnanians in the city and those waiting in ambush fell upon them, slaughtered a considerable number, and drove the rest back in panic. Cnemus and the Greek hoplites under his command formed up in a phalanx and were able to save the barbarians who sought shelter in their ranks, but they were unable to do more—for the people of Stratus did not offer battle. From a distance, moreover, the Acarnanian slingers proved a tremendous irritant. For, in the face of the artillery onslaught they unleashed, Cnemus' forces could not move about and forage for provisions without their armor. Mindful that the Acarnanians from the coast would in time rally and that his army would soon lose its numerical advantage, Cnemus marched that night, under cover of darkness, around the Acarnanian capital to a point on the river Anapus nine miles below Stratus. From there, the following day, he withdrew to Oeniadae, an Acarnanian city a short distance

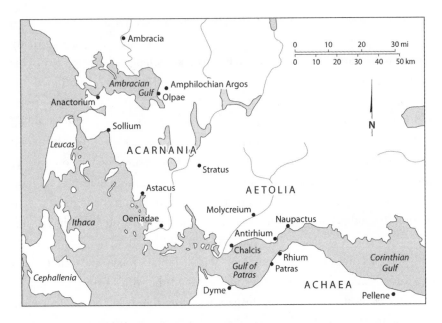

Map 13. Acarnania, the Gulf of Patras, and the Mouth of the Corinthian Gulf

upriver from that region's southern coast that Pericles had tried and failed to take in 454. It was from this anti-Athenian stronghold that the ships, which had been based at Leucas, conveyed the various contingents in his army home.[45]

While events were unfolding in Acarnania, another especially revealing drama was taking place near the mouth of the Corinthian Gulf in the Gulf of Patras. When the fleet, intended to support Cnemus' venture in the Ionian Sea, left Corinth for Leucas, Phormio monitored it closely, hoping to attack when it reached the open sea—where the superior skill possessed by his crews would give the Athenian fleet an edge.

Within a trireme, there were officers on deck to decide on and direct the ship's course, to dictate and sustain the tempo of the oarsmen's strokes, and to convey to them the orders of the trierarch awarded command. There was also a shipwright on board and a purser, and there were specialists trained in handling the sails as well as archers and marines fully equipped for combat. When fully manned—as it had to be if it was not to be underpowered, slow, hard to maneuver, and unlikely to survive a contest—this vessel was a formidable fighting machine. It took extraordinary grit, determination, discernment, and discipline on the part of a considerable number of men for a trireme to be operated in battle to advantage. The trierarch in command had to be a man of fine judgment—quick to sense danger, and no less quick in recognizing opportunity—and he had to have an intimate knowledge of the capacity of his ship and crew and of their limits. The helmsman [*kubernḗtēs*] stationed immediately below the trierarch's perch at the stern was in charge in the trierarch's absence and had to possess the same capacities. He also had to be skilled and precise in his use of the vessel's two steering oars. Everything depended on his ability to maneuver the galley into a position from which it could strike and not be struck in return, and an error or even a measure of imprecision on his part could quite easily be fatal to all concerned. When the trireme was in motion the archers and marines on deck had to remain seated lest they destabilize the vessel. In consequence they had to be able to shoot or hurl projectiles with great accuracy from an uncomfortable, sedentary position. With the help of a flutist [*aulḗtēs*] located amidships keeping time with his instrument, the exhorter [*keleustḗs*] situated on the gangway near the stern and his colleague, the bow-master [*prōrátēs*] stationed near the prow, had to drill the oarsmen in synchronizing their strokes and in rowing forward now at this pace, now at that. These two also had to teach them how to reverse themselves on the benches and back water without missing a beat, and they had to instruct them in the procedure of partially shipping their oars on command at a time when a few seconds delay on their part could result in the oars on one side being sheared off, in some of the men wielding them being killed by whiplash, and in the galley itself being left entirely disabled. In time of battle, moreover, these two officers had to convey the helmsman's orders quickly and accurately, and throughout they somehow had to sustain the morale of men whom they were driving quite hard.

Phormio had twenty triremes—about as many as the little harbor at Naupactus would accommodate. The Corinthians and their allies had fifty-seven—most of which doubled on this occasion as troop transports. The latter, confident in their numerical superiority, did not expect the Athenians to launch an assault. But they were cautious, nonetheless. Within the Corinthian Gulf, their fleet made its way along the Peloponnesian coast while Phormio's followed the northern shore. When the Corinthians and their allies reached Patras in Achaea, a few miles beyond the narrows at the mouth of the Corinthian Gulf, they paused. That night, under the cover of darkness, they tried to slip across the Gulf of Patras to the opposite coast—probably, to Kryonéri in

Aeolia or to Oeniadae in Acarnania further northwest. But Phormio was ready for them, and he was alert. His triremes, which were moored west of Kryonéri at Chalcis and in the river Evenus, he sent to confront the enemy.

The Peloponnesian commanders feared that the Athenians would resort to the *diékplous*—that they would row through their line, narrowly avoiding head-in collisions, shipping their own oars at the last minute, and shearing off the oars on one side of the triremes they passed. And they worried that the Athenians would then perform the *anastróphē* by swinging around to ram the remaining Peloponnesian galleys at the stern where they could most easily puncture and disable these ships. To render this maneuver unworkable, the Peloponnesian galleys formed what the Greeks called a *kúklos* or circle, as the fleet of the Hellenes had done in similar circumstances when they first confronted Xerxes' armada at Artemisium fifty-one years before. Their prows with the sharp metal rams attached they directed outward. Their sterns they tucked in. In the middle of this loose circle they lodged the smaller craft carrying their provisions and the five fast triremes, unburdened with hoplites, that they held in reserve.

There was ample sea room in the Gulf of Patras, and the Athenians, on this occasion, responded by imitating the Persians at Artemisium and resorting to the *períplous,* which required that they sail about the *kúklos,* keep up the pretense that they are about to attack, and move ever closer in an attempt to force the circle to contract. Phormio's goal was that the Peloponnesian ships run afoul of one another. And so, in the morning twilight as the sky above gradually came into view, he slowly tightened the ring and tarried until the wind coming out of the gulf suddenly picked up and there were swells, as still happens in those parts in the summer at dawn nearly every day.

The Peloponnesian galleys were overburdened with infantrymen, top-heavy, and hard to handle in the best of circumstances. When the swells were amplified, their crews lost control. The triremes began to drift and bump up against one another. Their oars, which the inexperienced rowers did not have the wit to raise, got caught in the chop. In the chaos that ensued—as crew members broke out poles to push the ships off from one another and there was shouting and swearing loud enough to drown out the commands issued by the helmsmen and repeated by the exhorters and bow-masters—Phormio gave the agreed-upon signal; and the Athenian triremes descended upon the Peloponnesian fleet. They sunk one of the command ships. Other galleys they rammed and disabled. In the confusion, they captured twelve triremes. The rest they chased back to Patras and to Dyme further west on the Achaean coast. It was from there that the remnants of this fleet made their way west, then south-southwest down the coast of the Peloponnesus to Cyllene, the principal port of Elis, where Cnemus soon presented himself with the fleet that had fought along the coast of Acarnania.[46]

In ordinary circumstances, those who have been badly and unexpectedly mauled in battle take a breather to lick their wounds, reflect on the source of their failures, and reconsider their options. The Spartans back home, however, were unaccustomed to losing, and they did not much relish the experience. That their navy was so inferior to that of the Athenians that a force of twenty triremes could easily whip a fleet nearly three times as large they simply could not imagine. The Peloponnesians must somehow have suffered "a theft of war." There had to have been "softness [*malakía*]"—a lack of spiritedness, vigor, and energy—on someone's part. So they supposed—and, in fury, to Cnemus they dispatched three Spartiates to serve as his *xúmbouloi* or "councillors," the first such of whom we have express knowledge. These men were empowered to make recommendations, which, in the circumstances, Lacedaemon's navarch would be ill-advised to ignore.[47]

One of the three was Brasidas, as we have already had occasion to note. No one could accuse the hero of Mothone of *malakía*. The others were named Timocrates and Lycophron, and they brought with them instructions from the authorities at Lacedaemon. At the first opportunity, they were to stage another naval battle. This time, they were to be better prepared. This time, they were to win. The Peloponnesian fleet was not to be driven from the sea by a handful of ships.

Mindful of their orders, Cnemus and his *xúmbouloi* sent messengers to the cities in their coalition, asking for additional ships; and they repaired and otherwise re-equipped the ones they had. In the interim, Phormio, anticipating a reprise, sent a messenger to Athens to report his victory and ask for more ships. His compatriots responded to the emergency in much the same fashion in which they had responded earlier to the prospect that Samians and Potidaeans might revolt. They sent off an insufficient number of triremes—only twenty in number—and they did not instruct them to make haste. Instead, they ordered them to make a stop in Crete en route to support a scheme de-

vised by the Athenian *próxenos* at Gortyn against the Aeginetan colony at Cydonia, from which privateers are apt to have been conducting operations.[48]

In consequence, when the onslaught came, Phormio had only the twenty
triremes that he had started with. Against this flotilla, Cnemus and his councillors conducted to Panormus in Achaea a fleet of seventy-seven triremes.
This time, the Peloponnesian galleys were not overburdened with infantrymen. This time, their sole aim was to win a battle at sea, and there was every
prospect that they would succeed—for their fleet outnumbered that of their
foe by almost four to one.

For six or seven days, the two sets of galleys faced one another across the
narrows, separated by a mile of water, and there was a standoff. Phormio's triremes were anchored southwest of Molycreium off Antirhium within the Gulf
of Patras with its broad expanse of waters, where he was intent that the battle
take place. Those of Cnemus and his councillors were situated ever so slightly
to the east of Achaean Rhium in the direction of Panormus, just inside the
Corinthian Gulf, where there was much less sea room and they hoped to use
their superiority in numbers to envelop and overwhelm the Athenians. Fearful that reinforcements would arrive, Cnemus, Brasidas, and the other two
councillors were reportedly eager for a decision.

The odds are good that Thucydides was exceedingly well-informed concerning these events. As we have seen, he was an adult—in his mid-twenties,
if not a bit older—at the beginning of the war, and he began working on his
history immediately after its inception. He was, moreover, an Athenian—born
into a prominent family related to Cimon son of Miltiades—and five years
after this battle, when he was in his thirties, he was chosen as a general and
assigned to Thrace, where Phormio had also served. In the early years of the
war, he was almost certainly in Athens when he was not abroad on campaign.
Athens was not a large place. A young man of this sort can hardly have escaped
becoming acquainted with the son of Asopius. If his account of the man's intentions and achievement sometimes reads like an eyewitness account, it is
either because he really was an eyewitness or because he later interviewed
Phormio at length.

It is also virtually certain that Thucydides later met Brasidas. The two men
were antagonists during the Athenian's brief tenure as general, and the son of
Olorus had an enduring interest in the theater of operations that concerned

the Spartan in his final years. He had almost certainly been given a command in that region because, as he tells us himself, he was well-connected in that part of Thrace. Like Cimon, he is apt to have been a descendant of the Thracian king whose name his father bore—which may help explain how he acquired the right to work certain gold mines in the Strymon basin. In 423, a year or more before Brasidas' death at Amphipolis, Thucydides was forced into exile—where, he tells us, he lived chiefly among the Peloponnesians. We have good reason to suspect that he resided for some of the following twenty years in Corinth—about which, his history shows, he was exceedingly knowledgeable. But there are no grounds for doubting that the Byzantine scholar Marcellinus was correct when he reported that the historian also spent time in the vicinity of Amphipolis, where he had interests in need of protection; and it is a reasonable guess that he did so in the first few years after he had been driven from Athens—for, as we shall in due course see, he was closely familiar with developments in that region after the Spartan's seizure of Amphipolis.[49] If his description of Brasidas' thinking and conduct throughout the man's career also quite often reads like an eyewitness account, it is almost certainly because he had also found occasion, while in exile, to interview the Spartan at length.

When Thucydides tells us that Cnemus, Brasidas, and the other Peloponnesian commanders tried to prepare their men for the battle to come—first, by explaining away their earlier defeat as the product of chance and by insisting that the innate courage the Peloponnesians supposedly possessed was of greater value in combat than the Athenians' superior experience and skill in the nautical arts; then, by emphasizing the advantage they gained from the fact that they outnumbered the Athenians; and, finally, by threatening to punish anyone who displayed cowardice and promising to reward those who distinguished themselves—there is no good reason that we should doubt that these arguments were among those made. Similarly, we should give Thucydides the benefit of the doubt when he tells us that Phormio became aware that fear had his crews in its grip, when he intimates that mutiny was in the air, and when he reports that, in his disquisition, the Athenian commander told his men that they were more than a match for the Peloponnesians in experience and skill, that their recent victory over the same men had them cowed, and that he hoped to stage the battle where there would be plenty of sea room so that they could run down enemy triremes and ram them, resort to the *diékplous,* follow it up with the *anastróphē,* and swamp the enemy triremes by striking them in the stern. It also makes sense that the Athenian commander should end his disquisition by reminding his men of the stakes: "This contest is of great moment for you. Either we destroy the hope that the Peloponnesians repose in their navy or we bring nearer to the Athenians the fear they entertain that they will lose control of the sea."[50]

Phormio had had options, as Thucydides makes clear. He could have ignored the Peloponnesian fleet and kept his triremes in reserve in the well-fortified harbor at Naupactus, and this would have been the prudent thing to do. What he did, instead, was gratuitous and reckless in the extreme. There was nothing at stake on this occasion other than Athens' ability for the nonce to blockade the Corinthian Gulf. Had Phormio hunkered down in his stronghold, the fleet marshaled by Cnemus, Brasidas, and the former's other two councillors would not have been in any position to storm that port. Phormio had, however, been instructed to put an end to traffic in the Corinthian Gulf. He had pulled off a remarkable coup in routing the Peloponnesian fleet earlier in the summer, and he was a true Athenian: anything but risk-averse.

Phormio's audacity afforded the Spartans an opportunity that they would not otherwise have had, and—no doubt at the urging of Brasidas and his colleagues—the Peloponnesian fleet seized it. They had spent six or seven days practicing maneuvers with an eye to training their crews, entertaining the Athenians, and giving them the jitters. Then, one day at dawn, they rowed out, formed up four abreast, and sailed east along the Peloponnesian coast with their twenty fastest triremes under the command of the councillor Timocrates in the lead. It was their hope that Phormio—fearing that their goal was to wheel, dash across the narrows near the entrance of the Corinthian Gulf into the undefended harbor at Naupactus, and seize the place—would sprint with his triremes in the same direction, find himself cut off from the harbor by Timocrates' division, and have to fight the entire Peloponnesian fleet in the shallows just off Aeolian coast where the agility of the Athenian triremes would be of no use.

For the most part, this maneuver worked. Phormio and his triremes did make a dash for Naupactus. Timocrates and his division tried to head them off, nine Athenian triremes were driven ashore along the Aeolian coast, and the Peloponnesians descended upon them—eager to slaughter or capture the crews, disable the triremes, and haul them away. Ten of Phormio's triremes, however, made it to Naupactus, turned about, and settled in at the entrance to the harbor to defend the place. There was one additional trireme, a laggard caught in between; and it found itself in distress. Or such was the pretense—for it was, we are told by a late source, captained by Phormio himself, and he was perfectly capable of dangling his galley as bait. It was vigorously pursued by a single Leucadian galley—carrying Timocrates himself—which rowed out well ahead of the rest; and the Leucadian would almost certainly have caught the Athenian galley had it not been for the presence of a merchantman anchored in the deep water outside the harbor of Naupactus.

In the event—whether on the spur of the moment or as calculated in advance—the Athenian trireme glided past the merchantman, wheeled suddenly around it and out of sight, and then unexpectedly darted out on the other side—whence it rammed the Leucadian galley amidships, swamping it and causing Timocrates, in shame and no doubt fearful of capture, to commit suicide. This maneuver so surprised and shocked the trierarchs on the other ships in Timocrates' division that they ordered a pause so that they could reconsider while the rest of the fleet caught up. And this ship's success and the confusion that gripped the Peloponnesians so excited those who commanded the Athenian ships in the harbor at Naupactus that they had their triremes sprint out and attack—which induced those in command of the Peloponnesian galleys to panic and order a retreat to Panormus. It was from there, the next day, that the Leucadians departed for the Ionian sea and the remaining triremes headed for Corinth.

While the battle at sea was under way, the Messenian hoplites—those who had accompanied Phormio's fleet on foot as it made its way to Antirhium and who had followed it back toward Naupactus—had plunged into the water along the Aeolian shore to rescue the triremes that had run aground, and they had managed to hoist themselves onto eight of the nine and save them. In consequence, Phormio's flotilla emerged from the struggle almost intact. They had achieved a remarkable victory. In a conflict with a fleet outnumbering them almost four to one, they had lost one galley with its crew. At a time when nine of their triremes were out of commission, they had not only hulled one trireme and captured six with the eleven still in operation; they had also routed the seventy Peloponnesian galleys that remained. In the process, as Asopius' audacious son had predicted, they had destroyed the hope that the Peloponnesians had reposed in their fleet. For no one could regard the humiliation that they had inflicted on their adversaries on this occasion as "a theft of war." When it was all over, the Athenians were once again in control of the narrows at the entrance to the Corinthian Gulf, and not long thereafter Phormio welcomed the relief fleet sent from Athens via Cydonia in Crete.[51]

Late in the winter, after the Peloponnesian fleet had broken up, Phormio paid a brief visit to Acarnania, taking with him four hundred Athenian and four hundred Messenian hoplites. There he discovered, to his dismay, that it was impossible in so wet a season to negotiate the Achelous River and launch an assault on Oeniadae—the one Acarnanian community hostile to Athens—and so he took care of other business, expelling from Stratus and other towns individual Acarnanians suspected of sympathizing with the Peloponnesians.[52]

The following spring, Phormio and his men sailed home in triumph to Athens with the eighteen ships they had captured in the two battles and those of their prisoners who, as free men, were eligible for ransom. In commemoration of their commander's achievement, his compatriots dedicated in a stoa near the temple of Apollo at Delphi shields and prows taken from the Peloponnesian triremes alongside an inscribed marble slab listing the eight *póleis*— Elis, Lacedaemon, Sicyon, Megara, Pellene in Achaea, Ambracia, Leucas, and Corinth—whose forces the son of Asopius had routed; and, when this indomitable figure died some time after his homecoming, the Athenians gave him a public burial and erected a statue in his honor on the Acropolis.[53]

We are not told whether the second contingent of triremes, the one sent as a reinforcement, remained in Naupactus to maintain the blockade after Phormio's departure. But, given Athens' aims in this war, it is unlikely that the narrows at the entrance to the Corinthian Gulf were left unguarded. If so, however, they were not expected to be unguarded for long. At about the time that Phormio headed home, an expeditionary force of forty triremes under the leadership of Cleippides son of Deinias and two other commanders was slated to circumnavigate the Peloponnesus.[54]

The Mytilenian Revolt

It speaks to Brasidas' capacities as a leader of men that he, Cnemus, and the other Peloponnesian commanders did what they could in the aftermath of Phormio's victory to bolster the morale of Sparta's allies and turn to advantage the confidence that the Athenians reposed in their command of the sea. By the time they reached Corinth, the long Greek summer was over; November had come or would soon arrive; and winter had set in. There, from the Megarians, Brasidas and his colleagues learned two things of great interest to the strategic imagination—that the Athenians were negligent and did not even bother to set a guard at the entrance to the Peiraeus; and that, in dry dock in the harbor at Nisaea, there were forty triremes which an enterprising commander might put to use. With these galleys, if the Peloponnesians were sufficiently bold and did not delay for the purpose of gathering their courage and making further preparations, they could mount a surprise attack aimed at burning Athens' dockyards, her ship sheds, and the bulk of her gigantic fleet. All that they had to do was to have their rowers shoulder their oars, lay hold of the fleece cushions on which they were accustomed to slide back and forth as they rowed, and bring with them the oarloops used to attach their oars to the trireme's tholepins by those on all three banks—by the *thranítai,* who rowed from the outriggers mounted above the galley's topwale; by the *zúgioi,* who were seated on the thwarts or crossbeams [*zúga*] running inside along the ship's hull; and by the *thalamíoi,* who rowed from deep in the hull. Then, all that they had to do was to stroll across the isthmus, make their way along the coast road to the Megarian port, and do the daring deed.

The journey they made. The oars, cushions, and oarloops they carted; and as planned—at night, under the cover of darkness—they launched the forty triremes. Collective leadership is, however, nearly always a synonym for timidity; and those in authority (no doubt, to the fury of Brasidas) lacked the audacity required for executing the original scheme. Instead, they settled for a descent on Salamis. There, they mounted an assault on the little fort that the Athenians had built on the Budorum promontory, towed off the three triremes kept there for the purpose of blockading Nisaea, and began laying waste the island. When the fire beacons on Salamis were lit and noticed in the Peiraeus, it produced a panic among the Athenians; and, at dawn, they launched their fleet. But, by the time that they reached the island, the Peloponnesians were gone. The Megarian triremes, which had been out of service for at least two years, had dried out, and the wood from which their planks were made had contracted. As a result, they were no longer fully watertight; and the commanders had decided that, in the circumstances, it would be prudent for them to count their blessings, make their way back to Nisaea with the booty they had gathered, and then head for hearth and home.

In the end, the raid, though brilliant, was entirely without strategic con-

sequence. Its chief effect was to awaken the Athenians from the slumber produced by overconfidence and put them on their guard.[55] It might, however,
have marked a turning point in the war. Had the Peloponnesian commanders
not been so risk-averse, had they possessed the audacity of a Phormio, they
might have done Athens untold damage, and they might have elicited from
the Spartan alliance the resolve required for tackling the Athenians at sea. Had
they done so, they might also have taken full advantage of the signal strategic
opportunity that presented itself early in the summer of 428.

When the war began, there were only two places left in the Aegean that
paid no *phóros* to Athens but supplied ships, instead: the one *pólis* on the island of Chios, and the five *póleis* on the island of Lesbos. Of the islanders, the
Chians and the Mytilenians alone were sufficiently well-provided with galleys
to put up a real fight should they launch a rebellion; and, as the authorities
at Lacedaemon were fully aware, the latter were in the winter of 429/8 making
preparations to take the plunge. They were repairing the walls of their city.
They were building triremes. They were constructing moles to protect their
harbor. And they were awaiting the archers and the grain that they had requested from their suppliers along the coast of the Black Sea.

The Mytilenians were also doing everything within their power to unite
the *póleis* of the island under their leadership—which was their undoing. The
citizens of Tenedos, the little island to the north, and those of Methymna, the
second largest of the cities on Lesbos, were alert; and there were Atticizers
within Mytilene itself—among them, as one would expect, the vice-consuls
[*próxenoi*] appointed by the Athenians to look after their interests in the *pólis*.
They all sounded the alarm: they informed the Athenians that the Mytilenians
were trying to bring Lesbos in its entirety under their control, and they suggested that, in cooperation with their kin in Boeotia, the citizens of Mytilene
were preparing a revolt which the Lacedaemonians would support.[56]

As usual, the Athenians were behindhand and slow to take heed. As Thucydides indicates, they had more than enough to cope with already. They did
not want more. They had only recently succeeded in bringing the Potidaean
revolt to an end, and they had suffered a gruesome and disheartening mishap
at home, which we will soon discuss. As a consequence of this mishap, they
were now short of manpower, and they did not want to contemplate having to
deal with another rebellion. The envoys that the Athenians dispatched to Lesbos failed to persuade the Mytilenians to give up their preparations for war

and abandon their attempt to effect a unification [*sunoíkisis*] of the island. So they took into custody the Mytilenians on the ten triremes that were to accompany Cleippides on his expedition around the Peloponnesus, and they rerouted to Lesbos the forty Athenian galleys in his fleet. If this force hurried, they might surprise the Mytilenians in the midst of the festival held outside the city every year in honor of Malean Apollo and bring them to heel. Short of that, the expedition's commanders could offer them a choice between facing war, on the one hand, and giving up their ships and razing their walls, on the other.

Unfortunately for the Athenians, their fleet did not move with the requisite speed, and word got out. A man sympathetic to the Mytilenians journeyed by land to Oropus; crossed over to Euboea; made his way on foot to Geraistos, the port of Carystus; caught a freighter to Lesbos; and tipped off the Mytilenians—who anticipated the surprise attack and evaded it, then refused to comply with the Athenian demands, put up a brief fight at sea, and proposed an armistice and negotiations, which the Athenian commanders accepted. In the time that this bought the Mytilenians, a trireme slipped out of their harbor, no doubt at night, and, unbeknownst to the Athenians, carried envoys to Lacedaemon, seeking help.[57]

The details of the revolt as such and of Athens' response need not detain us. In its rough outlines, it is an all-too-familiar tale. For the Athenians quickly took control of the sea, and they once again employed the *modus operandi* that they had used in dealing with the Naxians circa 470, the Thasians in 465, the Samians in 441, the Potidaeans in 432, and, no doubt, other rebels in the past. It should suffice to say that the negotiators failed to resolve the dispute, that the Mytilenians were not adequately prepared for the struggle to come, that on land they nonetheless put up a valiant fight, that the Mytilenian envoys made an eloquent appeal to the members of the Spartan alliance at a gathering held in the temple of Zeus at Olympia during the Olympic Games in mid-August, that the delegates voted to come to their aid, and that, in the autumn, the Athenians finally sent out a second expedition—this one carrying one thousand hoplites—which secured control of the countryside, built a wall of circumvallation around Mytilene, and mounted a proper siege.[58]

Had the Peloponnesians attacked the Peiraeus, as planned, at the beginning of the previous winter; had they burned Athens' dockyards and the fleet laid up in dry dock, as they might well have done given the arrogance and negligence of the Athenians—the tale we would now tell might well be quite different. For, on short notice, the Athenians would have had a hard time in coming up with a fleet adequate for the task of bringing the Mytilenians to heel; the Mytilenians, who were themselves capable of deploying a force of fifty galleys, would have been much more willing to risk their own triremes in an attempt to gain control of the sea and raise up a rebellion among their fellow islanders; and the Peloponnesians, full of hope, might have moved with greater enthusiasm and speed to deploy a fleet in support of the rebellion.

For the Peloponnesians, the revolt was, as the Mytilenian envoys insisted, a golden opportunity not likely to be repeated. Some in their number recognized as much. Thucydides tells us that, in the immediate aftermath of the decision to accept Mytilene into alliance, the Spartans summoned their allies to the Isthmus of Corinth to do what the Mytilenian ambassadors had asked: to conduct a second invasion of Attica, and to send an allied fleet into the Saronic Gulf to take command of Athens' home waters and then, presumably, sail on to Lesbos.

The Lacedaemonians were enthusiastic. Their aim was to attack the Athenians by land and by sea at the same time, to put them on the defensive, and to force them to recall their fleet from the Aegean. Archidamus was in charge. He understood the stakes. He knew that, if Sparta and her allies were to win the war, they would do so at sea. Thanks to his efforts and no doubt the enthusiasm of men like Brasidas, the Spartans moved on this occasion with unwonted alacrity. They arrived in the Corinthiad before the appointed time. They prepared slipways for hauling their alliance's triremes across the isthmus from the Corinthian to the Saronic Gulf, and then two things happened that put a damper on things. It was late August, and the Peloponnesians—who were busy with their own affairs, picking their grapes and gathering their olives—were slow in coming: so slow that Archidamus was forced to cancel the invasion of Attica, as we have already had occasion to note.

Even more important, however, the Spartans' attempt to launch a fleet came to nothing. Here, too, their allies dragged their feet. But this was not what disturbed the Lacedaemonians the most. At Olympia, the Mytilenians had told them that the Athenians had suffered a spine-chilling, debilitating calamity; that they were in dire financial straits; and that they lacked the strength to mount an effective resistance. In the event, the last of these three claims turned out to be false. For, alert to the enterprise in which the enemy was engaged and to its aim, the Athenians girded their loins and manned one hundred triremes, using as oarsmen not only the thetes who ordinarily rowed in the fleet but also men of hoplite status and the resident aliens. Then, with this fleet, they made a dramatic descent on the isthmus in a demonstration of power suggesting that any force launched in the Saronic Gulf would quickly be annihilated. When, in addition, the Spartans got word that thirty Athenian triremes under the command of Asopius son of Phormio were making their way around the Peloponnesus to Naupactus and that they were laying waste the maritime districts in Laconia as they advanced, they gave up and marched back home.[59]

In the aftermath, with an eye to sending a fleet to the Aegean to support the Mytilenians, the Lacedaemonians appointed as navarch a Spartiate named Alcidas and directed the cities in their confederacy to supply forty triremes. Had this fleet been gathered quickly and had Alcidas and the commanders chosen to lead its various civic units adequately grasped what would be squandered with the passage of time, the forty triremes stipulated would have set out in short order, they would have attempted to circumnavigate the Peloponnesus, and, if successful, they would have made their way through Ionia to Lesbos. There, they might well have caught off guard the Athenian fleet conducting the blockade at Mytilene, and they might have relieved the siege and, with the help of the Mytilenians, stirred up a rebellion throughout the Aegean. But they did none of this. Instead, they waited for spring. They no doubt recognized that to attempt such a journey in October, November, or December and to remain on post in Ionia throughout the winter would be to court danger. The risks associated with delay, however, they did not weigh. No one in authority at the time appears to have entertained a sense of urgency. The Corinthians were right about the Spartans. The presence of the helots had taught them a habit of caution.

In the meantime, the Mytilenians were working their way through the food they had in storage; and, as time passed, they began to wonder whether the Peloponnesians would ever show up. Late in the winter, early in 427, a lone Spartiate named Salaethus surreptitiously made his way on shipboard from Lacedaemon to Pyrrha on Lesbos, walked across the island to Mytilene, and slipped into the city via the bed of a watercourse, where there was a small gap in the wall of circumvallation. He promised that his compatriots would soon arrive; and, for a time, this put an end to the Mytilenians' consideration of a resort to negotiation. But, although Cleomenes, the younger brother of Pleistoanax, conducted a Peloponnesian army into Attica in what we would think of as the late spring with an eye to distracting the Athenians and although he saw to it that his men ravaged an enormous swath of land as yet untouched, Salaethus' promise was not honored by those in charge at sea. Alcidas wasted time en route; and, while he was loitering, time wasted the Mytilenians; and, in the face of starvation and the tensions within the city between the rich and the poor which it aggravated, the oligarchs who ruled Mytilene chose to negotiate a surrender.[60]

Eventually, of course, Alcidas did make it to Ionia—the long, slow way, one must suspect, by way of Crete. In time, he reached Delos and, then, moved on to Ikaria, Mykonos, and Embatum in the territory of Erythrae on the Anatolian coast—where the rumors that Mytilene had surrendered, which he had heard shortly after his arrival in Ionia, were confirmed. Teutaplius, who commanded the Elean contingent, reportedly urged Alcidas and his fellow commanders to launch a surprise attack on the Athenians celebrating at Mytilene. But Alcidas was unmoved. Some of the Ionian exiles and the Mytilenians in his entourage suggested that he seize an Ionian *pólis* or the Aeolian city of Cumae, instead, and use it as a base for stirring up a rebellion throughout the region. They were of the opinion that he might then be able to lure Pissouthnes, who was still the satrap at Sardis, into the fray.[61]

This was by no means a foolish notion. As these exiles knew, this Pissouthnes had been conducting a cold war of sorts against Athens for more than a decade. He had made considerable mischief for the Athenians in the course of the Samian revolt, and he had clearly done so, as we have seen, with the advice and consent of the Great King. This had not, however, been the end of it. The pertinent sources are scattered and fragmentary but highly suggestive. The outbreak of war in Greece seems to have occasioned a concerted attempt on the part of the Persians to recover control of the coastal communities in Anatolia. To this end, Pissouthnes appears to have been working hand in glove with a Persian general, also of Achaemenid stock, who was based at Caunus—a Carian city, near the border with Lycia, which had hitherto been a member of the Delian League. Tellingly, this general bore the name Hystaspes, which was shared by the fathers of Darius the Great and of Pissouthnes himself.

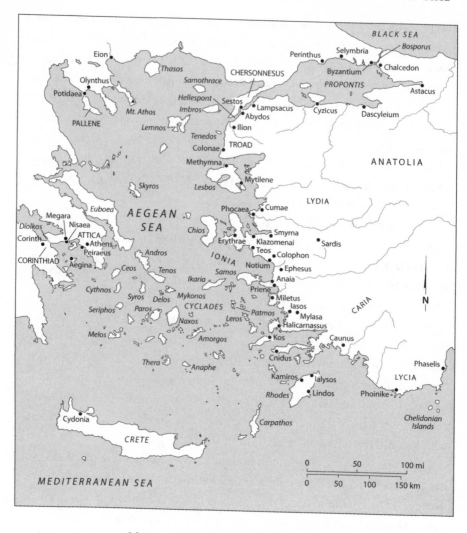

Map 14. Alcidas and the Mytilenian Revolt

In 430, for example, Pissouthnes' minions had cannily exploited the civil
strife that had broken out not only in the Greek city of Colophon, which was
situated at the base of the Erythraean peninsula, but also in its port Notium,
which lay on the Anatolian coast a few miles northwest of Ephesus—and in
this fashion they had managed to seize both towns. In the winter of 430/29,
the Athenians dispatched a general to southern Anatolia to extort silver from
communities in the region hitherto allied with Athens and to afford Phaselis
and Phoinike, which regularly exported to Athens timber suited to the build-

ing of triremes, protection against pirates sponsored by Lacedaemon—and
he met his end in the interior of Lycia at the hands of a force marshaled by a
Lycian notable from Phoinike who appears to been doing the bidding of the
Persians. Two years later, just a few months before Alcidas' arrival in Ionia,
we find Pissouthnes' bastard son Amorges—at the instance of Hystaspes in
Caunus—in command of an army made up of Carians and of the exiled Samian
oligarchs then based at Anaia in the Samian *peraía* on the Anatolian coast.
And with this army he massacred a force sent into the Maeander valley on a
money-collecting expedition by the increasingly cash-strapped Athenians. The
trouble directly or indirectly caused by this Hystaspes was of a such magnitude that the Athenians are said to have dispatched the exiled Persian notable
Zopyrus son of Megabyzus to the region along with an expedition aimed at
Caunus' recovery.[62]

Alcidas listened—no doubt with close attention—to the Ionian exiles who
urged that he take advantage of this ongoing, low-level conflict to effect an
alliance of sorts with the Persians. Again, however, the Spartan commander
was unmoved. Instead of intervening, he headed south. He circled about the
Erythraean peninsula to the town of Myconnesus in the territory of Teos,
where he slaughtered most of the prisoners he had captured en route.

When Alcidas reached Ephesus, envoys from the dissident Samians resident at Anaia further south reproached him for his conduct, arguing that "he
was not in a noble fashion liberating Hellas if he was killing men who had
neither raised their hands against him nor were his foes. They were allies of
the Athenians by necessity. If he did not cease, he would lead very few from
being enemies into friendship and would come to have more enemies from
among those who had been friends." By this he was persuaded, and he released the Chians in his custody and some of the others he had taken. Then—
fearing pursuit because his flotilla had been spied by those on Athens' two
fastest triremes, the *Paralos* and the *Salaminia*—he fled. This was the only
occasion in which Alcidas acted with dispatch, outrunning the Athenian triremes, which chased his fleet all the way to Patmos. From there—though
caught in a storm and scattered—the Peloponnesians made their way via Crete
back to Cyllene on the Elean coast, having accomplished nothing.[63]

We are not expressly told that on this occasion the Spartans became angry.
Nothing is said indicating that Alcidas was accused of *malakía*. But the Lacedaemonians cannot have been happy about the opportunity lost. Nor can they

have been pleased with the fecklessness of their navarch, and they expressed their discontent in familiar fashion by sending Brasidas to Cyllene to serve henceforth as Alcidas' *xúmboulos*. It is impossible to know what the outcome would have been in Ionia had the Spartans done this at the start. But one thing is certain: the Peloponnesians would not have been dilatory. Whether the son of Tellis could have persuaded Alcidas to put up a fight is, however, an open question.

Brasidas was like Archidamus in one particular. He understood the nature of the war. He knew that it was a conflict between a power fully in command of the land and a power virtually sovereign at sea. If stalemate was to be avoided and one side was to emerge victorious, that party would somehow have to seize control of the element controlled by the other—which would require cunning, resourcefulness, and audacity as well as good fortune. If, then, Brasidas' compatriots were to win this war, as he hoped they would, they would have to become dominant at sea; and this they could never achieve if their navarchs were risk-averse and had as their principal aim an avoidance of outright defeat. On the water, as he was aware, the Peloponnesians had little to lose and everything to gain—for, in the circumstances, failing to secure a decisive victory at sea was, as a strategic outcome, the equivalent of suffering a decisive defeat on that element. The Lacedaemonian navarch, whom Brasidas was sent to advise, had no such understanding of the stakes, and the son of Tellis had no doubt been prominent among his critics. As Alcidas' conduct suggests, he feared losing far more than he relished winning.[64]

On this occasion, the Lacedaemonians instructed Alcidas and Brasidas to proceed to Corcyra with the Peloponnesian fleet, reinforced by thirteen triremes from Leucas and Ambracia. On that island, civil strife had broken out between a faction loyal to the democracy and supportive of Athens and an oligarchic faction—led by some of the men captured at the battle off the Sybota Isles whom the Corinthians had persuaded to become their allies. At Corcyra, there was a considerable disparity of wealth, and the ordinary citizens seem to have played a minor role in the manning of their city's fleet. Of the mariners taken in the battle off the Sybota Isles, three-quarters, roughly eight hundred, were slaves. These the Corinthians sold. The remaining two hundred fifty citizens whom they seized—many of them wealthy and quite prominent—were eventually ransomed, and they returned home intent on effecting a change. We do not know when they returned. Nor do we know when the factional strife began. But it is striking that the Corcyraeans, who lived in the neighborhood of Acarnania and had a stake in that community's fate, were not in evidence in 429 when the residents of that district came under pressure and Phormio's little fleet at Naupactus could have used some help.

By the time in which Alcidas reached Cyllene, Phormio's son Asopius had himself lost his life in combat, and eighteen of his triremes had returned to Athens. As the Lacedaemonians knew, the only Athenian forces in the region were the twelve triremes remaining from Asopius' original thirty, which were stationed at Naupactus.

Under the command of Nicostratus son of Diitrephes, these twelve nonetheless managed to reach Corcyra before Alcidas and his fleet, and they brought with them five hundred Messenian hoplites. With the help of these forces, the democrats on the island managed, with difficulty, to retain control. The arrival of the fifty-three Peloponnesian triremes threatened, however, to tip the balance—especially, after they defeated the Corcyraeans and cowed the twelve Athenian triremes in a messy battle at sea. But despite the urging of Brasidas, whom he appears to have brushed off, Alcidas was characteristically hesitant and slow in following up on the Peloponnesian victory. As a commander, he seems never to have lost an opportunity to lose an opportunity, which is what he once again did on this occasion.

Soon thereafter, there arrived from Athens a relief force of sixty triremes commanded by Eurymedon son of Eucles—who appears to have been named after Cimon's great victory and who may well have been born circa forty years before, shortly after that remarkable battle took place. Toward the end of the campaigning season of 427, when this Eurymedon reached Corcyra, the democrats on the island were still in the ascendant, thanks to Alcidas' timidity; and the Peloponnesian galleys then quickly fled under cover of darkness, keeping close to the shore as they rowed toward the Gulf of Patras. In a desperate attempt to avoid being seen, instead of doubling the cape at Leucas, the Peloponnesians dragged their ships over the narrow and swampy isthmus linking that island to the mainland.

Eurymedon's arrival did not mark the end of the civil war at Corcyra. Its immediate consequence was a massacre of some of the oligarchs, and, as Eurymedon resolutely averted his gaze, further bloodshed followed.[65] Nor did his appearance on the scene mark the final chapter in the struggle between the Corinthians and their allies and the Athenians and theirs for dominance in the Corinthian Gulf and the western waters more generally. But, in these years, there was never again an occasion in which Peloponnesian triremes dared to fight a fleet action against Athenian galleys. Athens was still the lord of the sea.[66]

Part II

FORTUNE'S WHEEL

Never, never, never believe any war will be smooth and easy, or that anyone
who embarks on that strange voyage can measure the tides and hurricanes he
will encounter. The Statesman who yields to war fever must realize that once
the signal is given, he is no longer the master of policy but the slave of unfore-
seeable and uncontrollable events. Antiquated War Offices, weak, incompetent
or arrogant Commanders, untrustworthy allies, hostile neutrals, malignant
Fortune, ugly surprises, awful miscalculations—all take their seat at the Council Board on the morrow of a declaration of war. Always remember, however
sure you are that you can easily win, that there would not be a war if the other
man did not think he also had a chance.

WINSTON CHURCHILL

THE events of the first five campaigning seasons of the war confirm
Pericles' overall strategic analysis. These were for the Peloponnesians
years of frustration. The triremes promised by Lacedaemon's allies in
Italy and Sicily made no appearance. The Peloponnesians—presumably because the Spartans had religious scruples—built few, if any, galleys with money
borrowed or stolen from the treasuries at Olympia and Delphi. And the repeated approaches made to the Great King came to naught—in part, perhaps,
because of a plague that had struck the Persian empire and is apt to have taken
a terrible toll in the port cities that supplied him with his navy; and in part,
it appears, because of Lacedaemonian ambivalence. As the message borne by
an emissary of the King of Kings in the winter of 425/4 complained, no two
ambassadors from Sparta said the same thing.[1]

In these years, with the resources ready to hand, the Spartans and their allies had invaded Attica and ravaged its farmlands on four separate occasions—
but to no avail. In these years, with the galleys they already possessed, the
Peloponnesians had twice challenged at sea Athens' capacity to control the
entrance to the Corinthian Gulf—but to no avail. In these years, they had

repeatedly disputed Athens' dominance in the Ionian Sea—but to no avail. And, in these years, they had tried to take advantage of the rebellion of a powerful ally of Athens that regularly supplied to her fleet an impressive number of triremes—also to no avail. At the end of five years, Athens as a city had proved to be impervious to invasion by land, and she was still the sovereign of the seas. It would be very easy to suppose that Thucydides was correct when he contended that "Pericles had foreknowledge that the city would very easily win through [*perigenésthai*] in the war with the Peloponnesians if the latter were on their own."[2]

There was, however, one obstacle to Athens' triumph that Pericles had not foreseen, and it made "winning through" considerably less easy than he had anticipated. In the summer of 430, shortly after Archidamus arrived in Attica with the Peloponnesian army, the plague that was wreaking havoc within the Persian empire struck the Peiraeus, spread to Athens, and killed her citizens in massive numbers. Thucydides, who contracted and survived the disease, described in fine detail "what sort of thing it was," specifying its symptoms and analyzing the process by which it spread and sometimes failed to spread— and this he did, in a more accurate fashion than the medical profession would achieve for more than two millennia thereafter, by identifying for the very first time two processes of profound importance: person-to-person transmission and specific acquired immunity.

In this sphere, as in the sphere of war, the historian's purpose was to inform future generations of what to expect should a particular malady reappear; and his report has given rise over the last two centuries to an extensive literature, mainly in the medical journals, canvassing the possibility that the disease in question might have been smallpox; bubonic plague; scarlet fever; measles; typhus; typhoid; glanders; ergotism; leptospirosis; tularaemia; a coincidence of influenza, staphylococcal infection, and impetigo; and, most recently, Ebola. It is now known, however, that natural selection is pertinent: that bacterial and viral diseases evolve quickly and that their hosts also evolve, which suggests that it is unlikely that the plague which struck Athens just short of two and a half millennia ago can properly be identified with any malady known today.[3]

What we can infer, however, from Thucydides' report is that the disease was a horror to contract, a horror to monitor in others, and demographically devastating. Prayers and sacrifices were useless, the Athenian historian reports.

Physicians did no good and tended to contract the disease themselves as they tried to help others. Those who visited or nursed the sick were repaid for their kindness in a similar fashion. The contagion did not spare those who were in good health. It began with violent feverishness and an inflammation in the eyes and the throat or tongue, which produced bleeding. The breath of victims was unnatural and rank. Sneezing and hoarseness followed, and thereafter came coughing and chest pains, then queasiness, and discharges of every species of bile known to the physicians of the day. Often, there was ineffectual retching accompanied by violent spasms. Victims suffered from fever, their skin became flushed, and on its surface they developed blisters or pustules and ulcers. The lightest clothing gave rise to unbearable pain, they suffered from an unquenchable thirst, and none could sleep. Most died on the seventh or eighth day. In the case of those who lived longer, there was ulceration in the bowels and acute diarrhea, which produced weakness and eventually death. Of those who recovered, some lost their genitals, their fingers, or toes; some, their eyesight. Others suffered amnesia.

The crowding at Athens that the second Peloponnesian invasion produced and the squalid living conditions and lack of proper sanitation attendant thereon no doubt had something to do with the rapid transmission of the disease, as Diodorus suggests. But the malady was extremely infectious and might have spread quickly in any case. When, for example, later that summer, Hagnon and Cleopompus took command of the armada originally directed against Epidaurus and the other communities in the Argolic Acte and devoted forty days to a bootless attempt with siege engines to conquer Potidaea, one thousand fifty of the four thousand hoplites accompanying them died of the plague.

Thucydides was unable to gauge the number of Athenians that the pestilence killed, but he reports that—between 430 and 429, when it was at its height, and 427/6, when it returned with a vengeance, then disappeared—the malady eliminated three hundred of the city's twelve hundred cavalrymen and forty-four hundred of her thirteen thousand hoplites. This could be taken as evidence that the proportion of those felled by the disease was between a quarter and a third of the overall population, but the percentage is apt to have been considerably higher. The cavalrymen and hoplites who died were among the Athenians least likely to succumb. They were all fully grown men in their prime; and, to be eligible for the particular services that they performed, they had to be prosperous—which suggests that they were also well-fed. Children and poor Athenians who were malnourished will surely have been more vulnerable.[4]

Above all else, Thucydides' purpose was to examine the impact of the plague on "human nature." To this end he explored the manner in which the disease instilled in human beings at Athens a "spiritlessness [*athumía*]," which subverted the influence of honor and eliminated the capacity of convention [*nómos*]—whether sanctioned solely by custom or by force of law—to restrain human conduct. As Thucydides put it,

> Overpowered by the violence done by the evil [*huperbiazoménou gàr toû kakoû*] and not knowing what would become of them, human beings became neglectful of things alike sacred and profane. All the *nómoi* that they had formerly observed with regard to burials were confounded and each conducted the rites as best he could. And many, lacking what was required because of the number of those who had died before, resorted to the most shameless methods in disposing of the deceased. To funeral pyres piled up by others, some would add the corpses of their own relatives and, getting in ahead, they would set them afire; others would hurl the bodies they were carrying on top of other corpses already burning and then go away.
>
> In this regard and in others, the plague first gave rise to a marked increase in lawlessness [*anomía*]. Seeing the abrupt changes—the unforeseen demise of those who were flourishing and the manner in which the propertyless suddenly came to possess the substance of those who had died—the individual more readily dared [*etólma*] to do what he had previously kept hidden and had done in a manner contrary to the dictates of pleasure. And so they thought it worthwhile to reap the fruits quickly with an eye to their own gratification since they regarded their bodies and their money alike as ephemera. And no one was enthusiastic about persisting in what was deemed beautiful and noble [*kálon*] since they thought it unclear whether they would die or not before achieving it. So whatever gave immediate pleasure or seemed conducive to it in any way was regarded as both noble [*kálon*] and useful. No fear of the gods and no human law [*anthrópōn nómos*] held them back. With regard to the former they judged that it was the same whether they were reverent or not—seeing that all were equally likely to die; with regard to the latter no one expected lives to last long enough for anyone to come to trial and pay the penalty for his offenses since a much greater penalty had been passed on him and was impending—so that it was only fair and reasonable that he enjoy life a bit before that penalty befell him.

The mass graves that archaeologists have recently found survive as mute testimony to the breakdown that took place at this time in public decorum.[5]

The collapse of morals and manners described by Thucydides, the emancipation of individual daring [*tólma*], and the attendant disappearance of all respect for *nómos* (whether human in origin or putatively divine) deserve close attention. Not only does this development cast light on the erosion of the more generous instincts of the Athenians in particular and suggest that the disaster caused them to conduct their affairs at home as the Spartans characteristically did abroad by identifying honor with pleasure. The impact of the plague also helps explain why the Athenians panicked, removed Pericles from office in 430, tried him for embezzlement, fined him, and then foolishly sued for peace.[6]

It accounts as well for the fact that the Athenians did not prosecute the war in the first few years thereafter with the vigor that they had displayed in the summers of 431 and 430. They were in financial difficulties, as we shall soon see. Even more to the point, they were increasingly short of manpower— and their morale had suffered. On the eve of the war, as the Athenians knew, the oracle of Apollo was thought to have announced his support for the Peloponnesian cause. They were also aware of an old oracle predicting that, when they went to war against the Dorians, they would suffer from famine [*limós*]— or, some supposed, pestilence [*loimós*]. And, when the Peloponnesians invaded, the refugees from the country districts occupied land below the acropolis that Apollo had warned them to leave unworked. It is a reasonable guess that many an ordinary Athenian saw in the disease from which his compatriots suffered something analogous to the plague visited upon the Achaeans at Troy: a calamity inflicted on them by an angry god whom they had offended. Even the son of Xanthippus—who was anything but superstitious and who was sensitive to the manner in which "that which is sudden and unexpected and comes to pass largely in defiance of reason" is apt to "enslave the mind and spirit"—catalogued the malady among "the things demonic: sent by the gods."[7]

Aspiring Athenian statesmen were expected to have a comprehensive understanding of the city's resources—both military and fiscal—and Pericles was in this particular an exemplar. On the eve of the war, he provided his compatriots with a net assessment of Athenian strength, listing the number of hoplites, cavalrymen, and triremes that they commanded; specifying their annual income from the empire; and describing their reserves. They were, he made clear, prepared to fight the war—and their provisions would, in fact, have been more than adequate had it not been for the plague. Pericles did not expect the first phase of the epic struggle with Lacedaemon to last long. He presumed that, when the Spartans discovered that invading Attica had no real effect on the Athenians and when they and their allies learned just how much damage the Athenian fleet and the amphibious forces it carried could do, they would sue for peace. It never crossed his mind that the Athenians would be the first to flinch, and he had no idea that the city would soon be deprived of one-quarter to one-third or more of her citizens and that his compatriots would find it impossible to man expeditions on the scale he had envisaged.

When the Athenians did sue for peace, however, they did wonders for the morale of their foe. In the circumstances, it is no surprise that the Lacedaemonians responded by proposing terms unacceptable to their opponents. They were, they told themselves, fighting for the freedom of the Greeks, and they believed that they were on the verge of winning. All that it would take to crush the Athenians was a bit more patience and a renewed effort, and it would surely speed things up if they could inflict on them a defeat at sea. So they supposed.

There is this to be said for the Spartans' calculations. By 428, the Athenians had begun to feel the pinch. Twenty years before, on the acropolis, they had possessed reserves in silver of nine thousand seven hundred talents—which is to say, more than two hundred seventy-six tons. By May 431, a bit more than a third of this had been spent on the expedition to Potidaea and on the construction of the Parthenon, the Propylaea, and the other sanctuaries, scattered throughout Attica, which formed a part of Pericles' program. In May 431, Athens had six thousand talents (one hundred seventy-one tons) left in silver coin. In addition, the treasuries on the acropolis held other items that Pericles valued at something like five hundred silver talents (over fourteen tons): uncoined silver and gold derived from public and private dedications, the sacred vessels used in processions and games, the spoils from the Persian wars, and the like. To this they could add, in an emergency, the dedications which had been carted in from the treasuries of the other sanctuaries scattered throughout Attica as well as the forty talents—well over a ton—of pure gold that adorned the statue of Athena in the Parthenon.[8]

Each year, moreover, as Pericles explained—in *phóros,* in indemnities, and in other contributions made by the cities within their dominion—the Athenians took in something on the order of six hundred talents (which is to say, seventeen tons) of silver. If Xenophon is correct in reporting that Athens' total annual income in silver at this time amounted to something like one thousand talents (twenty-eight and a half tons), her additional income from internal sources—the silver mines at Laureium; harbor fees; the duty on exports and imports; the rents paid on sacred lands; the profits from the auction of property confiscated; the fines imposed by the law courts; the taxes she levied on metics, prostitutes, and the sale of land; and the like—must have come to something like four hundred talents (a bit more than eleven tons) in silver per annum.[9]

Had the war been over in two or three years, the drain on Athens' reserves would have been manageable. But the struggle went on and on and on, and the costs were immense. The campaign at Potidaea alone consumed in silver more than two thousand talents (fifty-seven tons). The sizable expeditions sent out in 431 and 430 were exceedingly expensive, and the smaller operations—to the coast of Locris in 431; to Naupactus, Acarnania, and Corcyra in 430, 429, 428, and 427; and to Mytilene in the last two of those four years—gobbled up funds. Most of Athens' income from internal sources was spent at home on the ordinary operations of the democracy—on festivals, on repairing the walls and dockyards, and on the salaries awarded the jurymen, the councillors, other officials, and the citizens who guarded those walls and dockyards. It is questionable whether, from domestic sources, even one hundred talents (a bit less than three tons) of silver was available each year for supporting the projection of power abroad. In the six-year period stretching from the battle off the Sybota Isles in 433/2 to the suppression of the Mytilenian revolt in 428/7, the Athenians received no more than forty-three hundred talents (more than one hundred twenty-two tons) of silver in ordinary income from foreign sources and in domestic revenues that were available for expenditure on the war and probably, given the rebellion at Potidaea and more generally in what was then called the Chalcidice, a good deal less—while their expenditures on the conduct of the war came to something like nine thousand ninety-one talents (two hundred fifty-nine tons) of silver. The discrepancy between current income and current expenditures was made up from Athens' rapidly dwindling reserves. It is, then, no wonder that, in the emergency occasioned by the Mytilenian Revolt in 428, the Athenians were forced to impose a capital levy on the more prosperous of their fellow citizens of two hundred talents (a bit under six tons) of silver and that they chose to reduce expenses by having the one thousand hoplites dispatched to Lesbos in the autumn do double duty as mariners and row themselves to the island. Nor should it be a surprise that in 425/4, when the ordinary quadrennial reassessment of the *phóros* was, in fact, overdue, the Athenians voted to increase the sum requisitioned from their subject allies to thrice what it had been at the beginning of the war. In the circumstances, they had no choice.[10]

One fact, nonetheless, stands out. The Athenians could get away with it. They could, if pressed, greatly increase their take. They did so, and no rebellions took place. They could double or even triple their demand for *phóros* and continue the fight; and, when they did so, nothing happened in the interim to make the Peloponnesians more effective in the struggle. As Plutarch intimates, the only real effect of the plague was to delay the day of reckoning.[11]

By high summer in 427, Spartan hopes had diminished. There was no reason to suppose that further invasions of Attica would ever force the Athenians to give in. The Mytilenian rebellion had collapsed; and, at sea, the Peloponnesians had more than once been so soundly thrashed that they now fled when informed of the approach of an Athenian fleet.

Of course, it is easier, as we have already had occasion to observe, to begin than to end a war—especially, when neither side has won a decisive victory. Above all, for the party that initiated the war and has to acknowledge failure, openly abandon its aims, and leave its allies in the lurch, the negotiations themselves are apt to be a public humiliation. This obstacle notwithstanding, there is evidence suggesting that the Lacedaemonians were drifting toward an acceptance of the inevitable and had begun contemplating not only the possibility but the likelihood that they would neither restore the Aeginetans and the Potidaeans to their ancestral cities nor free the Hellenes from Athens' yoke and that the war itself would be brought to an end by way of a negotiated peace.

That summer—when the Peloponnesians made an assault on the fortifications of Plataea, and the town's defenders were unable to repel the attack—the Spartan commander deliberately refrained from taking the town by storm. The authorities back home had instructed him to trick the Plataeans into surrendering the town voluntarily with a false promise—for, Thucydides reports, the Thebans hoped to be able to retain it should peace be made with Athens on terms specifying that each party "return the places seized in the course of the war." With these instructions the Lacedaemonian commander complied, promising the city's remaining defenders a fair trial, which, thanks to the Spartans' eagerness to please their Theban allies, is not at all what they received.[12]

There is one other indication that the tide was beginning to turn and that the Lacedaemonians were beginning to contemplate the negotiation of a peace. In the fall of 427, the Spartans voted to recall from exile Pleistoanax son of Pausanias—the figure chiefly responsible for the settlement Lacedaemon had reached with Athens in 446. For eighteen long, lonely years, this man had resided in Arcadia within the precinct of Zeus atop Mount Lycaeum. At some point in the interim—perhaps when it became clear that the war against Athens was not going at all well—the priestess at Delphi had begun responding to inquiries from Lacedaemon with a command backed up by a threat. The Spartans were "to bring back home the seed of the demigod son of Zeus—for, otherwise, they would have to plow with a silver plowshare." The meaning of the oracle was clear enough. The Lacedaemonians knew that one could not break up the soil with a plowshare made of so soft a metal, and they drew the obvious conclusion—that the setbacks they had suffered in the war were occasioned by the absence of the Agiad king. And so, in desperation, they did as they were told: they brought Pleistoanax back home and restored him to his office with, we are told, "the same choral dances and sacrifices with which they had instituted their kings at the time they first settled Lacedaemon."[13]

The Lacedaemonians evidently hoped that Pleistoanax' return would occasion on their part greater success in the war. But that the man would once again favor reaching an accommodation with Athens—this they surely also knew. In fact, in some quarters, the forging of peace may have been the principal aim; and there is reason to suspect that, at about this time, an attempt was made.

Early in 425, Aristophanes in his comedy *The Acharnians* alluded in passing to a proposal, initiated within recent memory by the Spartans on something like the terms anticipated by the Thebans. Therein, he tells us, the Athenians rejected the overture because they were unwilling to meet these terms and restore to the Aeginetans the island seized from them at the beginning of the conflict. By the winter of 427, the Spartans were certainly weary of war; and they may have supposed that the recurrence of the plague late in that year had rendered the Athenians once again eager for a respite. The reference in Aristophanes' play would have been especially poignant had the negotiations collapsed just a few months before the comedy was performed.[14]

CHAPTER 4

A Loss of Strategic Focus

Of the historians the most effective is the one who shapes his narrative as an image in the manner of a painting, depicting passions and portraying persons. So, in the account he gives, Thucydides always strives for vividness of this sort, eagerly hungering to make his auditor a spectator of sorts and to reproduce in his readers the feelings of astonishment and agitation experienced by eyewitnesses. For Demosthenes arranging his Athenians along the rocky shore at Pylos; Brasidas exhorting his helmsman to run his trireme onto the rocky shore, making his way to the ship's brow, suffering wounds, swooning, and tumbling onto the outrigger; the Spartans fighting a land battle from the sea and the Athenians a naval battle from land . . . —in such an arrangement and description of events there is the vividness of a painting.

PLUTARCH

THE plague was not the only misfortune that Pericles did not foresee. He failed as well to anticipate his own mortality and to prepare for his own departure from the scene. For this, there can be no excuse. He was, as far as we know, in good health when the war broke out, but he was not young. Had the plague not taken him in the autumn of 429—when he was, we have reason to suspect, in his mid-sixties—some other malady might well have done so, and his disappearance would have had profound implications for Athens' conduct of the war . . . as it did when the day of his demise finally came.

The strategy that Pericles intended to pursue required of his compatriots two qualities that were, at Athens, in short supply: patience and focus. The Athenians were, as the Corinthians had told the Spartans, a profoundly restless lot. But, as Thucydides explains when he records the great man's death, the son of Xanthippus had a stature, an intelligence, and a justified reputation for incorruptibility that enabled him to hold the people in check without flattering them or depriving them of their liberty. This made it possible for him, when necessary, to bring them to an intermediate state between being audacious to the point of insolence [*húbrei tharsoûntas*] and being fearful without reason [*alógōs*]. "As long as he presided over the city in time of peace," Thucydides tells us,

> he led her in a measured manner [*metríos*] and in safety; and in his time she was at her greatest. . . . What was, in name, a democracy was, in fact, rule by the first man. Those who came later were more on an equal plane with one another, and each desiring to be first, they sought to please the people and to them handed over public affairs. In consequence, as tends to happen in a great city also possessed of an empire, they blundered in many regards.

Pericles had urged his compatriots to embrace for the time being a policy of *hēsuchía* utterly foreign to their temperament. He had exhorted them to concentrate solely on the war then under way, to avoid risky ventures, and to resist the temptation to add to their dominion in ways not apt to contribute materially to Lacedaemon's defeat. After his death, Thucydides reports, "what they did was the contrary in all regards, governing themselves and their allies, even in matters seemingly extraneous to the war, with an eye to private ambitions and private profit in a manner quite harmful, pursuing policies whose success would be to the honor and advantage of private individuals, and whose failure brought harm to the city in the war."[1]

Pericles' demise did nothing to alter the geopolitical fundamentals. The plague notwithstanding, Athens still possessed the material resources needed for her to "win through." What she lacked was the requisite patience and focus; and for this, as Thucydides allows us to discern, Pericles was himself at least partially at fault. He may have had *pronoía* with regard to the war, but he seems to have lacked it with regard to the political community he had done so much to reshape. Thanks in considerable measure to legislation sponsored by Pericles in the 450s, Athens had become a "salaried city" dependent for the survival of her radically democratic regime on an income stream constituted by the *phóros* contributed by her subject allies. Her citizens had a deep and abiding interest in the expansion of her empire that was at odds with the policy of *hēsuchía* promoted by Pericles in and after 431.

Moreover, in his Funeral Oration, Pericles had deployed an arresting image, exhorting his compatriots to become the city's *erastaí*—lovers intoxicated by the community's beauty and nobility—and, in the course of his subsequent narrative, Thucydides intimates that such an eroticization of politics is apt to be a serious obstacle to the rational conduct of policy. For example, according to his report, in the debate that took place with regard to the punishment to be meted out to the Mytilenians after the collapse of their rebellion, the more discerning of the two principal speakers contended that the death penalty has little or no deterrent effect against crime at home or misconduct abroad. "No law [*nómos*] will prevent it," he argued. No form of punishment will be a sufficient restraint. "Hope [*elpís*]," he said, "and the eros for all [*érōs epì pantí*], . . . being invisible [*aphanḗ*], are more powerful than terrors which can be observed," and this is especially true in the case of "cities" concerned "with the greatest of things, freedom [*eleuthería*] and rule [*archḗ*] over others," in which "each citizen, acting in concert with all," is inclined, when led on by hope and by an erotic desire for grandeur, to overestimate his capacities "*alogístōs*—in a manner devoid of calculation and impervious to speech."

That eros and prudence are at odds Thucydides intimates in a later passage—where a speaker inveighs against an enterprise of some ambition (which, in the circumstances, Pericles clearly would not have undertaken) not only by stressing its magnitude and the difficulties and risks involved, but also by exhorting the Athenians not to become "lustful in a perverse manner [*dusérōtas*] for that which is far afield." What on this occasion was intended as a deterrent had, we are told, the opposite effect. In the immediate aftermath, as Thucydides observes,

> A lust [*érōs*] for the enterprise fell upon everyone alike: to the older men it seemed that they would either subdue the places against which they were sailing or, with so great a force, trip up not at all; those in their prime felt a yearning for sights and spectacles [*póthos ópseōs kaì theōrías*] far afield and were of good hope [*euélpides*] that they would be safe; the great mass of people and the soldiers presumed that they would secure silver in the short run and add to their possessions a power whence they would draw wages forever.

In the grips of greed and of the passion for grandeur promoted by Pericles, the Athenians substantially expanded the armada and brought on their city a catastrophe no less devastating than the Egyptian debacle. Such is Thucydides' claim, and it is clear that the genuine admiration which this kinsman of Cimon felt for the son of Xanthippus was tempered by a recognition that, as a statesman, the latter had failed and that the defeat ultimately visited on Athens on this occasion was to a considerable degree his handiwork. Like Xenophon's Socrates, the Athenian historian greatly admired the statesmanship of Themistocles, but Pericles, whose strategic brilliance and political talent could not be denied, he nonetheless found wanting.[2]

Imprudent Ventures

Pericles' death did not put an end to Athenian attempts to discomfit and bring pressure to bear on Lacedaemon and her Peloponnesian allies. In the years immediately following his demise, the Athenians continued to invade the Megarid twice a year. They maintained the blockade directed at Nisaea, Megara's port on the Saronic Gulf, and even tightened it by seizing the little island of Minoa just off the coast; and they continued to post a flotilla at Naupactus—in part, for the defense of their allies in the region; and in part, for the purpose of controlling and curtailing traffic in the Corinthian Gulf.[3]

But, while going through their accustomed motions, the Athenians did begin to flail. The war had gone on for four long, painful years. The Athenians had little to show for it, and there was now no one they trusted who could calm their frustrations. The disaster that would eventually strike was foreshadowed by their departures at this time from the strategy that Pericles had outlined. Thus, for example, late in the campaigning season of 427, at some point between August and October, the Athenians dispatched twenty ships to Sicily, under the command of Laches son of Melanopus and Charoeades son of Euphiletus, to support a coalition—made up almost entirely of Ionian cities under the leadership of Leontini—against a rival alliance of Dorian cities led by Syracusa. In ordinary circumstances, a modest venture of this sort might well have made sense. The Athenians had made their influence felt in the west earlier when they organized on the site of Sybaris the settlement called Thurii, when Diotimos intervened at Neapolis with an Athenian fleet, and when they forged alliances with Leontini and Rhegium. They had a foothold in the region to defend, and their allies genuinely needed help. This counted for something.

In 427, however, the situation was unpropitious—as Pericles would have insisted, had he survived. Thanks to the plague, Athens' manpower was much diminished. Thanks to the war with the Peloponnesians, the revolt at Potidaea, and the rebellion just suppressed at Mytilene, the city's reserves had dwindled—and that great war was by no means over. Of course, the Athenians could tell themselves that, with only twenty triremes in play, the risks were small and the cost, negligible; and Thucydides is no doubt correct in reporting that they saw the operation as exploratory. The Athenians coveted Sicily, as we have seen. Some day, they really might want to subjugate the island; and with this expedition they could test their allies, probe the weaknesses of their enemies, and learn more fully the geopolitical lay of the land. In their assembly, they could even prattle on about stopping the export of grain to the Peloponnesus, as, Thucydides reports, they did—though, given the number of cities involved and the fact that they were situated on the open sea, it is unclear how, absent the subjugation of Sicily and Magna Graecia as a whole, such a ban could have been enforced.

All rationalization aside, however, Athens' first Sicilian adventure was a sideshow; and, even more to the point, it was a waste of precious resources in a time of constraint. The Syracusans and their allies in Sicily and Magna Graecia may well have promised that they would contribute two hundred triremes to support the Peloponnesian cause, but four years had passed, and, as far as we can tell, they had not delivered a single ship. Nor were they ever likely to honor their commitment. They had never before ventured east—not even when Xerxes' Persians had penetrated deep into the Balkan peninsula—and they were no match for Athens' fleet. Moreover, as the conflict with Leontini and her allies indicates, the Syracusans faced challenges near home. And, had they succeeded in subduing their Ionian neighbors, they would still have had the Carthaginians across the water in North Africa and the Punic colonies in western Sicily to contend with.[4]

The expedition mounted in 427 was in one other particular injudicious. If it succeeded in thwarting Syracusan ambitions, as it did at first,[5] it would give rise to a temptation that the Athenians were ill disposed to resist. They would be apt to double-down on the endeavor—which is what they did early in 425, when they got word that the Syracusans were building a fleet to counter the Athenian flotilla, and they decided to dispatch to the west another forty triremes. To man a fleet of sixty triremes required twelve thousand men. If it was to be able to land an effective amphibious force, an additional complement of up to thirty marines per ship was required; and the cost of maintaining such an armada on station far from home—if it was not, in fact, borne by Athens' allies in the west—would have set Athens' treasury back at least seven hundred fifty talents (more than twenty-one tons) of silver per year. Given the further losses inflicted in the interim by the plague, which had returned to

Athens with a vengeance shortly after the dispatch of the first fleet to Sicily, the risks were exceedingly high—and the likely reward was modest.[6]

In the event, moreover, the dispatch of reinforcements proved counter-productive. Athens' allies in the west were already weary of war. In magnitude, the force sent from Athens was sufficient to make them nervous and to cause most of them to entertain salutary second thoughts concerning the motives of their benefactor. In consequence, when, at a congress held at Gela, the opposing coalition offered them peace on favorable terms, they accepted it in order to rid themselves of the threat, they thought, posed by their own ally.

In this venture, the Athenians were fortunate. Apart from the expense and the loss of a handful of triremes, they appear to have suffered little in the way of harm. As Thucydides makes clear, however, it speaks volumes about the megalomania to which they were prone that his compatriots not only refused to accept responsibility for the setback they had inflicted on themselves but blamed, instead, the generals whom they had put in charge. When an embassy arrived from Catana to lament Athens' withdrawal, they fined one general and the two others they exiled on the presumption that, had the three not been bribed, the force dispatched could not have failed to subjugate Sicily as a whole.[7]

This Sicilian enterprise was by no means the only questionable venture undertaken by the Athenians in these years. In 426, they dispatched the most successful and methodical of their generals, Nicias son of Niceratus, with sixty triremes and two thousand hoplites to Melos—with an eye, so it was said, to bringing that island community into the Delian League. There may have been more to this venture than Thucydides lets on. Melos was a Spartan colony, as he acknowledges. Although her citizens no doubt sympathized with the Peloponnesians, as a polity they had maintained a strict neutrality and professed to be on friendly terms with both sides. We do not know whether Alcidas and his fleet visited Melos while en route to and from Ionia in 427. Had he done so, however, he would surely have been graciously received. That the Peloponnesians had such an option anywhere in the southern Cyclades was from the Athenian point of view intolerable—which explains why, after being forcefully reminded of this fact, they made the Melians an offer that the latter were ill-advised to refuse.[8]

When the Melians did, in fact, refuse, Nicias had his soldiers and sailors, who were numerous, ravaged their farmland, which was not extensive. But he chose not to initiate a siege, for he had another, more pressing task to accomplish; and, in relation to it, the visit to Melos served as a feint. When he had done what he intended at Melos, he conducted his fleet to Oropus on the Greek mainland opposite Euboea—where, early one summer evening, his hoplites disembarked and marched westward roughly eleven miles to the outskirts of Tanagra in Boeotia. There, as previously arranged, they were met by the entire levy of hoplites from Athens, which had marched up under the command of Eurymedon and of Hipponicus son of and heir to Callias, the wealthy diplomat who had negotiated the peace with Persia in 449 and the settlement with Lacedaemon in 446. Outside the city they camped. The following day the Athenians ravaged the territory of Tanagra. The day after they met and defeated the Tanagraeans and those of the Thebans who had marched some ten miles to their defense—and then Nicias' hoplites returned to their ships and those of Eurymedon and Hipponicus marched back to Athens.

As a show of force, this last operation was impressive. It no doubt served a variety of purposes. It bolstered morale at home by ostentatiously taking revenge on at least some of the Boeotians for the support their cavalry had rendered the Peloponnesians on the occasion of the latter's invasions of Attica. It demonstrated for all to see Athens' formidable capacity for amphibious warfare and Sparta's inability to protect her allies from such raids. The operation may also in some measure have assuaged the awkwardness occasioned for the Athenians by the fall of Plataea. When the Peloponnesians had threatened a siege, the Athenians had encouraged resistance on the part of the Plataeans, as we have seen, by making a pledge, incompatible with Pericles' strategy in the war, that they would keep faith with their longtime allies and come to their aid to the best of their ability. This promise, they surely knew, they would not honor. In consequence, when Plataea fell, the Athenians tried to make up for their gross negligence by doing something which they had never done before— which is to say, by actually conferring full citizenship on the survivors, a number of them escapees from the siege. The brief foray into Boeotia projected by Nicias, Eurymedon, and Hipponicus appears to have been a compensatory gesture aimed at the same end.

The risks associated with this operation were, nonetheless, considerable and the potential rewards, negligible. Had word gotten out in advance, had this force been met on the plains of Tanagra by the entire levy of the Boeotian League, Athens' losses in a time when she was desperately short of manpower could easily have been devastating—and there was nothing of strategic value to be gained. The combined operation undertaken by Nicias, Eurymedon, and Hipponicus was no doubt magnificent. The casualties incurred were apparently not worth mentioning. But it might have been otherwise, and the entire endeavor was—from a strategic perspective—gratuitous.[9]

There was yet another dubious venture undertaken in 426, and this one ended in tears. At about the time that Nicias and his fleet left Athens for Melos, thirty triremes, under the command of Demosthenes son of Alcisthenes and Procles son of Theodorus, set out for Naupactus and the region nearby. Initially, they gathered a large force—drawn from Corcyra, which supplied fifteen triremes; from Zacynthus and Cephallenia, which sent hoplites; and from Acarnania (apart from Oeniadae), which called up its entire levy. With this sizable army they then attacked Corinth's ally Leucas, forcing her citizens to retreat behind the city walls and ravaging her territory. At this point, had Athens' generals followed through, as the Acarnanians requested—had they built a wall across the narrow causeway linking Leucas with the continent, cut her off from the fertile *peraía* she possessed on the mainland, and thereby secured the city's surrender—their conduct would have been fully consistent with the strategy devised by Pericles. His aim had been to consolidate Athens' hegemony over the maritime region stretching from the mouth of the Corinthian Gulf and the Gulf of Patras up the Balkan coast to Corcyra and beyond; to frustrate and further enrage thereby the Corinthians, who coveted control and thought preeminence in the district theirs by right; and to bring home to the latter once more the utter fecklessness of their Lacedaemonian ally.[10]

Instead, at the suggestion of the Messenians residing at Naupactus, the son of Alcisthenes infuriated Athens' Acarnanian allies by selecting a more distant object. Directly north of Naupactus and of Ozolian Locris more generally lay Aetolia—a hilly land of unwalled villages inhabited by a Greek people who eschewed the hoplite panoply, fielded light-armed troops brandishing javelins instead, and had a propensity for antagonizing their more fully civilized neighbors to the south. In the face of an attack by a hoplite army, if surprise precluded the timely arrival of reinforcements, the Aetolians could easily be subdued. So, the Messenians told Demosthenes, who reportedly envisaged such an operation as the prelude to a much grander scheme, culminating in an attack on and reconquest of Boeotia—effected, without aid from Athens, via a march from Ozolian Locris north-northeast through Aetolia to Cytinium in Doris and then east-southeast down the Cephisus valley to the land of the

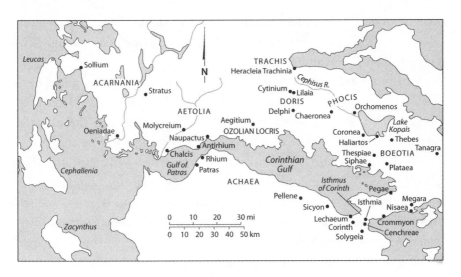

Map 15. From Leucas to Boeotia

Phocians, who had once been allied with the Athenians and who might easily, he supposed, be drawn in again.

This was an audacious enterprise. One might even call it foolhardy, for it was most unlikely to work. There were too many stages at which things could go wrong. If the attack on Aetolia failed, it might well imperil Naupactus. If it succeeded, the Athenians would find themselves deeply entangled in one more theater in yet another conflict of no real pertinence to the larger war against Lacedaemon in which they were engaged.

Demosthenes' scheme also made no strategic sense. As long as the Peloponnesians could march through the Megarid in support of the Thebans and their league, there was no way that the Athenians could conquer and hold Boeotia. Even more to the point, Pericles was right. As the Athenians in his generation had learned the hard way, Boeotia was, from a strategic perspective, peripheral. If, by some miracle, the son of Alcisthenes had accomplished its conquest, his compatriots would not have been, on balance, materially and strategically better off. The absence of the Boeotian cavalry would have rendered the ravaging expeditions that the Peloponnesians mounted against Attica considerably more difficult and less effective. That this was an advantage there can be no doubt. But that which was gained would have been more than offset by the heavy burdens assumed. Adequately garrisoning the cities of

Boeotia would have been a tremendous drain on Athens' depleted manpower. Moreover, rebellions—and there would have been rebellions—would have consumed both treasure and blood.

Most important of all, however, the subjugation of Boeotia would have been a diversion. It would not have contributed in any substantial way to Sparta's defeat. The Lacedaemonians were not dependent upon Thebes in the fashion in which they were dependent on Corinth and the other core members of their Peloponnesian alliance. Had they been deprived of Boeotian support, they could—and they surely would—have soldiered on, as they had under similar circumstances in their first Attic war. The Athenians might well tell themselves that, absent the Boeotian cavalry, the Peloponnesians would abandon their invasions of Attica. But, in a pinch, the Lacedaemonians could form cavalry units of their own, as, we know, they did later in the war.[11]

Demosthenes' scheme was, moreover, as tactically obtuse as it was strategically defective. By the time that he was ready to launch the attack, the Corcyraeans had withdrawn; and the Acarnanians, in anger, had refused to participate. Nonetheless, thinking sufficient the three hundred marines manning his ships and the Zacynthian, Cephallenian, and Messenian hoplites who had lent the enterprise their support, and being unfamiliar with the terrain and the species of warfare best suited to it, the son of Alcisthenes blundered on, leading his little army with impressive alacrity some nine miles inland and not pausing to wait for the arrival of his Ozolian Locrian supporters, the only light-armed troops then at his beck and call.

Near Aegitium, his army encountered a host of warriors, unencumbered with heavy equipment, who commanded the surrounding hills. From the heights, these nimble, light-armed troops scrambled down here, then there, to hurl javelins from one side, then another, into the ranks of his army; and, when his hoplites, weighed down with armor, sallied forth to repel the attack, these Aetolians danced back up, impervious to assault. For a time, the archers accompanying the expedition managed to keep these javelineers at a distance. Soon enough, however, they ran out of arrows, the Aetolian artillery began to take a toll—and, among those who succumbed early on was the army's principal guide.

Eventually, as was inevitable in the circumstances, Demosthenes' soldiers fled in a panic. Many of them were overtaken and killed. Others lost their way and sought refuge in the woods, which the Aetolians then set afire. When it was all over, Procles was dead, as were a great many Zacynthians, Cephallenians, and Messenians. Of the three hundred marines conveyed from Athens, no more than one hundred eighty were left alive. When the campaigning season ended, these survivors took to ship and returned to Athens. Demosthenes, for his part, chose to stay on at Naupactus. He had a pretty good idea of what would have been in store for him had he returned home. In 430/29, when the generals victorious at Potidaea had brought the siege to an end by allowing the Potidaeans to depart, the demagogue Cleon, who had accused Pericles of cowardice at the beginning of the war, had brought charges against them.[12]

Demosthenes Learns a Lesson

It was almost inevitable that the disaster which took place in Aetolia should attract the attention and interest of the Peloponnesians. Naupactus was a source of grief for the Corinthians and the other cities on the Corinthian Gulf, and the fleet the Athenians posted there had repeatedly humiliated the Lacedaemonians and their allies. While the Athenians were preparing to invade, the Aetolians had appealed for the Peloponnesians' help; and, given the number of Messenian infantrymen killed in Aetolia and the weakened condition in which Demosthenes' defeat had left their town, it was only natural that the Peloponnesians accept the invitation and join the Aetolians in an attempt to storm Naupactus from the landward side. This was an opportunity not apt to be repeated, and it might well lead to the expulsion of the Athenians from a region of great and lasting strategic interest to Lacedaemon's demanding Corinthian ally.[13]

This endeavor was made easier and all the more attractive by the fact that the Spartans had themselves recently become engaged in central Greece. Not long before these events, the Malians of Trachis, just a few miles from Thermopylae, had suffered grievously in a war with the Oetaeans to the north, as had their neighbors to the south in Doris. In desperation, with firm support from the citizens of the latter—which was thought to be the mother city of all the Dorians—these Trachinians had appealed to the Lacedaemonians for protection and had offered to hand over the city into their keeping. This offer the Spartans had accepted, thinking Trachinia well located for the conduct of war against Athens. And so, in 426, with an eye to controlling the pass at Thermopylae, exercising influence in central Greece, having a refuge on the road to

Athens' domain in Thrace, and basing a fleet there that could be used against Euboea, they embarked upon this venture. They sent off a host of Lacedaemonians as colonists, Spartiates and *períoikoi* alike. They invited the other Hellenes, apart from certain suspect peoples, such as the Ionians and Achaeans, to join them. Then, with a force approaching ten thousand, they refounded the *pólis* on a nearby site under the name Heracleia Trachinia. In the process, they built a wall across the pass at Thermopylae, and they began constructing docks.[14]

As autumn approached, the Lacedaemonians dispatched to Delphi twenty-five hundred Peloponnesian hoplites under the command of three Spartiates—Eurylochos, Macarius, and Menedaeus. There they were joined by an additional five hundred heavy infantrymen from Heracleia Trachinia; and it was from Delphi that Eurylochos, who appears to have been in charge, sent a herald to persuade the various communities of Ozolian Locrians to abandon their alliance with the Athenians and the citizens of Naupactus, to join his expedition, and supply him with hostages as a guarantee of their fidelity. Out of fear, nearly all of these communities complied, which greatly facilitated Eurylochos' march on Naupactus. There, the Aetolians joined him, and the allied army then laid waste the territory, seized an unfortified suburb of the town, and captured Molycreium to the west. Had the son of Alcisthenes not in the meantime demonstrated resourcefulness; had he not endeavored to persuade the Acarnanians, who were still for understandable reasons angry with him, that their fate was bound up with that of Naupactus; and had they not sent with him on shipboard a thousand hoplites to man the walls of the town, the Messenian exiles settled there would have lost their refuge, and Athens would have been deprived of her strategic foothold at the mouth of the Corinthian Gulf.[15]

Eurylochos, who had more in common with Brasidas than with Alcidas, was no less resourceful than Demosthenes. Though thwarted at Naupactus, he was undaunted. The Aetolians he dismissed. Then, he made his way west along the coast to the district called Aeolis. There, he lingered for some weeks with an eye to responding at the appropriate moment to a request from Corinth's Ambraciot colonists that he march up-country through Acarnania and help them take Amphilochian Argos. Early in the winter, when circumstances were propitious, three thousand Ambraciot hoplites marched boldly from the north into Amphilochia. There they occupied Olpae—a stronghold built by the Acarnanians on a hill near Amphilochian Argos not far from the sea, where a court of justice met to deal with the affairs of their people. The Acarnanians responded cannily, sending a part of their forces to defend Amphilochian Argos and the rest to a place in the interior where they hoped to intercept and ambush the forces marching north under Eurylochos' command. At this time, they also summoned the son of Alcisthenes and twenty Athenian triremes, under the command of two Athenian generals, which were making their way to Naupactus along the western coast of the Peloponnesus.

In response, the Ambraciot commanders sent a message to their compatriots, seeking reinforcements and imploring them to march forth immediately with their entire levy. Eurylochos, on his march from the south, managed to bypass the Acarnanian force awaiting him and to join the Ambraciots at Olpae. The Athenian triremes and Demosthenes, the latter with two hundred Messenian hoplites and sixty Athenian archers in tow, reached the Gulf of Ambracia soon thereafter.

The son of Alcisthenes was placed in charge. For five days, the two forces camped on opposite sides of a ravine, eyeballing one another. On the sixth day, they formed up for battle; and Demosthenes, whose force was outnumbered, set an ambush—just as the Acarnanians had done in response to the earlier invasion mounted by the Ambraciots, Leucadians, Anactorians, and Chaonians under the leadership of the Spartiate Cnemus. Along a sunken path overgrown with bushes, the Athenian situated four hundred hoplites and light-armed infantrymen. They were to rise up and attack the left wing of the enemy forces from the rear; and when, in fact, they assaulted the contingent commanded by Eurylochos, Demosthenes and his Messenians, who were posted opposite them on his army's right wing, cut that contingent to pieces. The Ambraciots on the other wing were, however, victorious, and they pursued the Acarnanians and Amphilochians all the way to Amphilochian Argos. When they returned, however, they were made to suffer heavy casualties as they worked their way back to Olpae. The only soldiers who without great loss fought their way through were the Mantineians, who never broke ranks.

In the aftermath, with an eye to humiliating the Peloponnesians and undermining Lacedaemon's prestige, the son of Alcisthenes struck a deal with the surviving Spartan commander Menedaeus, allowing the Mantineians and the other surviving Peloponnesians to slip away and, in a cowardly fashion, stealthily abandon their Ambraciot allies—which they did. The hoplites sent as reinforcements from Ambracia he then intercepted en route, falling upon them with his army at dawn as they slept. Those who escaped into the woods the light-armed Amphilochians under his command hunted down and killed. In the end, Demosthenes did to the reinforcements sent from Ambracia what the Aetolians had done to the army he had commanded the previous year. Thucydides tells us that this was the greatest disaster suffered by any Hellenic city in an equal number of days during the entire Peloponnesian War.

If Ambracia was not in the aftermath taken—if, instead, the Ambraciots were called upon to pledge that they would not in the future come to the defense of Anactorium, if a defensive alliance supposed to last a century was formed between Ambracia and Acarnania, and the Corinthians were subsequently allowed to insert into Ambracia a garrison of three hundred drawn from among their own citizens—it was because the Acarnanians had come to suspect that, if the city were captured and turned over to the Athenians, their own independence might be at risk. When the son of Alcisthenes, who had evidently learned an enormous amount from his experience in Aetolia, returned to Athens, he did so as a victor, not a loser; and he bore with him as a token of his achievement one-third of the spoils—including three hundred captured hoplite shields fit for dedication in the temples in Attica. Thanks to his generalship, at least nine hundred Ambraciots had lost their lives.[16]

In the summer of 425, after Demosthenes' departure, the Athenians based at Naupactus and the Acarnanians mounted an expedition against Anactorium, the joint Corcyraean-Corinthian colony in command of the entrance to the Gulf of Ambracia, which the Corinthians had seized and resettled on the eve of the war. This city, now unsupported by the Ambraciots, they took by treachery; and they resettled it with Acarnanians. A year later, shortly before the son of Alcisthenes returned with a fleet and marines, the Acarnanians forced Oeniadae to join them in alliance with Athens.[17] By this time, as we shall soon see, the Corinthians had lost what remained of their fleet, and they had failed ignominiously in the quest that had originally catapulted them into armed conflict with the Athenians. They had neither ousted the Messenians from Naupactus nor had they reasserted the maritime hegemony which they had once possessed in the Corinthian Gulf, the Ionian Sea, and the Adriatic along the coastal trade route linking the Balkans with Italy and Sicily. Though Ambracia and Leucas, where they also posted a small garrison, were still nominally theirs, the Corinthians no longer possessed any real leverage in the region, and there is reason to suspect that the frustration and anger that they felt

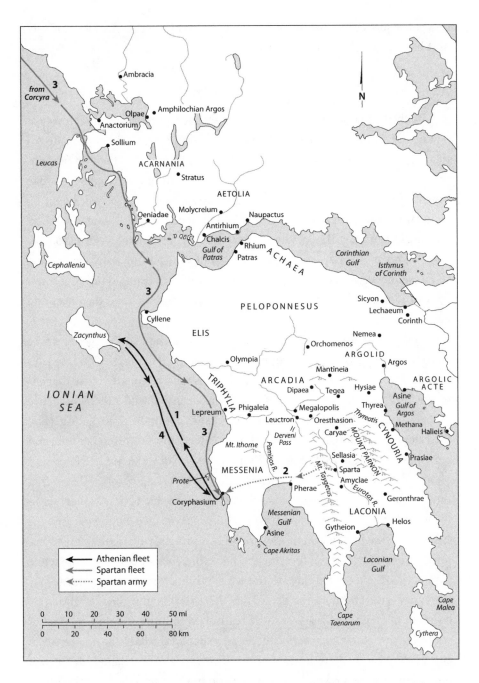

Map 16. The Athenian and the Peloponnesian Fleets in the Ionian Sea and the
Lacedaemonian Army Converge on Coryphasium in Four Stages

as a consequence was for the most part directed at their feckless Spartan ally, as it had been on the eve of the war in 432.[18]

Coryphasium

By the time that the campaigning season began in 426, Archidamus was dead. That spring the forces of the Peloponnesian League did not invade Attica. Agis, Archidamus' son and heir as Eurypontid king, led them to the Isthmus of Corinth, then turned back, taking a swarm of earthquakes as a bad omen. The following year, however, the Peloponnesians returned, intent on laying waste the countryside outside Athens, but this time they remained there for only fifteen days. The weather was, we are told, unfavorable—unseasonably cold, we must assume—and the grain was not yet ripe and ready for harvest. In consequence, the invaders soon fell short of provisions—and then their commander heard alarming news that caused him to dismiss the levies and hasten home.[19]

Agis was, as his response to the swarm of earthquakes suggests, a true Spartan—god-fearing and cautious in the extreme. His worries on this later occasion stemmed from yet another ambitious scheme cooked up by that enterprising Athenian Demosthenes—this one consistent with Athens' objective in the war and as sensible as it was audacious. At about the time that Agis and the Peloponnesians reached Attica, the reinforcements promised Leontini and her allies had set out from Athens. Pythodorus son of Isolochus had been sent on ahead to Sicily to succeed Laches, the sole surviving commander in that theater—who had been recalled and who would in due course be harried in the assembly, if not also brought to trial for malfeasance, by the demagogue Cleon. Eurymedon and Sophocles son of Sostratides, who had remained behind to organize the reinforcements, had other business to transact while conducting the forty triremes to the west. While en route, they were to pay Corcyra a visit and help the democrats there drive out a force of about six hundred oligarchic exiles—who had regrouped on the mainland and seized control of the Corcyraean *peraía* there, then slipped across to the northeastern end of the island where it came within two miles of the Balkan peninsula, burned their ships, and built a stronghold on the southern slopes of the Istone massif whence they had begun plundering their compatriots' farms in the lowlands below. The Athenian commanders may also have received word that the Peloponnesians were planning to dispatch a fleet of sixty triremes to the island in order to exploit the famine produced by the ongoing conflict and capture the city.[20]

On this voyage, begun early in the spring of 425, the wily son of Alcisthenes traveled as a passenger. He was not at the time a general but he would apparently take up that office again in short order near midsummer at the beginning of what counted in Athens as the new year; and he was contemplating an enterprise, dependent on surprise, that he had divulged to few, if any at Athens, and to none of those whom he accompanied on this stage of their journey—at least as far as we can tell. At his suggestion, Eurymedon and Sophocles had been instructed to allow him to employ their fleet as they rowed along the Peloponnesian coast in whatever way he wished.

That Demosthenes actually got the opportunity he had sought appears to have been fortuitous. Eurymedon and Sophocles had learned that the Peloponnesian fleet was already at Corcyra, and they were understandably eager to reach the island before it was too late. But the weather bedeviling the Peloponnesians in Attica came to Demosthenes' rescue. A storm descended on the triremes as they were laboriously working their way up the coast of Messenia; and the winds, which in those parts nearly always blew down the Adriatic from the northwest, drove the fleet back down the coast, where it found shelter in what was later called Navarino Bay. There, as luck would have it, the son of Alcisthenes, on one of his previous voyages along this coast, or Messenian raiders operating from Naupactus had spotted an inviting headland, replete with stone and timber and equipped with a spring from which fresh water flowed, which stretched out northward along the seacoast from the bay's northern shore for nearly a mile. This feature of the landscape the Athenian hoped, on this occasion, to examine in detail. If it proved suitable, he planned to return later with a host of exiled Messenians versed in the local dialect, primed to launch raids into the interior of what they regarded as their fatherland, and equipped to fortify and garrison the place. It was near this headland, along a sandbar at the north end of the bay, that the Athenian fleet found refuge from the storm.[21]

After exploring the headland and admiring its distinguishing feature— the rectangular ridge flanked by cliffs that guarded it along the landward side and that ran as well along much of the coast—Demosthenes judged the place well-suited to his purpose. And, thanks to the tempest then under way, he

realized that he was confronted with an unexpected opportunity. The headland beckoned, and about him there were men aplenty at leisure who might
be employed in its fortification. According to Thucydides, who seems to have
been exceedingly well-informed, neither Eurymedon nor Sophocles favored
the enterprise that their compatriot now proposed. Both were sensitive to the
sharp decline in Athens' reserves, and neither thought the project worth the
money that would have to be spent in its support. Nor were the taxiarchs and
the soldiers under their command initially attracted by the scheme of Alcisthenes' son, and it almost came to naught.

Scholars today, who suppose Pericles' strategy for the war dogmatically
and inflexibly defensive, tend to regard Demosthenes' project as a risky venture and a dramatic departure from what the deceased statesman had had in
mind. In fact, however, as subsequent events would demonstrate, the young
warrior's plan was perfectly consistent with the elder statesman's aims, and
it was brilliant. As a stratagem, it followed naturally from Pericles' insistence
that Athens' efforts be focused solely on bringing pressure to bear on Lacedaemon in such a manner as to persuade her to accept a humiliating peace, leave
her allies in the lurch, and abandon the pretense that she was on a quest to
liberate the Greeks from Athenian domination.

On the eve of the war, the Corinthians had advocated the establishment
of fortified positions in Attica. In the speech in the Athenian assembly in
which Pericles explained how the city would "win through," he had expressly
canvassed doing the like; and in the first year of the war, undoubtedly at his
instigation, the Athenians had established something of the sort on the island
of Atalante off the Locrian coast. A maneuver of this sort aimed directly at
Lacedaemon, which had been contemplated before the war even began (even
if, then, solely as an available mode of retaliation), would surely have been
considered a viable option, consistent with the original strategy, when patience
in the face of the annual Peloponnesian invasions of Attica—supplemented by
the semi-annual Athenian invasions of the Megarid, the sting of seaborne
raids, and the obstruction of Megarian and Corinthian trade—had failed to
achieve Pericles' aims.[22]

There were risks involved, to be sure. The site—named Coryphasium by
Spartans impressed by the size of the promontory [koruphḗ] and called Pylos
by outsiders mindful of the location nearby assigned Nestor's palace in Homer's
Odyssey—was isolated. It would not be easy to supply with provisions a garri-

son situated in so lonely a place. To do so from Athens, one would have to convoy merchantmen down the difficult and dangerous eastern coast of the Peloponnesus, around Cape Malea, through the high seas along the southern coast of the Peloponnesus, and some distance up the western coast of Messenia. To do so from Corcyra, Acarnania, Naupactus, Cephallenia, or Zacynthus, one would have to deploy a fleet of triremes sufficient to protect merchantmen, loaded with provisions, from the Peloponnesian fleet stationed at Cyllene in Elis. But if one could somehow manage this, one could place the Spartans in difficult straits. For the enduring presence on the coast at this site of an armed band of intrepid Messenian raiders would certainly attract runaway helots from among those of their compatriots who were made to farm the Pamisos valley on Sparta's behalf; and, as the Lacedaemonians understood only too well, it might also incite yet another general revolt on the part of this people, on whom they had long maintained a tenuous hold.[23]

If Thucydides is to be believed, it was boredom that finally induced the soldiers (and presumably also the rowers, who were similarly trapped in the bay for an extended period by the storm) to take up the task of fortifying the headland. This they accomplished—since it had not been supposed before the voyage that they would at any point be thus employed—without the benefit of possessing the tools proper for working stone. They hoisted boulders and fit them in place; they made mortar and, clasping it between their hands, they lugged it on their backs. For six days, we are told, these soldiers and sailors labored with vigor and increasing enthusiasm on the project, walling off the ridge on the headland thoroughly in the extreme northeast and the extreme southeast, where access was comparatively easy, and building less extensive fortifications along the western shore in the south, where this natural stronghold was protected not by cliffs but by the exceedingly rough and rocky character of the approach. Then, the fleet departed, leaving the son of Alcisthenes with soldiers and five triremes for raiding and for their fort's defense. The only thing requisite that the garrison lacked was an adequate provision of food—which Demosthenes no doubt hoped to secure, along with additional manpower, from Naupactus.[24]

The fact that Eurymedon and Sophocles provided Demosthenes with soldiers and with a handful of triremes is telling in one other particular, especially since we know that the Athenian fleet loitered in the neighborhood for a week some seventy miles up the coast at Zacynthus, the nearest harbor on a friendly shore of a size sufficient to shelter all of the galleys. Whatever reluctance the two generals may initially have displayed and whatever doubts they may have harbored regarding the long-term prospects of the enterprise, they had clearly come to realize that they had baited a trap and that there would soon be a showdown. The Lacedaemonians would cross Taygetus and initiate a siege, for they had no choice; and they would also recall the Peloponnesian fleet from Corcyra. On this the Athenian commanders banked, and so they situated themselves where they might most easily intercept and destroy that fleet.[25]

When the Lacedaemonians at Sparta learned that the headland was being fortified, they did not, initially, take the development seriously. The main body of their army was in Attica. Those at home were celebrating a religious festival, and the latter presumed that, at their leisure, they could capture the place or force a withdrawal.

When, however, word reached Agis in Attica, he rightly thought otherwise. Lacedaemon's Eurypontid king was not a man given to complacency. Believing the matter something "close to home [οἰκεῖον]," as Thucydides explains, he left immediately for Lacedaemon with the Spartiates under his command, paused briefly to regroup, then traversed Taygetus, and marched on to Coryphasium after collecting soldiers from among the *períoikoi* who lived nearby. In the meantime, the authorities at Lacedaemon summoned help from Sparta's allies within the Peloponnesus and sent word to the Peloponnesians in the fleet at Corcyra, who set off for Leucas, dragged their ships across the isthmus there to avoid notice, and then rowed south, slipping past the Athenian fleet anchored at Zacynthus unseen (no doubt at night).

Before the Peloponnesian fleet reached Coryphasium, the son of Alcisthenes had dispatched two of the triremes under his command to Eurymedon at Zacynthus to let him know that the Spartan army had arrived. He was, as Eurymedon no doubt knew, ill-provisioned. If soldiers and provisions were on their way from Naupactus, they had not yet arrived, and he was going to need help. In the meantime, suspecting that the Athenian fleet would soon descend on them, the Lacedaemonians selected by lot from their entire army a force of four hundred twenty Spartiates and *períoikoi* and stationed them, along with their helot attendants, on the narrow, wooded island of Sphacteria, which stretched nearly three miles from north to south along the bay, sheltering it in some measure from the sea. The Lacedaemonians recognized the risks and regularly rotated contingents on and off the island. It was, nonetheless, their supposition, so Thucydides reports, that—if they held the mainland and the island, which was very nearly unapproachable on the seaward side; if they situated their fleet within the great bay; and if they contested the entrances to that body of water with a couple of triremes in the shallow narrows north of the island and with the remainder of the fleet deployed in the broader expanse to its south—they would be able to deter attack and deny the Athenians on shipboard a place nearby in which to anchor, land, camp, prepare food, and secure fresh water. They surely also recognized that, if they controlled the island, they could post lookouts above and behind the little fort they had built on the heights at its northern end, and these could then alert them well in advance of the approach of an enemy fleet.[26]

In the meantime, before the Athenians in the fleet could come to its defense, the Lacedaemonians sought to storm Demosthenes' fort. In preparation for their attack, the Athenian and his men dragged the three triremes still in their possession up on the sandy shore of the little cove situated opposite the northeastern tip of Sphacteria immediately to the west of the sandbar on which the Athenian fleet had found shelter from the storm. There, where the fortifications constructed by the Athenians ran from the southeastern edge of the towering ridge down to the water and blocked access by land from the sandbar, they built a stockade to protect the ships.

In the interim between the Athenians' departure and the Spartan attack, probably in response to a summons dispatched to Naupactus by the son of Alcisthenes as soon as the storm abated, a small boat and a thirty-oared privateer piloted by Messenians had appeared. The wicker shields on board these ships Demosthenes distributed to the crews of the three triremes, and he added to his garrison the forty Messenian hoplites who manned the two vessels.

Demosthenes' headland was, in most respects, a natural fortress—unapproachable from the northwest and much of the west because of cliffs that dropped down to the sea and inaccessible from the east where it ended abruptly in a precipice no less sheer. Where the headland could be most easily be approached—from a small bay at its northeastern end and from the cove in the southeast—the Athenians had built extensive fortifications, as we have seen. Most of his men—some with arms, others without—the son of Alcisthenes posted on the fortifications on the southeastern edge of the headland on the landward side facing the sandbar at the northern end of Navarino Bay. They

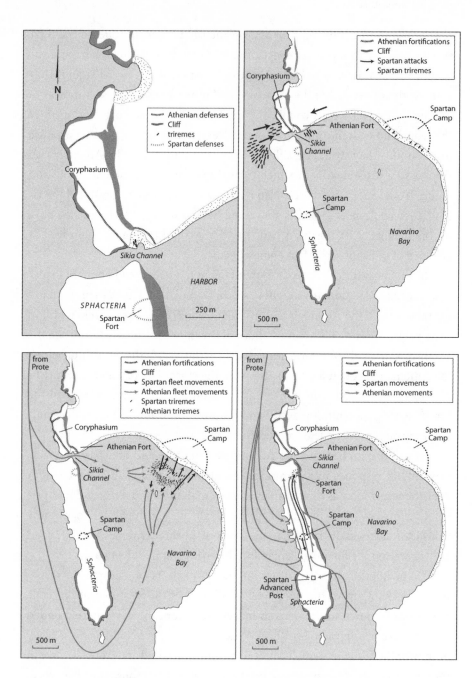

Map 17. Sequence of Events at Coryphasium and Sphacteria

were to repel any attempts made by the Spartans to scale the walls. The weakest part of the fortifications ran just inland for some distance along the southernmost part of the headland's rugged western shore just outside the entrance to the northern of the two channels leading from the Ionian Sea into that great bay. At the water's edge, outside these walls, Demosthenes stationed sixty hoplites and a handful of archers. They were to contest any attempt to make a landing.

It was here that the son of Alcisthenes expected an especially fierce attack, and it was here that he hoped to draw Lacedaemonian blood. Although, as he explained to his men, they were badly outnumbered, they were not at a tremendous disadvantage. The shore was long, to be sure, but there was no sand. It was a shelf of solid rock extending inland. The drop-off into deep water was sudden and severe, and there were only four or five places, if that many, suitable for an amphibious landing—which was too few for the Lacedaemonians to make their approach en masse. They would have to land in small detachments. It was incumbent on the Athenian and his infantrymen to beat back the waves of assault seriatim, catching and dispatching the individual Lacedaemonian hoplites as they tried to make their way from ship to shore and then attempted to clamber across the difficult, rocky shelf that stretched toward the great ridge from the watery expanse—and preventing their establishment of a beachhead. If they could do this, victory would be theirs.

In the event, Demosthenes' analysis of the tactical environment was proven correct. The attack made on the landward side across the sandbar went nowhere, and the assault launched along the southernmost part of the western shore by the Spartan navarch Thrasymelidas son of Cratesicles, although it was sustained throughout the first day and most of the next, also fell short. Not even Brasidas, who was trierarch of one of the triremes and who was as bold and brash as ever, managed to force a landing. To demonstrate to his fellow trierarchs what had to be done, he had his helmsman run the stern of his trireme aground. But, while attempting to negotiate the brow of his ship, he was himself wounded repeatedly, and he fainted from loss of blood, collapsed onto the trireme's outrigger, and lost his shield, which the Athenians later retrieved from the shoreline and proudly posted on the trophy they raised in celebration of their victory. In the end, the Spartans called off the assault and sent to Asine on the Gulf of Messenia for lumber with which to construct scaling ladders, battering rams, and the like.[27]

Figure 2. Spartan Shield Captured at Pylos, 425 B.C. (Athens, Stoa of
Attalus. Photographer: Giovanni Dall'Orto. Published 2020 under the
following license issued by Giovanni Dall'Orto: "The copyright
holder of this file allows anyone to use it for any purpose, provided
that the copyright holder is properly attributed. Redistribution,
derivative work, commercial use, and all other use is permitted.")

Late that same day, lookouts posted on the heights at the northern end of
Sphacteria must have alerted the Peloponnesians to the approach of Athens'
fleet—now perhaps as many as fifty in number, thanks to the addition of four
Chian vessels and some of the triremes posted at Naupactus. For, thanks to the
advance warning, when Eurymedon arrived, he discovered that the northern
entrance to the bay was blocked; and when he reached its southern entrance,
he not only found the island and the harbor shore bristling with hoplites. He
is also said to have seen a host of enemy ships moored at the harbor's entrance
with no sign that their commanders were willing to sally forth and fight a
battle in the open sea. Not knowing where to anchor and needing time to
contemplate his options, he then took his fleet roughly eight miles back up the

Messenian coast to the little island of Prote, where there was fresh water to be found and at least some of his triremes could be accommodated in the sizable, sheltered bays along its southern shores.[28]

The next day—almost certainly before dawn, when his fleet could not be spied by the lookouts on Sphacteria—Eurymedon had the Athenian galleys, fully cleared for battle, slip quietly down the coast. His aim was to catch the Peloponnesians flat-footed, and this he did. Some scholars explain the failure of the Peloponnesians to block the entrances by speculating that Thrasymelidas and his subordinate commanders thought that the Athenians had gone away for good. Others do so on the presumption that Athens' enemies had decided to stage a battle in Navarino Bay. Neither hypothesis is, however, plausible. The Spartans cannot have supposed that the Athenians had sailed away. At Prote, the Athenian fleet would have been visible to the Lacedaemonian lookouts posted on the heights at the northern end of Sphacteria. Nor can the Peloponnesians have thought that they stood a chance against the Athenians in a bay as large as the one at Coryphasium. They had been outmaneuvered by their opponents in open water too often in the recent past to want to endure yet another defeat.[29]

Their best bet was to post a couple of triremes at the bay's northern entrance to close it. Then, they could use the remainder of their fleet to block the southern entrance as had been their plan from the outset. This, scholarly opinion to the contrary notwithstanding, they could easily have accomplished by the simple expedient of lining up across that span of water fifty or more triremes facing the open sea in three or more lines abreast. In such circumstances, any Athenian trierarch who attempted a *diékplous* would have his trireme rammed by one of the galleys in the second or the third rank.[30] If, on this occasion, the entrances to Navarino Bay had been left unguarded overnight, it was thanks solely to gross negligence on the part of the Eurypontid king Agis, the navarch Thrasymelidas, and their colleagues; and it was their carelessness that allowed Eurymedon at first light to conduct his fleet, unimpeded, into the bay from its northern and southern entrances at the same time.

Once there, the triremes of Athens and Chios gathered in the center of the bay and descended on the enemy fleet, routing the ships that the Peloponnesians managed to man, seizing five triremes, disabling others, ramming some in the process of being manned, and towing off a number that were entirely empty. In a frenzy, Thucydides tells us, Sparta's hoplites then waded into the bay, laid hold of the empty vessels being towed off, and tried with considerable success to drag them back while the *epıbátaı* on board the Athenian and Chian triremes had at them. When the battle had come to an end and the confusion subsided, the Athenians set up a trophy, handed back the dead, secured the wrecks, and began circumnavigating Sphacteria, where they now had four hundred twenty Lacedaemonians trapped. The besiegers had become the besieged.[31]

CHAPTER 5

Lacedaemon at Bay

How often, . . . have statesmen and officers, even in the most harmonious conference, been unable to decide on a coherent plan of war from inability to analyse scientifically the situation they had to face, and to recognise the general character of the struggle in which they were about to engage.

JULIAN STAFFORD CORBETT

WHEN word reached Lacedaemon regarding their defeat in Navarino Bay, the Spartans voted to send "the authorities [tà télē]"—in all likelihood, the "little assembly" made up of the ephors, the *gérontes,* and the two kings—to Coryphasium to review the situation and decide what was to be done. Thanks to the Lacedaemonian infantrymen who had waded into the bay, the Peloponnesian fleet was for the most part intact. But it was apparently no longer deemed viable for combat—presumably because its trierarchs, who had repeatedly been outmaneuvered by the Athenians, were now thoroughly cowed. And the delegation from Lacedaemon concluded that their compatriots and allies were not in a position to come to the aid of the men on the island. Fearing that the latter, who were ill-provisioned, would be overcome by starvation or overwhelmed by the number of infantrymen that Athens could deploy on the island, they concluded a local truce with the Athenian generals and sent an embassy to Athens to negotiate a peace agreement. Their aim, Thucydides tells us, was to recover their men as soon as possible.

Mindful that the Peloponnesians with their remaining ships might in the interim mount a surprise attack or a rescue effort, the Athenian generals drove an extremely hard bargain, requiring that their opponents surrender for the duration of the truce not only the ships remaining in the bay but also all of the others that they possessed in Laconia, and stipulating that, if the truce was breached in even the slightest particular, the agreement would be null and void. In all other regards, the terms were what one would expect. Demosthenes' fort was to be left alone, and neither side was to attack the other. The Athenians would keep the island under guard, and, under the eyes of the Athenians, a fixed quantity of food and wine would be delivered each day to the Lacedaemonians on the island.[1]

The Spartans had a variety of motives for seeking peace at this time. The one most often mentioned by the Lacedaemonians was their desire to safeguard the men trapped on Sphacteria. Something like two-fifths of these were Spartiates; and among them, we are told, were a considerable number of scions of the leading families of Lacedaemon.[2]

The demographic implosion in and after 465 that the Spartans had undergone no doubt reinforced the Lacedaemonians' eagerness to recover these men. The great earthquake had more than halved the population—both female and male—and the losses in battle suffered by Lacedaemon during the helot revolt and at Tegea, Dipaea, and Tanagra had no doubt compounded the difficulties they faced. From such a demographic implosion, populations tend to bounce back tolerably quickly if, as in the case of Argos after Sepeia, there is no shortage of eligible women. When, however, their numbers have been dramatically reduced, as the Spartan women's numbers were, the rebound takes considerably more time.

It is also conceivable that the Spartans—who were notoriously reticent and, when it came to matters of political and strategic significance, quite secretive and even devious—suffered additional, possibly even catastrophic, losses at the time of the plague. Although Thucydides denies that the disease even reached the Peloponnesus, his informants among the denizens of that great peninsula were neither omniscient nor always entirely candid, and there is evidence suggesting that he may have been misinformed. We are told, for example, that the plague struck Troezen in the Argolic Acte and Cleonae to the north of the Argolid. We are told that it threatened Phigaleia deep in Arcadia; and it is telling that in 420, when the Spartans negotiated a peace agreement with Argos, it included an unprecedented clause contemplating the possibility that one or the other community might succumb to such an epidemic.

In the late spring of 425, although the Spartiate population may well have been larger than it had been in the immediate aftermath of the earthquake and helot revolt forty years before, it was not even remotely as large as it had been at the time of the battle of Plataea.[3] It is no wonder that the Spartans were intent on recovering the men stuck on the island.

The Lacedaemonians also entertained other concerns that may well have been too delicate for mention outside their own ranks. Coryphasium on the coast of their domain in Messenia remained in the hands of Demosthenes and his motley crew, and their efforts to wrest the headland from these men had come to naught. This province was the foundation of Spartan prosperity. Its possession and the labor of the helots who farmed it made possible a way of life that the citizens of Lacedaemon treasured. As one would expect, they were horror-struck that a fort in so strategically vital a location should be garrisoned by exiles eager to liberate their fellow Messenians from peonage and ignite a revolt; expel Lacedaemon from the fertile, well-watered Pamisos valley; and refound Messene as an independent *pólis*. This prospect really did touch them quite "close to home."

It was also true that the war was not going at all well. The Lacedaemonians and their allies had nothing to show for the divers ventures in which they had been engaged. The annual invasions of Attica had been without effect. The Peloponnesians' repeated attempts to assert their preeminence at sea in the Corinthian Gulf, the Ionian Sea, and the Adriatic had failed ignominiously. Aegina had been seized, and Potidaea had fallen to the Athenians. The Spartans had squandered the opportunity afforded by the Mytilenian revolt. The investment of time, manpower, and treasure in the operations undertaken at Corcyra and in Acarnania had been for naught. Meanwhile, the blockade imposed on Corinth and Megara remained in place, wreaking havoc within these two commercial cities; and Athens, though profoundly weakened by the plague, soldiered steadily on. It was with this record in mind that the Spartans had been persuaded to recall Pleistoanax from exile; and, if Aristophanes can be trusted, they had thereafter made an abortive attempt to reach an accord with the Athenians.

Demosthenes' construction of a fort in Messenia, Athens' naval victory in Navarino Bay, and the cornering of so many Spartiates on Sphacteria—in the circumstances, this was more than could be borne. Given what had happened, it is no surprise that the Spartans should now more seriously contemplate the possibility that they had brought all of this on themselves by incurring the wrath of the gods when they started a war and broke the oaths they had taken in ratifying the Thirty Years' Peace. And it stands to reason that they should now very much want to reach an agreement with the Athenians.

It was, nonetheless, exceedingly unwise for the Lacedaemonians to lose heart on this occasion and make a truce on the terms that the Athenians were willing to offer. When, at Sparta's behest, the Peloponnesians handed over their remaining triremes, they gave up the considerable leverage conferred on them by their capacity to launch a surprise attack and use those galleys to rescue their men and do the Athenian fleet harm—and, in the process, they left the men trapped on the island at Athens' mercy. If the Eurypontid king Agis was in overall command of the forces concentrated at Navarino Bay, as seems to have been the case, he allowed his inbred caution to get in the way of a proper assessment of the military situation.[4]

Sphacteria

Political regimes are worlds unto themselves. Each fosters a way of life, based on an idea of justice and the common good, that gives rise to an ethos which blinds its citizens to the preconceptions and predilections of those who live under markedly different regimes and embrace different ways of life and different notions of what constitutes justice and the common good. In his *Republic*, Plato rightly compares the regime to a cave inhabited by denizens chained in such a manner that they see nothing but the shadows of images crafted by artists and projected on the wall of the cave.[5]

It is not easy for those born and bred under one regime to properly and effectively address those born and bred under another. The former tend to deploy arguments that would persuade those just like themselves—which is what the Lacedaemonian envoys did when they reached Athens. The Spartans prided themselves on their possession of *sophrosúnē* and their avoidance of its opposite: *húbris*. They were, so they thought, moderate; and they had a healthy aversion to the arrogance that gives rise to insolence. Their *sophrosúnē* was a quality, Thucydides wryly intimates, most apt to be found in a people greatly outnumbered by their own slaves.[6]

In addressing the Athenian assembly, the Spartan envoys forgot what the Corinthians had tried to teach them on the eve of the war about the significance of regime differences. They themselves had a propensity for attributing success to fortune and the will of the gods. They were not cowed by Athens' victory at Coryphasium. They regarded it as "a theft of war," and they assumed that they could talk the Athenians into a species of *sophrosúnē* akin to their own—first, by getting them to attribute the victory they had achieved in Navarino Bay to good luck and, then, by persuading them to embrace peace as a means for avoiding the catastrophe that a change of fortune, which was notoriously fickle, might well produce. Thanks to the helots, the Lacedaemonians lived in constant fear and exercised extreme caution. That the Athenians lived, instead, on hope; that they were, for all intents and purposes, fearless; and that they enthusiastically embraced audacity—this the Spartans simply could not comprehend. Remembering the Athenians' eagerness for peace early in the war, they offered—in return for the release of the men trapped on Sphacteria—peace, friendship on equal terms, and an alliance, which would, they said, enable the two powers to share the hegemony and dictate to the other Greeks.[7]

There were no doubt some at Athens who at this time succumbed to nostalgia and dreamed of a return to the policy of dual hegemony once promoted by Cimon. There were certainly quite a few who strongly favored negotiating a peace. Prominent among these, Plutarch reports, was Nicias son of Niceratus, a man famously pious, who was as prone as the Spartans to attribute success to good fortune and the will of the gods. But, although the matter was vigorously contested in the assembly, those at Athens of Nicias' persuasion did not at this time constitute a majority.

According to Thucydides, the Athenians responded in a manner wholly in keeping with the portrait of them drawn on the eve of the war by the Corinthians. The Spartiates on Sphacteria were, they assumed, theirs for the taking. With these men in their keeping, they could secure peace whenever they pleased—and what they wanted in the meantime, above all else, was "more." At the instigation of Cleon, they issued a series of demands: first, that the men on Sphacteria surrender, hand over their arms, and come to Athens; and, then, that Lacedaemon return Nisaea, Pegae, Troezen, and Achaea, which the Athenians had ceded back in 446—in a time of catastrophe, when they themselves had suffered "a theft of war" and were more in need of terms than they were now. Only then, the Spartans were told, would they get their men back and secure peace for a period to be determined by the two sides.

These terms were designed as a public humiliation, and their being so brazenly stipulated put the Spartans in an exceedingly awkward position. As a preliminary to a settlement, they were being asked to announce in public not only the abject surrender of the men on Sphacteria but also their willingness to betray their allies Megara, Troezen, and Achaea—an act which would almost certainly have had the effect of alienating their other allies. But, tellingly, the

Spartans did not reject Cleon's terms outright. Instead, they suggested that the two sides appoint *xúnedroi*—negotiators to sit alongside one another and work out in private the details of a deal—which suggests that, on condition that the Athenians not play a game of bait and switch, the Lacedaemonians were willing to go a considerable distance in the direction of satisfying their demands.

It was at this point that Pericles, who had never had any faith in the policy of dual hegemony, would nonetheless have sought an agreement. As he understood, Athens and her allies could never on their own defeat Lacedaemon in the field. The only way to put an end to Spartan assertiveness once and for all was to do again what Themistocles had done while at Argos early in the 460s and to succeed where he had fallen short—by breaking up the Peloponnesian League, as he had, and by achieving a victory over Lacedaemon in the field with the help of her erstwhile allies of the sort that had eluded him. Had the Spartans gone even halfway toward meeting the Athenian demands—had they, for example, agreed to turn over Nisaea and Pegae—their prestige would have plummeted. Corinth would have bolted in fury from the Spartan alliance, as she had threatened to do on the eve of the war; and other cities within the Peloponnesus would have seized the opportunity to liberate themselves from the constraints imposed by the Lacedaemonians. Then, the Argives, sensing opportunity, would almost certainly have waded in.[8]

Thucydides conveys his opinion when he picks up on a propensity that the Spartans had warned against and tells us that the Athenians "reached out for more." Overreaching [*pleonexía*]—the propensity for always seeking more and more—is a term of powerful disapprobation in the Greek moral vocabulary, suggestive of *húbris;* and it is into this trap, he intimates, that the Athenians fell when, under Cleon's leadership, they rejected negotiating in private. It was this refusal that caused the Spartans to give up and return to war. In Pericles' heyday, the Athenians had boasted, "We are measured [*metriázomen*] in our conduct of affairs." Thucydides himself confirms their claim, reporting that Pericles had himself managed the city "in a measured manner [*metríōs*]." But on this occasion, he observes, the Spartans concluded that the Athenians were not willing to give them "on measured terms [*epì metríois*]" what they asked. They had, the Lacedaemonians implied, lost all sense of proportion; and Thucydides clearly agreed, as did his astute younger contemporary the comic poet Aristophanes.[9]

When the Athenians conveyed the Lacedaemonian envoys back to Coryphasium, they dispatched twenty additional triremes to bolster the force guarding Sphacteria. The return of the envoys put an end to the truce negotiated earlier; and, as the Peloponnesians should have anticipated, the Athenians refused to return the triremes that the former had provisionally placed in their keeping. The Athenians asserted that their opponents had broken the truce by launching an attack on the headland and that there had been other breaches of the agreement, which Thucydides did not even think worth mentioning. The Peloponnesians in turn accused the Athenians of injustice and of having acted in bad faith—which may well have been the case. The Peloponnesians had much to lose from a breach of the truce. The Athenians were functioning as judges in their own cause, and they had a tremendous amount to gain from eliminating the last vestiges of their opponents' power at sea.

The standoff was not, however, resolved by the Athenians' seizure of the Peloponnesian fleet. On the mainland, the Spartans intensified their attempts to scale the walls of Demosthenes' fort. At sea, the Athenians anchored their fleet around the island at night and had two ships, rowing in opposite directions, circumnavigate it over and over and over again during the day. Moreover, as it turned out, time was not on the side of Cleon's compatriots.

The Athenians had no place in the immediate vicinity of Coryphasium and Sphacteria where they could anchor their ships and easily go ashore, apart from the little cove to the west of the sandbar on the northern shore of the great bay—and this cove could not accommodate more than a small proportion of their fleet at any given time. The Spartans and their allies occupied the shoreline within the bay almost in its entirety. Sphacteria itself is mountainous and uninviting. There are very few landing places on its eastern coast, and the ground is anything but flat. Moreover, it was then so woody that the Athenians could not discover the extent or character of the forces they would encounter if they landed on the island; and the son of Alcisthenes, the general present with the most experience in irregular warfare, had no desire to risk defeat by repeating the blunders he had made in Aetolia. In the bay proper, it was solely along the eighty or so yards on the southeast corner of the headland protected from the Spartans by a wall that Athens' triremes could in relays land their men to prepare meals, secure fresh water, and stretch out to rest. It may well have been necessary, as one scholar has suggested, that they also send triremes in relays to the sheltered bays on the south shore of Prote, where water was available and the rowers could sleep on shore.

What bothered the Athenians the most, however, was that the Spartans managed to run the blockade and supply provisions to the men on the island. In rough weather, the Athenians could not safely anchor their triremes at night on Sphacteria's seaward side. In these circumstances, helots—promised their freedom and rich rewards—drove small boats, laden with food, onto what was an unfriendly shore apt to ruin the vessels; and there the cargo was gratefully received. Within the bay, divers swam across to the island under water, dragging by a cord skins filled with crushed linseed and with poppy seeds mixed with honey.

The news concerning this stalemate, when it reached Athens, caused consternation. They were, the Athenians knew, in danger of losing the advantage they had gained and with it their leverage over the Lacedaemonians. The situation had to be resolved before winter—when exceedingly stormy weather would of necessity bring their blockade of the island to an end. In that season, it would be impossible to convey provisions on the requisite scale around the Peloponnesus, and there were none to be had locally. Moreover, even if somehow the siege was sustained, the men on the island could wait for an extended bout of bad weather and escape on the little boats that brought in provisions. And to make matters worse, the Spartans apparently recognized that they now had the advantage. The fact that they had stopped sending envoys in quest of peace was ominous.[10]

All of this put Cleon on the spot. At first, we are told in an extended passage that reads like an eyewitness account, he simply poured scorn on the reports from the field. Then, when the emissaries from the fleet suggested that, if the Athenians did not believe them, they should send observers to see for themselves, he found himself threatened with what was apt to be an exceedingly awkward and embarrassing assignment. In an effort to dodge the responsibility about to be thrust upon him, Cleon urged that a relief expedition be sent instead—which is what appears to have been contemplated in the *proboúleuma,* drafted in advance by the Council of 500, that had occasioned the debate. Pointing to Nicias, whom he reportedly detested, Cleon suggested that, if the Athenians had as their generals real men, the latter would sail to Sphacteria and capture those on the island. Had he himself been assigned the command, he boasted, he would have done just that.

Nicias, to whom the *proboúleuma* appears to have provisionally assigned responsibility for the proposed expedition, should have ignored the demagogue's taunt, and he should have accepted the assignment. There was, after all, a great deal at stake. It was the prospect of losing their men that had forced the Lacedaemonians to sue for peace. They would not soon renew their appeal if they won them back. In the circumstances, it really was imperative that Athens take the island and seize a goodly number of Spartiates.

Nicias, who was risk-averse and loath to undertake so dicey an expedition, responded in a manner that later earned him mockery and that was, as Thucydides tacitly invites us to conclude, irresponsible and even disgraceful—though not surprising, given the circumstances. Instead of offering to go, he called Cleon's bluff and suggested that, if this was what his opponent really thought, he should go himself. When Cleon, who had hitherto never been in command of troops or a fleet, answered that it was Nicias, not he, who had been elected general, the latter pressed his advantage by offering to resign the proposed command in Cleon's favor. The more reluctant Cleon seemed, the more, Thucydides tells us, "the mob" pressed him to go—until, cornered, he finally agreed, saying that *he* did not fear the Lacedaemonians and that he would take with him not a single man from the city proper but only the Lemnian and Imbrian cleruchs who were present, the peltasts that had come in from Aenus, and four hundred archers from elsewhere; and boasting that, within twenty days, he would either bring back the Lacedaemonians alive or dispatch them on the spot.[11]

By this time, Cleon, who had a gift for invective and a well-honed instinct for cruelty, had earned for himself the loathing of a great many of Athens' leading men—including the poet Aristophanes and Thucydides himself. The son of Cleaenetus persistently struck a self-righteous pose. When he first entered the political arena, we are told, he sought to distinguish himself from his rivals by ostentatiously repudiating all ties of friendship, by presenting himself as a public-spirited devotee of everything that was upright and just, and by implying that his competitors were self-interested rogues—and Aristophanes' depiction of the man confirms that this is the posture he maintained from then on. We know that, in 427, Cleon had pressed in the most violent terms for the execution of every last Mytilenian and that he had cast aspersions on the motives of those who disagreed with him, intimating that they must have been bribed and were, in effect, guilty of treason. As the charges he lodged against the generals victorious at Potidaea and the troubles he later inflicted on Laches indicate, he was behind the growing propensity at Athens for men of ambition to use prosecution as a political weapon, to treat failure in the field as treason, to seek fines or exile for commanders who were less than fully successful, to brand political opponents as conspirators and would-be tyrants out to betray the city, and to prosecute magistrates and even private individuals on trumped-up charges.[12]

Cleon was not, to be sure, the first to have used the courts in this fashion. Pericles' father Xanthippus had prosecuted Cimon's father Miltiades when, after his victory at Marathon, he had mounted an abortive mission to Paros. Themistocles had later been treated in a similar fashion by Cimon's associates, and Pericles himself had done the like to Cimon when his initiatives in the Thraceward region had gone awry in the mid-460s. But these last two trials had been exercises aimed at softening up an opponent and preparing the way for his ostracism. Cleon appears to have eschewed ostracism and temporary exile as a political weapon. Instead, he had adopted a policy of intimidation, making prosecutions aimed at fining, permanently exiling, or executing his foes the norm. This was no small matter. There is evidence, drawn from the first nine decades that followed the outbreak of Sparta's second Attic war, strongly suggesting that something on the order of one-fifth of Athens' generals were tried for treason and that most of those accused were executed or exiled.

Already by this time, Cleon had so thoroughly poisoned political life in Athens that, when he uttered his boast, those who prided themselves on being "men of moderation [*sóphrones*]" reportedly took comfort in the thought that one of two goods was in prospect. The more likely of the two was that they would be rid of Cleon. But, if they were cheated out of this expectation, they would have the Lacedaemonians in their hands. As Thucydides lets us see without being openly didactic, at Athens something truly terrible was unfolding: domestic quarrels had begun to outweigh the desire for victory in the war.[13]

Had Thucydides lived longer—had he been able to finish his history, review his narrative, and make adjustments to the text—he might well have tweaked his account at this point. For he tells us that Cleon had learned quite a number of things: that the soldiers in Navarino Bay were fed up with their situation and eager to have it out; that Demosthenes now had it in mind to make a landing on the island and bring things to a head; that—thanks to a fire unwittingly set by an Athenian soldier, which had ripped through the underbrush and burned down the trees—this veteran commander had discovered the character of the Lacedaemonian force he was up against; and that he had sent to Athens' allies in the region for additional soldiers and was making other preparations. With this in mind, he adds, the demagogue persuaded the assembly to appoint the son of Alcisthenes as his colleague. It can hardly, then, be an accident that the peltasts and archers requested by Cleon were precisely what was needed for combat on the type of terrain predominant on Sphacteria. Demosthenes must have included a request for specialists of precisely this sort in the report delivered before the assembly by the emissaries sent to Athens from Coryphasium—and, had he had the time to reread and rewrite, Thucydides would very likely have corrected his failure to mention the fact.

When Cleon arrived with these men, he and Demosthenes sent a herald to the Spartan camp on the mainland, suggesting that whoever was in command (in all likelihood, the Eurypontid king Agis) order the men on the island to surrender, and promising that, if this were done, the captives would be kept "under terms of imprisonment that are measured [*phulakê hē metría*]." The second day after this proposal was rejected, in the dark a bit before dawn, the two generals landed about eight hundred hoplites on the island in the south—one group on the landward side, the other (no doubt with more difficulty) on the seaward side. Dashing forward, these commandoes overran the advanced post set up nearby by the Lacedaemonians and slaughtered the thirty hoplites quartered there. Then, at dawn, the remainder of the army came ashore.

Included in their number were eight hundred archers; a like number of peltasts; Messenian reinforcements from Naupactus; all of the other infantrymen at Coryphasium, apart from those garrisoning the fort; and more than two-thirds of the rowers on the seventy triremes in the Athenian fleet (all but the *thalamioí* situated deep in the hold of each vessel, who remained with the ships). It was a massive show of force involving something like eleven thousand men.

The son of Alcisthenes then divided them into groups of two hundred and sent them to occupy the high ground on every side in order to surround the main force of Lacedaemonian hoplites—which its commander Epitadas had deployed on flat ground near a freshwater well in the middle of the island— and subject it to cross fire, as arrows, darts, stones, and javelins rained down upon them. It was Aetolia all over again—this time with the positions reversed. If pursued, Demosthenes' men would flee; and, when the pursuers gave up the pursuit and turned, his men would be on them again. On the flat ground, his hoplites advanced a certain distance toward the main body of Epitadas' hoplites. Then, with the enemy pinned down, they halted while the light-armed troops on their flanks and behind the Lacedaemonians had at them, shouting in such a manner as to make it impossible for the latter to hear Epitadas' commands.

Eventually, the Lacedaemonians retreated in good order to the little fort that they had built and garrisoned on the heights of what is now called Mount Elias, near the northeastern end of the island, where they could no longer be outflanked—or so they assumed. There, for an extended period of time, the Lacedaemonians held their own until the Messenian contingent, led by an individual of some ingenuity named Komon, managed to worm its way unseen along the precipices above the sea (almost certainly on the island's less forbidding western side) to a point at Sphacteria's northeastern end behind the little fort, then climb to the heights above it, and from there rain down on its defenders projectiles of every conceivable sort.[14]

At this point, Cleon and Demosthenes called a halt and issued a proclamation inviting the Lacedaemonians' surrender. The Spartiates among the survivors were worth far more to the Athenians alive than dead. Their surrender would undercut Lacedaemon's prestige, and their value as hostages was incalculable.

Epidatas had been killed, and the next in command, though alive, had been left for dead. Styphon son of Pharax, who was in charge, requested permission to send a herald to the mainland to ask for instructions; and the Athenians, instead, summoned a herald from the Lacedaemonian camp on the edge of the bay. After this herald had traveled back and forth multiple times, Styphon and his men were told to deliberate among themselves concerning the matter but to do "nothing shameful." The point should have been crystal clear. No one had forgotten the example set at Thermopylae by Leonidas and the Three Hundred. But the men on the island had lost their commander and, with him, their bearings. They were defeated, dazed, and at a loss—and so, in despair, they resolved to do the unthinkable. Acknowledging defeat, they opted to hand themselves over with their arms.

Some seventy-two days after the Athenians had rowed into Navarino Bay, two hundred ninety-two Lacedaemonians were taken into custody—of whom roughly one hundred twenty were Spartiates. Mad though his promise had seemed, Cleon kept it, conveying them to Athens within the stipulated twenty days; and the assembly responded to this astonishing achievement by honoring him as if he were an Olympic victor. For him, they reserved a front seat at the theater, and to him they offered free meals in the prytaneum in company with the probouleutic council charged with setting the assembly's agenda. As Thucydides allows us to see, Aristophanes was right the following year when he had a character who almost certainly represents the son of Alcisthenes quip that he had himself prepared a cake and that Cleon had then filched it and successfully presented it to the people of Athens as his own confection.[15]

As Thucydides intimates, at this moment, the aura that the Lacedaemonians had acquired at Thermopylae began to dissipate. Of all the events that took place in the war, the historian observes, the surrender of the Spartans on Sphacteria was the one most contrary to what everyone took for granted. No one had hitherto believed that, in the face of starvation or any other species of necessity, the men of Lacedaemon would think it proper to hand over their weapons. They were expected to hold onto them, to fight, and die.

Many at Sparta and elsewhere found it hard to get their minds around the fact that those who had surrendered were *hómoioi*—"equal" to those who had been killed. When, in due course, the Athenians released the captives, the Lacedaemonians, who had long sought their release, did not quite know what to do with the returnees; and for a time they treated them not as fellow *hómoioi*, but as inferiors unworthy of the rights and prerogatives they had hitherto exercised as Spartiates. In the same spirit, someone from a city allied with Athens contemptuously asked one of the captives whether those who had fallen were not the *kaloì k̓agathoí*—"the gentlemen beautiful (or noble) and good (which is to say, brave)"; and from the Spartiate whom he had mocked, he elicited an answer no less redolent of disdain. Within the moral horizon of the hoplite, archery was work thought fit for women, not men; and so, substituting for arrow a term that conveyed its purportedly effeminate character, the man in captivity replied that "the spindle" that could single out the *agathoí* from the rest would be worth a lot.[16]

Athens on a Tear

In the aftermath of this victory, the Athenians doubled down on their commitments. First, at the suggestion of a member of the Council of 500 named Thudippus, who appears to have been a son-in-law of Cleon, they sharply increased the *phóros* demanded, bringing it to three times the sum required at the beginning of the war, dramatically raising the assessment on many (but not all) of the cities within their alliance, and demanding *phóros* from communities situated on the Black Sea and in the Aegean that had not hitherto been called upon for contributions. Then, at the insistence of Cleon himself, they increased by half the pay awarded jurors under the Periclean dispensation, and at this time they very likely voted to provide comparable compensation to the members of the Council of 500.[17]

Most important of all, however, the Athenians opted at this point to ratchet up the pressure they had brought to bear on Sparta and her allies. They announced that, if the Peloponnesians invaded Attica, they would put to death their prisoners; and promptly the invasions ceased. The "most suitable" of the Messenians from Naupactus they then conducted to Coryphasium, whence they began making exceedingly destructive incursions into the heartland of Messenia; and the Spartans, discovering that their helots were deserting and fearing a general uprising, began sending envoys again to Athens seeking peace and offering generous terms—despite, Thucydides emphasizes, a marked reluctance on their part to betray to the Athenians the degree to which they were vulnerable. To this, he adds, the Athenians, "reaching out for more," responded by sending embassy after embassy away with empty hands.[18]

Late in the campaigning season of 425, after Sphacteria had been secured, Nicias and two other generals set out for the Corinthiad from Athens with eighty triremes, two thousand Athenian hoplites, and two hundred cavalrymen and their mounts on horse transports, supported by an unspecified number of infantrymen sent from Miletus, Andros, and Carystus. The Corinthians had been forewarned and were out in full force awaiting the arrival of the Athenians, but Nicias and his colleagues nonetheless landed their troops in the dark and thereby caught them unawares, and there was a hard-fought battle near the village of Solygeia south-southwest of the isthmus—which the Athenians won, in large part because they had cavalry to deploy and the Corinthians had none. Then, after killing two hundred twelve Corinthians and their general and losing fifty of their own men, Nicias' force weighed anchor and struck at Crommyon, east of the isthmus, where his infantrymen ravaged the countryside and spent the night.[19]

The next day, they slipped down the coast, ravaged the farmland of Epidaurus, and set to work fortifying the narrow causeway linking the Argolic Acte with the little peninsula on which Methana was situated. The garrison they left at Methana, which lay between Epidaurus and Troezen opposite Aegina, subsequently mounted forays aimed at laying waste not only the territory of those two *póleis,* but also that of Halieis, which was situated nearby, at the entrance to the Gulf of Argos. It was not long before Troezen and Hermione found their way into alliance with Athens, as they had in the previous war, and Halieis followed suit.[20]

The Athenians were active as well in the Ionian Sea, where they consolidated their position of dominance. After the capture of Sphacteria, Eurymedon and Sophocles conducted their fleet to Corcyra, where, with the help of the city's democrats, they ousted the oligarchs from their stronghold on Mount Istone, forced their surrender; and, in keeping with Eurymedon's conduct two years before, put on a charade, feigning an attempt to prevent the massacre that the Corcyraean democrats then perpetrated. It was while the fleet commanded by these two men made its way from Corcyra to Sicily that the Acarnanians, with the help of the Athenians at Naupactus, seized Anactorium.[21]

The Athenians did not slacken the pace one iota during the campaigning season of 424. Early on, Nicias, Nicostratus, and Autocles son of Tolmaeus—whose patronymic suggests that he may have been a grandson of the Tolmides who had three decades before pioneered circumnavigating the Peloponnesus—set out from Athens with sixty ships, two thousand hoplites, a handful of cavalrymen, and additional hoplites from Miletus and elsewhere. Their aim was to seize Cythera—an island of modest size, inhabited at this time by Lacedaemonian *períoikoi,* governed by an official called the *Kuthērodíkēs* dispatched each year from Sparta, and defended by a garrison of Lacedaemonian hoplites. Situated, as it was, opposite Cape Malea, Cythera was of considerable strategic value. It was there that merchant ships from Egypt, Libya, and no doubt Phoenicia, Rhodes, and Crete landed. From there, as Tolmides had demonstrated after seizing the island thirty-two years before, ships could land ravagers at will in the Gulf of Laconia and the Gulf of Messenia; and the island was extremely useful also as a stopping point for ships circumnavigating the Peloponnesus.

As a feint, the Milesians and some of the Athenians landed in the little harbor at Scandea on the island's eastern shore while the rest landed on its northern shore, fought a battle for control of the lower city of Cythera, and drove the survivors into the upper city. Thanks in part to connections that Nicias had established in advance with certain of the island's residents, the

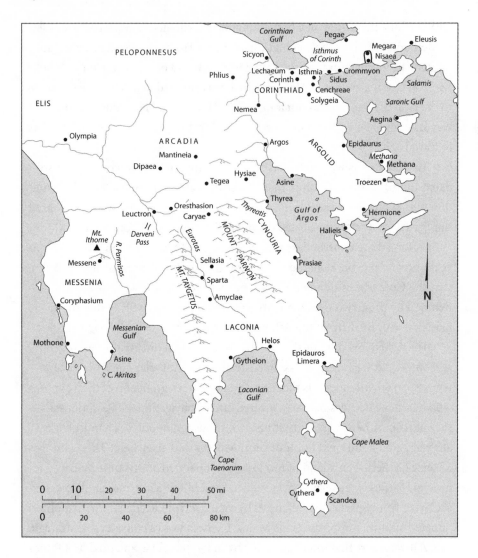

Map 18. The Athenians in the Corinthiad, at Epidaurus, on Cythera, in the Gulfs of
Messenia and Laconia, at Epidauros Limera, and at Thyrea

upper city soon surrendered on terms; and, after occupying the harbor at
Scandea, placing a garrison in the town of Cythera, and making the island
tributary, the Athenians spent a week ravaging places on the mainland nearby,
including Asine on the Gulf of Messenia, and Helos on the Gulf of Laconia.

By their defeats, the Spartans were, we are told, thrown into "the greatest
consternation," and these left them "bereft of the audacity requisite for battle."

So nowhere did they resist the Athenian attacks. They did establish garrisons of hoplites at various strategic locations near the coast, but their aim was less to oppose incursions than to deter rebellion. According to Thucydides, the Spartans' deepest fear was that the Athenian raids would set off a helot uprising. It was with this danger in mind that, contrary to established practice, they raised a cavalry troop of four hundred and a force of archers; and it may have been at this time that they freed a few hundred helots, armed them, and deployed them against those still in servitude. If the Athenians "always supposed something not attempted an achievement squandered," the Lacedaemonians (who had always been cautious) were now, we are told, "in matters of war far more hesitant than before."[22]

While en route back to Athens, the fleet commanded by Nicias, Nicostratus, and Autocles paused at Epidauros Limera on the eastern coast of Laconia with an eye to ravaging that town's territory. Then, moving north, these three generals landed a force on the coast of Cynouria, marched inland a mile to Thyrea, and pillaged and burnt the town. The Lacedaemonian commander stationed there they captured and added to the Spartiates incarcerated at Athens, and they killed or seized for execution the Aeginetan exiles whom they encountered.[23]

Not to be outdone, Demosthenes and his colleague, Pericles' nephew Hippocrates son of Ariphron, mounted an attempt that same summer to seize Megara. The blockade and the semi-annual invasions of the Megarid had produced the intended results. The political community was wracked by civil strife. A democratic uprising in the city had driven the ruling oligarchs out; and, after being settled by the Thebans in temporary quarters at Plataea, the latter had seized Pegae, the Megarian port on the Corinthian Gulf. From there, they had then conducted raids on the farmland tilled by their opponents—which served only to redouble the Megarians' misery. When the people in the town began discussing the possibility of reaching a reconciliation with the oligarchs at Pegae, the leaders responsible for the original uprising began to fear for their lives, and in desperation some of them turned to Demosthenes and his colleague, thinking it less dangerous for them that they betray the city to the Athenians than that a reconciliation take place. Their plan was, first, to let the Athenians seize the Long Walls linking the town with Nisaea, its port on the Saronic Gulf, so that they could slaughter or drive out the Peloponnesian garrison lodged there and prevent the Corinthians and the other Peloponnesians from marching to the city's defense. Once the Athenians controlled these walls, they calculated, it would be easy to persuade those dwelling in Megara to surrender.[24]

In its first stage, this plan was implemented without a hitch. At night, in the harbor at Nisaea, Hippocrates landed on the tiny island of Minoa with six hundred hoplites while the son of Alcisthenes with light-armed troops from Plataea and a mobile force of young frontier guardsmen stationed himself closer to the walls. Shortly before dawn, as planned, when the gates in the Long Walls were opened as on previous nights to let out a rowboat on a cart that the Megarians who had invited Athens' intervention ostentatiously employed for nocturnal raiding, the Athenians rushed in and the Peloponnesian garrison panicked and fled to Nisaea. In Megara, however, the plot was betrayed, the gates of the city were at the crucial moment kept shut, and the four thousand hoplites and six hundred cavalrymen who had made their way stealthily by night from Eleusis in Attica were unable to force their way in. The Athenians did, however, manage to invest Nisaea; and the garrison that had fled there, being bereft of provisions, surrendered on terms and turned over their Spartan commander to the Athenians.

The town itself might have capitulated had Brasidas not been nearby in the vicinity of Sicyon and Corinth, recruiting a mercenary force. But, when alerted, he summoned the Boeotians, who feared being cut off from their allies in the Peloponnesus; and he rallied the Corinthians, Phliasians, and Sicyonians, who lived nearby. Though unable initially to persuade the Megarians to allow him into the city, he quickly enough had in hand a force of six thousand hoplites and a sizable contingent of Boeotian cavalry. With this he confronted the Athenians—whose generals flinched, telling themselves (and no doubt others thereafter) that they had gained most of what they wanted and that the remaining rewards were not worth the risk.

This was a grave blunder on the part of Demosthenes and Hippocrates. The remaining rewards were of tremendous strategic worth. They included not only the capacity to obstruct, if not block, egress from the Peloponnesus—but also an ability to impede, if not prevent, entry into that great peninsula by the Thebans and their Boeotian allies should they be summoned to defend Lacedaemon against a helot rebellion or a local anti-Spartan coalition like the one led by Argos in the 460s and 450s. Moreover, had the Athenians been defeated, they could have fallen back on Nisaea. As a consequence of the Athenian generals' failure of nerve, Brasidas and his men were admitted into Megara. Then, the Atticizers fled the city; the exiles in Pegae returned; and, ignoring their promise that there would be a general amnesty, they staged a coup, executed roughly one hundred of their enemies, established in the city a narrow oligarchy profoundly hostile to Athens, and succeeded in stabilizing the regime. Not long thereafter, they seized control of the Long Walls linking the city with Nisaea and tore them down. Thanks to a lack of strategic comprehension on the part of Demosthenes and Hippocrates, the effort that Athens had put into blockading Megara and ravaging her territory year after year had come to little.[25]

Had Pericles been alive, he would no doubt have seized on the victory at Sphacteria to negotiate a peace with Lacedaemon favorable to Athens' ambitions and fatal to the Peloponnesian League. Had peace not been an option, however, he would have favored everything, thus far mentioned, that the Athenians did in the aftermath of that victory—above all, the attempt to seize Megara. For anything that put pressure on the Lacedaemonians, that humiliated them, and that encouraged their allies in the Peloponnesus (Corinth, first and foremost) to abandon them was consistent with his long-term aim.

In only one particular would the son of Xanthippus have been critical. Lacedaemon's center of gravity lay not on the coast, where Athens was harrying her and her allies, but in the interior. It mattered what Halieis, Troezen, and Hermione did—but not a lot. From a defensive perspective—and also from an offensive perspective, given the proximity of Pegae to Lechaeum, Corinth's port on the Corinthian Gulf—Megara was much more strategically significant, but she was important chiefly for the defense of Attica. She was not essential to Sparta's security. The key to Lacedaemon's survival was the hoplite army that she could gather from Corinth, Epidaurus, Sicyon, Phlius, Elis, and the communities, both large and small, scattered throughout Arcadia. If they remained loyal and if she managed to keep her helots under control, she would be secure, and she would have the wherewithal to make a comeback, as she had in 446. All that would then be required of her was patience and cunning, which the Spartans possessed in abundance.

Cleon, who appears to have directed Athenian policy in this period, was by no means oblivious to the sources of Spartan strength. We have evidence, in fact, that he was dickering with the Argives—one of the keys to attracting Lacedaemon's core allies away from her alliance. As we have seen, in 451, when Cimon negotiated a truce between Athens and Sparta, Argos, which suddenly found herself isolated, had made a peace of thirty years' duration with the Lacedaemonians. By the late 420s, that agreement had very nearly run its course; and, in 424, in his comedy *The Cavalrymen,* Aristophanes alludes to negotiations that Cleon was conducting with Sparta's ancient enemy. It is possible that these discussions were already taking place the year before. For we are not only told that, early in that campaigning season, the Corinthians were forewarned regarding Nicias' descent on the Corinthiad; Thucydides also indicates that the warning that they had received had come from Argos. There are various ways that certain parties in Argos could have learned of Nicias' plan, but the most likely is that the Athenians had sought Argive participation in their expedition against her neighbors Corinth and Epidaurus.[26]

Cleon did not, however, understand the manner in which a peace pact can be deployed as an instrument of war. He had not reflected on the damage that a humiliating settlement of the outstanding differences would have done to relations between Lacedaemon and Corinth, and he did not recognize the damage that a breach between those two cities would have done to the Spartan alliance more generally. Cleon was quick-witted, to say the least. But indirection was not his strong suit, and patience was not among his virtues. When the Peloponnesians first invaded Attica in 431, he was among those who advocated marching out to fight and who railed against Pericles' policy of strategic restraint.

The Road to Delium

Even worse, however, Cleon and his compatriots seem not to have grasped the dangers attendant on risky ventures in peripheral areas. Had they understood what Pericles had learned from the Egyptian debacle and from the massacre attendant on Tolmides' defeat at Coronea, they would certainly have put a stop to the scheme cooked up late in the summer of 424 by Demosthenes and Hippocrates.

These two had their eyes on Boeotia. For Demosthenes, this was nothing new, as he had demonstrated when he conducted his abortive invasion of Aetolia. Boeotia was also a concern of Pericles' nephew, who had ostentatiously

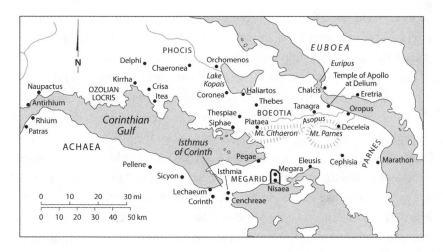

Map 19. The Corinthian Gulf, the Megarid, and Boeotia

championed the interests of the Plataeans. He it was who had introduced the decree making these refugees citizens of Athens. Now, the aim of the two was to revive and improve upon the ill-fated enterprise that the son of Alcisthenes had undertaken two years before.

This time, Demosthenes was to conduct his incursion into Boeotia by sea. He was to take forty triremes to Naupactus. There he was to raise an army from among the Acarnanians and Athens' other allies in the region. Then, in November, with this army aboard his fleet, he was to descend on Siphae, a harbor town in the territory of Thespiae, situated in the bay of Crisa on the Corinthian Gulf—which a local faction, intent on instigating a democratic revolution, had promised to betray. Soon thereafter, a similar faction in Orchomenos, Thebes' chief Boeotian rival, was to seize Orchomenos' dependency Chaeronea—with the aid of some exiled Orchomenians and their associates from across the border in Phocis.

While this was causing a commotion in northwestern and southwestern Boeotia, Hippocrates was to lead an army from Athens into the territory of Tanagra in the southeast. There, he was to occupy the sanctuary of Apollo at Delium—situated a mile beyond Oropus near the Gulf of Euboea opposite Chalcis—and fortify the place, as Demosthenes had the headland at Coryphasium. Had this scheme worked, the enemies of Thebes would have had three bases in different parts of Boeotia from which to launch raiding parties and foment revolution. If this series of preliminary maneuvers worked, there would soon be a general uprising against the hated Thebans throughout Boeotia. So, at least, the instigators supposed.[27]

In so complex an enterprise, there is much that can go amiss; and, on this occasion, the son of Alcisthenes had once again failed to gauge accurately the likelihood of success and the risks involved. The consequence was a disaster. To begin with, a Phocian who had gotten wind of the plan betrayed it to the Lacedaemonians, who in turn alerted the Thebans. Thanks to this, the uprising at Siphae and the attempt on Chaeronea were nipped in the bud, and what was supposed to take place simultaneously took place seriatim. Demosthenes, who may have learned in advance about the betrayal, arrived at Siphae earlier than planned—but not early enough, for he found the place already occupied by the partisans of Thebes.

By the time that Hippocrates reached Delium with a full levy from Athens—not only of the citizens but also of the metics and of the allied forces present in the city—the Thebans and their associates were finished with their work at Siphae and Chaeronea. Thus, while for five days the host of light-armed troops accompanying Hippocrates' army busied themselves digging a trench and constructing a wall of mud, timber, and stones to fortify Delium, the enemy was mustering at Tanagra—apparently, unbeknownst to the Athenians. Then—persuaded, against the counsel of the other Boetarchs, by their Theban commander Pagondas son of Aeolidas—they marched east and fell upon the Athenian hoplites as the latter were making their way toward home. The battle took place a mile or two south of Delium between two ravines in the hill country of Oropus, on the Athenian side of Athens' border with Boeotia, at a moment when the unwitting Hippocrates was short of cavalry and had already sent his light-armed troops ahead. The Boeotians had seven thousand hoplites in the field as well as one thousand cavalrymen, five hundred peltasts, and more than ten thousand light-armed troops. The Athenians had a like number of hoplites, many fewer cavalrymen, and no light-armed troops worth mentioning; and oblivious to the danger, while their commander was dawdling at Delium, they had paused to wait for his arrival at the bottom of a hill—where they were especially vulnerable to assault.

In the battle that followed, Pagondas outgeneraled Hippocrates—in part, by employing a technique that, to the best of our knowledge, had never before been tried. Ordinarily, at this time, the hoplite phalanx was formed up at all points in the line in precisely the same fashion—eight men deep—and that is what the Athenians did. On the right of the Boeotian army, however, where the Thebans were posted, Pagondas did something unprecedented. Thanks to the two ravines on either side, the space available for battle was confined. There was no danger that either army would be outflanked. So he had the hoplites on his right form up twenty-five men deep. In this fashion, they could bring their superior weight to bear against one section of the enemy line.

On their own right, the Athenians put most of the Boeotians posted opposite them to flight. The Thespians—who distinguished themselves from the Tanagraeans and Orchomenians posted alongside them by stubbornly holding their ground—they surrounded and slaughtered; and in the confusion, as they closed in on the Thespians, they killed a number of their own compatriots. Then, when, at Pagondas' direction, two squadrons of Boeotian horsemen suddenly appeared from behind a hill, these Athenians, already in disorder, panicked and ran.

On their left, the Athenians remained in formation, with their interlocking shields forming a wall. But they were shoved back and back again and again by the Thebans, precisely as Pagondas had calculated—until, startled by the collapse of their right wing, they, too, took flight. The Athenians then scattered and fled—some toward Mount Parnes, some back toward Delium, and others east toward Oropus (among them the philosopher Socrates, the once and future general Laches, and a gallant young cavalryman of noble birth named Alcibiades son of Cleinias, about whom we shall soon have much to say). Along the way many of those in flight were caught and cut down by the Boeotian cavalry and by the horsemen whom the Boeotians had summoned from Opuntian Locris to the north. Had it not been for nightfall, we are told, the casualties would have been much more numerous than they were.[28]

Seventeen days later, the Boeotians recovered Delium. First, they constructed a primitive flamethrower—the first of which we have any knowledge. It consisted of a tube through which, with the help of bellows, they could hurl fire into the timbers sustaining the wall that the Athenians had built to fortify the sanctuary. Then, with help from abroad—darters and slingers from the Gulf of Malia, two thousand Corinthian hoplites, the garrison that had evacuated Nisaea, and a handful of Megarians—they overran the sanctuary, captured two hundred Athenians, and slaughtered everyone else on whom they could lay their hands. When the two battles were finally over, Pagondas, whom his kinsman the poet Pindar had memorialized as a youth, had much to celebrate. The Boeotians had lost no more than five hundred men (most of them Thespians and Tanagraeans); and the Athenians, close to one thousand (including their general, Hippocrates). Demosthenes had also lost a handful of men when, having been turned away from Siphae, he led his armada against Sicyon and the soldiers he landed on shore suffered a rout. The Thebans had a vast trove of discarded shields, breastplates, grieves, and helmets to display and sufficient booty and ransom money to allow them to build a stoa in their market and to establish a festival in honor of Apollo of Delium.[29]

Delium was a severe setback for the Athenians. In part, this was material. In 431, the full levy of citizen and metic hoplites had been thirteen thousand. Thanks to the plague and the losses that the Athenians and Athens' metics had suffered in battle, that number had by 424 declined to fewer than seven thousand. The loss of a thousand more at Delium, 14 percent of the phalanx, was a serious blow—exceeding in the overall proportion of heavy infantrymen killed on the field every other pitched battle of which we have detailed knowledge.

In part, the setback was moral. It put an end to the euphoria to which Demosthenes' victory at Sphacteria had given rise. Moreover, like the debacle at Coronea in 446, it appears to have inspired a rebellion on the part of the Eretrians and Chalcidians just across the straits in Euboea. If, however, the report we have is accurate, the Athenians quickly crushed the uprising, and Thucydides did not consider it even worth mentioning.[30]

There were, however, worse developments under way. Cleon and his compatriots had miscalculated in another important particular. Athens' refusal to negotiate a peace and the pressure she had brought to bear on Lacedaemon had had the effect of strengthening politically those among the Spartans who had all along argued that they had to be much more aggressive. The Lacedaemonians might be timid and hesitant, but they were not cowards. When they were cornered and pummeled, the handful in their number who were prepared to imitate in audacity Sparta's Athenian foe came to the fore.

The Lacedaemonians and their allies did not have the resources requisite for striking at Athens by sea. The remnants of the Peloponnesian fleet had been handed over to the Athenians in Navarino Bay. There was, however, one district of importance within Athens' dominion that the Spartans might be able to reach by land. Early in the war, there had been a rebellion in western Thrace at Bottiaea and in what was then called the Chalcidice; and, though the

Athenians had retaken Potidaea, they had not, despite repeated efforts, been able to quell the larger uprising and seize the Bottiaean stronghold at Spartolus and the city of Olynthus, where the Chalcidian rebels had found refuge.[31] This the Spartans had noted; and, when they founded Heracleia Trachinia near Thermopylae on the Gulf of Malia, they did so, as we have seen, in part with an eye to having a station on the way to Thrace.

In 424, when Demosthenes and Hippocrates had tried to take Megara and Brasidas happened to have been nearby in the vicinity of Corinth and Sicyon, he was there with a host of liberated helots, mustering a supplementary force of mercenaries with which he intended to march on and beyond western Thrace—and it was this that he did with his little army of seventeen hundred hoplites shortly after saving Megara from seizure by the Athenians.[32] Demosthenes, Hippocrates, and their compatriots would have been well-advised to forgo their pointless quest to restore Athens' hegemony within Boeotia and to focus their attention, instead, on the enterprise undertaken by the man who had almost single-handedly forestalled their attempt to recover for Athens the strategically vital Megarid corridor. There are times when an individual has more sway than a multitude; and Brasidas was, as we shall soon see, that sort of man.

Part III

A Peace to End All Peace

He will win who knows when to fight and when not to fight.

SUN TZŪ

THE resources that Lacedaemon devoted to Brasidas' endeavor amounted to next to nothing. Tellis' brave son was almost entirely on his own. There were, as far as we can tell, no other Spartiates and no *períoikoi* in his company. The seven hundred able-bodied helots whom he took with him—these men the Spartans were happy to be rid of. As we have had occasion to note, spirited young fellows of this class they regarded less as an asset than as a threat.[1]

Apart from Brasidas himself, the only resources put at risk in the summer of 424 were the funds required for feeding his helots and hiring mercenaries, and there is no reason to suppose that any of this money was supplied by Lacedaemon. There were no doubt individuals at Sparta who had high hopes regarding the expedition. As a warrior, the son of Tellis was much admired. But there is no indication that the hopeful were numerous, and the political community as such was not willing to wager much of anything on his success.

What Brasidas had going for him was an invitation and a promise of financial and military support from the Chalcidian rebels and from Perdiccas of Macedon, who feared that the Athenians, who were then on a roll, would once again renew their pacification efforts in the Thraceward region. The son of Tellis could rely as well on the longing for full freedom secretly communicated by many within the subject communities of Athens' empire, on the resentment to which the dramatic increase in the *phóros* assessed on the cities in the Thraceward region must have given rise, and on his own abundant enthusiasm, courage, and resourcefulness.[2]

The Road to Amphipolis

Brasidas was not behindhand. As soon as affairs at Megara were settled, he completed his recruitment effort; and, at about the time that Demosthenes sailed for Naupactus, he and those under his command set out through Boeotia and Phocis for Heracleia Trachinia. From there, with the help of his *xénoi*—his guest-friends—at Pharsalus and of Perdiccas, who exercised considerable influence in Thessaly, he and his men crossed into that region, bamboozled those who initially challenged their presence there, and then hotfooted it some seventy miles, managing to pass through the entirety of Thessaly, which was nominally allied with Athens, and to reach Dium in Macedonia in three long days—before serious opposition could be concerted.[3]

The Athenians were not oblivious to Brasidas' venture. He may well have made it to Heracleia Trachinia unremarked, but his progress through Thessaly is bound to have been reported, and we are told that the Athenians responded once he reached western Thrace. To the best of our knowledge, however, they took no serious countermeasures—apart from declaring war on Perdiccas and instructing their commanders in the region to keep a close watch on Athens' allies. To have dispatched an infantry force to counter Brasidas' efforts would have been to reduce the resources available for the venture in Boeotia projected by Demosthenes and Hippocrates. As they had been earlier in the runup to the rebellions at Samos, Potidaea, and Mytilene, the Athenians were once again overconfident and slow to take heed.

While the Athenians were wasting precious time, making preparations for a risky, strategically insignificant enterprise, Brasidas was making excellent use of every available minute. When Perdiccas sought to employ his army as an instrument for resolving the quarrels internal to the Macedonian monarchy, he brushed his paymaster off and marched without further ado all the way across what we now call the Chalcidice to Acanthus, a colony of Andros situated between the Strymonian Gulf and the Gulf of Singos at the entrance to the Acte peninsula—a few miles from the narrow point where Xerxes had had a canal cut through the isthmus linking Mount Athos with the mainland. The year was 424, and it was mid-August or very early September when Brasidas and his army arrived—and, as he no doubt knew when he abandoned Perdiccas, in those parts the grape harvest was about to begin. Recognizing that the year's vintage was at stake, even those in Acanthus who were risk-averse were willing to listen to the interloper. And hear him out they did. For Thucydides was correct when he observed that Brasidas "was, though a Spartan, not incapable as an orator"; and he provides us with a comprehensive summary of the seductive line of reasoning that the Lacedaemonian articulated to good effect both there on this occasion and elsewhere as he made his way through western Thrace.[4]

Brasidas was not just eloquent. He was a smooth talker—perfectly willing to stretch the truth. He approached the Acanthians and the members of the other political communities he encountered in much the same manner as Archidamus had approached the Plataeans in 429—with a promise and a threat. It was liberty that he promised. The Lacedaemonians had gone to war, as they had claimed at the outset, to free the Greeks. If their arrival in Thrace had been delayed, it was only because they had wrongly supposed that they could effect a defeat of the Athenians without putting the cities of Thrace in danger. So he said.

Brasidas also feigned surprise and dismay that the Acanthians had shut their gates against him. He and his compatriots had thought them allies apt to extend a warm welcome to their liberators, and this was why he and his men had taken the risks associated with their long and dangerous march through Hellas to Thrace. He could not imagine that a city like Acanthus, so worthy of note, boasting citizens "supposed to be in possession of intelligence," would take a stand in opposition to her "own freedom and that of the other Greeks." He feared that, if the Acanthians did so, it would make his task of persuasion harder elsewhere, causing others to suppose that the cause he professed was unworthy of trust; that his promise of liberty was false and his intentions unjust; or that the little army with which he had recently forced the Athenians to back off at Megara was inadequate for their defense.

To the Acanthians, Brasidas promised autonomy, and he claimed that he had made the authorities at Lacedaemon swear to honor this promise. He firmly denied that he and his compatriots would act as they often had in the past and install oligarchies in the cities that joined their alliance. It was not their purpose to turn Acanthus over to the few or the many. If the Spartans failed to honor these commitments, he acknowledged that they would rightly become more hated than were the Athenians.

Finally, this eloquent Spartan issued a warning, pledging that if, after coming all this way to confer on the Acanthians a benefit, he was rejected, he would under the constraint of necessity lay waste their land—without in any way supposing his action unjust. For if they continued to contribute funds to the Athenians, they would be harming the Lacedaemonians and preventing their fellow Greeks from throwing off servitude. The Spartans had, he asserted, no desire for dominion. They had come to destroy an empire, not to build one. And he would be doing the great majority of the Hellenes a grave injustice if he were to overlook the opposition of the Acanthians to their autonomy.[5]

Such was the argument advanced by Brasidas. It was beguiling and inspiring. It was deceptive and threatening. It appealed to the interests and the pride of those who heard it—and it worked at Acanthus where the citizens debated the question, then voted by secret ballot to admit his forces on one crucial condition reflective of their conviction that the Spartans really were god-fearing men: that this Spartiate warrior solemnly confirm with his own oath that the authorities at Lacedaemon had actually sworn to respect the autonomy of those in the Thraceward region who became their allies. The same mixture of enticement, deception, and threats proved effective later elsewhere—in late summer, for example, at Stagira and in the winter at Argilos, both of them also colonies of Andros; then at Amphipolis; at the Edonian city of Myrcinus; at the Thasian colonies Galepsos and Oisyme; and eventually at Torone, Scione, Mende, and no doubt elsewhere within what we now call the Chalcidice.[6]

Of the cities that went over to Brasidas, Amphipolis was by far the most important. As we have already had occasion to note, this settlement was situated on an exceedingly well-fortified site of great strategic importance located on the eastern bank of the river Strymon, astride the great road linking Epidamnus in the west with Byzantium in the east. All traffic passing from western to eastern Thrace had to negotiate the bridge that spanned that river nearby at its narrowest point. This strategically vital crossing lay roughly eleven hundred yards northwest of the inner circuit built by Hagnon around Amphipolis' acropolis and a short distance north of the northwestern corner of the much more extensive walls the Athenian had planned, which were at this time in the north near completion. By means of these fortifications, the Amphipolitans and their mother city were not only in a position to regulate the commerce that ran up and down that river. Thereby, they also dominated a region replete with timber, including fir well-suited to the construction of triremes; and they exercised considerable leverage over the Daton valley to the northeast, where, on the slopes of Mount Pangaeum, there were rich mines in which gold and

Map 20. The Delian League's Thraceward Region

silver could be found in abundance. Although Athens did not collect *phóros* as such from Amphipolis, she drew income from her colony on a considerable scale.

Had Hagnon, the oecist charged by the Athenians with the city's foundation, been able to populate Amphipolis to any great extent with his compatriots, this great fortress would have become a permanent anchor for Athens' dominion in Thrace. But, in 437, as we have seen, Athens was short of manpower, and Hagnon had to look elsewhere for settlers. Many of those who volunteered came from Argilos nearby and even more, we have reason to suspect, from the cities said to have been founded long before in what we now call the Chalcidice by Euboean Chalcis and her neighbor Eretria. As one would expect, these Amphipolitans shared the predilections of their erstwhile compatriots, and this rendered them no less susceptible than the Argilians and Chalcidians had been to the blandishments on offer from the Spartan interloper.

The Athenians were not entirely unprepared for what was to come. At the time of Brasidas' attack, two of the ten generals elected for the year 424/3 were stationed in the Thraceward region. Eucles was situated at Amphipolis, where he presumably had a number of Athenian infantrymen in his entourage but, to all appearances, no proper garrison under his command. Thucydides the historian was operating from Thasos with a flotilla of seven triremes. The ordinary complement of infantrymen per trireme was ten. Where amphibious

landings were contemplated, there might be as many as forty. The son of Olorus had no more than two hundred eighty marines under his command, and
he is apt to have had no more than seventy.

It is conceivable that these two generals were dispatched from Athens
when word arrived that Brasidas had reached western Thrace. But it is far
more likely that they were sent out earlier when they assumed office and that
this division of labor, their posting, and the limited military resources placed
at their disposal reflected in a rough and ready way the dispositions that we
know the Athenians had made at the beginning of the war with an eye to securing their empire. As we have seen, something of the sort appears to have
been Athens' practice with regard to other strategic locations, such as Atalante
and Naupactus. Thucydides' testimony concerning these dispositions overall
suggests that modest precautions of this sort were the norm; and when Thucydides tells us that Eucles was "guardian [*phúlax*]" of Amphipolis, he may be
indicating that the man bore a title analogous to that of the "Guardians of the
Hellespont [*Hellespontophúlakes*]" known to have been stationed at Byzantium in the early years of the war.[7]

To counter Brasidas and the Macedonians, Bottiaeans, and Chalcidians
allied with him, the Athenians should have immediately dispatched two or
even three thousand hoplites, a corps of cavalry, and a fleet to convey them
from one place to another under the command of two or more experienced
generals. Instead, in the months in which Brasidas was working his way toward
Amphipolis, those in charge were preoccupied with the Boeotian distraction.

Once he was ready, Brasidas moved, as was his wont, with breathtaking
celerity. It was now December. In this season, the temperature in Thrace can
be exceedingly cold; the days are invariably short; and the nights, long. On this
particular occasion, the weather was stormy—and the Spartan took full advantage of the situation. He started from what we now call the Chalcidice and
made his way to Bromiscus, where Lake Bolbe empties into the Aegean. Come
evening, he then journeyed twelve miles further to Argilos, which, thanks to
negotiations that had taken place before his departure, went over to him without a struggle. Finally, ripping a page out of the Athenian playbook, in the wee
morning hours, under cover of darkness, he marched with guides from Argilos the six miles separating that community from the bridge leading over the
Strymon to Amphipolis.

At first, everything went according to plan. Shortly before dawn, in the midst of a light snowstorm, Brasidas surprised the small squadron posted to guard the bridge. Its defenders, with the help of treachery, he quickly overwhelmed. Then, he crossed the span and seized control of the countryside outside the inner circuit surrounding the acropolis and the other high ground making up what Thucydides calls the Amphipolitan *pólisma*. There, in the suburbs, a substantial proportion of the community's population was domiciled and had been left vulnerable, thanks to the fact that the more extensive walls envisaged by Hagnon were as yet in the north incomplete. It was Brasidas' hope that those secretly enlisted in advance by Perdiccas and by the Chalcidians and Argilians would immediately throw open the gates of the inner circuit and betray the *pólisma* to him.

Eucles, the Athenians in his entourage, and those of the Amphipolitans not privy to the conspiracy were caught napping. Within the inner circuit, there was great confusion and mutual distrust; and some, in the aftermath, suspected that, had Brasidas pressed his advantage by immediately launching an attack, he would have succeeded. Instead, however, mindful of what he could gain from nurturing a reputation for eliciting consent, the Spartan tarried, hoping that those recruited by his allies within the community would prevail and deliver the citadel to him. That this did not happen right away was due to the presence of a number of erstwhile Athenians in the citizen body, to others fearful of the invader and accustomed to Athens' dominion, and to the efforts of Eucles and his companions, who soon dispatched a message—perhaps, as some scholars have suggested, with the aid of a signaling device—to Thucydides on Thasos half a day's sail away.

The historian was a man of some influence in the region, and that is no doubt why he was stationed there. He had, he tells us, the right to work certain gold mines nearby, and he appears to have been in part of Thracian descent. We know that he was related to Cimon, and his father Olorus bore the name of the Thracian prince who had been Cimon's maternal grandfather. It is conceivable that, if Amphipolis had held out and he had been allowed some weeks, he might have been able to rally his Thracian kinsmen against the Spartan invader. At Amphipolis, however, Brasidas soon learned what he might be up against; and, in his eagerness to secure the town before Thucydides could reach it from Thasos, he resorted, as he had at Acanthus and elsewhere, to persuasion.

We are not told everything that the proclamation which Brasidas issued contained, but it is highly probable that in it he made in brief the same pitch that had worked elsewhere. What we do know with certainty is that he followed through on what he had done at Acanthus and offered the Amphipolitans generous terms. The citizens were to retain their civic rights. Those captured outside the *pólisma* would, we must assume, be released. Moreover, those who wished to withdraw were accorded five days in which to do so, and they were told that they could take their personal property with them.

As Brasidas and the Amphipolitans surely knew, there was no one nearby capable of coming quickly and effectively to their rescue. Some scholars insist that Thucydides should have been stationed at the stronghold and trading post maintained by the Athenians some three miles south-southeast of Amphipolis at Eion on the Aegean coast, where the Strymon flowed into the Aegean. Some even contend that he could then have defended the city.

None of this makes any sense. The Athenians had not one but two prize possessions in the region—one on the Strymon in Thrace and the other offshore—and they had quite appropriately posted one general at each. Amphipolis was not the only place that needed watching. Given her wealth in gold, silver, lead, copper, marble, and timber, there was always a possibility that Thasos would once again rebel; and the well-protected and well-equipped military harbor on the island's north shore was, in fact, the perfect place for posting a small Athenian fleet prepared at short notice to intervene anywhere in the region. Moreover, with the breakwaters, moles, and shipsheds still in evidence today, the military harbor at Thasos was an excellent place in which to wait out the winter—when one northeaster after another descended on the northern Aegean—and there, at leisure, one could recaulk, repair, and refit one's galleys.

In any case, had Thucydides been stationed at Eion, there is little that he could have done of immediate practical use once the Spartan and his men had stormed the Strymon bridge. The son of Olorus did not have on hand or at his beck and call a force of footsoldiers capable of driving off in short order the seventeen hundred hoplites under Brasidas' command. The most that he might have accomplished had he marched up from Eion with his marines and managed to slip past Brasidas' men and into the *pólisma* would have been to bolster Amphipolitan morale and reinforce Eucles' promise that help would eventually come.

As it turned out, however, in the time that it took for Thucydides to equip his fleet and in the five to six hours required for the flotilla under his command to make its way from Thasos to Eion, the Amphipolitans had calmed down. Like the Acanthians before them, they then deliberated concerning what it would cost them to resist the invader and what might be gained from rebellion. And upon sober consideration—mindful, above all else, that many of their kinsmen and fellow citizens were hostages at the mercy of the invader—a majority voted to let the Spartan and his men enter the *pólisma* and take control. Thucydides did manage to prevent Brasidas from seizing Eion, and he repelled a subsequent attack on that stronghold mounted soon thereafter by that enterprising man.[8]

We do not know what happened to Eucles in the aftermath. He may have been killed at Amphipolis. He may have been allowed to leave. Cleon may well have seen to it that he was exiled by the Athenians—which is what, a late source tells us, he did in the case of Thucydides. Eucles had certainly been remiss. The Strymon bridge was of crucial importance for the defense of Amphipolis and eastern Thrace; and, especially given Brasidas' presence in the region, it should have been properly guarded. But Eucles had not been nearly as remiss as his compatriots at Athens—who, when they learned of Brasidas' venture, had failed to take appropriate countermeasures. It was, in fact, only at this point, after they had lost their most important strategic asset on the Thracian mainland, that the Athenians began to pay serious attention to the threat posed by the Spartan interloper. As they quickly recognized, eastern Thrace—including, we must suppose, the Thracian Chersonnesus, Sestos, Byzantium, and the umbilical cord running through the Hellespont, the Propontis, and the Bosporus, which linked Athens with the Black Sea—was now within the Spartan's reach. Although it was winter and travel by sea was perilous, the Athenians now, finally, sent garrisons to the cities still in their control. Even at this point, however, the number of hoplites dispatched was unequal to the task, as we shall soon see.[9]

Torone and Scione

In the meantime, Thucydides tells us, Brasidas was deluged with clandestine invitations from within the cities under Athens' yoke. To Lacedaemon, he sent dispatches requesting reinforcements; and in the shipyards along the Strymon—where, we must suspect, the Amphipolitans had for some time been building triremes for the Athenians—he began producing these great galleys for his own use. It was at this time that he began having grain stored and panoplies produced for the young men of the region whom he hoped to recruit for service as hoplites and that he roped in Myrcinus, Galepsos, and Oisyme and brought over most of the cities on the Acte peninsula.[10]

Thereafter, Brasidas marched on Torone, a prosperous settlement, then already quite ancient, of considerable strategic importance. This city, which advertised her viticulture on her coins, was situated at the top of a headland that curled out from the western shore of Sithonia, the central of the three prongs extending south-southeast from what we now call the Chalcidice. Located a few miles north of that long peninsula's tip, this *pólis* was blessed with two harbors. One of these (called "the Quiet Harbor" then and, by the same token, Porto Koupho today) was an inlet, situated a mile or so down the coast from the town, which was so well protected from the sea by the mountainous terrain to the east and by a high ridge to the west that it was proverbially sheltered from noise even in the midst of the greatest blow. The other harbor was located in a bay (more extensive and inviting in antiquity than it is now) just to the east of a narrow promontory, shaped like an oil bottle and called for that reason Lekythos, which stretched out in a northwestern direction from the town into the gulf separating Sithonia from the Pallene peninsula just nine miles to the west.

In the northern Aegean, squalls and tempests are by no means infrequent. The prevailing winds blow from the northeast; and thanks to the forbidding coast along the southern half of the eastern shore of the Acte peninsula, in antiquity, the waters about what we now call the Chalcidice were, as the Persian commander Mardonius learned to his dismay, perilous in the extreme. The canal subsequently cut through that peninsula on the orders of the Achaemenid king Xerxes was still at this time in operation, and it reduced the dangers considerably. But it was nonetheless necessary that maritime travelers risk the open sea while rounding Sithonia and Pallene, and there disasters could and did take place.

Torone's importance stemmed in part from the fact that hers were quite literally the perfect ports in a storm. Both harbors were sheltered from northeasters by the mountain range that formed a ridge down the center of the peninsula, and we can surmise that the community profited handsomely from the harbor dues she was in a position to charge, which may explain why the

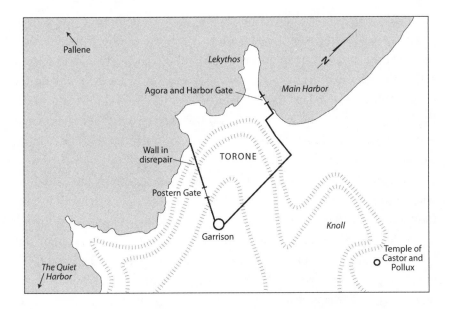

Map 21. Torone

Athenians thought it appropriate to impose on the city in 425 an annual assessment in silver of fifteen talents (more than two-fifths of a ton). As a refuge from bad weather of all kinds, Torone is still treasured by mariners today.[11]

As was his wont, Brasidas proceeded, in the manner of the Athenians, by stealth. To reach the town of Torone, he had to conduct his hoplites and the one hundred or more peltasts supplied by his local allies down the long, slender peninsula on which the city was situated. To avoid being spotted from her walls, he conducted his march at night, and he is apt to have chosen as his route the comparatively smooth path that ran along Sithonia's eastern shore—where, thanks to the peaks at the center of the peninsula, travelers were sheltered from Toronaean surveillance. If this was, indeed, the route he chose, then, when he neared the city, he must have slipped quietly across the spine that runs down the center of the peninsula. For we are told that, shortly before dawn, he called a halt at the temple of Castor and Pollux, which appears to have been located behind the knoll just over a quarter-mile east of the city's walls.

From there, Brasidas dispatched twenty peltasts under the command of a Chalcidian from Olynthus named Lysistratus. Guided by conspirators who had made their way out of Torone, they were to slip into the city at a place where the wall facing south-southwest, as it neared Lekythos, ran quite near the open sea and was in an advanced state of disrepair—thanks to seismic activity and human negligence. Then, they were to make their way up the ridge sloping down to Lekythos, on which the city sat, and climb to the town's highest point, where the wall which they had traversed met at a sharp angle another such wall facing east, and there they were to slay those stationed in the garrison. Thereafter, they were to return to the wall looking south-southwest, where it faced the open sea, and there break open a postern gate built long before with an eye to allowing a small group of the city's defenders to sally forth and catch off guard anyone who had the effrontery to attack the town.

When directly confronted with the considerable danger attendant on this bold and complex enterprise, thirteen of the twenty peltasts balked; and Lysistratus slipped quietly over the broken-down segment of the city wall with the remaining six. Perhaps because these stalwarts were far fewer in number than anticipated, the tasks assigned them took them longer than expected. But, after dispatching the garrison, opening the pertinent postern gate, and bringing in through it additional troops on the south side of town, they managed to rendezvous with Brasidas' local partisans. With their help, they then sawed through the wooden bar securing the main gates of the city, which interrupted yet another wall (this one facing the harbor to the north) and led directly from Torone's marketplace out to her docks. Through those gates, they then let in the remainder of the peltasts, who had been waiting impatiently just outside the walls; and they raised a fire signal to alert Brasidas to their achievement. In response, he then roused his hoplites and led them swiftly through the harbor gates into the city. His aim was to seize the high ground and take the town from top to bottom, from the spine of the ridge at its high point to its lower levels on all three sides—and this he did.

There was a garrison of fifty Athenians bivouacked in the marketplace near the saddle of land separating the ridge on which the city was situated from Lekythos. These men the invaders found fast asleep. A few they killed right away. The others fled—some to the two Athenian triremes anchored in the harbor; others to Lekythos, where there was a fort in which they had stationed a small squadron of troops—and the survivors all then gathered on that promontory, where they proposed to make a stand. There they were joined by the Toronaeans most closely associated with Athens.

In the meantime, Brasidas mollified the astonished and terrified people of the town by adjusting to the peculiar circumstances of the place and time his usual pitch, promising pointedly, among other things, that the Toronaeans who had sought refuge with the Athenians on Lekythos would be left unharmed if they rejoined their compatriots and remained faithful thereafter to the cause of Greek liberty. Then, he negotiated a two-day truce, which gave him time to consolidate his control of the community and the Athenians time to repair the fortifications on Lekythos; and, when it was over, he turned his attention to the promontory and the fort on it.

On the first day, the Athenians and Toronaeans cornered there managed to repel his attack at the narrow isthmus on the saddle of flat land linking the promontory with the town. On the second day, however, Brasidas brought up a flamethrower—constructed, we can presume, on the same lines as the one deployed by the Boeotians against the Athenian fort at Delium some months before. The Athenians responded by hastily constructing a tower on top of a nearby house from which they intended to hurl great jars of water and heavy stones onto the siege engine and the men wielding it. When the building unexpectedly collapsed under the weight, panic gripped a great many of the Athenians; and, as they fled, Brasidas' men surged forward, killing those whom they caught while the rest found refuge on the two Athenian ships anchored nearby, which their crews then conducted across to Pallene without further ado.[12]

Not too long thereafter, Brasidas embarked on a similar journey. While he was busying himself at Torone, settling affairs, the citizens of Scione—which was located in the south high in the hills overlooking the western shore of the Pallene peninsula—voted to break with Athens. When he learned of the revolt, he immediately took to the sea and, under cover of night, made his way across the bay of Torone and around Cape Castarnaeum at the tip of Pallene in a small boat, trailing a trireme deployed as a decoy and prepared, if his boat came under attack, to come to his defense. After landing in the small harbor below Scione, he summoned an assembly at which he welcomed the rebels into the Spartan alliance, and there he delivered an address modeled for the most part on the speeches he had delivered at Acanthus and Torone. In it, he singled out the Scionaeans for special praise, celebrating the audacity and courage they had displayed, noting that they had not been in any way pressed to revolt, and drawing attention to the considerable dangers they now faced. As he pointed out, the Athenian cleruchs ensconced at Potidaea controlled all traffic by land between the cities to the south on Pallene and the mainland to the north, which rendered Scione, in effect, an island and made her especially vulnerable to a siege mounted by those who ruled the sea.

The Scionaeans were, Thucydides tells us, elated. Even those who had opposed the rebellion were emboldened by Brasidas' brave words. In the assembly, the citizens voted to crown him with a wreath of gold and welcome him formally as the liberator of Hellas. Individuals decked him out with ribbons and garlands as if he were an Olympic victor. The son of Tellis left a small garrison at Scione, crossed back to Torone, and dispatched a more substantial force. It was 423, and the winter was at an end. It would not be long before the weather improved and the Athenians fitted out a fleet for the Thraceward region. This he knew. Scione was doomed if he did not in the interim gain full control of the long, slender peninsula on which it lay. It was his intention to forestall the Athenian attack by making attempts on Mende and Potidaea, further north on Pallene, before their fleet could arrive. To this end, he was actively seeking the betrayal of both cities.[13]

At this point, however, a trireme unexpectedly arrived, carrying an otherwise unknown Athenian named Aristonymos and a Spartiate, well known to Brasidas, named Athenaios son of Pericleidas. The latter was, we have reason to believe, Athens' *próxenos* at Lacedaemon. It was his father who had sought and secured Athenian help at the time of the great helot revolt four decades before, and he and Aristonymos had news for the son of Tellis that this warrior no doubt found most unwelcome.[14]

CHAPTER 6

Mutual Exhaustion

If, like the Spartans, one were to rear one's sons in the country, make them sleep in the open, go with head and feet uncovered, and wash in ice-cold water in order to harden them, render them able to withstand woes, and make them love life and fear death less, one would be mocked and supposed a wild animal rather than a man.

NICCOLÒ MACHIAVELLI

HAD Brasidas' compatriots responded in the wake of his initial victories to his appeal for additional help by immediately dispatching reinforcements and by encouraging him to build ships, launch a fleet, and march into eastern Thrace, it is by no means clear just how far he might have been able to extend his reach. The Persians had not been in evidence for a very long time. It was easy to suppose that the league founded more than half a century before to keep them at bay was an anachronism, and it was clear to everyone long before the late 420s that what had once been a genuine alliance had been transformed into an imperial protection racket. The Athenians openly acknowledged as much. They no longer even went through the motions of pretending that there was an alliance. In the speeches they are said to have delivered, in the inscriptions recording their decrees, and even in the comedies performed at their festivals, they spoke of their league as an "empire [*arché*]," and they described its members as "the cities which we rule." In these cities, their dominion provoked deep resentment (especially among the well-to-do and the ambitious), as they were perfectly prepared to acknowledge; and their prestige had quite recently suffered a series of damaging blows—at Megara, at Delium, and in the Thraceward region—which encouraged on the part of the restive populations within that district still subject to Athens an audacity that many would in due course rue.[1]

At the start of the war, the Lacedaemonians had adopted as their slogan "the freedom of the Greeks." With the expedition conducted by Brasidas, they seemed now finally to be making good on that promise. The son of Tellis was not a xenophobe. He seemed, in fact, a philhellene. He was not reluctant and hesitant in the manner of the Eurypontid king Leotychidas. He was not brutal in the manner of the regent Pausanias son of Cleombrotus. Nor was he blood-thirsty in the manner of the navarch Alcidas. He was, to all appearances, a gentleman: *kalòs k'agathós.* Everywhere he went, we are told, he was "mea-sured [*métrıos*]" in his treatment of those invited to join the Spartan venture. He displayed what appeared to be a genuine willingness to respect the auton-omy of those who turned against the Athenians, and the disgruntled subjects of the latter flocked to his standard. Brasidas was—at least, he seemed to be—as good as his word, and the Thracian Chersonnesus and the Hellespont were within reach. He had everything he needed to make further trouble on a con-siderable scale for the Athenians—everything, that is, except for the one thing he needed most: firm, enthusiastic support from the authorities back home.

Republics give rise to rivalry and engender jealousy; and, at Lacedaemon, where the two kings tended to be exceedingly wary of overmighty subjects, this propensity was especially pronounced. This occasion was not an excep-tion. The leading figures at Sparta are said to have envied Brasidas, and the majority of the Lacedaemonians were weary of war, fearful of a helot revolt, eager to recover the men captured on Sphacteria, and ready to forge a peace. The Spartans were also aware that their thirty years' peace with Argos would in two years come to an end, that in the interim the Argives had prospered, that a new generation had come of age, and that there was every reason to suppose that Lacedaemon's ancient enemy would then enter the war on the Athenian side. In February or early March 423, the Spartans and the Athe-nians sat down to negotiate a truce. The latter, Thucydides reports, wanted time so that they could make arrangements to forestall further revolts, and many in their number contemplated the possibility of forging a settlement if things went well for them in the negotiations. Those in both cities who favored peace, though they recognized the chief aim of the majority of Athenians, were also aware that the latter were now "more receptive" than before to the idea of bringing the conflict to an end "on equal terms"; and they hoped and suspected that the respite would soften antagonism and render the Athenians more amenable to a general settlement.

The Spartans were not, like the Athenians, prone to overconfidence. In keeping with their instincts and their customary outlook, they chalked up

Brasidas' successes to good fortune. Thrace was—they told themselves—far, far away; and it was not at all clear that they could secure passage through Thessaly for the reinforcements that their fellow Spartiate had requested. In any case, they no longer believed it possible to win the war, and they suspected that, in breaching the terms of the Thirty Years' Peace, they had incurred the wrath of the gods. They even doubted—and with reason—Brasidas' capacity to hold onto the cities in and near what we now call the Chalcidice that he had so recently won over; and they wanted to cash in, regain their men, and put paid to the fort at Coryphasium and the Athenian presence on Cythera before their compatriot's luck turned.[2]

The truce that the two sides worked out was not universally popular. Brasidas was appalled, and he had admirers and now supporters aplenty back home—especially, we have reason to suspect, among the hot-blooded young. The truce was for him a crippling blow. It robbed him of momentum, which is in wartime a precious commodity; and it dispelled illusions and altered calculations. It suggested to those in western Thrace and at Amphipolis who had thrown in their lot with the man that his promises were worthless and that his compatriots could not be trusted—that, in return for concessions from Athens, they would readily betray their newly acquired allies. It almost certainly put a damper as well on the enthusiasm and confidence of Hellenes, eager to throw off the Athenian yoke, who lived to the east of the Strymon River along the Thracian coast, the Hellespont, the sea of Marmara, and the Bosporus; and thereby it must have rendered it far more difficult for Brasidas to lure their cities into rebellion. The prospect of becoming someone else's bargaining chip is not an enticement.

The truce also sowed division within the Spartan alliance. The Lacedaemonians managed to persuade the Corinthians, the Sicyonians, the Megarians, and the Epidaurians to join them in accepting its terms. But the Thebans resolutely refused to fall in line. Militarily, they were full of confidence in the wake of their victory at Delium. Politically, however, they were fearful that, if the Spartans withdrew from the war, the Athenians would once again exploit the political divisions within Boeotia that had bedeviled them in the past. Their Phocian allies to the north followed their lead, and the Opuntian Locrians may have done so as well.

There may have been a similar reluctance within the Peloponnesus. We hear nothing of the Eleans and the Phliasians. Nor is there mention of Mantineia, or Tegea, or of any other community in Arcadia; and it is telling that in the winter following the promulgation of the truce, while it was still in effect, there was a bloody and inconclusive battle fought at Laodokeion in south-central Arcadia, just south of the future site of Megalopolis, between Lacedaemon's Tegean and Mantineian allies.

There is reason to suspect that the Athenians were divided as well. Cleon is notably absent from the list of those who swore on Athens' behalf to uphold the truce. Those known to be his enemies were, by way of contrast, very much in evidence. The proposal was put forward by ambassadors sent from Lacedaemon and elsewhere in the Peloponnesus. It was Laches, whom Cleon had harried, who moved in the assembly that it be adopted; and he did so, we are told, in a manner reminiscent of the Spartans, invoking, as was sometimes done in Athens, "the good fortune of the Athenians." Moreover, it was Nicias, whom Cleon loathed, and Nicostratus and Autocles, who had served with him on the expedition to Cythera, who formally ratified the agreement by pouring libations and taking the oath on Athens' behalf.

The oaths were administered at Athens in late March 423—in the immediate aftermath of the City Dionysia at which Aristophanes had mocked Socrates in *The Clouds*. The Spartan envoys—among them Athenaios son of Pericleidas—are apt to have been entertained at that festival on a grand scale as honored guests and to have gotten an eyeful. They almost certainly would have been in attendance in the theater when the comedies were staged. They would also have watched with amazement as the Athenians displayed in that venue the *phóros* dispatched that spring from the subject cities within their league, and they would have looked on with interest as the now adult sons of citizens who had lost their lives fighting on Athens' behalf were paraded before the *pólis*. These young men had been reared with support from the city; and now, in the year in which they reached maturity, the Athenians solemnly conferred on each a hoplite panoply.

The terms of the truce were, for the most part, what one would expect. First came the gods. The Spartans pledged to do everything within their power to persuade the Boeotians and Phocians to allow the Athenians what they had apparently on occasion been denied: free access to the oracle and temple of Pythian Apollo. In addition, all were agreed that those, presumably on the Peloponnesian side, who had stolen treasures from the god would be punished. Both sides promised to remain at rest within the territories they possessed and to honor for the time being one another's acquisitions. The Athenians at Coryphasium, on Cythera, in the territory of Troezen, on Minoa, and at Nisaea were to cease their raids and to be confined within specified limits. Deserters and runaway slaves and helots were to be received by neither side. The Lacedaemonians and their allies were allowed to journey along their own coasts in galleys of restricted tonnage, such as triaconters, but not in proper warships; and assemblies were to be held and embassies exchanged with an eye to forging a lasting peace.[3]

A Truce Subverted

It is, as I have more than once had occasion to remark, far, far easier to initiate a war than to negotiate one's end. After years of conflict, trust and goodwill are apt to be in short supply. On this occasion, Brasidas was in a position to stoke animosity and distrust; and to this end, within limits, he was even prepared to play fast and loose with the authorities back home. When Aristonymos and Athenaios arrived to announce the truce, he ostentatiously acquiesced—by recalling the force he had dispatched to Scione for use against Mende and Potidaea, and presumably also by persuading the cities that had come over to him to accept the terms of the agreement.

Nonetheless, a difficulty soon arose. When Aristonymos counted the days, he discovered that Scione's revolt had taken place after the two sides had formally ratified the agreement, and he therefore denied that the terms of the truce applied to Scione. This put Brasidas, who had made commitments to the Scionaeans, in an exceedingly awkward position; and he seized on the situation as an opportunity to drive a wedge between Athens and Sparta. He spoke, we are told, at length, falsely asserting that the rebellion had preceded the truce. He announced that he would not relinquish the city; and his compatriots, who trusted him and did not have the means with which to test his claims, believed him. In consequence, when the Athenians began making preparations to dispatch an expedition against Scione, the Lacedaemonians sent an embassy to lay claim to the city and to assert that an Athenian attack would be a breach of the truce, and they suggested that the dispute be arbitrated as stipulated in that instrument.

Thucydides' account is compressed. He does not describe the discussions that then took place in the Athenian assembly. He tells us merely that the Athenians were unwilling to risk arbitration. They were furious, he explains, (and no doubt anxious) that, "even within" a city located among what they regarded as "the islands," there were those "who thought a revolt worthwhile, trusting in the strength of the Spartans on land"; and he reports that Cleon succeeded in persuading his compatriots to pass a decree stipulating that the Scionaeans be expelled from their city and killed. If there was a struggle going on at Athens between those who envisaged the truce as a step on the way to peace and those opposed to the truce and favorable to a renewal of the war, Brasidas' maneuver had the effect of reviving the fortunes of the latter—which may well have been what the canny Spartan had hoped to achieve.[4]

In the meantime, thanks to Brasidas' resolute support for Scione, another opportunity for mischief-making presented itself. Up the Pallene peninsula to the northwest of Scione a bit more than two miles east-southeast of a prominent headland bearing a sanctuary dedicated to Poseidon lay Mende—a prosperous city, famous for her wine. While the Athenians were preparing to sail against Scione, some of the Mendaeans took courage from the Spartan's fidelity to their neighbor and persuaded or forced their compatriots to rebel, and Brasidas accepted them into the Spartan alliance.

According to Thucydides, in his eagerness for victory, the Spartiate commander indulged in self-deception, telling himself that his conduct with regard to this city "was not unjust." He had not exercised force. He had not even brought pressure to bear. "She had come over to him openly under the truce." In any case, he thought, "the Athenians had broken the agreement in certain particulars." It was presumably with this species of casuistry in mind that in the winter of 423/2, before the truce had come to an end, Brasidas led an army up Sithonia from Torone with an eye to mounting a surprise attack at night on the Athenian colony at Potidaea and opening a way by land to Scione and Mende.

There was, we are told, a night watch posted on the ramparts at Potidaea. To maintain discipline, prevent sleep, and promote watchfulness, its members passed a bell about the walls. Brasidas tried to take advantage of this procedure by exploiting the moment when a post was briefly left unguarded by a watchman who was bearing the bell to his neighbor. While this was going on, a handful of his soldiers placed a scaling ladder against the wall where, they hoped, it would not be noticed. The next time that post was left unguarded Brasidas' commandos would then scale the wall at that point, descend from it, and break open a gate. On this occasion, however, the ladder was discovered; soldiers were summoned; and the opportunity was lost.

In the interim, between his forging of an alliance with Mende in the late spring or early summer of 423 and his abortive attempt on Potideia the following winter, the Spartan came under intense pressure from his paymaster Perdiccas. He was not deluded with regard to what the Athenians were likely to do should he absent himself from what we now call the Chalcidice. But he was evidently quite short of funds, and his options were limited. Earlier when he had left Perdiccas in the lurch and had marched on Acanthus, the Macedonian monarch had retaliated by substantially cutting the subsidy he had promised, and by this expedient he had apparently now brought the proud Spartan to heel. Nonetheless, before doing as he was bid and departing with most of his troops to join the expedition the Macedonian monarch was about to mount against Arhaebus, king of the Lyncestians, Brasidas took precautions indicative of his fears—first by conveying the women and children of the Mendaeans and the Scionaeans to Olynthus, and then by sending to the two cities five hundred Peloponnesian hoplites and three hundred Chalcidian peltasts, under the command of an otherwise unknown figure named Polydamidas—who was presumably the captain of one of the mercenary bands that Brasidas had hired.[5]

The support that Brasidas provided to the two communities on Pallene was inadequate, as he evidently feared it might be. While the Spartan was in Lyncus, Nicostratus, who appears to have been well connected in the Thracian region, and his frequent colleague Nicias—acting, one must suspect, in defense of the truce they had both sworn to uphold—made their way to Potidaea with fifty triremes (ten of them from Chios) and with one thousand Athenian hoplites, six hundred archers, one hundred Thracian peltasts, and additional peltasts drawn from the old Eretrian colony at Methone on the Thracian coast to the south of Macedon and from elsewhere nearby. From there the Athenian forces rowed down to the headland on Pallene's western shore topped by the sanctuary dedicated to Poseidon. There they disembarked in the bay to its north and tried in vain to dislodge a Mendaean force from a nearby hill and make their way around the headland to Mende. After this setback, they returned to their ships, sailed around the headland, landed south of Mende, and began ravaging the city's farmland. Then, they got lucky. Polydamidas, who was intent on sallying forth against them, committed an offense against an outspoken Mendaean dissenter; this gave rise to civil strife within the city; and, while this was going on, the Athenians managed to slip through the gates and sack the place. Then, they left it to the popular party to punish those who had staged the rebellion and turned their attention to Scione. There, after dislodging the Scionaean infantry and their Peloponnesian auxiliaries from a high hill they had occupied, the Athenians began investing the town. By the end of the summer, when the bulk of the force returned to Athens, a full-scale siege was under way.[6]

While these events were taking place, Perdiccas and Brasidas marched into Lyncus in Upper Macedonia. There, they skirmished with Arhaebus' cavalry and defeated his hoplites. But Perdiccas' Illyrian allies betrayed him and joined his Lyncestian foe; his Macedonians soon thereafter panicked and fled; and Perdiccas followed suit, leaving Brasidas and his hoplites behind, bereft of cavalry and initially unaware of the grave danger they faced. Although the resourceful Spartan managed to form his beleaguered Greeks into a hollow square so that they could fight their way out of Lyncus, the experience did not endear Perdiccas to Brasidas or to his men. The two leaders had already quarreled; and, as Brasidas' hoplites marched back through Lower Macedonia to what we now call the Chalcidice, their commander apparently did nothing to prevent them from venting their anger against those who had abandoned them, and so they slaughtered the oxen and cattle they encountered and looted the abandoned baggage they found on their way.

By indulging his men in this fashion, Brasidas may in some measure have satisfied his own as well as their sense of grievance, but this cost him dearly. For Perdiccas, who was cut from similar cloth, was a spirited man no less inclined to allow indignation to get in the way of a sober calculation of his long-term interests—and he responded to this provocation in kind by exacting revenge. By the time that Brasidas had reached Torone, Perdiccas was busy negotiating an alliance with Nicias, who demanded as proof of his change of heart that the Macedonian use his influence to prevent Peloponnesian reinforcements from making their way through Thessaly to Macedon and western Thrace—which is what he did in the fall of 423 or the winter of 423/2 when three Spartan notables named Ischagoras, Ameinias, and Aristeus tried to conduct an army overland to join Brasidas.[7]

Though blocked in this important particular, the threesome was otherwise successful. Ischagoras was, we have reason to believe, a proponent of peace apt to regard Brasidas' larger ambitions with a jaundiced eye. One or both of his colleagues may have been friendlier to the man's enterprise. For, in composing embassies and, one must suspect, commissions sent abroad, the Spartans, intent on promoting consensus and solidarity, tended to strike at a balance between men inclined to different views. The three had been instructed to take a close look at affairs in Thrace, to assess the strategic situation, and to report back to the authorities at Lacedaemon. They had also been asked to convey a few young Spartiates to Brasidas so that the latter would have, ready to hand, subordinate commanders—who were abler and more politic than the "chance persons," such as the hapless Polydamidas, on whom he had hitherto had to rely; and who could, in the great warrior's absence, rule over and defend the cities that he had brought over to Lacedaemon. These two parts of their mission Ischagoras and his colleagues accomplished with aplomb.

The third of the three tasks assigned the trio deserves special notice—for, as Thucydides intimates, it was a portent of things to come. It involved a breach of the law, fundamental to the Spartan regime, specifying that young men under the age of forty-five not be sent outside the Lacedaemonian domain except when they marched alongside their peers as hoplites within the Spartan army. As far as we can tell, this regulation had never before been broken, and it is easy to see why. It reflected a keen awareness on the part of Sparta's ruling order that their regime was fragile and that the cultivation of the intense self-forgetfulness and public-spiritedness which distinguished Lacedaemon as a political community required a considerable measure of isolation. No outsider visited Sparta and no Spartiate went abroad without express permission from the ephors; and these officials were not allowed to extend this privilege to those under age for fear that these impressionable young men might be exposed to temptation, fall into corruption, and lose their élan.

If the rule was relaxed on this one occasion, it was no doubt because Lacedaemon was short of manpower and presumably also because the particular young men chosen were enthusiastic supporters of Brasidas' enterprise whose dispatch he had expressly requested. When, however, this brave warrior put Clearidas son of Cleonymus and Pasitelidas son of Hegesander in charge of Amphipolis and Torone, he did much more than set a precedent. He took the first step toward reconfiguring the Lacedaemonian regime for empire and fundamentally altering the city's grand strategy. It was, to be sure, a small step, and it had, as far as we can tell, no immediate consequences. But it reflected an awareness that, if Sparta were to assert herself in the larger world of the

Aegean, she would have to change; and the fact that Thucydides pointedly draws our attention to it as a breach of Lacedaemonian norms suggests that among his Spartan informants there were some who had voiced misgivings.[8]

A Truce Extended

Had there been no squabbling, it is unlikely, but not impossible, that the truce initiated in the spring of 423 would have eventuated in the forging of a settlement. Except in Thrace, its terms seem to have been observed. But what Brasidas did in what we now call the Chalcidice rendered the situation at Athens of the minority who longed for peace untenable; and, by the end of the summer, everyone must have realized that in the following year the war would almost certainly be renewed. It is this that explains the belated Spartan attempt to deliver reinforcements to Brasidas, and it is this that explains the care Nicias took in advance to deny them access to Thrace.

As Ischagoras and his colleagues no doubt discovered, Brasidas' situation at this time was unenviable. Mende was lost, and Scione, doomed. The Spartan was in no position to come to the latter city's defense. As for the surprise attack on Potidaea, that he had had to abort. Moreover, the little army that he had led from the Peloponnesus had suffered considerable attrition. Five hundred of his hoplites were dead or trapped in Scione; others had died in Lyncus. The reinforcements that he had requested had been forced to turn back. Perdiccas was no longer contributing at all to the support of the forces that the Spartan had left; and, when their pay was curtailed, some of the mercenaries in Brasidas' employ are apt to have abandoned his service. He could rely on the Chalcidians and perhaps also the Bottiaeans, on some of the Toronaeans and Acanthians, on the people of Stagira and Argilos, and on the Amphipolitans. If the Athenians returned to the Strymon basin, he might even be able to rally some of the barbarians who resided in the neighborhood. But what his supporters had to offer was not sufficient to enable him to defend everything he had gained. So he concentrated his attention on the most valuable and defensible of his acquisitions: Amphipolis.

We do not know when Brasidas left Pasitelidas in charge of Torone and withdrew to Amphipolis. It is plausible to suppose that he did so during the winter of 423/2 and that the attempted surprise attack on Potidaea was undertaken while he was conducting the main body of his forces from Sithonia to the Strymon basin. Subsequent to Brasidas' seizure of Amphipolis, considerable work was done on the fortifications of that city, completing the extensive walls of the outer circuit in the north and extending them by way of a palisade in such a way as to include the bridge over the Strymon River.[9] If Brasidas oversaw this work himself, as seems likely, the one extended period in which he is not known to have been engaged elsewhere was in and after this particular winter.

The truce formally came to an end at the time of Athens' City Dionysia in late March 422. But the war was not renewed until late August after the Pythian games had been held at Delphi. This much is clear, but we are not told why. Thucydides' text, which seems to be corrupt, offers us no explanation.[10] It is possible that the truce was formally extended to allow for negotiations. It is also conceivable that both sides simply remained at rest. In either case, however, it is highly likely that the Athenians were waiting for news from another quarter. They were undoubtedly eager to recover Amphipolis and the other cities that Brasidas had taken, and by this time they were surely ready to try. But elsewhere there had been an unsettling event, and it is apt to have given them pause.

The Mission of Epilycus

In the winter of 425/4, an Athenian commander had captured at Eion a Persian ambassador named Artaphernes, who was on his way from the court of Artaxerxes to Lacedaemon. Later, in the spring of 423—perhaps as a consequence of the setbacks they had suffered in the interim at Delium, Acanthus, Amphipolis, and Torone—the Athenians dispatched to the Great King an embassy of their own in the company of this Artaphernes. We are not told the purpose of this particular diplomatic venture, but its aim was surely to shore up relations with that monarch and forestall any cooperation on his part with the Spartans. It was by no means the first such embassy dispatched by the Athenians in the course of this war, but they may have acted on this occasion with a greater sense of urgency than in the past. When, however, their envoys reached Ephesus, they learned that Xerxes' son and heir had died, and for this reason Athens' envoys returned home for consultation.

The Babylonian evidence indicates that Artaxerxes, who had ruled the Achaemenid empire for more than forty years, had met his end early in 424, shortly after or shortly before Artaphernes was captured, at a time of year when the Great King was almost certainly in residence at Susa. Not long thereafter, his sole legitimate son and heir Xerxes II was assassinated by one of his seventeen bastard half-brothers. A civil war then broke out; and, in the course of the year that followed, a figure named Ochus, who was the son of one of Artaxerxes' Babylonian concubines, fought his way to the throne, ousted the assassin, and assumed the throne-name Darius.

It was to this man that the Athenians subsequently sent an embassy, and it was with him that a wealthy and well-born Athenian named Epilycus is said to have forged an agreement extending and perhaps amending the peace negotiated with Artaxerxes by Callias in 449. The Athenians were not at this time as cocky as they usually were, and the news of Artaxerxes' demise no doubt made them exceedingly nervous. They knew that, where there are new men, there are often new measures; and, for understandable reasons, they cannot have relished the thought that the Persians might in the circumstances then pertaining renew their bid for control in the Aegean. For this reason, they are apt to have dispatched Epilycus and his colleagues to pay their respects in or soon after the beginning of summer in 423—as soon as it became evident that Ochus had won the initial civil war.[11]

Epilycus and those who accompanied him on this trek may have had a certain amount of leverage. Ochus' claim to the throne was tenuous, to say the least. He was not the son of one of Artaxerxes' wives. He was a bastard. Moreover, the Achaemenid regime was emphatically Persian; the Persians were ethnocentric in the extreme; and Ochus was a half-breed. His mother was not an Achaemenid. She was not a descendant of one of the seven conspirators who had placed Darius on the throne. She was not even a Persian nor, for that matter, a Mede.

Moreover, there were others among Artaxerxes' bastards with as good a claim to the kingship as Ochus; and, with the help of Megabyzus' enterprising son Artyphius, Ochus' full brother Arsites is said to have staged a rebellion— almost certainly, as Megabyzus had in the 440s, in Syria. Twice this Artyphius is said to have defeated armies dispatched by Ochus; and twice he reportedly did so, as his father appears to have done, with the help of mercenary hoplites from Greece.

There were also pure-bred Achaemenids with a far better claim to the kingship than any of Artaxerxes' bastards. One among these was Pissouthnes, a direct descendant of both Cyrus and Darius who was, as we have seen, the legitimate son of Xerxes' younger brother Hystaspes. This Pissouthnes was, moreover, a man of some experience, as we have also seen. He had long been satrap of Sardis. As such, he had at his beck and call a substantial military force—which he supplemented with a host of Greek hoplites led at this time by an Athenian mercenary captain named Lycon. In consequence, like Artyphius, he was in a position to deploy against the half-breed in Susa a formidable army combining Persian cavalry with Greek infantry, like the one that Megabyzus seems to have deployed against Artaxerxes in Syria in the 440s.

We know that Pissouthnes staged a rebellion at some point in the early years of Ochus' reign. We are not told the date, but there is reason to suspect that the revolt began in 423 and that Ochus' present or future son-in-law Tissaphernes son of Hydarnes was dispatched to Anatolia that year or the next to put it down. And there can be no doubt that its prospects and those of Artyphius' rebellion would have been greatly enhanced had the Athenians facilitated either's hiring additional mercenaries or otherwise lent either man their assistance.

Of course, the Athenians owed Pissouthnes nothing—apart from ill will. But, in the circumstances, past antagonism cannot have much mattered. Politicians really do make strange bedfellows; and, especially in foreign affairs, yesterday's foe can easily become tomorrow's ally. With Megabyzus' son Artyphius, the Athenians may well have been on good terms, as they apparently had been with his father. He was, in any case, Zopyrus' brother—which surely counted for something.

In the end, however, the Athenians appear to have given aid and comfort to neither rebel. To gain what Athens wanted from Persia, Epilycus and his colleagues are apt to have suggested to the bastard in Susa a quid pro quo. It is telling that both rebellions collapsed when the minions of the monarch we now call Darius II managed to bribe the Hellenic mercenary bands marshaled against them.[12]

Epilycus' journey from Athens to Susa and back will have eaten up at least four months and quite possibly an additional span of weeks or months. If the negotiations with the new king and the attendant formalities took some time, as such things nearly always did, Athens' ambassadors are unlikely to have made it back home prior to the summer of 422.[13] It is, then, easy to see why the Athenians should have wanted to put off a renewal of their war with Lacedaemon until they had received assurances that the new King of Kings would remain on the sidelines.

Brasidas no doubt profited from the extra time this five-month delay allowed him. He had fortifications to build, and he needed time in which to rally support. But, as he must have known, the hand he had been dealt was weak. Although, in any circumstances, this man would undoubtedly have played his cards with consummate skill, the odds were not in his favor. Had the Athenians at this time sent a set of veteran generals to recover their possessions in Thrace, they would almost certainly have met with success.

Cleon in Thrace

Instead, however, the Athenians listened to Cleon; and, at his urging, they sent him to the Thraceward region after the Pythian Games, quite late in the campaigning season, with thirty triremes, twelve hundred Athenian hoplites, three hundred Athenian cavalrymen, and "an even larger force" supplied by Athens' allies. If Thucydides' reference to this "larger force" means what it seems to mean, Cleon may have had with him an army of twenty-five hundred hoplites.

This was, as far as we can tell, the man's first independent command. His only known previous stint as a general in the field had been at Sphacteria, and there he had shared responsibility with the son of Alcisthenes, to whose judgment he had sensibly deferred. Of course, Cleon was by no means stupid, and he cannot have been unfamiliar with the exigencies of war. He was wealthy and had no doubt done service himself as a hoplite in the ranks and perhaps also as a trierarch in the fleet. But, as a military strategist and, above all, as a tactician, he was a man of limited experience. All that could be said in his favor is that in 426 he had recognized the obvious: that a great deal could be gained for Athens from the capture of the Spartans trapped on Sphacteria and that the man who had defeated the Peloponnesians and annihilated the Ambraciots at Olpae was a skilled tactician. It was a grave error on the part of the assembly to give Cleon a major command and send him alone against an opponent as wily as was Brasidas, and it is no surprise that the hoplites assigned to the enterprise recognized as much and were decidedly reluctant to accompany him on the venture.[14]

We are not told where the son of Tellis positioned himself and his army when he first got wind of the Athenian expedition. He cannot have known where Cleon would strike first. So he may have situated himself in between Torone and Amphipolis at Acanthus. From there he could without difficulty dash west to Sithonia or north and east to the Strymon.

In the event, Cleon chose to attack Torone first; and there, Thucydides' narrative suggests, he handled the operation with aplomb. First, he paid a brief visit to Scione, whence he withdrew from the residual force conducting the siege a small body of hoplites. Then, he crossed from Pallene to Sithonia and sailed into the "Quiet Harbor," a short distance to the south of Torone. Thucydides must later have interviewed one or more of the individuals in Cleon's immediate entourage—perhaps in the course of speaking with the Athenians captured in the course of the battle that later took place at Amphipolis. For he professes to know considerably more about the thinking and intentions of the Athenian commander than could be inferred from what he tells us about the man's conduct. Thus, for example, he tells us that it was upon learning that Brasidas was absent and that the garrison which the Spartan had left with Pasitelidas was insufficient to do battle with the Athenian force on the flat ground outside the city walls that Cleon did two things. First, he sent ten triremes to land marines in the harbor lying immediately east of the Lekythos promontory and north of the city proper. Then, with his remaining hoplites, cavalry, and light-armed troops, he marched on the town from the south.

Brasidas had partially pulled down the city wall at one point and had used the stones to build fortifications out from the wall to take in a suburb. Initially, Pasitelidas attempted to mount a defense from behind these new fortifications—but to no avail. Fearing rightly, when he learned of their arrival, that the marines in the harbor would take the town and that the outer fortifications, which were apparently incomplete, would also be taken, he fled back to the city with Cleon's Athenians at his heels. The latter clambered over the remnants of the original city wall and entered the town right behind the Spartan; and Torone fell before Brasidas, who had marched to its relief and was then less than five miles up the peninsula, could arrive. The women and children Cleon sold into slavery; the men of Torone and the Chalcidians and Peloponnesians stationed there for the city's defense, seven hundred in all, he dispatched to Athens.[15]

After settling affairs at Torone, Cleon conducted his fleet around Cape Amphelos. Then, mindful that Brasidas' allies at Acanthus might obstruct his use of the canal dug through the Acte peninsula at the behest of Xerxes, he had his crews row their galleys past the towering heights of Mount Athos and on to Eion at the mouth of the river Strymon. From there, with an eye to the terms of the alliance forged the previous year, he dispatched envoys west to summon Perdiccas, who had pledged his support, and east to Polles, king of the Odomantians, who had promised to supply a host of Thracian mercenaries. In the meantime, Cleon attempted in vain to seize Stagira to the west on the Gulf of Strymon, and he managed to overrun Galepsos to the east on the coast opposite Thasos. Then, for a time, he paused, hesitant to approach Amphipolis without the reinforcements he had been promised.[16]

Cleon was right to wait. Amphipolis was much better fortified than Torone. Under Brasidas' direction, the Amphipolitans had completed the outer circuit to the north of the acropolis, which had been projected fifteen years before by Hagnon. To conquer the city, the Athenians would have to storm it, which was no easy task. Amphipolis' only weakness lay in the length of that circuit and in the vast number of men required if it was to be defended at every point. To seize the town, Cleon's forces would have to overwhelm the defenders by attacking the walls simultaneously at multiple points with the scaling ladders and battering rams they had brought with them—which would require a great deal more manpower than had accompanied the Athenian to Thrace.[17]

Brasidas knew a great deal about Perdiccas' propensity for ignoring his obligations, and he may have entertained doubts about the reliability of the Odomantian king. It was, in any case, his conviction—so Thucydides tells us—that, out of a disdain for the relatively small number of soldiers then lodged at Amphipolis, Cleon would eventually march on that city with the forces he had ready to hand. On this supposition, the Spartan did two things. First, he acted to increase the size of his army, by calling upon his local allies for aid. To this end, he summoned fifteen hundred Thracian mercenaries and the cavalry and peltasts of the Edonians to join the one thousand peltasts supplied by the Myrcinians and the Chalcidians and the two thousand hoplites and three hundred cavalrymen under his immediate command. Then, with fifteen hundred of the hoplites, he made his way across the bridge spanning the Strymon and situated himself atop Cerdylium—a high hill close by in the territory of Argilos near the west bank of the river—from which it was possible to look down on Eion and the surrounding lowlands and observe the Athenians' every move. In this fashion, if and when Cleon set out with his army to march up the eastern bank of the Strymon, Brasidas would have sufficient time in which to size up the enemy, return to Amphipolis, and marshal his own troops.[18]

According to Thucydides, it was not so much contempt on Cleon's own part, directed at the force under Brasidas' command, which induced the Athenian general to make that short journey. It was mainly scorn directed at him by the men under his command which finally forced his hand. They grew restless while they dawdled at Eion; and they grumbled, as soldiers will. It was, moreover, late October, and they no doubt knew that the time which remained to them was short. The campaigning season of 422 was, in fact, drawing to a close.

Many of the Athenians present no doubt loathed their commander. Especially among the propertied classes which supplied Athens with her hoplites, the violent rhetoric in which he engaged and his propensity for harrying his opponents and for treating disagreement, not to mention failure in the field, as treason had naturally earned him a level of dislike bordering on hatred. Nor were they as impressed as are Cleon's modern apologists by their general's deft handling of the skeleton force defending Torone. It is, as they knew, not all that difficult to take a city inadequately fortified and poorly defended. Having sized up their commander's capacity for leadership in the field, these Athenians are said to have drawn a sharp contrast between "the experience and daring" of his opponent and "the ignorance and *malakía*" that their own general displayed. When he learned of their discontent, Cleon reportedly decided to distract their attention by breaking camp and marching upriver to conduct a reconnaissance in force.[19]

There was nothing in principle wrong with such an enterprise. Something of the sort was no doubt needed. Amphipolis' defenses were not what they had been. The outer circuit, now in the north complete, needed examination. It is, moreover, vital that a commander know the terrain on which he will have to operate, and this was surely part of Cleon's purpose—if not, in fact, as many scholars assume, his prime concern. Nonetheless, such a maneuver requires vigilance and care—for armies on the march are much more vulnerable to attack than are armies arrayed for a fight—and on this occasion neither vigilance nor care was in evidence.

On one point, Brasidas was right. The Athenian commander was full of himself, and he did regard the enemy with disdain. He was, we are told, no less self-confident than he had been at Pylos. It did not even cross his mind that

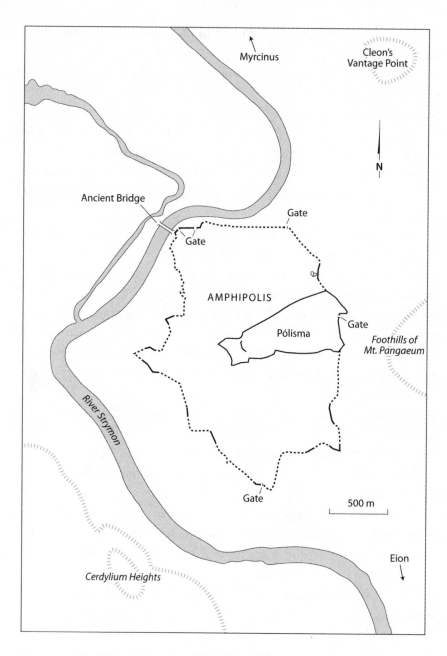

Map 22. Amphipolis and Her Walls, ca. 424–422

his opponent might seize upon his foray as an occasion in which to launch a surprise attack. He acknowledged that he might well need reinforcements to encircle and storm Amphipolis. But he denied that he needed them to safely win a victory if he was forced to fight on the open ground outside the city's walls.[20]

While Cleon and the men under his command were marching three miles up the Strymon and making their way along the road through the valley lying between the eastern wall of Amphipolis and the westernmost foothills of Mount Pangaeum, Brasidas returned from Cerdylium with his men. Concerning this man's thinking, Thucydides appears also to have been exceptionally well-informed—thanks, we must suppose, to what he later gleaned from conversations with Clearidas and others in Amphipolis.[21]

Brasidas was not eager to stage a formal hoplite battle with the Athenians and their allies. At this point, with the arrival of the Thracian mercenaries and the Edonian cavalry and peltasts, the numbers in the two armies may have been more or less equal. But he did not think his ragtag army of hoplites (many of them, we have reason to believe, recent recruits) a match for the considerably larger phalanx made up of Athenian citizens and the most formidable of their Lemnian and Imbrian cleruchs. Victory could be achieved, he was persuaded, but only by means of art and stealth. Moreover, if he showed to his opponents the number of men under his command and the fact that many of them possessed only the minimally necessary equipment, it would not, he thought, be to his advantage—for he would earn their contempt. So he did what he could to render his forces invisible, and he waited and watched while Cleon led his men up the large, steep hill a mile or two north-northeast of the city—where, some scholars believe, the Athenians in Cimon's day had made their abortive attempt to found a settlement at Ennea Hodoi. From the top of this great hill, it was possible to peer into the city of Amphipolis.

At this point, the son of Tellis summoned his infantrymen and delivered a speech in which he drew attention to the degree to which Cleon's army, which was itself visibly engaged in looking around, was in disarray; and this he took as a sign that the Athenians were psychologically unprepared for battle. Then, after explaining to his men the character of his plan and reminding them that their own liberty and that of the Greeks more generally were at stake, he split his force in two. One hundred fifty of his hoplites he posted at "the first gates," which were situated at the northwestern corner of Amphipolis' outer circuit where, under his direction, the Amphipolitans had built a palisade linking the city's walls with the bridge a short distance to the north—and there he joined his men. The remainder, the vast majority, he assigned to Clearidas, whom he sent to "the Thracian Gates," which were located either at the northeastern corner of the outer circuit or further south on the city's eastern wall alongside its acropolis. At the appropriate time, Brasidas hoped to deliver a one-two punch.[22]

While Brasidas was marshaling his men and making his preparations, Cleon blundered on, oblivious to the danger he was in. When he had posted his men on the hill, he ascended to the vantage point at its top and he looked all about, noting the extensive marshland to the north and the south along the Strymon and studying the situation of the city more generally with respect to eastern Thrace. He figured that he could withdraw without doing battle whenever he wished. For on the walls of Amphipolis, he spied no one, and no one was coming out of her gates, which were shut. He even expressed regret that he had not had his men cart in the scaling ladders and battering rams they had brought from Athens. Had they done so, he supposed, they could have taken the city—for it was empty.[23]

When Cleon proceeded a bit further to complete his reconnaissance of the city's outer circuit, one of his subordinates approached him with a disturbing report. An army could now be seen in the city, and at least one of his men had apparently approached the Thracian Gates; and, under them through the gap between their lower edge and the roadway beneath, he had spied the feet of horses and men poised and ready to burst out.

Cleon went to look and confirmed the report. Had he rallied his men at this point and ordered them to descend into the plain and form up in a phalanx facing the Thracian Gates, Brasidas would have been left with two choices— neither of them palatable. He could have called off the attack, or he could have led an army inadequately trained and poorly equipped into a battle it was almost certain to lose.

Cleon did not, however, order his hoplites to form up for battle. Instead, supposing that his men had time in which to stage a withdrawal, he played into Brasidas' hands by sounding the retreat and directing his army to head southward toward Eion. This required that his men descend in stages from the steep hill where they had been posted, make a quarter-turn to the left, and

Figure 3. Greek Hoplites Marching in Column (Black-Figure Kylix, National Archaeological Museum, Taranto, Italy. Photograph by Mark Cartwright / Ancient History
Encyclopedia [www.ancient.edu], courtesy of the photographer).

march in column south—initially to and then through the valley running
along the eastern wall of Amphipolis.

This maneuver left the Athenians and their allies exposed and open to
attack. A hoplite deployed outside the phalanx was like a duck out of water.
The *aspís* he bore was a large, round, concave shield designed solely for use in
the phalanx. When hoplites were lined up in formation facing the enemy, the
aspís covered the left side of its bearer and the right side of the man ranged
beside him on the left. When, however, hoplites marched in column, the right
side of each hoplite was unshielded and the *aspís,* which was not light, robbed
its bearer of agility and speed. In such circumstances, these heavily armed infantrymen were vulnerable to assault not just by other hoplites, but even more
so by cavalrymen and archers as well as peltasts and other light-armed troops
armed with javelins, who could easily outpace them, outmaneuver them, and
cut them down.

When presented with such an opportunity, Brasidas was inclined to seize it—and that is precisely what, on this occasion, he did. After sizing up the intentions of the Athenians on the basis of a perusal of their body language and after telling his companions that there was no way that men conducting themselves in this fashion would stand up to assault, he ordered those with him at the gates near the bridge to make a sortie and charge the Athenian center. This attack caught the Athenians, who were marching in less than perfect order, completely off guard. It startled them and gave rise to fear. Then, when Clearidas and the remainder of Brasidas' strike force burst forth from the Thracian Gates and bore down in large numbers on the left wing of the Athenian army, this fear turned into panic. This body of Athenians, which was in the lead, fled down the valley running along the city's eastern wall to the Strymon and on toward Eion. Those on the right wing, where Cleon had stationed himself, were trapped as Brasidas' hoplites turned in their direction. Many of them courageously chose to stand their ground, pulling back to the hill from which they had just descended. From that position, they repulsed Clearidas' hoplites, when they came up, twice or even thrice—before finally giving way when they were surrounded by the Myrcinian and Chalcidian cavalry and by a host of peltasts who hurled javelins at them from all sides.

Cleon, who should have taken charge and organized the resistance, panicked and fled immediately, instead. And, predictably, he was cut down by a Myrcinian peltast who outran him. In suffering this fate, he was one among many. Twelve hundred Athenian hoplites had joined him on this expedition. Thanks to his arrogance, negligence, and incompetence, nearly half of these and an untold number of Lemnians and Imbrians were killed at Amphipolis that day—which did not deter his devotees in Athens from subsequently seeing to it that his name was placed at the top of the inscription listing and honoring those of their fellow citizens who had lost their lives at Amphipolis.[24]

The casualties on the other side were negligible. It speaks volumes about Brasidas' brilliance as a commander that only seven of his men died. It speaks volumes about his personal courage and audacity that he himself was one of the seven—fatally wounded during the initial sortie. As one would expect, Amphipolis accorded him a public burial, and all of the allies joined together in honoring him with an armed procession. All that it had taken to humiliate Athens was the sacrifice of a single highly distinguished Spartiate.

In part out of a desire to distance themselves from the Athenians and curry favor with the Lacedaemonians, the Amphipolitans also tore down the

Figure 4. Brasidas' Final Resting Place (Archaeological
Museum, Amphipolis, Greece. Photographer: Harrygouvas.
Published unchanged in 2020 under the following license
issued by Harrygouvas: Creative Commons Attribution-
Share Alike 3.0 Unported).

buildings constructed in connection with the Hagnon cult, and they erased
every reminder of the role that the Athenian had played in the city's foundation. Henceforth it was Brasidas—the Spartan Achilles—whom they treated
as the city's founder, regarding him as their savior.

Brasidas' tomb the Amphipolitans located in front of what became the
city's agora, and they fenced it off as a sacred precinct. There, it was the subsequent practice of individuals to slay victims as offerings to him as a hero or
demigod. There, the city staged games and conducted sacrifices each year in his
honor. And there, more than two thousand four hundred years later, when the
Greek Archaeological Service had foundations excavated for the museum it
had chosen to build, a two-room temple-like building was found covering a cist
grave—and within that grave a silver larnax with carved feet was discovered.
It contained the cremated bones of a man topped by a single gold wreath.[25]

A Treaty of Peace

While Cleon was tarrying at Eion, three Spartiates—Ramphias, Autocha-ridas, and Epicydidas—set out from the Peloponnesus with a force of nine hundred hoplites, intent on making their way to the Thraceward region. While the battle at Amphipolis was raging, these men were taking their ease at Her-acleia Trachinia—where there had apparently been civil disorder, and the three Spartiates had been instructed to introduce reforms while en route. It was not until winter, Thucydides reports, that this threesome led these infantrymen into Thessaly; and, when they reached Pierium and the Thessalians betrayed an inclination to oppose their further advance, they lost heart and turned back. After all, they reportedly told themselves, Brasidas was dead; and, with the Athenians' defeat and withdrawal, the crisis had passed. In any case, they thought themselves unequal to the pursuit of that great warrior's larger proj-ect, and they had known before they even set out from Lacedaemon that what their compatriots most wanted was peace.[26]

On this last point, there can be no doubt that Ramphias and his colleagues were correct. For some time, as we have seen, the Spartans had been resolutely fishing for a settlement, and nothing had happened in the interim to change their minds. As Thucydides explains, they had long before recognized that invading Attica would not bring the Athenians to their knees. The defeat at Sphacteria had profoundly shaken their confidence. From Coryphasium and Cythera, the enemy was with impunity plundering their land. The helots were deserting; there was reason to fear that, with the help of the deserters, those who remained behind would rise up in rebellion, as they had not much more than forty years before—and, of course, the Lacedaemonians wanted back the men captured on the island.

Now something new, which had long been on the horizon, presented it-self; and it could no longer be ignored. The Thirty Years' Peace with Argos was about to expire. The Argives announced that they were willing to renew it—but only if the Spartans were prepared to restore Cynouria to them. In addi-tion, Thucydides pointedly adds, the Lacedaemonians had begun to suspect—and with good reason—that some of the cities in their Peloponnesian league were contemplating rebellion and an alliance with the Argives. This was an old story. Argos had been neutral at the time of the Persian Wars, and the Man-tineians and the Eleans had absented themselves in a highly suspicious manner from Plataea in 479. Moreover, in the 460s, the Argives had lured the Tegeans into an alliance aimed at overthrowing the Lacedaemonian hegemony. But to understand the perils that the Spartans now faced one did not have to be old enough to remember these developments. In the late 420s, it was obvious that the condition of Lacedaemon's alliance required close attention.[27]

The ancient Greeks took it for granted that one community's freedom presupposed the subjection of others. In consequence, within leagues, as we have seen, those charged with the leadership often found it necessary to protect weak communities from those that were strong, and the ambition of the latter more often than not expressed itself within the alliance as a centrifugal force. When the Thasians and, as we have seen, the Samians and the Mytilenians sought to withdraw from the Delian League, it was because Athens stood in the way of their extraterritorial ambitions.[28]

As the hegemon of a league, Lacedaemon repeatedly faced the same challenge. While she was preoccupied with Athens, one of her most important allies—Mantineia—had constructed a little empire within Arcadia by subjugating her neighbors, and another no less significant—Elis—had mounted a campaign to reassert her control of a district that the Spartans had come to regard as important to their own security. It was the first of these two developments that had occasioned the bloody battle that had taken place in south-central Arcadia between Mantineia and Tegea during the truce in 423, and it had led the Mantineians thereafter to consider jettisoning their connection with Lacedaemon in exchange for an alliance with Argos. If the Eleans thought along similar lines, it was because Sparta stood in the way of their ambition as well. The citizens of both communities knew that, when Lacedaemon was no longer preoccupied with Athens, she would intervene to break up or prevent the reestablishment of their little dominions—and Thucydides' testimony suggests that the Spartans were sensitive to their growing unease.[29]

This time, the Athenians were also ready to negotiate in earnest. Delium had been for them, as Thucydides points out, a terrible blow; and it opened up the possibility that the Thebans would invade and ravage Attica. Amphipolis had made things considerably worse. We can flesh out the details. Coming on top of what the plague had done, the loss in hoplite manpower they had suffered in these two battles was devastating; and we can be confident that their financial reserves, apart from the thousand talents in silver set aside for an emergency, were much reduced.

It was one thing to triple the *phóros* assessed, as the Athenians had done between 432 and 425/4; it was another to collect it. Some of the cities from which *phóros* was demanded in 425/4 are not known to have ever in the past made a single contribution. Moreover, by 422, there were many wealthy communities that had once provided substantial support to the Athenian alliance which were no longer doing so. When the Athenians expelled the Aeginetans and Potidaeans from their cities and sent their compatriots to take their place, they chose to forgo the *phóros* they had once collected. After they put down the Mytilenian revolt and established a cleruchy there, the citizens of that *pólis* ceased supplying ships and made no compensatory contributions to the coffers of the Delian League. The rebellions in the Thraceward region on the eve of the war and those instigated later by Brasidas cut sharply into Athens' take from that rich region, and that canny Spartan commander also deprived the Athenians of the considerable revenue they had derived each year from the colony they had established on the Strymon at Amphipolis. The reassessment of 425/4 notwithstanding, it is conceivable that Athens' overall income from abroad was less in 423/2 than it had been ten years before.

After their seizure of Sphacteria, Thucydides tells us, his compatriots had entertained high hopes, trusting in their strength. At that time, thanks to their good fortune, they were confident that they would have the upper hand. Now, however, they feared that their allies, elated at Athens' defeats, might rebel; and they greatly regretted that they had not reached an agreement with Lacedaemon "after the business at Pylos when it had been in their power to do so in a manner consistent with the dictates of honor."

The Athenians had good reason to entertain such regrets, as we have seen. But they were nonetheless ill-advised to enter into serious negotiations at this particular time. They were, we must remember, unchallenged at sea. There was next to no chance that their subject allies in the Aegean and along its coasts could mount a revolt and sustain it. The blows that the Athenians had suffered were grievous, to be sure. But they had weathered worse. Their financial resources may have been to a considerable degree depleted, but they were by no means exhausted; and, thanks to their command over the sea, they still had a steady stream of income. If they were patient and parsimonious, their coffers could be replenished.[30]

Even more to the point, the Athenians had a great deal to lose at the negotiating table. In 425, as we have seen, they could have employed a treaty of peace as an instrument of war. But, in 421, there was no longer much of anything to be gained by such an expedient. Thanks to the truce and the eagerness for a settlement repeatedly and abjectly displayed by the Lacedaemonians both before and after, the damage to Sparta's prestige (and to the leverage she exercised over her allies) that a humiliating settlement would have inflicted in 425 had by 421 already for the most part been incurred. Lacedaemon's allies in and near the Peloponnesus were close observers of their hegemon. Brasidas' brave efforts in Thrace to the contrary notwithstanding, they can hardly have supposed that Sparta still seriously contemplated bringing Athens to her knees, liberating the Hellenes, and redressing the grievances of those in her league whom the Athenians had harmed; and they must have known that she was ready to concede to Athens the gains she had made in the Saronic Gulf and the Ionian Sea.

In 421, moreover, the Athenians were afforded a golden opportunity. The Argives were poised to enter the fray; the Peloponnesian League was coming apart at the seams; and "thanks to the disasters she had suffered, the city of the Lacedaemonians was," as Thucydides puts it, "ill-thought of in the extreme and regarded with contempt." It was time to succeed where Themistocles had fallen short—first, by making an alliance with the Argives, rallying Sparta's disaffected allies, and deploying a hoplite army against her deep in the Peloponnesus where she would have to defend her fragile dominion with outside support greatly reduced; and then by annihilating her phalanx in battle, freeing the Messenians, and confining Lacedaemon within the Eurotas valley east of Mount Taygetus.[31]

Unfortunately for the Athenians, Themistocles' Peloponnesian venture, which had been undertaken half a century before, no longer loomed large in the public imagination. At Athens, strategic vision was in short supply, and there was no man of great influence left who thought as Pericles had.

The domestic political situation in both Athens and Sparta was, in fact, highly favorable to the forging of a settlement. The war's two most influential and intransigent proponents were out of the way, and the two most ardent proponents of peace had suddenly and unexpectedly gained the ascendancy. All four were, Thucydides believed, actuated chiefly by personal motives. None of them had a clear and coherent understanding of the long-term interests of his own political community. Brasidas and Cleon had wanted the war to continue. Although they may have flattered themselves that they were being public-spirited, the Athenian historian wryly observed that the former had enjoyed success in and had gained honor from the war and that the latter feared that if there was quiet he would be more conspicuous as a wrongdoer and more mistrusted as a slanderer.

Nicias and the Agiad king Pleistoanax no doubt also thought themselves public-spirited, but Thucydides harbored doubts in their case as well. As he was aware, his former colleague, who had enjoyed more success and good fortune as a general than any Athenian in his generation, was an exceedingly pious man who attributed his accomplishments largely to luck and divine favor. While still undefeated and honored, thinking peace less risky than war, he wanted an end of toil and trouble for himself and for his fellow citizens; and he also desired to leave behind for himself a name for never having caused the city to trip up. For his part, the latter figure shared his Athenian counterpart's conviction that little could go wrong in time of peace, and he wanted to silence those of his countrymen who were constantly blaming him for the martial setbacks that Lacedaemon had suffered since his return from exile. They alleged that his brother had committed a sacrilege and had broken the law by bribing the Pythia to press for his restoration, and they intimated that it was this impious act that had caused the gods to turn against Sparta.[32]

On this occasion, under the influence of Nicias and Laches at Athens and of Pleistoanax at Sparta, each city appointed *xúnedroi* to sit alongside one another and work out in private the details of an accord. The Athenians elected ten dealmakers, one from each tribe, including Hagnon; and the Spartans selected ten as well, in all likelihood two from each of Lacedaemon's five constituent villages. Included in their number were Philocharidas son of Eryxilaidas, one of the two Spartans who had taken the oath at the time of the truce; Ischagoras; and a man named Tellis, who may well have been Brasidas' father . . . or his son.

As was bound to happen, the negotiations, which took place during the winter of 422/1, met with obstacles. Eventually, in desperation, the Lacedaemonians intimated their willingness to up the ante one more time and sacrifice the men held captive at Athens—by ordering the cities in their alliance to make preparations for the construction of a fort in Attica, from which to ravage Athens' territory all year long. This gambit worked as intended, rendering the Athenians more willing to compromise. At the end of the winter, the two sides settled on an agreement intended to last for fifty years; and in the immediate aftermath of Athens' City Dionysia in mid-March 421—ten years and a few days after the outbreak of the war—the two kings, the five ephors, and the ten *xúnedroi* from Lacedaemon met with their seventeen counterparts from Athens to swear to the peace pact's terms. Foremost among the Athenians were the sometime generals Nicias, Laches, Lamachus, and Demosthenes.[33]

Like the truce of 423, the instrument ratified in 421 gave first place to the gods. All were guaranteed access to the common sanctuaries and to the oracles, and Delphi itself was accorded autonomy. The two sides agreed to desist from doing damage to one another and to submit disputes for arbitration. The Boeotians were to retain Plataea and the Athenians, Nisaea. Potidaea, Aegina, Corcyra, Sollium, Anactorium, and Acarnania were politely ignored. Otherwise, territory taken was to be returned. The Spartans and their allies were to restore Amphipolis to the Athenians, and the Athenians were to allow anyone in any cities restored to them who wanted to depart to do so with his personal property. Argilos, Stagira, Acanthus, Scolus, Olynthus, and Spartolus were to enjoy the autonomy promised by Brasidas on condition that they paid the *phóros* assessed at the time of the Delian League's foundation or soon thereafter by Aristeides son of Lysimachus. Otherwise, they could be neutral or ally with Athens as they saw fit. The citizens of Mecyberna, Sane, and Singus were to reside in their own cities undisturbed, as were the citizens of Olynthus and Acanthus. The Spartans and their allies were to restore to Athens the fort of Panactum, which the Boeotians had seized by treachery in 422 after the end of the truce; and the Athenians were to return to the Lacedaemonians and their allies Coryphasium, Cythera, Methana, Atalante, and a place called Pteleum, of which we have no knowledge. Both sides were to release their prisoners, and the Peloponnesians and the other Spartan allies trapped in Scione were to go free. The future of Scione, Torone, Sermylia, and the other rebellious cities that had come back into Athens' possession was left for the Athenians to decide. The treaty was to be renewed each year and solemn oaths were then to be retaken; and, if anything was left out, the Athenians and the Lacedaemonians were authorized to make the requisite changes.[34]

On the face of it, the agreement that came to be called Peace of Nicias would seem to display all of the features necessary if a treaty is to be conducive to a lasting settlement. It reflected the balance of power. It addressed all of the outstanding issues. It dealt with virtually every likely source of future dispute. It provided for arbitration, and it left room for adjustment.

There was, to be sure, one thing obviously amiss. Four of Lacedaemon's allies, including three of the most important, had voted against its acceptance; and, in the aftermath, the Boeotians, Megarians, Corinthians, and Eleans announced that they would refuse to abide by its terms. The same would in due course prove true as well for the Chalcidians at Olynthus and for Lacedaemon's other allies in the Thraceward region.[35] In practice, their intransigence meant that Sparta had made promises to Athens that it was not in her power to keep. But, as we shall soon see, there was much more amiss than this.

Athens, though battered and demoralized, was the victor; and the Lacedaemonians were humiliated—but they were by no means cowed. Coryphasium and Sphacteria they regarded as "a theft of war" not apt to be repeated. Moreover, the anxieties that had given rise to the conflict had not been dispelled. If anything, they had been intensified. The growth in Athens' power was a brute fact. Despite the painful setback she had suffered in the Thraceward region, that growth had continued during the war; and, as anyone could see, it had left Lacedaemon even more vulnerable than before.

The Spartans were by no means unaware of their plight, and they surely knew well before the event that a peace agreement along these lines would sow division within their alliance and make it harder for them to cope should there be a servile revolt. The Corinthians were at their wits' end. Nothing had been done to redress the grievances that had induced them in 432 to threaten to bolt from their league and take others with them. Instead, they had been deprived of Potidaea; and, in the region they deemed vital for their security—the Corinthian Gulf, the Ionian Sea, and the Adriatic—they were now considerably worse off than before. Moreover, thanks to the losses they had suffered in battle and to the Lacedaemonians' surrender of the allied galleys they had led into Navarino Bay, the Corinthians no longer had a navy of consequence; and the blockade imposed by the Athenians appears to have deprived them of the resources requisite for building another great fleet.[36] If Corinth now made good on the threat she had issued in 432, there were, as we have seen, communities of significance within the Peloponnesus that were apt to follow her lead. To this we can add that nothing had happened since the Thebans' refusal in 423 to agree to the truce to calm the fears, assuage the anger, and satisfy the ambitions of that proud people.

In 425, when the Lacedaemonians first displayed their willingness to accept a humiliating peace, they had proposed not only a cessation of hostilities and a set of mutual concessions, but also an alliance by means of which Athens and Sparta could share the hegemony and dictate to everyone else. This possibility had no doubt also been discussed at some length during the winter of 422/1. It received strong support, we are told, from Nicias; and a draft of just such an instrument was almost certainly produced. But the two sides had initially stopped short—perhaps because the Lacedaemonians feared that such an accord would be fatal to the league they had long led. If so, the degree of intransigence displayed by the Corinthians, Megarians, Eleans, and Thebans when they learned in detail the terms of the treaty of peace caused the Spartans to reconsider; and, when in these circumstances the Argives once again rejected a proposal that the peace between the two Peloponnesian rivals be renewed, the Lacedaemonians opted to suggest to the Athenians that the two communities forge a defensive alliance, providing for their mutual defense and specifying that neither without the other could go to war or, by pouring libations, make peace or form an alliance. This would, the Spartans reportedly thought, isolate the Argives and render them insignificant as a threat; and it would make it far more likely that the political communities within the Peloponnesus contemplating rebellion would choose to "remain at rest."

The terms of the alliance, which was slated to last for fifty years, suggest that another concern, not singled out for emphasis by Thucydides, may in fact have been paramount. For that instrument not only specified that the two cities were to defend one another from attack and to treat the attackers, after their repulse, as enemies. It also included a pledge that, should Lacedaemon's servile population rebel, the Athenians would come to the Spartans' defense.

Next to no time passed between the ratification of the peace pact and the forging of a bilateral alliance. The fact that those within Lacedaemon and Athens who ratified the two agreements by pouring libations and taking the oaths were the same proves that the alliance went into effect before the new archons took office at Athens in late June. The fact that, in his narrative, Thucydides situates the second of the two agreements prior to the beginning of his summer makes it clear that no more than a couple of weeks separated the treaty of peace from the promulgation of the alliance. Moreover, we have reason to believe that, during this period of intense diplomatic activity, the delegations from the members of Sparta's league which had been summoned to Lacedaemon to approve and subscribe to the treaty of peace, though released, had remained on the spot—presumably with an eye to further negotiations and to

agitating against and derailing the alliance with which they were now threatened. Had the Corinthians, Megarians, Eleans, and Thebans given way and
subscribed to the treaty of peace when the full consequences of their intransigence were brought home to them, the Lacedaemonians might well have
abandoned their quest for an alliance with Athens. But this they did not do.[37]

Though separately ratified, the peace pact and the alliance formed a single
package aimed at bringing to an end an enduring strategic rivalry. That much
is clear from the long duration specified in both. In reality, however, as Thucydides points out, like the Thirty Years' Peace, the new arrangement was little
more than "an armistice attended by jealousy and suspicion." It was a product
of mutual exhaustion, and it was inherently unstable. Moreover, to the extent
that it disrupted the Spartan alliance, it fostered the very troubles it was meant
to avert, and it left Lacedaemon dangerously dependent on Athens' goodwill.
When the two sides recouped their strength, they would both have occasion
to reconsider and rue the terms of the deal they had made.[38]

CHAPTER 7

The Peloponnesus in Flux

WARRE, consisteth not in Battell onely, or the act of fighting; but in a tract of time, wherein the Will to contend by Battell is sufficiently known: and therefore the notion of Time, is to be considered in the nature of Warre; as it is in the nature of Weather. For as the nature of Foule weather, lyeth not in a showre or two of rain; but in an inclination thereto of many dayes together: So the nature of War, consisteth not in actuall fighting; but in the known disposition thereto, during all the time there is no assurance to the contrary.

THOMAS HOBBES

THE arena that we now call the international realm is, in principle, ungoverned. To the extent that there is nonetheless a modicum of order within that arena, that order is imposed. It is a construct, a work of art, a product of statesmanship. It is a function of submission forced on the weak by the strong, of alliances forged in the face of a common fear, and of negotiations backed by a credible threat on one or both sides that, if a settlement is not achieved, there will be unpleasant consequences. It is only natural that, where so artificial an order emerges, it should require constant tending—and be, even then, fragile and fleeting.

Enduring strategic rivalries tend, within the geographical space wherein they play out, to bring a semblance of order out of the reigning chaos by imposing a structure on the relations between political communities. It would be an exaggeration to say that, in an enduring bipolar system, every polity knows its place and each hegemon disciplines its adherents—but for communities not on the margins this does come tolerably close to being true, and this was the case, as we have seen, within ancient Hellas.[1]

When, however, such a rivalry between great powers comes to an end—or even appears to do so—the old intercommunal order that accompanied it is apt to dissolve. When this process takes place, chaos regains its edge, and new possibilities present themselves. The promulgation of the Peace of Nicias and the institution of a bilateral defensive alliance between Sparta and Athens did not put an end to their rivalry. But that was the pretense; and, as all of those experienced in intercommunal affairs know, what begins as pretense can easily become reality. Moreover, even where the pretense is never more than a pretense, the illusions to which it gives rise can dramatically affect calculations and unsettle affairs—as happened in this particular case.

If the settlement worked out over the winter of 422/1 left the Athenians' league unmoved, it was solely because Athens retained her command over the sea and, with it, the capacity to impose her will on the communities within that league while the cities themselves—mindful of the punishment meted out to Naxos, Thasos, Chalcis, Eretria, Histiaea, Samos, Potidaea, Mytilene, Torone, and the like—had the good sense to do as they were told. It was within the Peloponnesus that anarchy reemerged within the Hellenic world. For there, by common consent, Lacedaemon had for generations reigned supreme and directed affairs—but she did not rule.

Corinth was the instigator. Eleven years before, she had issued a threat, and by this means she had bullied the Lacedaemonians into launching a war. Now in fury, after having been left in the lurch, she intended to make good on that threat by rallying the other discontents, "setting in motion that which had been settled [*diekínoun tà pepragména*]," and otherwise fomenting "trouble and disorder [*taraché*]" within the Spartan alliance. This was her only recourse. She had to show the Spartans that their well-being was dependent on satisfying her legitimate security needs. Otherwise, if she could not demonstrate her capacity to wreak havoc within the Peloponnesus and thereby force Lacedaemon to attend to her concerns and renew the war, she would have to accept as permanent Athens' denial to her of the position of strength, security, and proud independence that she had long enjoyed.[2]

There was nothing surprising about Corinth's conduct on this occasion. Pericles had not only anticipated it. He had banked on it. As we have seen, provoking her fury had been his focus from the moment he had advocated that Athens make a defensive alliance with Corcyra; and, while he was alive (and, as a consequence of inertia, long afterward as well), the Athenians had done everything within their power to frustrate, damage, and bring pressure to bear on Corinth—all, at least in Pericles' case, with an eye to stoking a wrath that would be unleashed in due course on her feckless hegemon.

Fortunately for us, Thucydides, who understood Pericles' objective better than anyone since, appears to have responded to this new set of circumstances by abandoning his refuge in the Thraceward region and taking up residence at Corinth; and he devoted himself thereafter to tracing in detail the breakdown of the inherited intercommunal order within the Peloponnesus and to puzzling over the conflicts and confusion to which the reemergence of intercommunal anarchy gave rise. If for the most part, in dealing with this period, Thucydides ignored Athens' initiatives in the Thraceward region as well as developments elsewhere, it was because he thought them comparatively insignificant and wanted to underline the profound importance of the troubles that emerged in Lacedaemon's backyard.[3]

If the Athenian historian does not tell us in his text everything he surmised, it was for three reasons. When he died, Thucydides left behind in draft a narrative account of this period that he clearly had not had the time to revisit and fully recast and rewrite. Had he returned to polish his rendering of this story, he would no doubt have eliminated the inconsistencies and fleshed it out to some degree. Nonetheless, in the draft account that he managed to jot down, he clearly wanted to reproduce for his readers the uncomfortable experience of being at a loss, of not knowing what is going on, of being caught up in a situation that one cannot not fully comprehend, much less control—which gripped those in the actual situation and caused them to oscillate between elation, on the one hand, and anxiety, dread, and panic, on the other. At the same time, he was inclined, as he was throughout his history, to set puzzles for prospective statesmen to sort out for themselves. His purpose, as I have said before, was not to tell his readers what to think but to induce them to do their own thinking and to provide them with raw factual material on which to exercise the political and strategic imagination.[4]

Corinth on a Rampage

When the bilateral alliance between the two erstwhile antagonists was ratified in late March or early April 421, and the various delegations that had remained at Lacedaemon while that instrument was being negotiated finally withdrew and headed for home, the envoys from Corinth took a brief detour and approached "some of those in authority at Argos." We are not given their names—as scholars have noticed, Thucydides is exceedingly parsimonious with Argive names—and the principle by which they were singled out is not specified. Thucydides is well informed concerning Argive institutions and practices, and he was surely capable of naming names. But, when he brings us into that community, we are repeatedly made to enter a shadowy world of conspiracy and intrigue. Thucydides' purpose is to inspire curiosity, elicit suspicion, and force us to put the pieces of the puzzle together ourselves.

There were—Argos' ancient antipathy to Lacedaemon, notwithstanding—figures of importance in that *pólis* who were decidedly unsympathetic to the Athenian cause. One such was caught early in the war by the Athenians, accompanying in a private capacity an official delegation composed of three Spartans, a prominent Corinthian, and a Tegean headed for Susa in search of support against the Athenians. Another is known to have tipped off the Corinthians in advance regarding the invasion of the Corinthiad that Nicias staged at Solygeia in 425. It was almost certainly to men of this stamp—some of them, would-be oligarchs and secret Laconizers—that these envoys now turned. There was at Argos, as Thucydides eventually informs us, a faction, decidedly hostile to that city's democratic order, more than willing to be "serviceable [*epitédeioi*]" to the Lacedaemonians and to do their bidding; and, thanks to the institution of guest-friendship and to the occasions for conviviality at the athletic contests held at regular intervals at Olympia, Delphi, Nemea, and Isthmia, there were networks that linked the members of Hellas' ancient aristocracy, and men of this particular political orientation were well known to the like-minded abroad.[5]

Upon arrival, no doubt to the surprise and delight of their hosts, their Corinthian visitors set aside the ancient antagonism that had hitherto pitted these two Dorian communities against one another. Then, they put forward a proposal that would, they rightly suspected, set off a diplomatic revolution within the Peloponnesus.

These Corinthians were mercantile men, skilled in the ways of diplomacy; and they knew how to make mischief. At Argos, they told the select individuals whom they approached precisely that, which they recognized, the people of Argos had for a very long time most wanted to hear. According to Thucydides, they beguiled their interlocutors with the prospect that Argos might regain the leading position within the Peloponnesus that she had lost to Lacedaemon well over a century before. In making peace, they charged, and, above all, in forging an alliance with those who had "hitherto" been "their worst enemies," the Spartans were "up to no good." Their real aim, they said, was "a subjugation of the Peloponnesus," and "it was incumbent on the Argives to see to it that the Peloponnesus was saved."

To this end, the Corinthian envoys urged their Argive interlocutors to secure the passage of a decree inviting "any Greek city which was self-governing and prepared to submit to judgments consistent with equity and common practice" to join them in "forging a defensive alliance." To this end, they suggested that the Argives appoint "a few men fully empowered" to conduct negotiations, and they urged them not to handle this business in the public assembly before the people lest the overtures of those not accepted be made public. "Out of a hatred for the Lacedaemonians," they predicted, "many communities will come forward."[6]

The calculations that had originally led the Spartans to suppose that their negotiation of a defensive alliance with Athens would cow the Argives and reduce the restlessness that threatened their league were not, on the face of it, unsound. Had the Corinthians not given way to rage, had they not dangled this tempting bait, it is by no means certain that the Argives would at this time have mounted a bid for regional hegemony. In the event, however, the citizens of Argos swallowed the bait and acted precisely as urged. The Argives were a proud lot. Even those who hated Athens and greatly admired Lacedaemon also dreamed of surpassing the latter. Mindful that their thirty years' peace with that power was about to expire, convinced that war was on the horizon, and hopeful that they might recover the hegemony within the Peloponnesus that every red-blooded patriot thought rightly theirs, the Argives issued the requisite decree of invitation, and they elected a twelve-man commission authorized to negotiate, without reference to the assembly, a defensive alliance with any city, apart from Athens and Sparta, that met the pertinent criteria.

The Argives had known nothing but peace and prosperity for thirty years. They had, as Thucydides observes, suffered none of the "disasters" that had caused the Lacedaemonians to be "ill-thought of in the extreme and regarded with contempt." They had, in fact, "done exceedingly well in every particular." Moreover, they had taken no part in "the Attic war"; and, being at peace with both sides, "they had reaped the fruits."[7]

It was at this time that the Argives, mindful of Sparta's marked superiority in hoplite warfare, are also said to have set up an elite heavy infantry force of one thousand young men—as, we have reason to believe, they had done on occasion in the past. Chosen from among those who were "the strongest in body and preeminent in wealth" and provided by the city with sustenance and support, they were expected to exercise constantly and train in the manner of the Lacedaemonians so that, like them, they could become "athletes in war-like deeds."

Militarily, this was a sensible move. Politically, given the fact that some leading Argives greatly admired Sparta and strongly disliked their own city's democratic order, this decision was unwise. In spirit, this arrangement was aristocratic, not democratic. The esprit de corps that the Argives hoped to foster could easily turn an elite unit made up of men from such a background into an instrument for overthrowing the existing regime—as, we later learn, it did.[8]

The Mantineians were the first to take up the Argive offer. Argos was, they knew, a fellow democracy and a city of consequence forever at odds with the Lacedaemonians. They feared that the Spartans, now that they were at leisure, would dismantle the little empire which they had constructed in Arcadia—and they were right to do so. That diminutive dominion threatened everything that the Lacedaemonians held near and dear. It included not only Parrhasia, which lay directly to the north of Messenia, but also Cypsela, which was situated within the high plateau in south-central Arcadia between Sciritis, just north of Laconia, and the Derveni Pass leading into Messenia. There, as if to provoke the Lacedaemonians, the Mantineians had built a fort, which dominated the strategically vital wagon road leading from the Eurotas valley within the narrow confines of what we now call Laconia across south-central Arcadia and down into the Pamisos valley in Messenia.[9]

Mantineia's defection caused a great uproar within the Peloponnesus, inducing the other cities to consider imitating her example. The furor, which the Corinthians vigorously stoked, was occasioned, we are told, in part by the suspicion that the Mantineians must know something that had escaped the attention of everyone else and even more so by the suspect clause in the treaty of peace authorizing the Lacedaemonians and the Athenians to amend the instrument, without reference to their allies, as these two great powers thought fit. This clause led at least some of Sparta's longtime allies to fear that the two cities had conspired to achieve for Lacedaemon in the Peloponnesus what Athens had accomplished in the Aegean: the reduction of the self-governing cities within her alliance to subject status.[10]

The Lacedaemonians were keenly aware of the uproar, and they knew that the Corinthians were the purveyors of this conspiracy theory and the chief

Map 23. Boeotia, Megara, and the Peloponnesus

promoters of the Argive alliance. To Corinth, therefore, they sent an embassy in an attempt to bring the disintegration of their league to a halt. Their envoys accused the Corinthians of being the originators of the entire mess. They solemnly warned them that, if they defected and made an alliance with Argos, they would be in violation of the oaths they had taken long before—adding that they had already committed an injustice in refusing to accept the treaty of peace with the Athenians after having agreed that whatever the majority of the allies decreed would be authoritative unless something pertaining to the gods or the heroes proved an impediment.[11]

In anticipation of this exchange, the Corinthians had invited as witnesses to the parley those who had joined them in refusing to abide by the treaty. In response to the Spartans, they could have rehearsed the genuine grievances that had, in fact, occasioned their intransigence. In particular, as Thucydides makes clear, they could legitimately have zeroed in on the fact that, in tacitly sanctioning their loss of Sollium and Anactorium, the peace treaty was incompatible with another agreement that had been made on the eve of the war to promote solidarity within the alliance—a solemn pledge that in the course of the struggle none of the powers allied would lose any of the holdings that they had possessed before the war began.

Instead, however, knowing to whom and before whom they spoke, the Corinthians set aside the grievances peculiar to their own community and cannily presented themselves as public-spirited defenders of decency and the common good and as loyal supporters of their allies, insinuating, without ever openly asserting, that it was the Lacedaemonians who had betrayed their allies and that they were the true oath-breakers. On the eve of the war, the Corinthians explained, they had sworn to come to the assistance of the Chalcidians in Thrace; and the gods, they asserted, would not look kindly on their abandonment of these allies. That the Spartans had incurred the wrath of the gods by betraying the Chalcidians and the others in the Thraceward region recruited by Brasidas—this they did not say. In the circumstances, there was no need.[12]

In the immediate aftermath of this altercation, an embassy arrived in Corinth from Elis. Its members negotiated an alliance with the Corinthians. Then, with the encouragement of the latter, they went on to Argos to do the same. Like the Mantineians, the Eleans had a little regional empire to defend— one that had first emerged in the archaic period—and though this dominion, in which members of the subject communities are tellingly called *períoikoi* in the ancient literary sources, was clearly modeled on that maintained by Lacedaemon on the margins of Laconia and Messenia, the Eleans also found themselves at odds with the hegemon of their league. The reasons were strategic.

To the south of Elis, along the west coast of the Peloponnesus, lay a region, thought to have been settled early on by Minyans and others, which came at some point to be called Triphylia—"the land of three tribes." In the archaic period, this district is said to have come under Elis' control. In the late fifth century, if not well before, she and others abroad regarded it, like the other districts under her control, as part of the Eleia; and it was her practice—when a citizen of Lepreum, the principal *pólis* in Triphylia, won an Olympic contest— to proclaim the victor as an Elean from Lepreum.

At times, to be sure, Elis' right to rule was contested. In 479, for example, Lepreum was sturdily independent; and, while the Eleans dithered and, we must suspect, flirted with Medism, the Lepreates contributed two hundred hoplites to the fight at Plataea. Later, however, at some point within the lifetime of Herodotus, the Eleans reasserted their claim, as we have already had occasion to note, by seizing and sacking a majority of the Triphylian towns.[13]

With regard to Lepreum, everything turned on an obligation incurred at an unspecified moment in the past—whether before or after the Persian Wars, no one now knows. On that occasion, the citizens of Lepreum are said, in desperation, to have asked the Eleans to help defend them against an Arcadian incursion, offering half of their land as recompense. With this request, the Eleans had purportedly complied. But the land on offer they had left in the hands of its original owners—on condition that forever after, once a year, the Lepreates formally acknowledge their debt and, with it, their subordinate status as *períoikoi* by paying a talent of silver in rent to the treasury of Zeus at Olympia—which, as it happened, the Eleans controlled.[14]

During the war with Athens, the Lepreates had withheld this contribution, citing the conflict as a pretext. Demanding payment, the Eleans had then resorted to force. In response, the Lepreates had appealed to Lacedaemon. At first, the Eleans appear to have accepted their hegemon's arbitration. But when they came to doubt the impartiality of the court, they withdrew from the proceedings and laid waste the territory of Lepreum. In response, the Lacedaemonian tribunal ruled that the Lepreates were not *períoikoi* after all; that they were properly autonomous and self-governing; and that the Eleans had done them wrong. To enforce this ruling and protect the Lepreates, they then introduced into Lepreum a garrison of hoplites.

This was, as the Eleans vehemently pointed out, an egregious breach of the agreement that none of Lacedaemon's allies would be deprived of anything that they had possessed before the great war began. In the face of this principled objection, however, the Spartans were unmoved. As Thucydides allows us to see (but does not say), Athens' establishment of the fort at Coryphasium had made the Lacedaemonians much warier than before; and they had come to think Lepreum, which abutted the northern border of westernmost Messenia, almost as strategically vital as the corridor that ran through south-central Arcadia. It was this change in perspective that had occasioned the squabble pitting them against their longtime ally.[15]

Elis' adherence gave the Corinthians the confidence to take the plunge and join in—which is what they soon thereafter did, in tandem with the Chalcidians, who, faced with Athenian ire, were now no doubt eager to find support. And, when the alliance of these two peoples with the Argives had been solemnized, the Corinthians and the Argives sent a joint embassy to Tegea. If, they reportedly thought, the Tegeans were to join, the entire Peloponnesus would follow.

But the Corinthians had miscalculated. This was not to be. The Tegeans were a proud, fiercely independent community with a strong sense of common identity rooted in legend and genuine historical events. Moreover, Tegea and Mantineia were close neighbors and had long been rivals—separated, as peoples (such as the Argives and the Corinthians) sometimes are, by a common language and ethnicity. When divisions emerged within the Peloponnesus, these two *póleis* could rarely be found on the same side; and, in fact, they had fought a savage, inconclusive battle over south-central Arcadia no more than two years before. It may also have mattered that Mantineia, Elis, and Argos were democracies, instinctively unfriendly to the domination of the many by the few. Decades before, when Cleandridas had put an end to the Tegean rebellion, he had installed in the city a ruling oligarchy dependent on and fiercely loyal to Lacedaemon.[16]

Up to this point, the Corinthians had acted zealously in promoting the Argive alliance. When, however, the Tegeans bluntly rejected their blandishments, sobriety set in; and, Thucydides tells us, they lost "the love for victory [*philonikía*]" that had thus far animated them, and they "shrank back in horror" at the prospect that none of Lacedaemon's other allies would join in, fearing not only that they would be unable to bully her back into the war, but also that they might soon find themselves isolated and subject to reprisals.

This loss of nerve did not prevent the Corinthians from vainly making the same pitch to the Boeotians, who, in company with the narrow oligarchy now dominant in Megara, found the prospect of breaking with Lacedaemon and forming an alliance with a democracy distasteful in the extreme. But it did cause them to ask two favors when the Boeotians rejected the invitation: that, for the Corinthians, they obtain from the Athenians what they had obtained for themselves—a ten-day, renewable truce—and that, if the Athenians denied their request, they themselves break off that truce.

Where they had once been enraged, the Corinthians were now diffident—and with reason. It was not at all clear that they had the leverage that hitherto they had supposed they possessed. In venting their frustration and fury, they now feared that they had gone too far. Argos could not accomplish for them what Sparta had failed to achieve, and she was not even likely to want to try. It was, moreover, unwise for a Peloponnesian *pólis* profoundly at loggerheads with Athens to infuriate the only community that might come to her rescue. When the Boeotians put their request to the Athenians and the latter demurred, observing that, as far as they were concerned, the treaty with Lacedaemon included Corinth, and when the Boeotians then renewed their truce with Athens, the anxiety that had the Corinthians in its grip did not abate.[17]

If anything, their fears must have grown. For, that same summer, the Spartans demonstrated their capacity to act against both Mantineia and Elis. First, Pleistoanax son of Pausanias, Lacedaemon's Agiad king, led the entire levy of the Lacedaemonians into Parrhasia to liberate the Arcadians there from their Mantineian overlords; and, though the Mantineians placed their city in the hands of an Argive garrison and marched out in full force to defend their little empire, they could neither save Parrhasia nor prevent the Spartans from tearing down the fort they had built at Cypsela in south-central Arcadia.[18]

A bit later, when the survivors from among the soldiers who had accompanied Brasidas to Thrace returned from that posting, the Lacedaemonians settled the liberated helots in their number (whom they termed *Brasídeioi*) at Lepreum alongside a considerably smaller group of manumitted helots who had in the interim done them good service nearer home. The latter batch of freedmen, who had almost certainly assisted their former masters in fending off the raiders from Cythera and Coryphasium and in keeping the remaining helots under control, the Spartans termed *neodamódeis*—"new citizens." It was apparently at this time that the Spartans decided to restore full equality to the men who had surrendered on Sphacteria. They had begun to suspect that they were going to need all of the manpower they could get.[19]

A Stillborn Peace

In the meantime, relations between Athens and Sparta had become fraught. When the treaty of peace was signed, the two sides drew lots to determine who was to make the first move in implementing the agreement. Thanks perhaps, as Theophrastus later claimed, to chicanery on the part of Nicias, it fell to Lacedaemon to take the lead by releasing the prisoners she held, by restoring Amphipolis to Athens, and persuading the cities in the Thraceward region to comply with the treaty's terms. Those held captive she immediately let go, and she dispatched Ischagoras, Menas, and Philocharidas to Thrace to order Clearidas to hand over Amphipolis to the Athenians and to instruct the other cities mentioned in the instrument to fall in line.

The latter, however, refused to comply, thinking the terms inconvenient and unsuitable. Clearidas, whom Thucydides appears to have interviewed, was reportedly eager to please the Chalcidians; and so he, too, balked, claiming that it was impossible to hand over the city in the face of forceful opposition on the part of her citizens.

With expedition, Clearidas then journeyed to Lacedaemon, taking with him with envoys from Amphipolis. There, before the ephors, he defended his act of disobedience against the accusations which, he suspected, Ischagoras and his colleagues would lodge; and he sought to find out whether there was still a chance to alter the treaty. When he discovered that the matter was settled, he returned to Thrace with no less haste, having been dispatched by the authorities at Lacedaemon with strict orders to hand over the place and, if this proved impossible, to withdraw however many Peloponnesians there were in the town—and it was, of course, the latter, not the former task, that he performed.[20]

As a political actor, Clearidas was a worthy successor to Brasidas—outwardly obedient to the authorities while he passively resisted their policies and rendered them unworkable. The fact that the ephors let him get away with this bit of skullduggery suggests that they sympathized with him—that, although they regarded Lacedaemon's betrayal of Amphipolis and her abandonment of her allies in the Thraceward region as a necessity, they bitterly regretted the fact and found the orders they were called upon to issue a source of humiliation. In effect, however, thanks to their toleration of obstruction on Clearidas' part and to their failure to make good on their subsequent promises, the peace that they had sponsored was stillborn.

If Theophrastus' report is accurate and somehow, by way of bribery, the son of Niceratus saw to it that the Spartans had to go first, it was a smart move on his part. But what the Athenians had then gained, either by good fortune or by his underhandedness, they subsequently sacrificed when—at his suggestion, as Plutarch reports—they generously responded to Lacedaemon's release of her captives and to the promulgation of a treaty of alliance by swiftly sending home the men who had surrendered on Sphacteria and the other Spartiates who had come to be imprisoned with them. As Nicias and his compatriots surely knew, it was the capture of these men that had brought the Lacedaemonians to the negotiating table. This was for them the chief object of the peace; and, had the Athenians insisted on holding onto these prisoners of war until they had Amphipolis in their possession and the cities in Thrace had knuckled under, the Spartans would have seen to it that the terms of the treaty were strictly enforced against their allies.[21]

As one would expect, Lacedaemon's failure to deliver on her commitments quickly gave rise to suspicion and ill will. In the course of the summer of 421, that suspicion was repeatedly compounded as Athens' new ally promised again and again to unite with Athens in compelling the cities that had rejected the treaty to comply with it, and as time after time she fixed a date when these cities would be declared enemies of both allies—and never made good on either pledge. As the Athenians came to doubt the honesty of the Lacedaemonians, Thucydides reports, they came to regret having released the men captured on Sphacteria, and so they resolutely refused to give up the fort at Coryphasium. In time, they were persuaded to withdraw the Messenians of Naupactus from Coryphasium and to evacuate the runaway helots and the others who had fled Sparta's domain—and the latter they resettled nearby at Cranae in Cephallenia. In the circumstances, however, this was as far as the Athenians were willing to go.[22]

There had been in Athens no effective opposition to the peace. But there had been opposition, nonetheless. There is mention in Aristophanes of the objections raised by the demagogue Hyperbolus, but he was not preeminent among the treaty's opponents. That role was reserved for a dashing young man, just over thirty, named Alcibiades son of Cleinias, who had distinguished himself as an exceedingly young infantryman at Potidaea. He was, by all accounts, a charming rogue—breathtakingly handsome, brave, clever, wealthy, and given to ostentatious displays of magnificence—and his pedigree could

Figure 5. Bust of Alcibiades (Capitoline Museum, Palazzo
dei Conservatori, Hall of the Triumphs, Rome. Photographer: Marie-Lan Nguyen. Published unchanged in
2020 under the following license issued by Marie-Lan
Nguyen: Creative Commons Attribution 2.5 Generic).

hardly have been bettered. On his mother's side, he was of Alcmeonid stock, like Pericles. On his father's, he stemmed from an old aristocratic line that had for generations served as *próxenoi* of the Lacedaemonians, and the name he bore was a Spartan name, reflective of that ancient and honorable connection. The son of Cleinias was also, however, reckless, self-indulgent, and unscrupulous, as rich and well-born young whelps often are.

This Alcibiades was as well prepared for political life as anyone in his generation. He had studied with the sophists. He had spent a great deal of time in the company of the philosopher Socrates; and, in 425, he had served along-side Thudippus on the commission that had dramatically increased the *phóros* demanded from Athens' allies. Even more to the point, he had grown up in the household of Pericles. His father Cleinias had been one of the great states-man's closest friends; and when that brave man died fighting for Athens at Coronea, Athens' principal leader had taken charge of his four- or five-year-old firstborn son and of that boy's younger brother. Most of what he intuited about Athenian politics Alcibiades had learned from intimate and sustained contact with his guardian—the city's most successful practitioner of the polit-ical art.[23]

There was, Thucydides tells us, an element of personal pique in the pos-ture that Alcibiades adopted toward Lacedaemon. In 461, when Athens re-nounced her alliance with Sparta, his like-named grandfather had resigned his family's Spartan *proxenía*. The younger Alcibiades, who had cultivated the captives from Sphacteria with an eye to regaining that office, had taken it as an affront when, in 422/1, the Lacedaemonians had neglected him because of his youth and had chosen to treat with Athens through his elders Nicias and Laches. When the treaty came up for a vote, feeling slighted, he had spoken against it, arguing that the Lacedaemonians were unworthy of trust—that they sought peace solely in order to crush Argos with his compatriots' help and then, with Athens isolated, to turn again on her. In fact, Thucydides re-marks, the young man actually believed something of the sort. For he thought an alliance with Argos preferable, and it was he who insisted—against, we must suspect, the advice persistently proffered by Nicias—that Coryphasium should not be surrendered until and unless Amphipolis was returned.[24]

Things Come Apart

At the end of the summer, the ephors who had subscribed to the peace and the alliance with Athens left office; and it happened, as Thucydides tells us, that some members of the board that replaced them were opposed to the peace. This has often been taken as evidence for a shift of opinion at Lacedae-mon; and were the ephors directly elected, as most scholars now assume, such an inference would be more than merely plausible. But if, as Plato asserts and I believe, the prerogatives reserved for these magistrates came "near to being an allotted power," the character of this new board must in considerable measure have been fortuitous. Their lack of a mandate did not, however, prevent the two members of that board who were most eager to subvert the settlement from making mischief.

Winter was a time for diplomacy. During that season in 421/0, the Athenians, the Boeotians, the Corinthians, and Lacedaemon's loyal allies sent envoys to Sparta; and extensive, inconsequential discussions took place. As these embassies were departing, Cleobulus and Xenares son of Cnidis, the two ephors in question, met in private with the envoys from Boeotia and Corinth and urged that the two communities, both opposed to the peace, make common cause. It was the aim of these two magistrates to engineer two things in close succession: first, a removal of the chief impediments that prevented their compatriots from contemplating a renewal of the war and, then, a rupture of the agreements with Athens. To this end, they first sought to recover Coryphasium from the Athenians and to draw Argos into an alliance with the Lacedaemonians on "honorable terms" compatible with the latter's sense of what was their due.

The initiative was to come from the Boeotians. It was proposed that they enter into an alliance with Argos. Then, presumably with the help of the Corinthians, they could inveigle the Argives into negotiating an accord with Sparta. In the meantime, Cleobulus and Xenares also asked that the Boeotians hand over Panactum to the Lacedaemonians so that they could then trade it for the fort at Coryphasium.[25]

The ephors' plan was, as we shall soon see, more complex than the instructions they gave the Boeotians revealed. It may, in fact, have been too complex to be fully practicable. But it was ingenious, nonetheless—and with regard to Argos, thanks to quick-wittedness and flexibility on the part of some of the plan's partisans, it came exceedingly close to success. The principal obstacle lay in the need for a measure of deceit, which presupposed on everyone's part both secrecy and dispatch. The Corinthians, if it had been up to them, could perhaps have managed something of the sort. They were governed by a relatively narrow oligarchy, and very little business was transacted in their public assembly. But for the cities of Boeotia, which were broadly based oligarchies governed under a complex constitution designed to elicit consent and promote solidarity, machinations of the requisite sort were well-nigh impossible.[26]

Cleobulus and Xenares were not, we soon learn, working entirely on their own. Lacedaemon had collaborators in Argos who held high office—*xénoi* of the two ephors, we must suspect—and they, too, appear to have been party to the plot. This, however, the ephors did not vouchsafe to the Boeotian envoys. Instead, they simply sent them on their way, perhaps in the wake of the Corinthians, who may have been asked to tip off Sparta's Argive admirers—and the Boeotians therefore thought it an astonishingly lucky accident when, on the road north, they came upon two high-level Argives officials, who were waiting for them there with an eye to persuading them to negotiate just such an alliance. These Argives argued (no doubt with a knowing grin) that, if such a confederacy were formed, the Boeotians, Eleans, Mantineians, and Argives "could easily, if they wished, make war *or peace* with Sparta—*or, if need be, with anyone else*"—and the Boeotians envoys responded by encouraging them to send an embassy to Thebes, where, on the Cadmeia, the Boeotian government had its seat.[27]

The Boeotian federation was governed by an executive board of eleven Boetarchs working in close cooperation with a series of four rotating probouleutic councils. When summoned to deliberate in common, these councils constituted an assembly with the authority to make public policy. The returning envoys could afford to be fully frank with the Boetarchs, and from them they elicited enthusiastic support. This was the break the Boeotian leadership had been looking for—a plan to lure Sparta back into the war. Accordingly, when the embassy arrived from Argos, the Boetarchs endorsed the Argive proposal and they promised to send envoys to negotiate.

Then, in consultation with envoys who arrived from Corinth, Megara, and the Chalcidians of Thrace, the Boetarchs proposed that the four powers involved in this conference exchange oaths with one another to provide aid when required and not to make war or accept peace except in common. When this was done, they supposed, the Megarians and the Boeotians, who had for some time been acting in concert, could join the alliance that the Corinthians, Chalcidians, Mantineians, and Eleans had forged with Argos.

The outcome was, predictably, a comedy of errors. The Boetarchs could not afford to divulge before the four councils the full ramifications of the plot cooked up by Cleobulus and Xenares. Had they done so, word would almost certainly have gotten out; the Argives not privy to the plot would have been tipped off; and Pleistoanax and the other Spartan proponents of peace would have learned of the mischief being promoted behind their backs by the two wayward ephors. In consequence of the reticence required of the Boetarchs, when the first proposal was presented to the assembly, its members out of ignorance dug in their heels, fearing that a pact of this sort with a city as notorious as Corinth—which had abandoned Lacedaemon for Argos and was known to be stirring up trouble in the Peloponnesus—would unnecessarily offend the Spartans. The Boetarchs knew better than to attempt, in these circumstances, to get approval for sending envoys to negotiate joining the Argive alliance—and so the matter was neglected and put off.[28]

In the meantime, the Spartans had been conducting conversations with the Athenians about exchanging the fort at Panactum for its counterpart at Coryphasium; and, to this end, they sent envoys to Boeotia to ask that they hand over to them the Athenian prisoners in their possession as well as the fort. This the Boeotians, pressed by those most opposed to the treaty of peace, resolutely refused to do until and unless the Lacedaemonians made a separate alliance with them akin to the one negotiated with the Athenians. Although doing so was a clear breach of their agreement with Athens, the Spartans, desperate for the contemplated exchange, complied.

The Boeotians then responded by razing the fort at Panactum to the ground. By way of explanation, they subsequently cited a supposedly ancient agreement that neither they nor the Athenians would inhabit the Skourta basin on the Attic-Boeotian border between the peaks of Mount Parnes and Mount Cithaeron, where the fort was located, and that both could use it for grazing. This was their excuse. The Boeotians' actual purpose was, of course, provocation; and their aim was a subversion of the peace. As the Spartans surely knew, when they made with the Boeotians a separate alliance, they had in effect publicly renounced the possibility of forcing them into compliance with the treaty. The demolition of the fort, which could easily be rebuilt, merely added insult to the injury the Boeotians had persuaded the Lacedaemonians to inflict.[29]

When summer arrived, the Argives lost heart. No envoys had come from Boeotia, and they knew not what to think. They had also heard that the Lacedaemonians and the Boeotians had negotiated an alliance and that the border fort at Panactum was being demolished. This last fact should give us pause, for it suggests that something underhanded was under way. The Argives can only have learned about the fort's demolition from someone in the know—for neither the Athenians nor the authorities at Lacedaemon were at this point aware that Panactum was being torn down. And yet, in other regards, the Argives appear to have been seriously ill-informed.

It is possible that the Boetarchs kept Cleobulus and Xenares privately informed and that these two conspirators had passed this information on to their associates in Argos. It is even conceivable that the two were party to the Boeotian decision, as some scholars assume. But neither possibility is at all likely. The two ephors were exceedingly eager for the return of Coryphasium, and this news would have infuriated them. It was, from their perspective, the worst possible moment in which to stir up the Athenians.

It is more likely that the Corinthians were the purveyors of this tale. They were in close touch with the Boeotians and with certain, select Argives; and they were master manipulators—quick to make the best of what might otherwise have been regarded as a disappointing situation.

With regard to the implications of the two facts divulged to them, the Argives came to be misinformed in a fashion suggesting that they were the object of a concerted disinformation campaign. They reportedly thought—and, I suspect, they had been told—that Athens had consented to this arrangement. They are said to have supposed—and again, I suspect, they had been told—that the Boeotians were now party to the peace with Athens. The informants of the Argives were trying to railroad them, and they almost certainly had collaborators within the city.

Given the misinformation that had been fed them, it was only natural that the Argives should worry that an alliance with Athens was no longer for them an option; and they are also said to have feared that the Eleans and Mantineians would go over to Sparta and that they would find themselves alone at war against a coalition of Lacedaemonians, Tegeans, Boeotians, and Athenians. In consequence, they panicked and succumbed to the blandishments of those within their own community who were eager for an arrangement with Sparta and privy to the plot hatched by Cleobulus and Xenares, and so they dispatched to Lacedaemon to negotiate the best terms that could be obtained Eustrophus and Aeson, the two Argives "they thought most acceptable to the Spartans."[30]

Cynouria was, as always, the main impediment. The Argive envoys suggested that the ancient territorial dispute be settled by arbitration. This, however, the Lacedaemonians were not willing to risk. But, when it was brought home to them that some such accommodation was required if they were to sideline the Argives via a peace of fifty years' duration, they acquiesced in an agreement, which they considered ridiculous, hearkening back to a duel that had taken place in the distant past—and they agreed that, at any time when neither party was involved with a war or suffering from the plague, either could issue a formal challenge, calling for the dispute to be settled by a battle in which pursuit would be allowed up to but not beyond the frontier of the loser.[31]

While the Argives were so engaged, the Spartans sent three envoys to Boeotia to take charge of the fort and the Athenians held as prisoners of war and to return both to Athens. They were reportedly surprised when they learned that the fort had been torn down. But, upon reflection, they did not think the fact material. So, they were subsequently taken aback when the Athenians were indignant that the fort had been razed and accused the Lacedaemonians of having done them a double injustice—first, in failing to restore to them the fort at Panactum intact and, second, in making a separate alliance with the Boeotians. There was no way, the Athenians said, to reconcile the latter act with the Spartans' previous promise to join with the Athenians in compelling adherence to Nicias' peace; and the envoys they angrily sent home empty-handed.[32]

It was at this point, Thucydides reports, that the Athenians opposed to the peace first vigorously asserted themselves. It was at this point, moreover, that Alcibiades first took command of affairs; and now that a breach with Sparta had taken place, he pounced. Privately, he sent a message to his guest-friends, his *xénoi*, at Argos, summoning the Argives to come to Athens with the Mantineians and Eleans, and telling them that the time was propitious for the formation of an alliance.

At Argos, this missive had an immediate and dramatic effect, undercutting the disinformation campaign to which the Argives had been subjected and putting paid to the effort mounted by Eustrophus and Aeson to forge an alliance between Argos and Lacedaemon. Now the Argives warmed to the idea of renewing their old alliance with Athens. She was, after all, they reportedly thought, "a city friendly to them of old, democratically governed, and possessed of a great capacity to engage in the conduct of war at sea." Then, as Alcibiades had urged, they dispatched an embassy to Athens accompanied by envoys from Mantineia and Elis.[33]

Before these envoys reached Athens, however, a Spartan embassy arrived in great haste. It consisted of three Spartiates—Philocharidas, Leon, and Endius—all of them known to be well-disposed to the Athenians. Leon we do not know, but Philocharidas is apt to have been a confidant of Nicias. He had been a party to the truce, the treaty of peace, and the alliance; and he had been one of the three Spartiates dispatched to Thrace to see that Clearidas turned Amphipolis over to the Athenians and that the Greek cities in the region complied with the terms of the treaty. Endius, whose patronymic was Alcibiades, was, we later learn, a hereditary guest-friend of the young Athenian notable bearing that name. The pairing of Philocharidas with Endius was entirely in keeping with the Spartan propensity to appoint to embassies men different in outlook.

The envoys' charge was to head off an accord with Argos, to secure Coryphasium in exchange for Panactum, and to reassure the Athenians that Lacedaemon's alliance with Boeotia had not been made with an eye to harming them; and to this end, with Endius' help, they apparently hoped to enlist as supporters Alcibiades as well as Nicias. In the circumstances, absent the former's support, they stood little chance of success, as they surely knew; and they had reason to think that the son of Cleinias might be accommodating. His ancestors had been Spartan *próxenoi*. He was not himself hostile to Lacedaemon as such. He had, in fact, gone out of his way to ease the conditions of the men who had surrendered on Sphacteria; and he had kept up the ancestral *xenía* which bound him to the family of Endius. The envoys may have been aware that personal pique had something to do with the posture Alcibiades had adopted; and everyone understood that, if the young man shifted his stance and helped arrange an Athenian evacuation of Coryphasium, a *proxenía* might well be his reward.

Alcibiades was, without a doubt, self-interested. But he was not a fool. He knew that these negotiations were going to end in bitter disappointment. The Spartans were not going to join with his compatriots in securing for the latter a recovery of Amphipolis, and they were not going to force their allies to comply with the terms of the treaty. For so paltry a personal gain, the son of Cleinias was not about to sacrifice the trust and respect of the Athenian public. He can hardly have failed to grasp what the envoys intended. And, in his dealings with the three, it was on their expectations in his own regard that he relied.

In the circumstances, it is by no means clear that these envoys could have succeeded in persuading the Athenian assembly. But the son of Cleinias was worried, and he was not inclined to take any chances. Technically, the three-some had come endowed with full power to settle all outstanding issues; and, before the Council of 500, they had trumpeted this fact. Were they to do the like before a meeting of the assembly, Alcibiades feared, they might well be able to persuade his compatriots that they could, in fact, commit Lacedaemon to doing that which, he knew, she would not do. Moreover, if, with Nicias' help, they managed to fool the Athenians yet again—even for a short time— the moment, propitious for luring Argos into an alliance, might pass; and the Argives might, in desperation, settle on a Spartan connection, as they had very nearly just done.

In consequence, in a private meeting with the envoys, Alcibiades is said to have pledged that he, hitherto the chief defender of Athens' retention of Coryphasium, would see to the delivery of that fort to the Lacedaemonians. But he insisted on one condition: that, in the public assembly, Philocharidas, Leon, and Endius sidestep acknowledging the extent of the authority con-ferred on them—and we can be confident that Endius pressed his colleagues to act as his Athenian *xénos* had urged. If Plutarch can be trusted, the son of Cleinias justified what might otherwise have seemed a decidedly odd request by explaining that Athens' assembly was apt to be far more contentious than the Council of 500 (as was no doubt true) and that, if the members of the for-mer were told that the envoys were fully empowered to make agreements on Lacedaemon's behalf, they would make extreme and outlandish demands— which, the envoys did not need to be told, would put their prospective bene-factor in an untenable position.

To Alcibiades' request, the Spartan envoys agreed. Then, after the envoys had done as he asked, he turned on them, publicly exposing the inconsistency in their statements and denouncing them as tricksters comparable to the other Spartiates with whom the Athenians had dickered in the recent past. Then, he saw to their being dismissed.[34]

Thanks to an earthquake—which, taken as a portent, prevented the Athe-nians from immediately ratifying the alliance with Argos—Nicias managed to get his compatriots to delay their deliberations. It was his contention—and no doubt his conviction as well—that the actually existing peace, imperfect though it might be, was greatly to Athens' advantage; and his stature was such that he managed to persuade his compatriots to send an embassy to Lacedaemon, on which he proposed to serve himself. The envoys' charge must, however, have been composed by Alcibiades and his associates. They were to invite the Lacedaemonians, if they were genuinely sincere, to restore to the Athenians Panactum intact as well as Amphipolis and to abandon the alliance with the Boeotians as a commitment inconsistent with the peace and alliance they had made with Athens. They were also to threaten that, if the Spartans refused, the Athenians would make an alliance with the Argives, the Mantineians, and the Eleans.

Thanks to the efforts of Xenares and of those who agreed with him, the Lacedaemonians refused to renounce the Boeotian alliance. Nicias succeeded solely in having the oaths renewed, and at Athens Alcibiades subsequently had his way. On the presumption that, if the Spartans could make a separate alliance, they could do so as well, the Athenians then negotiated bilateral defensive pacts of one hundred years' duration with Argos, Mantineia, and Elis modeled on the earlier instruments linking Lacedaemon with Athens and Boeotia. Each city subscribed not only on her own behalf but also, tellingly, as an imperial power acting on behalf of "the allies over whom she held sway."[35]

The Corinthians, who had from the outset aimed at drawing the Spartans back into war with Athens, were not a party to this alliance. Nor had they joined in, a short time before, when the Argives, Mantineians, and Eleans transformed their defensive alliance into an offensive and defensive alliance. Although they did not renounce the defensive alliance they had made with the three Peloponnesian powers, they reportedly "stood aloof from their allies and once again took thought regarding the Lacedaemonians."[36]

Technically, the Athenians did not go to war with Lacedaemon at this time. Indeed, for almost six more years, the two cities sedulously kept up the pretense, pouring libations and exchanging oaths at regular intervals while punctiliously avoiding attacks on one another's territory. By this time, however, their alliance was, for nearly all practical purposes, defunct. No one on either side expected that either city would answer a summons for aid. Moreover, their peace agreement the two powers repeatedly dishonored in the breach. Amphipolis was not restored to Athens. Nor was Coryphasium returned to the Lacedaemonians. There was a truce with the Boeotians that was renewed every ten days; and, in the Peloponnesus, open warfare soon broke out. "Outside the territories" of the two great antagonists, Thucydides remarks, "the cessation of hostilities was anything but firm, and they did a great deal of harm to one another."[37]

CHAPTER 8

An Opportunity Squandered

Money is not the sinews of war. . . . That what we are saying is true every history shows in a thousand places, notwithstanding the fact that Pericles advised the Athenians to make war against the Peloponnesus in its entirety, asserting that they could win that war with industry and with the force of wealth. For although the Athenians did well in that war for a time, in the end they lost it; and the counsel and good soldiers of Sparta were worth more than the industry and the wealth of Athens.

NICCOLÒ MACHIAVELLI

D IPLOMACY and dissimulation are almost inseparable. The alliance linking Athens with Argos, Mantineia, and Elis was only nominally defensive. Its real aim was the opposite, and everyone knew it. The four cities were as one in wanting to destroy the foundations of Lacedaemon's power.[1] With this in mind, they set out to break up Sparta's Peloponnesian alliance, knowing full well that, in the end, the question could only be settled on the battlefield.

The Olympic Games, scheduled to be held under the presidency of Elis in August 420, provided an occasion for ritually humiliating and provoking the Lacedaemonians. The latter had apparently attacked Fort Phyrcus in Triphylia and dispatched some of their hoplites to Lepreum shortly after the Olympic truce had been proclaimed in Elis. The Eleans seized upon this purported infraction to charge the Spartans with a breach of the truce, which barred attacks on the presiding city in the general period of the Olympic festival; and the tribunal at Olympia, which was under their control, levied a fine in silver of two thousand *minae* (nineteen-twentieths of a ton)—two *minae* per hoplite, as the Olympic law prescribed—which was to be divided between Elis and the treasury of Zeus at Olympia.

The Spartans might have objected that Triphylia did not belong to Elis, but they knew better than to suppose that this would be accepted. Instead, they relied on a technicality, protesting that they had dispatched the hoplites before the Elean herald, sent to proclaim the truce, had reached Lacedaemon. The Eleans, in turn, rejected their plea but offered to give up their share of the fine and to pay what was owed the god if the Lacedaemonians would restore Lepreum to them. When the Spartans balked at this, they sought to soften the blow (or, at least, assume a posture of reasonableness) by offering the Lacedaemonians a second option—that they swear before the Hellenes that they would pay the fine at a later time.

When this overture was also rejected, the Eleans barred the Lacedaemonians from the temple of Zeus, the opening sacrifice, and the games. Fearing that the Spartans would resort to force, they posted at Olympia or nearby a guard of their own soldiers supplemented by a thousand Argives, a thousand Mantineians, and some Athenian cavalrymen. Although the Lacedaemonians refrained from violence, they did, with the help of the Boeotians, attempt to make a mockery of the proceedings.

There was a well-known, wealthy, senior Spartiate named Lichas son of Arcesilaus. His father had twice been an Olympic victor in equestrian events; and, as one would expect, Arcesilaus' son owned a splendid team of horses. These he loaned to the Thebans, who ran them and were proclaimed the victors when this team won the chariot race. Then, however, Lichas stepped forward to claim the victory as his own by crowning his charioteer with a headband— and the umpires gave him a taste of the whip.

It is conceivable, but most unlikely that Lichas was acting on his own. The fact that he was the *próxenos* of the Argives at Lacedaemon made this gesture and the savage response of the Eleans especially poignant. In effect, Elis and her allies had thrown down the gauntlet. For the time being, we are told, the Spartans did not stir. They appear to have shared the modern French view that revenge is a dish best eaten cold; and, as we shall see, when the moment was propitious, they took up the challenge.[2]

In the meantime, the Eleans and their allies tried to cash in on Lacedaemon's humiliation by luring Corinth into their alliance—but to no avail. The following winter, the Spartans suffered another setback. The tribes in the neighborhood of Heracleia Trachinia had harried that Lacedaemonian colony from the moment of her foundation. Now, in battle, they inflicted a devastating defeat on her citizens and killed Xenares son of Cnidis, who had been dispatched from Sparta as their commander. In the aftermath, the Boeotians, who did not welcome Sparta's presence in their near abroad, occupied the town, expelled its governor, Hegesippidas, and sent that Spartiate home in disgrace.[3]

Themistocles Redivivus

Early in the summer of 419, Alcibiades, whom the Athenians had made a general the previous June, did what Themistocles had done fifty years before. He journeyed to the Peloponnesus, taking with him a couple hundred Athenian hoplites and some archers; and, in concert with the Argives and Athens' other allies, he traveled about, meeting with the men who counted and settling matters at this place and that with an eye to shoring up and expanding the anti-Spartan confederacy. Thucydides singles out only one enterprise for comment, noting that Alcibiades visited Achaea. There he apparently added Patras to the alliance and persuaded her citizens to build Long Walls from the town down to the sea. Nearby, at Achaean Rhium, he also attempted to build a fort but was stymied by the efforts of the Corinthians and the Sicyonians.

Why these two powers were concerned Thucydides does not explain. But it was surely material that Achaean Rhium on the southern shore of the Corinthian Gulf is located directly opposite Antirhium (sometimes called Molycreian Rhium) on that body of water's northern shore, that the two are situated astride the narrows where the Gulf of Patras to the west gives way to the Gulf of Corinth to the east and only a mile of water separates the two shores, that a coalition with ships stationed both at Patras on the south shore to the west and at Naupactus on the north shore to the east can quite effectively monitor and regulate traffic into and out of the Corinthian Gulf, and that Athens had controlled both shores and had no doubt used this to advantage against Corinth and Sicyon in the 450s. The prospect that suffering inflicted on one in the recent past will be inflicted once again concentrates the mind wonderfully.[4]

Later that same summer—almost certainly in August—the Argives, with moral support from Alcibiades, launched an attack on Epidaurus. The pretext was religious; the purpose, political. The temple of Apollo Pythaeus was situated at Asine on the coast in territory seized by Argos from the local Dryopian population centuries before. By way of this conquest, the Argives had come to preside over the associated amphictyony, which they had made a vehicle for asserting their hegemony within the Argolid, the Argolic Acte, and beyond. On this occasion, the Epidaurians were accused of not having sent a victim for sacrifice that they owed—perhaps as a thank offering for the pasture land where their livestock grazed. In demanding that they meet the obligation to Apollo Pythaeus that they had long before incurred, the Argives were doing to the Epidaurus what the Eleans had done to Lepreum: they were demanding from a onetime client a symbolic acknowledgment of her subordinate status.

In seeking to conquer this city, Alcibiades and the Argives were also reportedly focused on forcing Corinth, which was situated to the north of Epidaurus across some rugged terrain, to "remain at rest"; and they were no less eager to secure for the Athenians a shorter route than the voyage around Scyllaeum into the Argolic Gulf by which to deliver to Argos aid at short notice from their stronghold on Aegina.[5]

This maneuver was no doubt also intended as a provocation. Epidaurus was an ally of Lacedaemon. If the Spartans failed to come to her defense, and the Argives and Athenians seized and sacked the city, it would occasion a further, precipitous decline in Lacedaemon's prestige; and. though intangible, this might well give the Corinthians, the Sicyonians, and the Tegeans pause and induce them to reconsider their allegiance.

The Spartans understood the consequences, and they knew that they had to intervene. So, in response to Argos' invasion of the Epidauria, Agis son of Archidamus was dispatched with the city's full levy up the Eurotas valley to a place called Leuctron (in all likelihood, modern Leondari) in the Alpheios basin on their frontier opposite Mount Lycaeum. From there, one could head almost anywhere—north-northwest toward Elis, for example, or north-northeast toward Mantineia or even Argos.

On this occasion, Lacedaemon's Eurypontid king was no doubt acting at the behest of the ephors or of the "little assembly" constituted by the ephors meeting in consultation with the *gerousía*. For next to no one knew where this army was going, and all of the Spartiates would have been fully informed had the campaign been discussed and voted on at a meeting of the assembly.

At the frontier, it was the Spartan practice to conduct sacrifices called *diabatéria* and to examine the victim's entrails before crossing from the domain of one set of heroes and gods to that of another. When the signs were unfavorable, it was the duty of the seer to inform his commander and of the commander to heed his warning. Of course, there were times when circumstances required audacity and others when they argued for caution; and, in one fashion or another, this may have influenced calculations. Moreover, some commanders and some seers were habitually more risk-averse than others.

As we have already had occasion to note, Agis appears consistently to have erred on the side of caution. The same can be said for his seer. Time and again, after Archidamus died, his elder son and heir marched out, examined the signs in consultation with his seer, and then turned back—which is what he did on this occasion, perhaps in part because the nine-day festival of the Carneia, when the Spartans would be barred from campaigning, would before long be upon them. When Agis once again reached Sparta, word was sent to Lacedaemon's allies to be ready to march after the month of Carneios, which was among Dorian peoples a time sacred to Apollo.[6]

Three days before that month began, the Argives, as a gesture of contempt, initiated their invasion of the territory of Epidaurus and began ravaging it. To make this right with the gods—given that they, too, were Dorians—the Argives resorted to intercalation, cynically adding a day to the month previous to Carneios for every day they spent on campaign. The allies summoned by the Epidaurians were more scrupulous. Either they begged off, citing the month, or they marched to the Epidaurian frontier and did not cross.[7]

While the ravaging was going on, the Athenians summoned the Peloponnesian cities to a peace conference at Mantineia—almost certainly once again with an eye to persuading the Corinthians to join the four-power alliance and deny Sparta's Boeotian allies access to the Peloponnesus. Accordingly, when a Corinthian named Euphamidas son of Aristonymos—an experienced general who had subscribed to the truce of 423 on his city's behalf and who may have favored subscribing to the peace of 421—objected that it made no sense to be discussing peace while the Argives were in arms against the Epidaurians and their allies, Athens and her allies were quick to oblige. Delegates from the two sides were dispatched to separate the two armies, and the Argives actually withdrew from the Epidauria.

Of course, when the conference failed, the Argives conducted a second invasion, and, when the festival of the Carneia and the month of Carneios were over, the Spartans marched out again—this time to Caryae on the main thoroughfare leading via Tegea and Mantineia in eastern Arcadia to the Argolid. On this occasion, however, as on the previous occasion, the sacrifices conducted at the frontier were judged unfavorable, and so the Lacedaemonians returned home. Shortly thereafter, Alcibiades arrived in the Argolid with a thousand Athenian hoplites; and, upon learning that there was not going to be a showdown with the Spartans, he and they returned home. By the time that the campaigning season had come to an end, we are told, the Argives had ravaged a third of the Epidauria.[8]

This fencing match continued in the winter. Early on, the Lacedaemonians managed to slip into Epidaurus by sea a garrison of three hundred under the command of the Hegesippidas expelled from Heracleia Trachinia shortly before. When the Argives upbraided the Athenians for having failed to prevent this and pressed them to reintroduce the Messenians and the runaway helots into Coryphasium, Alcibiades persuaded his compatriots to inscribe at the bottom of the pillar recording Athens' treaty of peace with Lacedaemon that the Spartans had not kept their oaths. Then, he convinced them to conduct the fugitive helots back from Cranae to the fort at Coryphasium. In the Epidauria, toward the end of winter, there were raids and ambushes; and the Argives even approached the walls of Epidaurus with scaling ladders, hoping to find the city unguarded—but, thanks in part no doubt to the presence of Hegesippidas and his garrison, they did so to no avail.[9]

The Spartans cannot have been entirely happy with Agis and his seer. They could not afford to allow the Athenians and the Argives a free hand indefinitely, and they knew it. As Thucydides observes, by the summer of 418, they were acutely aware "that the Epidaurians, their allies, were suffering hardship and that the remaining powers in the Peloponnesus had either revolted or were ill-disposed, and they thought that if they did not with expedition get out in front of events, seize the occasion, and arrest the evil the situation would grow even worse." They did not, however, march out at the beginning of the summer, as they had in the past when they mounted invasions of Attica. Instead, they waited until midsummer—perhaps because it took some time to rally their allies; perhaps, as some scholars suggest, because they wanted to give their allies abroad and their helots at home (many of whom they intended to take with them) time to bring in the harvest; and perhaps, as others insist, because they thought that the Athenian generals slated to take office in late June were apt to be less enthusiastic regarding Alcibiades' Peloponnesian venture than was the young man himself.

This last possibility needs emphasis. In March, perhaps because they were not themselves as excited about the enterprise as its progenitor, the Athenians had not reelected Alcibiades as general. The new board included Laches and Nicias, the chief promoters of the peace negotiated with Lacedaemon, as well as Nicias' colleagues in various campaigns Nicostratus and Autocles, not to mention Callistratus and Demosthenes, who had both sworn on Athens' behalf to observe the terms of peace and those of the alliance. The Spartans had good reason to suppose that Alcibiades intended their undoing. They knew that, if they lost the great battle which they intended to stage, it might well mean the total collapse of their alliance, the liberation of the Messenians, an erosion of the economic foundations of their regime, and an end to their way of life—and it was their hope that Athens would not make a wholehearted effort to effect their defeat.[10]

Lacedaemon Stirs

The Spartans could hardly turn to the Agiad king Pleistoanax son of Pausanias for military leadership in such circumstances. He had been timid and, many believed, treasonous in dealing with the Athenians in 446; and he had championed the Peace of Nicias three years before. As such, he was suspect. So, it was his Eurypontid colleague Agis on whom they once again relied when they dispatched their full levy against Argos, accompanied by the helots in great numbers for the first time since the battle of Plataea. Along the way, he picked up the Tegeans and Lacedaemon's other Arcadian supporters.

Those of Sparta's allies which were situated either along the north coast of the Peloponnesus or beyond the Isthmus of Corinth gathered at Phlius—a city, fiercely loyal to Lacedaemon, situated near Nemea not all that far from the Argolid, which most of them could easily reach via Sicyon without having to cross any territory controlled by Argos or her allies. Notable among those who gathered at this mustering place were the Corinthians with two thousand hoplites (three thousand fewer than they had been able to send to the battlefield at Plataea), the Phliasians with every last man they could spare (at least one thousand heavy infantrymen), and, most important of all, the Boeotians—who dispatched five thousand hoplites, a like number of light-armed troops, and five hundred horsemen with as many light-armed infantrymen trained to operate in cooperation with their cavalry. There were also Sicyonians and Achaeans from Pellene to their west (who could march directly to Phlius), and there were Megarians and Epidaurians as well. It is also conceivable that there were contingents from Troezen, Hermione, and perhaps even Halieis in the Argolic Acte—though, since they pass unmentioned and were located on the coast of the Saronic Gulf where, as they knew only too well, the Athenians could do them great harm, they probably thought discretion the better part of valor.

All in all, with perhaps fifteen hundred Tegeate hoplites (the number sent to Plataea), another fifteen hundred Arcadians, as many as three thousand from Sicyon, and perhaps another fourteen hundred from Pellene, Megara, and Epidaurus in attendance, as well as something like fourteen hundred forty Spartiate hoplites and two thousand one hundred sixty *períoikoi,* the army of the Lacedaemonians and their allies is apt to have approached, if not exceeded, nineteen thousand hoplites with five hundred cavalrymen and an untold number of light-armed troops.[11]

"This was the most splendid Hellenic army ever yet assembled by far." So says Thucydides, who appears to have been an onlooker. "It should have been seen while it was still intact at Nemea—the Lacedaemonians there with their whole army, the Arcadians, Boeotians, Corinthians, Sicyonians, Pellenians, Phliasians, and Megarians—all of these the picked troops from each city, seeming a match in battle for the alliance of the Argives and for another such added to it."[12]

The forces available within the Peloponnesus for the defense of the Argolid were far fewer. There were three thousand Elean hoplites. This much Thucydides tells us, but he does not indicate how many hoplites the Argives and Mantineians with their subject allies could field. Given what we know of Argos' capacity at an earlier time when the city was also flourishing and at a later time, seven thousand is a reasonable estimate of what they and their allies could turn out at home to defend their own territory, and we are told by Diodorus Siculus that the Mantineians (with, we must suspect, their subject allies) supplied just under three thousand hoplites. Without Athenian help, these three powers cannot have been in a position to field a great many more than thirteen thousand hoplites, if even that.[13]

The Argives knew about the Spartan preparations well in advance of their departure from Lacedaemon, and they were not behindhand in alerting their allies. There is, in fact, evidence strongly suggesting that the Athenians had set aside funds for the expedition before their political year ended in late June. Nonetheless, when the crisis came, they were unconscionably slow in responding to the Argive plea for help—which had not been the case the previous year when Agis marched to Caryae and Alcibiades quickly brought reinforcements to Argos. Moreover, when the Athenians finally arrived, they were insufficiently numerous. The thousand hoplites and the three hundred cavalrymen that Athens eventually sent would surely have been most welcome had they arrived in time. But, in the circumstances, a great many more were needed. For Athens, as for her Peloponnesian allies, the stakes in this struggle were extremely high.[14]

There had not been a genuine opportunity to eliminate Lacedaemon as a great power in half a century; and Alcibiades resembled the Themistocles of that earlier period in more ways than one. Like his illustrious predecessor, he knew where Sparta's center of gravity lay, and he had an admirably clear understanding of the strategic situation. Moreover, like that great statesman, he did not fully command the support of his compatriots. In one respect, Alcibiades was better positioned than Themistocles had been. He had not been ostracized, and he was not operating from exile. He could appear in the assembly and make his case, and there he wielded considerable influence. But there were others—Nicias was their leader—who, in 418, commanded at least as much respect as he did (and quite possibly more), and they lacked the keen strategic insight that Pericles' ward possessed.

Alcibiades' compatriots were halfhearted. It would have taken a man graced with his late guardian's stature and eloquence to instill in them the requisite resolve. They were prepared to pursue victory on the cheap, which is apparently the prospect that the son of Cleinias dangled before them. But, as he seems to have recognized, thanks to the plague and the losses they had suffered at Delium and Amphipolis, they were too exhausted and too weary of war to take the considerable risks they should have embraced.[15]

That the tardiness of the Athenians was a function of the political conflict at Athens is certain. We know that there was fierce opposition to the expedition. In his play *The Demes,* the comic poet Eupolis tells us as much. The omens were bad, he reports. The generals were decidedly reluctant; and, to get them on the move, an unnamed proponent of the venture had to stand up in the assembly and threaten the expedition's prospective commanders with the stocks.[16]

The Argives, Eleans, and Mantineians were undaunted, and their commanders were not without intelligence. Their heavy infantrymen outnumbered

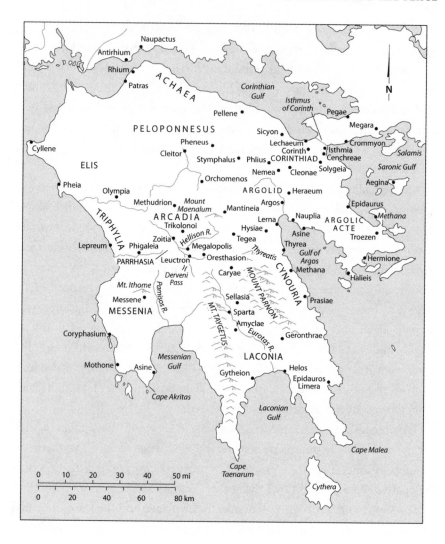

Map 24. The Peloponnesus

by more than two to one the sixty-six hundred or so hoplites making their way
north toward Phlius from Lacedaemon, Tegea, and elsewhere in Arcadia. As
they recognized, their best chance for victory was to intercept this force en
route. Agis understood the danger. It would have been foolhardy take the normal route from Caryae up the valley shared by Tegea and Mantineia. The latter
city, which was situated astride that well-beaten path, stood squarely in the
way. It was a virtual certainty that the Argives and their allies would take the

Lacedaemonians' appearance in the territory of Mantineia as an opportunity to force a decision before the great army could coalesce.

Mindful of all of this, Agis opted to bypass Mantineia and led the Lacedaemonians, Tegeans, and associated Arcadians through the plain in south-central Arcadia that would eventually be dominated by Megalopolis; then north-northeast through Zoitia and Trikolonoi on a roundabout route that ran initially to the west of Mount Maenalum; and finally, we have reason to believe, north and east from there to Arcadian Orchomenos—which had remained resolutely loyal to her hegemon. On Agis' path, directly north of Trikolonoi and across from Mantineia, lay the Arcadian city of Methudrion. There, the Argives, Mantineians, and Eleans gathered from the eastern and the western parts of the Peloponnesus; and there, no doubt to his great dismay, Agis found them waiting. For a brief moment, it looked as if there might be a battle. Each army occupied a hill, and the rival captains eyed one another warily. But Agis' defect was not audacity, and he was anything but tactically obtuse. So at night—while the Argives, Eleans, and Mantineians were asleep—he broke camp and, thanks to negligence on the part of the Argive commanders in charge of the coalition forces, he managed to slip off toward Orchomenos and the rendezvous at Phlius further east-northeast.[17]

In the aftermath, the Argives and their allies pulled back to Argos. Then, after a brief pause, they marched up through the Trestus pass along the main thoroughfare that stretched from that city to Corinth. Then, at Cleonae, they turned off onto the ancillary road that led to Nemea and Phlius in the west. It was their presumption that this was the path that the army concentrated at Phlius would have to take, and they may have supposed that they could stage a battle in a location near Nemea where the numerical superiority of the enemy and the cavalry they possessed would afford them no great advantage.

This was a bold and foolish maneuver. The proper station for an army intent on defending the Argolid was near the Heraeum at the point where an invader would emerge in column and in some disarray from the narrow Trestus pass. An army placed there could fall back on the city of Argos if the enemy chose one or more of the roads or paths less well-traveled—which is what a majority of those in Agis' army, in fact, did.

Instead of proceeding as expected, the son of Archidamus divided his army into three and had the separate contingents make their way to the Argive plain by different routes at distinct intervals. With the Arcadians and the Epidaurians, he and his fellow Lacedaemonians appear to have broken camp late at night, taking what Thucydides describes as a difficult path, which was no doubt seldom used. The Corinthians, Pellenians, and Phliasians then set off at first light, some two hours before dawn, following another, similar route. Last to leave were the Megarians, Sicyonians, and Boeotians with roughly eighty-five hundred hoplites, who took the main highway through Nemea past Cleonae and down through the Trestus pass, which was the only road suited to the Boeotians' five hundred mounts and to the carts bearing the army's provisions.

Agis' aim in staging this elaborate maneuver was to lure the Argives, Eleans, and Mantineians into a position in which they were surrounded and he could take maximum advantage of his army's great numerical superiority and of the cavalry in its possession. Thanks to the fact that the coalition army commanded by the Argives had marched up the Nemea road, this stratagem worked brilliantly.

As was planned, the Lacedaemonians, Arcadians, and Epidaurians—roughly seven thousand in number—were the first to enter the Argive plain—almost certainly from the west by way of a path that ran west or east of the main summit of Mount Keloussa. At dawn, when the Argive commanders learned that at least part of the enemy army had taken the route in question, they reversed course and hotfooted it back down the Nemea road—aware that there was a hostile army situated between them and the city of Argos.

Shortly after reentering the Argolid, the Argives, Mantineians, and Eleans encountered—to the northwest of the forces under Agis' direct command—the Corinthians, Pellenians, and the Phliasians, whose heavy infantry contingent cannot have numbered many more than thirty-five hundred. After a brief skirmish in which they killed a few Phliasians and lost a few men in encounters with the Corinthians, they brushed them aside; and, seeing that their territory was being plundered, they made a beeline for the Lacedaemonian, Arcadian, and Epidaurian marauders, whose heavy infantry theirs also greatly outnumbered. It was their local numerical superiority and the apparent opportunity with which they had been presented that made the greatest impression on the Argive rank and file.

The coalition's commanders no doubt knew better. They cannot have been unaware that something on the order of nine thousand Boeotian, Megarian, and Sicyonian hoplites and cavalrymen were unaccounted for. They knew that rough terrain rendered it difficult, if not impossible, to conduct cavalry by any route other than the main road running down from Phlius via Nemea, Cleonae, and the Trestus pass; and they must have anticipated being assaulted by twelve thousand hoplites and five hundred cavalrymen from their rear.

It is, of course, conceivable that the Argives, Mantineians, and Eleans could have routed the Lacedaemonians, Arcadians, and Epidaurians and then wheeled about to take on the Corinthians, Pellenians, and Phliasians to the northwest and the Boeotians, Megarians, and Sicyonians advancing from the northeast; and, since the odds are good that the latter contingent was not yet visible on the horizon, this may well be what the rank and file had in mind. But, in the best of circumstances, the achievement of successive victories of this sort would have been an astonishing feat, calling for iron discipline, astonishing endurance, and dispatch on a scale rarely achieved in classical antiquity except by the Lacedaemonians; and it would also have required time— time that, Thucydides intimates (if I and most scholars read him correctly), the Argives and their allies simply did not have. If the discernment ordinarily attributed to the Athenian historian is sound, as it seems to be, the soldiers in the Argive coalition were caught between two fires, and they were apt to be badly burned. Moreover, the Lacedaemonians, Arcadians, and Epidaurians were situated between the coalition army and walls of Argos. So, there was nowhere to flee.

This entire scenario is testimony to the tactical genius of Agis son of Archidamus. He had maneuvered the Argives, Mantineians, and Eleans into a position where, if he wished, he could see to their slaughter. Not since the battle of Sepeia had the Argives been in such terrible straits, and the situation of the Mantineians and Eleans was no less dire.[18]

The Eurypontid king was not, however, as astute politically as he was militarily. Just as the armies were about to do battle, when the Argive commanders asked for a parley, he agreed to a pause. This was on his part quite sensible. It afforded the Boeotians, Megarians, and Sicyonians more time in which to close in. But then, when an Argive named Alciphron, who was the *próxenos* of the Lacedaemonians at Argos, and another named Thrasylus, who was one of the five Argive generals, announced to him that the Argives were prepared to settle by "judgments consistent with equity and common practice" any complaints that the Spartans had to make and that they were ready and willing to pour libations and agree to a treaty providing for a lasting peace, he did what Pleistoanax had done vis-à-vis the Athenians in 446. He embraced their initiative. He informed "one of those in authority who was accompanying the army" (almost certainly one of the two ephors customarily assigned to keep an eye on a king sent out on such a command). But he did not consult his fellow Lacedaemonians—and he granted to the Argives a four-month truce in which to fulfill their promises. Then, without offering any explanation to Lacedaemon's allies, he led his tripartite army off to Nemea.

The Spartans and their allies followed their commander's lead dutifully, as the law required. But, in their conversations with one another, they reacted as they had when they marched out of Attica in 446. They showered blame on their king—in this case "thinking," as Thucydides puts it, "that, with the enemy hemmed in on all sides by cavalry and footsoldiers, they had happened upon a fair prospect for converging and striking a great blow and that they were now departing, having done nothing worthy of the preparations that had been made." It is in this context, as if to drive the point home, that Athenian historian describes in wonder the splendid quality of the army that camped at Nemea that night. In these circumstances, as in those that pertained in 446, it is hard not to sympathize with the Spartan and allied rank and file.[19]

Thucydides does not tell us what the son of Archidamus intended on this occasion. His reticence could be an indication that he had no idea. There is, however, a great deal that he does not tell us because he supposed divulging his thinking pedagogically counterproductive. He does not, for example, explain why Alcibiades encouraged the citizens of Patras to build Long Walls down to the sea, and he does not spell out why the Athenian attempted to construct a fort at Rhium. His aim throughout was to give his readers the tools with which to sort out such questions for themselves. It is an error to suppose that, if Thucydides was of a certain opinion or even knew something to be true, he would have told us as much. His silence is more often than not an invitation to us to puzzle over the information that he did, indeed, provide.

Agis' willingness to strike a deal with Alciphron and Thrasylus could be a function of caution. He does seem to have been risk-averse, and he may have had the good sense to recognize that, even in the most favorable of circumstances, going into battle makes one a hostage to fortune. Not one precious Spartiate and not one citizen from a community allied with Lacedaemon lost his life on that particular day because of the son of Archidamus.

There may, however, have been more to Agis' calculations than an aversion to danger. He may have hoped for an outcome more favorable to the long-term interests of his city than a mere massacre of the Argives, Mantineians, and Eleans. Alciphron the *próxenos* and Thrasylus, who was acting on behalf of his fellow generals, promised that there would be a settlement of disputed questions and a lasting peace. Such an arrangement would be a great boon for Lacedaemon. It would mean that Argos would remain quiet for an extended period; that Mantineia and Elis, once deprived of Argive support, could be forced to fall in line; and that Athens would lose her foothold within the Peloponnesus. It would restore within that great peninsula what must have seemed like the natural order, which had existed as long as this Eurypontid king could remember.

Alciphron may, moreover, have been Agis' *xénos*. If not, he was almost certainly the guest-friend of Lichas, the Argive *próxenos* at Sparta, or of another leading Lacedaemonian. Otherwise, he would never have been awarded the *proxenía* he held. He was a friend to Sparta, and it was through such friends abroad—those whom they termed "serviceable men [*epitédeioi*]"—that the Lacedaemonians provided guidance to the cities within the Peloponnesus and maintained their alliance.

Thrasylus may have been cut from similar cloth. He may have been well-known at Lacedaemon as a sympathizer. He, too, is apt to have been the *xénos* of an important Spartan. That such Laconizers existed at Argos and that some of them held high office is, as we have seen, an established fact; and Thucydides, who is nothing if not coy in his account of the flurry of diplomacy that took place in the wake of the Peace of Nicias, provides us with numerous clues suggesting their presence and importance. In the early summer of 421, the Corinthians knew to whom, among those in authority at Argos, they should in private turn. Later that summer, Cleobulus and Xenares knew whom at Argos they should alert to the willingness of the Boeotian envoys to discuss the forging of an alliance.

The Argive generals who sanctioned this overture were surely aware that Alciphron would be welcome in Agis' entourage, and they may well have been of the same opinion regarding their colleague Thrasylus. After all, in 420, there had been influential Argives who had lent a hand in trying to stampede their compatriots into the alliance with Lacedaemon that Eustrophus and Aeson, the two Argives then judged "most acceptable to the Spartans," had been dispatched to Laconia to negotiate. Within three or four months, there would be a briefly successful attempt, concerted between the Lacedaemonians and certain Argives, to install an oligarchy in Argos. The movement that produced a coup d'état in the fall of 418 did not come from out of the blue—and, as will become clear in the next few pages, in August 418 the royal son of Archidamus was prepared to protect such men.[20]

A Decision at Mantineia

The Spartans were sane and disciplined; the Argives, neither. The latter had far less reason than the former to be enraged about the four-month truce. Alciphron and Thrasylus had rescued them from a catastrophe. But they were furious nonetheless, "thinking," as Thucydides puts it, "that the Lacedaemonians had escaped and that they would never again have so fine an opportunity." Moreover, where the Lacedaemonians reined in their anger and operated within the framework of the rule of law, the Argives took out theirs on the person of Thrasylus. In the bed of a watercourse called the Charadrus, which was dry except after a heavy rain, the army of Argos ordinarily paused to try deserters and the like before making their way into the city. There, on this occasion, however, they sidestepped the formalities of justice; and they turned on Thrasylus, hurled stones at him, and would have taken his life had he not fled to the altar. His property they later confiscated.

Of course, the catastrophe from which the Argives had just escaped really had been a product of defective military leadership. Thrasylus and his colleagues could justly have been taken to task for letting Agis give them the slip at Methudrion and for marching up the Nemea road. Had they positioned the coalition army in the Argolid, they would have been in a position to take on the three contingents of Agis' army seriatim, and they would have had the city of Argos as a refuge. A commission of inquiry was certainly in order, and there was a case to be made for cashiering the generals, but not for a lynching.[21]

Not long thereafter, Laches and Nicostratus arrived with one thousand Athenian hoplites and a cavalry force of three hundred. They were not warmly welcomed. The leading Argives knew who they were. Laches had been one of the two principal sponsors of the peace with Lacedaemon; Nicostratus was an associate of Nicias; and, if Eupolis can be trusted, the two may well have borne some responsibility for the expedition's delay. The Athenians were bluntly asked to leave—in part, one must suspect, out of resentment that they had left their allies in the lurch; in part, we are told, because those in charge at Argos were loath to break the agreement so recently contracted with the Lacedaemonians; and in part, we know, because those responsible for setting the assembly's agenda did not want the Athenians to address the people of Argos. When, in fact, the Athenians leaders asked for a hearing, those in charge flatly refused—and that would perhaps have been the end of it all had the Mantineians and Eleans, who were still there, not made a great fuss and forced them to give way.[22]

We are not told with whom at Argos the Athenians at first dealt. The odds are good, however, that initially Laches and Nicostratus conferred with their peers—the four remaining Argive generals. This would have been in accord with the dictates of protocol, and it helps explain the cold welcome the Athenians received. Argos' generals will have been particularly upset about the Athenians' failure to show up. Moreover, when Alciphron and Thrasylus negotiated the truce, they were not, in fact, acting entirely on their own. Thrasylus was a spokesman for the entire board of generals, and the four remaining had no desire to renounce the engagement which he had negotiated on their behalf. They had had a sobering—one might even say, terrifying—experience. They had seen with their own eyes what the Lacedaemonian confederacy was capable of, and even those on the board who in no way sympathized with Sparta must have been wary of tangling with her again.

If the Argive democracy was anything like the one at Athens, the city's generals had it in their power to call a special meeting of the assembly. This they not only refused to do. They appear also to have persuaded Argos' probouleutic council, which certainly had such a prerogative, to take the same stand; and its members had held firm—until the Mantineians and Eleans caused a ruckus.

Alcibiades was present—not this time as a general nor even as a soldier, but as an ambassador—and he it almost certainly was who spoke on behalf of the Athenians before the Argive assembly. The oration was aimed at saving the enterprise that he had set in motion two years before. The individual who delivered it chided the Argives for making a truce, arguing that they had no right to do so under the terms of the alliance without the consent of their allies, and he suggested that, now that at so propitious a moment the Athenians had arrived, the war ought to be resumed. This argument carried the day, and the Eleans and Mantineians soon marched off against Arcadian Orchomenos in company with the Athenian hoplites. The Argives were, however, slow to follow—presumably because they were still at odds with one another regarding the truce—but follow they did; and the coalition forces mounted a siege and assaulted the walls of the town.

Their principal aim may have been to secure the hostages from Arcadia lodged in the town. But their goal was surely also strategic—for the wagon road that ran through the valley beneath Orchomenos and that it commanded was almost certainly the route that the Lacedaemonians had taken when they made their way north, then east from Methudrion in the direction of Phlius. They had undoubtedly passed that way—either en route to Phlius, on the way back from Nemea, or on both journeys—for it was they who had deposited the Arcadian hostages there, and, as we shall soon see, the Mantineians, Eleans, Argives, and Athenians had in mind a plan that required that they be able to obstruct, if not block, all of the main thoroughfares leading from the northern to the southern Peloponnesus.

The citizens of Orchomenos were aware that their walls were weak, and they were persuaded that the town was apt to be stormed before a relief expedition could be mounted. So, like the citizens of Acanthus and Amphipolis in similar circumstances, they took counsel and made the best deal they could. The hostages in their keeping they handed over, the alliance they joined, and they turned over to the Mantineians as security hostages of their own.[23]

When the news reached Lacedaemon that the Argives had broken the truce and that Orchomenos had capitulated, the criticism and anger directed at Agis grew more intense. Earlier in the summer, the Spartans had gone to a great deal of trouble in assembling an enormous and splendid coalition army. The rank and file knew that it would be almost impossible to duplicate that feat, and all along they had heaped blame on the Eurypontid king for squandering an opportunity to lay their hands on Argos of a kind never before afforded them. Nonetheless, despite the fact that many supposed Agis guilty of *malakía,* as a community, the Lacedaemonians had refrained from acting against the man—perhaps because the ephors and the *gérontes,* who functioned as a court in such cases and who cooperated in setting the agenda for the assembly, were well-informed concerning the presence of Laconizers in Argos and thought Agis' political stratagem worth the risk.

Now, however, the members of "the little assembly" gave way; and, in their fury, the Spartiates in "the common assembly" broke with their ordinary mode of conduct and deliberated whether they should first impose on the son of Archidamus a fine in silver of one hundred thousand Aeginetan drachmas (which is to say, twenty-three Attic talents, nearly two-thirds of a ton) and then, in ceremonial fashion, raze his house—as the Spartans had done almost sixty years before when his great-grandfather, the Eurypontid king Leotychidas, had been caught on a campaign in Thessaly taking bribes. Agis begged his compatriots not to do this, pledging that he would lead out the army and rescue himself from blame by the good service that he would do. If he fell short, they could, he told them, do with him as they pleased.

This induced the Lacedaemonians to suspend the fine and put off the razing of his house, but they did pass a measure, hitherto unprecedented in the case of a king, imposing on the royal son of Archidamus for the time being ten Spartiates as *xúmbouloi*. It is unclear just how far the brief of these ten men extended. Without the permission of these "councillors," Thucydides tells us, Agis did not have the authority to lead the army back home from a war with the enemy. Diodorus, no doubt following Ephorus, goes further, insisting that the king was instructed to do nothing contrary to his councillors' advice. This may be a distinction without a difference. For, in either case, it would have been a grave imprudence on Agis' part not to consult these ten men at every turn.[24]

While these developments were taking place at Lacedaemon, the Argives, Athenians, Mantineians, and Eleans were deliberating with regard to their next move. Everyone agreed that it was high time that they took the struggle to the southern Peloponnesus. This they had no doubt decided before the march on Orchomenos. As far as we know, however, no one had yet done what a Corinthian leader would do early in the fourth century—which was to compare Sparta's strategic position with a stream. No one had first observed that, "at their sources, rivers are not great and they are easily forded, but the farther on they go, the greater they get—for other rivers empty into them and make the current stronger" and then gone on to say of the Lacedaemonians, "There, in the place where they emerge, they are alone; but as they continue and gather cities under their control, they become more numerous and harder to fight." No one is known to have suggested that prudence dictates that enemies seek battle with the Spartans in or near Lacedaemon where they are few in number and relatively weak. But everyone at Orchomenos that summer's day in August 418 surely understood the principle. They were all aware that, if they now moved with all due speed, they could get the jump on the Spartans and force them to fight without the very considerable support that they had enjoyed in July from the Boeotians, Megarians, Corinthians, Sicyonians, Phliasians, and Epidaurians; and one of their reasons for seizing Orchomenos was to delay, if not deny, this coalition access to the southern Peloponnesus.

Greek cities tended to be parochial in their outlook. It is this in part that explained the Argive obsession with Epidaurus, and it no doubt helps explain why, at Orchomenos, the Mantineians proposed that they march on Tegea and the Eleans, that they first make their way to Lepreum. The Argives and the Athenians were the arbiters, and they opted for an assault on Tegea—with good reason.

Lepreum mattered to Elis. But, in the larger world, this tiny *pólis* counted for little. She occupied an outpost on the Neda River near the western coast of the Peloponnesus. This outpost was near and dear to the Eleans, and it was on the border with Messenia. But, although they had gone to some trouble to secure it, the Spartans could do without it. They had done so for decades before the Archidamian War; and, as we shall see, they would forsake it again within a couple of years. For Lepreum, they might well not fight, and they might take the isolation of the coalition army in the southwestern Peloponnesus as an opportunity to send an army up north again to meet with their allies in that part of the Peloponnesus and attack Mantineia or Argos.

Tegea was not like Lepreum. She was one of the two great cities in Arcadia; and, as the Corinthians and the Argives had recognized when they approached the Tegeans in 421, the plain which Tegea and Mantineia shared was the fulcrum of the Peloponnesus. The great power that secured hegemony over Arcadia would have enormous leverage everywhere else. As Themistocles had recognized fifty years before, Arcadia was the key to everything. It was sizable, populous, fiercely martial, centrally located, and bitterly divided; and Sparta's security depended on keeping it divided in this fashion. If Tegea and Mantineia were to come together and join forces, they could easily carry with them the remaining communities within Arcadia. If they did this and a proper Arcadian League was established, it would control south-central Arcadia—the strategically vital district through which the wagon road ran linking the Eurotas valley, where the Spartans resided, with the Pamisos valley, which the Messenians farmed on their behalf. Lacedaemon's hold on the latter valley would not be secure if Arcadia escaped her grasp—and without Messenia and the foodstuffs produced therein she could not support her regime and sustain her peculiar way of life. For Tegea, Sparta would fight without a doubt.

There was one further fact favoring an assault on Tegea. Civil strife was as much the bane of the ancient Greek city within the Peloponnesus as it was elsewhere. Thanks, in particular, to the influence of Homer, the *pólis* was an agonistic community in which the struggle for primacy and honor often trumped everything else—including civic loyalty. There were three further complications which added intensity to the rivalries that arose. First, resources were scarce, and poverty was the norm. Second, the Greek cities were slave societies, membership in the ruling order was regarded as a privilege, and the cultural ethos was anything but egalitarian. In consequence, the battle for primacy and honor was especially fierce, and it was often reconfigured by the political opportunities presented by the tension which existed between the propertied and those without property at all and by that between those who thought themselves especially worthy of inclusion within the ruling order and those to whom they wished or had managed to deny access. Third, in wartime, factions could look to outsiders for support—in this case, to Athens and Argos, on the one hand; and to Lacedaemon, on the other—and these connections could very easily play into the divisions having to do with class and regime. Rare in this time of war, deprivation, and political temptation was the city not rent by domestic strife. Athens escaped it for a time. So, as far as we can tell, did Corinth for an even longer period—and Sparta, thanks to her peculiar regime, was very nearly immune. But Tegea cannot be placed on this exceedingly short list; and, in 418, as the conferees at Orchomenos soon learned (if they were not already aware), there was a faction of self-described democrats at Tegea ready, willing, and eager to hand over the city to the Argives, Athenians, Mantineians, and Eleans and establish themselves in power.

These considerations, though they should have been dispositive, were not sufficient to satisfy the Eleans. They desperately wanted what *they* wanted, as most human beings do. Moreover, they had risked their lives for the Argives, whom they had come to think unworthy; and now they thought that they had been cheated. They were furious—and in their anger they grew short of sight and forgot a fact fundamental to rebellion: that rebels who do not hang together are apt to hang separately.

Had Laches and Nicostratus been enthusiastic supporters of Alcibiades' Peloponnesian venture, had their level of commitment been widely known, and had they arrived in a timely fashion with the one thousand hoplites and three hundred cavalrymen dispatched from Athens, they might have commanded goodwill, trust, and respect sufficient to allow them to mediate. Had Alcibiades himself been present, his charm might have worked wonders (as it often did), and his fervor for the cause might have given him the moral authority with which to get the Eleans to calm down and think soberly about their long-term interests. But his name is not mentioned in connection with this campaign, and there is reason to suspect that he may have returned to Athens to drum up support for sending further reinforcements to the coalition army.

For their part, the Mantineians were an interested party, to whom the Eleans would not listen; and, thanks to their strategic incompetence and the truce, the Argives had squandered much of the respect and goodwill that they had hitherto commanded. So, the Eleans, fed up, went home in a huff while everyone else marched off to Mantineia to prepare for the reckoning to come.[25]

While the three coalition members with soldiers at Mantineia were making their preparations, a message reached the Spartans from those "serviceable [*epitédeioi*]" to them at Tegea that, if they did not show up in short order, the city would go over to the Argives and their allies (if she did not defect in the interim). In response to what was taken as a great emergency, a relief force of Lacedaemonians and helots on a scale never before seen immediately set out from Sparta. Word went out for the Arcadians in alliance with the Lacedaemonians to join them at Tegea. Messengers were dispatched to the Corinthians, Boeotians, Phocians, and Locrians, asking that they come to Mantineia as soon as possible; and, though Thucydides does not mention the fact, couriers were no doubt sent on a similar errand to Sparta's Megarian, Sicyonian, Phliasian, and Epidaurian allies as well.

When these Lacedaemonians reached Oresthasion in Maenalia, where the helots and *períoikoi* from Messenia could join them and the road for wheeled transport leading up from the Eurotas valley came to an end, Agis sent back the oldest and youngest (one sixth of the whole) to guard their homes—perhaps, as one scholar suggests, because he had learned that, with the Eleans absent, his hoplites would have fewer combatants to confront. Then, upon arrival at Tegea, the Spartans and their Arcadian allies marched up through the eighteen-mile-long valley, shaped like an hourglass, that the Mantineians and Tegeans shared. They passed through the stretch—three miles south of Mantineia, where the plain is at its narrowest and a mere two miles separates the Mytikas ridge to the west from the Kapnistra ridge to the east—and marched on a mile or so to the temple of Heracles, where they made their camp and began in an almost ritual fashion to plunder the Mantineian countryside. If, by marching against Orchomenos, the coalition had issued a challenge, Lacedaemon and her allies had now taken it up.[26]

The Argives, Mantineians, and Athenians, when they became aware of this, did nothing to interfere, for it was August. The fields had been harvested well before, and there was little damage that the Lacedaemonians could do. Instead, they stationed themselves a couple of miles to the north on a hill, steep and hard to approach—almost certainly, on the lower slopes of what the ancients called Mount Alesion—from which they could intervene should Agis attack the city of Mantineia. And there they formed up for battle. They could afford to wait. The allies summoned by the Spartans were not going to arrive any time soon. They would first have to rendezvous at Corinth, Sicyon, Phlius, or Nemea and then proceed en masse. For, thanks to the coalition's conquest of Orchomenos, Lacedaemon's enemies were in a position to obstruct travel by small contingents on the main roads.

Agis was in a more difficult position. He needed a decision. He had been charged with *malakía;* his office as king was at stake; and Tegea might switch sides at any time. He needed to demonstrate the spiritedness, vigor, and energy he had hitherto seemed to lack. In consequence, he immediately led the Lacedaemonians toward the enemy and reportedly came "within a stone's throw or javelin's cast" of the army on the hill. This advance was, however, an extremely risky, even foolhardy maneuver, and it met with a stern rebuke. One of the senior Spartiates (quite possibly a *xúmboulos,* though not identified as such), seeing that the position on which they were advancing was unassailable, yelled out to Agis that he was "intent on curing one ill with another," intimating that he could not properly make amends for his blameworthy withdrawal from Argos with an eagerness for immediate battle that was ill-timed. Then, with celerity, Agis suddenly reversed course and led his army back without engaging; and after withdrawing into the territory of Tegea, he spent the rest of the day diverting onto land farmed by the Mantineians a stream, which had long been a bone of contention between the two Arcadian communities situated in that flood-prone, exceedingly well-watered upland valley. His aim was to force the enemy to come down from the hill and fight it

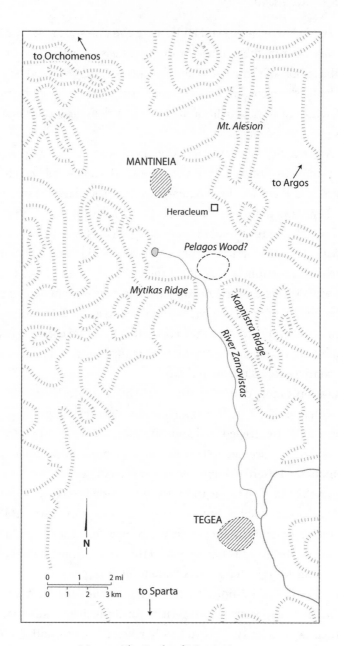

to Orchomenos

Mt. Alesion

MANTINEIA

to Argos

Heracleum

Pelagos Wood?

Mytikas Ridge

Kapnistra Ridge

River Zanovistas

N

0   1   2 mi
0   1   2   3 km

TEGEA

to Sparta

Map 25. The Battle of Mantineia, 418

out in the plain. In August, when the streams were relatively dry, such a maneuver was not apt to elicit as quick a response as it would have in the spring. But, in time, it would assuredly have an effect.

The Argive commanders found Agis' advance and sudden withdrawal puzzling, and, for understandable reasons, they at first had no idea how to respond. Like Agis, however, they were under severe pressure—for the rank and file within their army still thought them at fault for their earlier failure to attack the Lacedaemonians in the Argolid, and they blamed them now for not pursuing Agis' army. Moreover, *malakía* was not the charge that these ordinary Argives were inclined to lodge. In a fashion suggesting on their part an awareness that some of their leaders were Spartan sympathizers, they intimated that treason might well be the reason for their commanders' lack of enterprise. Disturbed by the wellspring of anger they encountered, the generals led their army into the plain and camped for the night, intent on engaging the enemy on the morrow.[27]

While these two armies were maneuvering for advantage, the Eleans had had time to calm down and reconsider the foolhardy decision they had made at Orchomenos, and they were on their way to Mantineia—as were another thousand Athenian hoplites. Had the Argive commanders been aware that reinforcements on such a scale would soon arrive, they would surely have explained the situation to the soldiers under their command, and they would have put off seeking a decision on the battlefield—as was in their power.[28]

Instead, however, on the next morning, the Argives and their allies formed up for a fight on the presumption that they might soon encounter the enemy, and, we are told, they entirely escaped notice. The Mantineians must have controlled the high ground in their territory—the Mytikas and Kapnistra ridges—where there are the remains of ancient guardhouses and Agis would undoubtedly have posted scouts had he been able to do so. And either the Argives had drawn up their army behind one of the two ridges where it could not have been seen from the south by an army about to pass between the two on its way north from the territory of Tegea back to its original encampment at the Heracleum, or there was in the plain a visual obstruction unmentioned by Thucydides, Xenophon, and, later, Polybius in their respective descriptions of battles that took place in this valley—such as the grove of trees that the travel writer Pausanias came upon between the Heracleum and the border with Tegea more than half a millennium after the battle described by Thucydides. What is crystal clear is this: The Spartans, when they marched back from their hydrologi-cal labors toward their original camp near the Heracleum, stumbled upon the enemy phalanx unawares and were, we are told, "astonished and panic-stricken on a scale greater than anyone could remember."[29]

Thucydides' report should give us pause. Something is missing that he would no doubt have supplied had he lived to rewrite his draft. Not only does he not explain why Agis and his officers failed to spy the Argive army until they were well-nigh upon them. His report concerning the intentions of the Argive commanders is also inadequate. One does not deploy a hoplite army for battle in preparation for a march. One does so only on the expectation that hand-to-hand fighting is about to take place. The details of Thucydides' de-scription make sense only on three presumptions: first, that the Argive com-manders knew precisely where the Lacedaemonians were and where they were going (about which Mantineian scouts posted up on the Mytikas and Kapnis-tra ridges could easily have kept them well-informed); second, that they had prepared an ambush; and third, that the Spartans were clueless—that a visual obstruction, in all likelihood one of the two ridges, was cannily exploited by the Argives; that it prevented Agis and those in his entourage from recogniz-ing that they were marching into a trap; and that this stratagem explains why the Spartan commander's men were "astonished and panic-stricken."

Startled though they were when they stumbled into the Argives' ambush, the vast majority of Agis' hoplites were Lacedaemonians and, as such, up to the challenge. Despite the shock that had been administered to them and with virtually no time for preparation, they are said to have redeployed "immedi-ately, in haste," from column to phalanx and to have "come into fine order—with Agis their king taking the lead in everything precisely as the law di-rected." This maneuver, by which something like *cháos* quickly gave way to *kósmos,* was, from Thucydides' perspective, a remarkable achievement; and, to underline its importance, he pauses briefly to describe the Spartan chain of command, in order to indicate that the rapid transmission of orders from the king to the polemarchs, on to the commanders of the regiments [*lochagoí*], then on to the "leaders of fifty men," the "leaders of the sworn bands," and, finally, the "members of the sworn bands" was a phenomenon duplicated in no other city.[30]

When two armies lined up, the Sciritae, who lived in the rough country just to the north of the Eurotas valley, occupied the extreme left in the Spartan line, as they always did. Brigaded with them were the *Brasídeioi,* the survivors from among the seven hundred freed helots who had accompanied Brasidas to Thrace, and the considerably smaller contingent of *neodamódeis.* After them came the Lacedaemonians in regiment [*lóchos*] after regiment, then the Arcadians of the city Heraea, the Arcadians from Parrhasia and the southern districts of Maenalia, and, finally, on the army's right, the Tegeans (with a few Lacedaemonians as reinforcements); and, of course, there were cavalrymen posted on both wings. In the opposing army, the Mantineians—in whose territory the battle was about to take place—occupied the post of honor on the right (opposite the Sciritae), followed by their Arcadian subject allies, the thousand picked men from Argos, the rest of the Argives, their Cleonaean and Ornean subject allies, and finally, on the extreme left of their line, the Athenians with the cavalry they had brought. Such was the order of battle.

In one passage, Thucydides reports that the Lacedaemonian army appeared to be the larger of the two forces; in another, he suggests that it really was the larger. He was nonetheless hesitant to hazard the size of either force—in part because of "the secretiveness of the regime [*tês politeías tò kruptòn*]" ruled out candor on the part of the Lacedaemonians, and in part because elsewhere men tended to be boastful and their estimates could not be trusted. But he also claims to have penetrated the veil of secrecy in the Spartan case; and, by specifying the number of men in the first rank and the number of files behind them, he indicates that their contribution must have come to roughly three thousand five hundred eighty-four Lacedaemonian hoplites. To this we must add an additional six hundred Sciritae, something like six hundred *Brasídeioi,* and perhaps another four hundred *neodamódeis*—as well as the three hundred *hippeîs* who functioned as a royal bodyguard.

With regard to the rest, we are left to guess. On this occasion, which they regarded as a grave emergency, the Spartans sent five-sixths of their levy. Ordinarily, however, when dispatching expeditions abroad, Lacedaemon and the cities in her alliance retained one-third of their hoplites for homeland defense and sent two-thirds, and this seems to have been the general expectation elsewhere as well. This would suggest that the Tegeans, who had dispatched fifteen hundred hoplites to Plataea, could field an army of something like two thousand two hundred fifty heavy infantrymen when defending their own territory, as they were doing on this occasion. The Arcadians of Herae and the Parrhasians and Maenalians in the south, who had supplied fifteen hundred hoplites for the invasion of the Argolid and who were similarly fighting in their own defense, should also have been able to come up with two thousand two hundred fifty additional hoplites.

The Argives and their subject allies had hostile neighbors—including the Epidaurians, who were itching for revenge and who were eager, therefore, to plunder their territory; and we are told that the Argives left behind a force for the defense of the Argolid. If, as was the norm, they sent two-thirds of their ordinary levy against the Lacedaemonians, they should have been able to field something like four thousand hoplites in addition to the elite unit of one thousand that we know they sent—while the Athenians are known to have provided one thousand and the Mantineians and their allies, just under three thousand additional heavy infantrymen. If these estimates are anywhere near correct, the two armies were tolerably well-matched—with Sparta and her Arcadian allies fielding at least ninety-seven hundred hoplites and quite possibly two hundred fifty more and the Argive alliance, not many fewer than nine thousand.[31]

In describing the two armies as they converged, Thucydides drew a sharp distinction between them. At the last minute, each side sought to buck up morale, and each then marched into battle—but they did not do either in the same way.

The Mantineian leaders are said to have exhorted their troops by arguing that they were fighting for their fatherland and that this contest would decide whether they were destined for enslavement or empire. The Argive commanders urged their hoplites to take revenge on the enemies and neighbors who had done them many wrongs and to battle for the "ancient hegemony" that was theirs in the time of Agamemnon and for "the equal portion" allotted to them when the Heraclids divvied up the Peloponnesus.

The Athenians were reminded that glory was at stake and that victory would safeguard their empire, expand it, and end once and for all the prospect that Attica might be invaded. In contrast, the Lacedaemonians eschewed oratory. Instead, they resorted to their traditional songs of war, exhorting one another in this fashion to remember what they, as brave men, already knew: that the extensive drill and training that they had undergone for so long would be more likely to save them than words of exhortation eloquently delivered on the spur of the moment.

After this, while the Argives surged forward eagerly and in a great lather, the Lacedaemonians are said to have advanced at a pace slow, deliberate, and—one might even say—majestic. This they did to the sounds emitted by the multitude of hereditary pipers in their midst, who were charged with maintaining a steady rhythm so that the hoplites could march in formation and not break ranks as the soldiers in sizable armies were wont to do. If, at this time, the Lacedaemonians all had lambdas emblazoned on their shields, as was certainly the practice a few years thereafter, they will have seemed all the more fearsome as they were piped into battle and inexorably bore down on their foe.[32]

Thucydides' account of the battle itself turns initially on a pattern of behavior inherent in all hoplite warfare. As he explains, the hoplite phalanx is a system of interlocking shields; and, because the *aspís* borne by each hoplite covers its bearer's left but not his right side and he relies on the *aspís* of the man to his right for protection in this regard, there is in every phalanx a soldier posted at the right end of the front rank whose right side is unshielded and dangerously exposed. In consequence of the fear to which his predicament gives rise, this hapless individual tends to drift to the right and to draw everyone to his left along with him in a slow but inexorable chain reaction—as one by one his fellow hoplites are forced by the empty space he originally opened up on his left to move in his direction and close ranks. This in turn tends to cause each phalanx to outflank the other on that wing, and there are times in which the threat this poses to the opposing army's left flank forces its commander to take compensatory action.[33]

This is precisely what happened at Mantineia—where, thanks to the chain reaction described above, the Sciritae and the liberated helots on the Lacedaemonian left and the Athenians on the Argive left found themselves dangerously outflanked. Agis, who was stationed in the center, took note of the danger. Judging that the units immediately to his right would be more than strong enough, even at reduced strength, for the challenge they faced, and fearing that the men on his left flank would be surrounded and overwhelmed, he ordered the Sciritae and the *Brasídeioi* to shift to their left, and he instructed the polemarchs Hipponoidas and Aristocles to bring in two *lóchoi* from among the units to his right to fill the yawning gap opened up when the Sciritae and *Brasídeioi* made their move. No one but the Lacedaemonians would have attempted so complex a maneuver at such a time, but they were well-drilled in the making of such adjustments, and Agis apparently thought the maneuver worth the risk.

The two polemarchs took a different view, thinking it unwise, if not impossible, to move large units about at the very moment of the onset, and they
refused to budge. Agis responded to the crisis by ordering the Sciritae back to
their original station, but it was too late for them to close the gap. On this
occasion, as Thucydides wryly observes, the Lacedaemonians proved defi-
cient in tactical skill and inept, and for this they paid a price. When the hand-
to-hand combat began, the Mantineians on the Argive right flank rolled over
the Sciritae and the *Brasídeioi* while the remaining Mantineian troops, their
subject allies, and the thousand-member elite force of the Argives poured
through the gap in the enemy line; routed the Lacedaemonians to their immediate left, encircling and slaughtering many; then drove the rest back to the
wagons that made up their baggage train, where they killed some of the older
men stationed there as guards.[34]

Elsewhere, however, as Thucydides emphasizes, the Lacedaemonians
demonstrated that they were anything but inferior in courage. In the center,
where Agis was posted with the three hundred *hippeîs,* and to his right, the
Spartans fell upon the five *lóchoi* fielded by the Argives, the Cleonaeans and
Orneans, and the Athenians posted with them, and they drove them off. When
the hand-to-hand combat began, most of those in the Argive army immediately fled the fight, and their panic was so severe that some were trampled
underfoot. On Agis' right flank, the Tegeans and the handful of Lacedaemonians posted with them curled about the Athenians whom they had outflanked; and, when the Argives, Cleonaeans, Orneans, and the Athenians
posted with them, who were stationed on their army's left immediately to the
right of the main body of the Athenians, cut and ran, those on the flank found
themselves caught between two fires. Had it not been for their cavalry, Thucydides reports, his compatriots would have suffered greater losses than any
other part of the Argive army.[35]

At this point, Agis ordered his army to wheel about and come to the defense of his own left wing. This enabled the Athenians and the defeated Argives to escape, and it caused the Mantineians and the members of the elite
Argive unit to take to their heels. The former suffered grievously. But, according to Thucydides, the majority of those in the elite Argive unit survived. The
disparity does not appear to have been an accident. Diodorus Siculus, following the fourth-century historian Ephorus, reports that Agis had these Argives
surrounded, could easily have slaughtered them, and would have done so had

he not been restrained by one of the *xúmbouloi,* a distinguished Spartiate named Pharax, who instructed him to let them escape.[36]

In the aftermath of the battle, Agis sent one message to Tegea to Pleistoanax, who had brought up the rest of the Spartan levy in case they were needed, and another to Corinth—announcing the victory and indicating that the Spartans would no longer need help. Later, he led his army back to Lacedaemon to celebrate the Carneia. But, first, the Spartans at Mantineia collected the enemy dead, laid them out, stripped the corpses, and set up a trophy as a memorial of their victory. Their own dead they then conveyed to Tegea and buried them there; and those of the enemy they returned, as was the custom, under a truce.

The losses suffered by those in the Argive coalition were heavy. The main body of the Argives and their subject allies had sacrificed seven hundred lives (perhaps 17.5 percent of the hoplites they fielded); the Mantineians, two hundred; and the Athenians and their Aeginetan colonists, another two hundred—including the generals Laches and Nicostratus—which is to say one man in five. Although no one really knew how many Lacedaemonians died, Thucydides reports that it was supposed that they had lost roughly three hundred men. Most of these were, we must suspect, Sciritae, *Brasídeioi,* and *neodamṓdeis.*

At Mantineia, the result was by no means a foregone conclusion. Had the Eleans and the Athenian reinforcements arrived in time, the Argives and their allies would have outnumbered the Lacedaemonians and theirs by a ratio of four to three, and they almost certainly would have won. Had the Mantineians and the elite Argive unit acted in the manner in which the Spartans were trained to act—had they exercised self-restraint and remained in formation after routing the Sciritae and the *Brasídeioi* and had they then wheeled to the left and attacked the center of Agis' army from behind—the Spartans might well have lost. It is even conceivable that, if the polemarchs Aristocles and Hipponoidas, who were subsequently exiled for *malakía,* had obeyed Agis' orders, the Lacedaemonian contingent to his right would have been so weakened that, in the face of the main body of the Argives, it would have collapsed.[37]

But the Spartans did win, and they won in the old-fashioned way by displaying strategic vision and by exhibiting the virtues of courage, steadfastness, discipline, self-restraint, solidarity, and respect for the law that they had been taught. They not only stood up to the Argives, they cowed them; and when they routed them, they did not do what the Mantineians and the elite Argive unit did. They did not break ranks and pursue those they had defeated. They remained in formation, as was their practice; they awaited orders; and they then wheeled about to take on those of their opponents who had thus far enjoyed success.

By the same token, the Argive alliance lost in the old-fashioned way by displaying strategic incomprehension and by exhibiting the vices of cowardice, half-heartedness, indiscipline, faction, and lawlessness. The Eleans conducted themselves in a foolish, childish, and self-destructive manner. The Argive generals were tactically astute, but their compatriots were inadequately trained, morally unprepared, politically divided, and afflicted with a propensity for becoming a lynch mob. The Mantineians possessed courage but lacked the requisite tactical focus and restraint.

And the Athenians? Their failure stemmed from strategic incomprehension. As in the late 470s and the 460s, when they spurned the advice of Themistocles, they badly misjudged the strategic stakes, and on this occasion they squandered the best chance that they had had in half a century to eliminate the one power in Hellas that posed to them a serious threat. It seems to have been their fate to take great risks which they should never have even considered and to exhibit caution when the rewards on offer were of supreme value. Within five years, the Athenians would come to rue the day that they had thrown away the golden opportunity afforded them in the aftermath of the Peace of Nicias.

Epilogue
The End of the Athenian Challenge

Battles are the principal milestones in secular history. Modern opinion resents this uninspiring truth, and historians often treat the decisions in the field as incidents in the dramas of politics and diplomacy. But great battles, won or lost, change the entire course of events, create new standards of values, new moods, new atmospheres, in armies and in nations, to which all must conform.

WINSTON CHURCHILL

THE contest at Mantineia was, Thucydides tells us, "the greatest battle" to have taken place "in the Hellenic world in quite a long time," and it involved "cities especially worthy of consideration." In it, he adds, "by a single deed," the Spartans "acquitted themselves of both the charge of *malakía*, lodged against them by the Hellenes as a consequence of the disaster on the island, and the charge of imprudence [*aboulía*] and sluggishness [*bradutḗs*], which had also been brought. It was now supposed that they had been brought low by ill fortune. In spirit and determination, however, they were still the men they had always been."[1] This is a telling observation—for victory in war is ultimately achieved by persuasion, and combat is nothing more than violence deployed in an attempt to convince everyone concerned that resistance is futile. Prestige is a force multiplier, a commodity as invaluable as it is intangible. The respect bordering on awe that the Lacedaemonians had once commanded and that they had squandered in the course of the Archidamian War by their slowness, their hesitation, and the surrender on the island of Sphacteria they regained at Mantineia by a single stroke.

The consequences were dramatic, and they were almost immediately evident. In the aftermath of the battle, Alcibiades was present in Argos, and an attempt was made—involving the Argives, the Athenians, and Argos' other allies—to bolster morale and hold the coalition together by means of yet another attack on Epidaurus.[2] When, however, the Lacedaemonians were done celebrating the Carneia, they once again marched out on campaign; and from Tegea, where they paused, they sent on to Argos conciliatory proposals. It was in response to this overture that the Laconizers—"the serviceable men [*epitḗdeioi*]" intent on overthrowing the Argive democracy—first reportedly took heart. Their immediate aim was to persuade their compatriots to accept a treaty of peace, then an alliance. With the aid of the Spartans, they then hoped to effect a change of regime and establish at Argos the dominion of the few over the many.

When Lichas son of Arcesilaus, the Argive *próxenos* at Lacedaemon, reached Argos, he offered her citizens a choice between war and peace, and a great debate took place, in which he tangled with Alcibiades. Had Thucydides lived to revise this section of his narrative, we might well have a full-scale, penetrating report concerning what was no doubt a memorable clash. As things stand, we will have to settle for a summary account of what happened. It was at this point, we are told, that "those doing the bidding of the Spartans first dared to come out in the open"; and, despite the presence of the son of Cleinias, in short order they succeeded in persuading their demoralized compatriots to accept the conciliatory offer of the Lacedaemonians and make peace, then to renounce the confederacy that linked them with the Mantineians, Eleans, and Athenians and contract an alliance with Sparta.

Soon thereafter, the Mantineians gave up their little empire and made terms with the Lacedaemonians. Then, an army, made up of one thousand Spartans and of the elite unit of one thousand Argives, set out in a joint operation. In advance, the Lacedaemonians paid Sicyon a visit, and there they remodeled the constitutional regulations defining that city's ruling order and recast the regime on more narrowly oligarchic lines. Then, the joint expedition returned to Argos and installed there an "oligarchy serviceable [*oligarchía epitḗdeia*] to the Lacedaemonians." The following summer, the Spartans intervened in Achaea and settled affairs there "in a manner" they deemed "more serviceable [*epitēdeíōs*]"; and, at some point, they reached an accommodation of sorts with the Eleans in which Lepreum was restored to the latter, the Spartans were no longer barred from Olympia, and the Eleans no longer participated in Lacedaemon's wars.[3]

The oligarchy which the Spartans and those "serviceable" to them imposed on Argos did not last—in large part because the Spartans were not prepared to make the long-term commitment necessary to prop up the Argive Laconizers.[4] But the other arrangements instituted at this time had staying power—and the Athenians were never again able to mount a challenge to Lacedaemon's hegemony in the Peloponnesus. Winston Churchill's dictum concerning "great battles, won or lost," is apt. Sparta's victory at Mantineia really did "change the entire course of events"; and within the Peloponnesus, where it mattered most, it created "new standards of values, new moods, new atmospheres," in the armies and cities to which all had to "conform."[5]

This victory also marked a turning point in the ongoing struggle between Athens and Sparta. Up to this moment, for more than forty years, as this volume and its predecessor make clear, Lacedaemon had been on the defensive. Even when she had launched an attack, its aim had been the preservation of the old order. No one knew it at the time. But Sparta's victory at Mantineia had brought to an end once and for all the threat to Lacedaemon's security and well-being posed by Athens. When the Lacedaemonians reentered the struggle in earnest five years later, their aim was not to contain and restrain Athens' dominion. It was to destroy and replace it.

The chief legacy of the Athenian challenge and of the concerted effort mounted at intervals by Themistocles, Pericles, and Alcibiades to break up the Spartan alliance and redeploy Lacedaemon's erstwhile allies in a grand effort to subvert her hegemony over the Peloponnesus and destroy thereby the foundations of her power was a dramatic change in the grand strategy of Sparta. In this regard, in the wake of their victory at Mantineia, while reflecting on their experience in their first two Attic wars, the Lacedaemonians came to recognize that they, too, had to "conform" to "new standards of values, new moods, new atmospheres."

Abbreviations and Short Titles

In the notes, I have adopted the standard abbreviations for classical texts and inscriptions, for books of the Bible, and for modern journals and books provided in *The Oxford Classical Dictionary,* 4th edition revised, ed. Simon Hornblower, Antony Spawforth, and Esther Eidinow (Oxford, UK: Oxford University Press, 2012); *The Chicago Manual of Style,* 15th edition (Chicago: University of Chicago Press, 2003), 15.50–53; and the bibliographical annual *L'Année Philologique.* Where possible, the ancient texts are cited by the divisions and subdivisions employed by the author or introduced by subsequent editors (that is, by book, part, chapter, section number, paragraph, act, scene, line, Stephanus page, or by page and line number). Cross-references to other parts of this volume refer to the prologue, part, or chapter and specify whether the material referenced can be found above or below.

Unless otherwise indicated, all of the translations are my own. I transliterate the Greek, using undotted i's where no accent is required, adding macrons, accents, circumflexes, and so on. When others—in titles or statements quoted—transliterate in a different manner, I leave their transliterations as they had them.

For other works frequently cited, the following abbreviations and short titles have been employed.

AT	John S. Morrison, John F. Coates, and N. Boris Rankov, *The Athenian Trireme: The History and Reconstruction of an Ancient Greek Warship,* 2nd edition (New York: Cambridge University Press, 2000).
Badian, *FPP*	Ernst Badian, *From Plataea to Potidaea: Studies in the History and Historiography of the Pentecontaetia* (Baltimore: Johns Hopkins University Press, 1993).
Badian, *Outbreak*	Ernst Badian, "Thucydides and the Outbreak of the Peloponnesian War: A Historian's Brief," in *Conflict, Antithesis and the*

	Ancient Historian, ed. June W. Allison (Columbus: Ohio State University Press, 1990), 46–91.
Briant, *CA*	Pierre Briant, *From Cyrus to Alexander: A History of the Persian Empire,* trans. Peter T. Daniels (Winona Lake, IN: Eisenbrauns, 2002).
Brunt, *SGHT*	Peter A. Brunt, *Studies in Greek History and Thought* (Oxford: Clarendon Press, 1993).
Brunt, *SPSAW*	Peter A. Brunt, "Spartan Policy and Strategy in the Archidamian War," *Phoenix* 19:4 (Winter 1965): 255–80.
Cawkwell, *CC*	George Cawkwell, *Cyrene to Chaeronea: Selected Essays on Ancient Greek History* (Oxford: Oxford University Press, 2011).
Cawkwell, *TPW*	George Cawkwell, *Thucydides and the Peloponnesian War* (London: Routledge, 1997).
Crux	*CRUX: Essays Presented to G. E. M. de Ste. Croix on His 75th Birthday,* ed. Paul Cartledge and F. D. Harvey, *HPTh* 6:1/2 (1985).
Debnar, *SSL*	Paula Debnar, *Speaking the Same Language: Speech and Audience in Thucydides' Spartan Debates* (Ann Arbor: University of Michigan Press, 2001).
Geske, *Nicias*	Norbert Geske, *Nicias und das Volk von Athen im Archidamischen Krieg* (Stuttgart: Franz Steiner Verlag, 2005).
Holladay, *AFC*	A. James Holladay, *Athens in the Fifth Century and Other Studies in Greek History: The Collected Papers of A. James Holladay,* ed. Anthony J. Podlecki (Chicago: Ares, 2002).
Hutchinson, *Attrition*	Godfrey Hutchinson, *Attrition: Aspects of Command in the Peloponnesian War* (Stonehouse, Gloucestershire: Spelmont, 2006).
IAE	*Interpreting the Athenian Empire,* ed. John T. Ma, Nikolaos Papazarkadas, and Robert Parker (London: Duckworth, 2009).
Kagan, *AW*	Donald Kagan, *The Archidamian War* (Ithaca, NY: Cornell University Press, 1974).
Kagan, *Outbreak*	Donald Kagan, *The Outbreak of the Peloponnesian War* (Ithaca, NY: Cornell University Press, 1969).
Kagan, *PNSE*	Donald Kagan, *The Peace of Nicias and the Sicilian Expedition* (Ithaca, NY: Cornell University Press, 1981).
Kallet-Marx, *MENP*	Lisa Kallet-Marx, *Money, Expense, and Naval Power in Thucy-*

	dides' History 1–5.24 (Berkeley: University of California Press, 1993).
Lafargue, *BP*	Philippe Lafargue, *La Bataille de Pylos: Athènes contre Sparta, 425 av. J.-C.* (Paris: Alma, 2015).
Lafargue, *Cléon*	Philippe Lafargue, *Cléon, Le Guerrier d'Athéna* (Paris: Diffusion de Boccard, 2013).
Lazenby, *PW*	John F. Lazenby, *The Peloponnesian War: A Military Study* (London: Routledge, 2004).
Lendon, *SoW*	Jon E. Lendon, *Song of Wrath: The Peloponnesian War Begins* (New York: Basic Books, 2010).
Lewis, *AW*	David M. Lewis, "The Archidamian War," in *CAH* V² 370–432.
Lewis, *SP*	David M. Lewis, *Sparta and Persia* (Leiden: Brill, 1977).
Lewis, *TYP*	David M. Lewis, "The Thirty Years' Peace," in *CAH* V² 121–46.
Morton, *RPEAGS*	Jamie Morton, *The Role of the Physical Environment in Ancient Greek Seafaring* (Leiden: Brill, 2001).
O&R	*Greek Historical Inscriptions, 478–404 BC,* ed. Robin Osborne and Peter J. Rhodes (Oxford: Oxford University Press, 2017).
Paarmann, *A&P*	Bjørn Paarmann, "*Aparchai* and *Phoroi*: A New Commented Edition of the Athenian Tribute Quota Lists and Assessment Decrees," Dissertation, University of Fribourg, 2007.
Podlecki, *PHC*	Anthony Podlecki, *Perikles and His Circle* (London: Routledge, 1998).
Rahe, *PC*	Paul A. Rahe, *The Grand Strategy of Classical Sparta: The Persian Challenge* (New Haven, CT: Yale University Press, 2015).
Rahe, *RAM*	Paul A. Rahe, *Republics Ancient and Modern: Classical Republicanism and the American Revolution* (Chapel Hill: University of North Carolina Press, 1992).
Rahe, *SFAW*	Paul A. Rahe, *Sparta's First Attic War: The Grand Strategy of Classical Sparta, 478–446 BC* (New Haven, CT: Yale University Press, 2019).
Rahe, *SR*	Paul A. Rahe, *The Spartan Regime: Its Character, Its Origins* (New Haven, CT: Yale University Press, 2016).
Roisman, *Demosthenes*	Joseph Roisman, *The General Demosthenes and His Use of Military Surprise* (Stuttgart: Franz Steiner Verlag, 1993).
Rood, *Thucydides*	Tim Rood, *Thucydides: Narrative and Explanation* (Oxford: Oxford University Press, 1998).

SAGT   W. Kendrick Pritchett, *Studies in Ancient Greek Topography*
                               (Berkeley: University of California Press, 1965–89; Amsterdam:
                               J. C. Gieben, 1991–92).

Ste. Croix, *OPW*   Geoffrey Ernest Maurice de Ste. Croix, *The Origins of the
                               Peloponnesian War* (Ithaca: Cornell University Press, 1972).

Salmon, *WC*   John B. Salmon, *Wealthy Corinth: A History of the City to 338
                               B.C.* (Oxford: Clarendon Press, 1984).

Samons, *EO*   Loren J. Samons II, *Empire of the Owl: Athenian Imperial Finance*
                               (Stuttgart: Franz Steiner Verlag, 2000).

Samons, *PCH*   Loren J. Samons II, *Pericles and the Conquest of History: A
                               Political Biography* (New York: Cambridge University Press,
                               2016).

Shepherd, *PS*   William Shepherd, *Pylos and Sphacteria, 425 BC: Sparta's Island
                               of Disaster* (Oxford: Osprey, 2013).

Stadter, *CPP*   Philip A. Stadter, *A Commentary on Plutarch's Pericles* (Chapel
                               Hill: University of North Carolina Press, 1989).

Wade-Gery, *EGH*   Henry Theodore Wade-Gery, *Essays in Greek History* (Oxford:
                               Basil Blackwell, 1958).

Westlake, *Essays*   Henry D. Westlake, *Essays on the Greek Historians and Greek
                               History* (Manchester: Manchester University Press, 1969).

Westlake, *Individuals*   Henry D. Westlake, *Individuals in Thucydides* (Cambridge:
                               Cambridge University Press, 1968).

Westlake, *Studies*   Henry D. Westlake, *Studies in Thucydides and Greek History*
                               (Bristol: Bristol Classical Press, 1989).

Wilson, *AC*   John B. Wilson, *Athens and Corcyra: Strategy and Tactics in the
                               Peloponnesian War* (Bristol: Bristol Classical Press, 1987).

Notes

Introduction. An Enduring Strategic Rivalry

1. Punic Wars: Donald Kagan, *On the Origins of War and the Preservation of Peace* (New York: Doubleday, 1995), 232–80, and Barry Strauss, "The War for Empire: Rome vs. Carthage," in *Great Strategic Rivalries: From the Classical World to the Cold War,* ed. James Lacey (Oxford: Oxford University Press, 2016), 81–102. War of the League of Augsburg and War of the Spanish Succession: Winston S. Churchill, *Marlborough: His Life and Times* (London: Harrap, 1947), I 424–84. World wars: Kagan, *On the Origins of War and the Preservation of Peace,* 81–231, 281–436, and Williamson Murray, "Versailles: The Peace without a Chance," in *The Making of Peace: Rulers, States, and the Aftermath of War,* ed. Williamson Murray and Jim Lacey (Cambridge: Cambridge University Press, 2009), 209–39. Situation of power defeated and consequences: Polyb. 3.12.

2. A part of the Green Pamphlet was eventually published as an appendix to the 1988 reprint of Julian Stafford Corbett, *Some Principles of Maritime Strategy* (London: Longmans Green, 1911), where he had elaborated on the idea of grand strategy without using the term: see Julian Stafford Corbett, *Some Principles of Maritime Strategy,* ed. Eric J. Grove (Annapolis, MD: Naval Institute Press, 1988), 305–25. For the history of the term, see Lukas Milevski, *The Evolution of Modern Grand Strategic Thought* (Oxford: Oxford University Press, 2016).

3. See J. F. C. Fuller, *The Reformation of War* (London: Hutchinson, 1923), 211–28 (esp. 218–21). For a recent discussion of the pertinent concept's application to ancient history, see Kimberly Kagan, "Redefining Roman Grand Strategy," *Journal of Military History* 70:2 (April 2006): 333–62 (esp. 348–50).

4. See Edward N. Luttwak, *The Grand Strategy of the Roman Empire: From the First Century A.D. to the Third* (Baltimore: Johns Hopkins University Press, 1976), and *The Grand Strategy of the Byzantine Empire* (Cambridge, MA: Harvard University Press, 2009), as well as A. Wess Mitchell, *The Grand Strategy of the Hapsburg Empire* (Princeton, NJ: Princeton University Press, 2018).

Prologue. A Sudden Reversal

Epigraph: Plato, *Leg.* 1.626a.

1. For further details and a full citation of the primary sources and the secondary literature, see Rahe, *SR,* Chapter 1 and Appendix 1.

2. Aristotle on Laconian helots: *Pol.* 1269a36–39. Note Critias ap. Lib. *Or.* 25.63.

3. See Rahe, *SR,* passim.

4. Formation of alliance system: Rahe, *SR,* Chapter 4. Corinthian leader on Spartan weakness nearer home: Xen. *Hell.* 4.2.11–12.

5. Pausanias' misconduct and Athens' assumption of the leadership at sea: Rahe, *SFAW,* Chapter 1. For subsequent misconduct on his part, see Chapters 2–3.

6. For the details, see Rahe, *SFAW,* Chapters 2–3, preface to Part II, and Chapters 4–5.

7. See Rahe, *SFAW,* Chapter 6.

8. For further details, see Rahe, *SFAW,* Chapter 6.

Part I. The Hatch and Brood of Time

Epigraph: William Shakespeare, *Henry IV, Part Two,* ed. René Weiss (Oxford: Oxford University Press, 1998), 3.1.79–85.

1. For the details, see Rahe, *SFAW,* Epilogue (with note 1, where I cite the ancient evidence and discuss the secondary literature).

2. Dream of lasting peace: Immanuel Kant, "Zum ewigen Frieden: Ein philosophischer Entwurf" (1796), in Kant, *Werke in Zehn Bänden,* ed. Wilhelm Weischedel (Darmstadt: Wissenschaftliche Buchgesellschaft, 1971), IX 193–251.

3. Homer the educator of Hellas: Pl. *Resp.* 10.606e. Primacy of war: *Leg.* 1.626a.

4. Polybius' distinction: 3.12.

5. City of salarymen: Rahe, *SFAW,* Chapter 6.

6. Theft of war: note Thuc. 4.21.3, and consider Lendon, *SoW,* 78–82, in light of David Whitehead, "*Klope polemou:* 'Theft' in Ancient Greek Warfare," *C&M* 39 (1988): 43–53. Conflict: Dion. Hal. *Thuc.* 10–12.

Chapter 1. An Uneasy Truce

Epigraph: Thuc. 1.76.2.

1. Cleruchs and colonists to the Chersonnesus, Naxos, Andros, Thrace, and elsewhere: Plut. *Per.* 11.5 with Stadter, *CPP,* 138–43. On the Chersonnesus, note also Plut. *Per.* 19.1 with *ML* 48 = *IG* I³ 1162 = *O&R* no. 129 and Meiggs, *AE,* 159–61. Evidence for reconquest of Euboea, expulsion of Histiaeans, and dispatch of cleruchs to Histiaea and Chalcis: Thuc. 1.114.3, Ar. *Nub.* 211–13 (with the scholia), Philochorus *FGrH* 328 F118, Plut. *Per.* 23.3–4. Confirmation that Athenian cleruchy of one or two thousand installed at Histiaea in 446: Thuc. 1.114.3, 7.57.2, 8.95.7; Philochorus *FGrH* 328 F118; Theopompus of Chios *FGrH* 115 F387; Diod. 12.22.2. Note Andoc. 3.9 and *IG* I³ 41. Chalcis also: Plut. *Per.* 23.4. *IG* I³ 14 (*ML* no. 40 = *O&R* no. 121), 40 (*ML* no. 52 = *O&R* no. 131) and 41 as well as Ar. *Pax* 1047 may well be pertinent—as Gomme, *HCT,* I 341–47; J. R. Green and Robert K. Sinclair, "Athenians in Eretria," *Historia* 19:5 (December 1970): 515–27; Meiggs, *AE,* 178–82 (with 565–70); and Jack M. Balcer, *The Athenian Regulations for Chalcis: Studies in Athenian Imperial Law* (Wiesbaden: F. Steiner, 1978), suppose. But some believe that these inscriptions date to 424/3, and they may well be right: for, although the letter forms used on the stones were once thought to be chronologically dispositive, it is now clear that they are not: see Peter J. Rhodes, "After the Three-Bar 'Sigma' Controversy: The History of Athenian Imperialism Reassessed," *CQ* n.s. 58:2 (December 2008): 500–506, and "What Remains of Periclean Imperialism?" in *Athēnaiōn Episkopos: Studies in Honour of Harold B. Mattingly,* ed. Angelos P. Matthaiou and Robert K. Pitt (Athens: Ellēnikē Epigraphikē Etaireia, 2014), 39–49; Nikolaos Papazarkadas, "Epigraphy and the Athenian Empire: Re-Shuffling the Chronological Cards," in *IAE,* 67–88; and Lendon, *SoW,* 426–30. Colony dispatched to Brea in Thrace: *IG* I³ 46 = *ML* no. 49 = *O&R* no. 142 with *IACP* no. 624, and Sélène Psôma, "Thucydide I, 61, 4: Béroia et la nouvelle localisation de Bréa," *REG* 122:2 (July–December 2009): 263–80. Note Hornblower, *CT,* I 104–5. All in all enormous numbers involved: Plut. *Mor.* 349c–d. Concomitant reductions in *phóros:* Lewis, *TYP,* 121–46 (esp. 127–29, 135–36).

2. That participation is apt to have been restricted to thetes and *zeugítai* can be inferred

from the provisions for the colony established at Brea (*IG* I³ 46 = *ML* no. 49 = *O&R* no. 142), which confirms Plutarch's description of Pericles' aims (*Per.* 11.6 with Stadter, *CPP,* 142–43) and supports Antiphon's claim: F6 (Blass/Thalheim): see Hornblower, *CT,* I 399–400. For an overview, see Peter A. Brunt, "Athenian Settlements Abroad in the Fifth Century B.C.," in *Ancient Society and Institutions: Studies Presented to Victor Ehrenberg on His 75th Birthday,* ed. Ernst Badian (Oxford: Basil Blackwell, 1966), 71–92, reprinted with a postscript in Brunt, *SGHT,* 112–36; and note Kurt A. Raaflaub, "Learning from the Enemy: Athens and Persian 'Instruments of Empire,'" in *IAE,* 89–124.

3. Themistocles' daughters: Plut. *Them.* 32.2–3. Threat of withdrawal to Siris (*IACP* no. 69): Hdt. 8.62.2. See Ste. Croix, *OPW,* 378–79.

4. Wealth of archaic Siris and Sybaris (*IACP* no. 70): Hdt. 6.126.2–127.1. From Sybaris to Thurii (*IACP* no. 74): consider Arist. *Pol.* 1303a25–33; Strabo 6.1.13; and Diod. 11.48.4, 90.3–4, 12.10.1–11.2, 22.4, 35.1–3 in light of Dion. Hal. *Lys.* 1, Plut. *Mor.* 835d, and the evidence presented by Colin M. Kraay, "The Coinage of Sybaris after 510 BC," *NC* ser. 6, 18 (1958): 13–37. Pericles as progenitor: Plut. *Per.* 11.5 with Stadter, *CPP,* 141–42. Lampon as a front man for Pericles: Plut. *Mor.* 812d with Arist. *Rhet.* 1419a2–5 and Plut. *Per.* 6.2–3: see Podlecki, *PHC,* 88–91. Additional evidence for role at Thurii: Schol. Ar. *Clouds* 332, Schol. Ar. *Birds* 521, Photius s.v. *Thouriománteis.* Hippodamus' role: consider Diod. 12.10.6–7 and Hesychios s.v. *Hippodámou némēsis* in light of Arist. *Pol.* 1267b22–30, 1330b21–31, and Strabo 14.2.9; and see Vanessa B. Gorman, "Aristotle's Hippodamos (*Politics* 2.1267b22–30)," *Historia* 44:4 (4th Quarter 1995): 385–95; Emanuele Greco, "Ippodamo e Thurii," *Ostraka* 6:2 (1997): 435–39; Emanuele Greco and Silvana Luppino, "Ricerche sulla topografia e sull-urbanistica di Sibari-Thuri-Copiae," *AION* (*Archeol.*) n.s. 6 (1999): 115–64; and Podlecki, *PHC,* 91–92. Protagoras' role: Heraclides Ponticus ap. Diog. Laert. 9.8.50. Cf. Diod. 12.11.3–4. An associate of Pericles: Plut. *Per.* 36.4–5. See Podlecki, *PHC,* 93–99. Cleandridas at Thurii: Thuc. 6.104.2, Diod. 12.23.2, Polyaen. *Strat.* 2.10.1–2, 4. His hero cult: Paolo Zancani Montuori, "La Campagna archeologica del 1932 nella piana del Crati," *Atti e Mem. della Soc. Magna Grecia* n.s. 4 (1962): 7–63 (at 36–40), and Günther Zuntz, *Persephone: Three Essays on Religion and Thought in Magna Graecia:* (Oxford: Clarendon Press, 1971), 287 (with n. 2). Herodotus: Arist. *Rh.* 1409a28, Plut. *Mor.* 604f, *Suda* s.v. *Hēródotos.* Cephalus and sons: consider Dion. Hal. *Lys.* 1 and Plut. *Mor.* 835c–d, which need correction in light of Pl. *Resp.* 328b–331d. Cf. Henry Theodore Wade-Gery, "Thucydides the Son of Melesias: A Study of Periklean Policy," *JHS* 52:2 (1932): 205–27 (esp. 217–19), reprinted in Wade-Gery, *EGH,* 239–70 (esp. 255–58), who fails to see how Panhellenic gesturing could serve the fierce imperial ambitions he rightly attributes to Pericles, with Victor Ehrenberg, "The Foundation of Thurii," *AJPh* 69:2 (1948): 149–70, reprinted in Ehrenberg, *Polis und Imperium: Beiträge zur alten Geschichte,* ed. Karl Friedrich Strohecker and Alexander John Graham (Zurich: Artemis Verlag, 1965), 298–315; Meiggs, *AE,* 185–86 (with 278–80, 303–4); Ste. Croix, *OPW,* 381; Antony Andrewes, "The Opposition to Perikles," *JHS* 98 (1978): 1–8 (esp. 5–8); Lewis, *TYP,* 141–43; and Podlecki, *PHC,* 81–84, 88–98, who recognize the connection, and note *ATL,* III 305 n. 20. Cf. Kagan, *Outbreak,* 154–69 (with 382–84), who thinks Pericles' Panhellenic gesture an attempt to promote cordial relations with Sparta and Corinth, with Lendon, *SoW,* 82–83, who is as sensitive to the manner in which generosity of this sort tends to be an assertion of superiority as was Pericles himself: Thuc. 2.40.4–5. On the import of Athens' shortage of manpower for the venture, see Samons, *PCH,* 107–8, 127–28.

5. Ethnic divisions produce stasis in Thurii and a turn against Athens: Diod. 12.35, 13.3.4; Thuc. 6.104.2, 7.33.5, 57.11, 8.35.1; Dion. Hal. *Lys.* 1; Plut. *Mor.* 835e. Consider Arist. *Pol.* 1307a27–33 and 1307b6–19 in light of Shlomo Berger, "Revolution and Constitution in Thurii: Arist. *Pol.* 1307a, b," *Eranos* 88 (1990): 9–16.

6. Renewal of alliances with Ionian cities Rhegium (*IACP* no. 68) and Leontini (*IACP* no. 33) in 433/2: consider *ML* nos. 63–64 = *IG* I³ 53–54 = *O&R* no. 149 in light of Thuc. 3.86, and see Terry E. Wick, "Athens' Alliances with Rhegion and Leontinoi," *Historia* 25:3 (3rd Quarter 1976): 288–304; David M. Lewis, "The Treaties with Leontini and Rhegium," *ZPE* 22 (1976): 223–25; and Lewis, *AW,* 375, who infer the existence of earlier alliances from the fact that the prescripts have been erased and reinscribed. I find the alternative explanation suggested by Silvio Cataldi, "I Pre-

scritti dei trattati ateniesi con Reggio e Leontini," *AAT* 121 (1987): 63–72, implausible. Lampon at Catana (*IACP* no. 30): Justin 4.3.4. Evidence suggesting that Metapontum (*IACP* no. 61), Naxos (*IACP* no. 41), and the other Chalcidian cities may also have been approached: Thuc. 3.86, 4.25.7–11, 6.50.2–3, 74.2, 75.2, 88.3, 7.33.5, 57.11. Diotimos in the bay of Naples at the invitations of the Neapolitans: Lycoph. *Alex.* 732–35 (with the scholia), Timaeus *FGrH* 566 F98. Athenian settlers at Neapolis: Strabo 5.4.7 with *IACP* no. 63 and Hornblower, *CT,* III 5. See Martin W. Frederiksen, *Campania,* ed. Nicholas Purcell (London: British School at Rome, 1984), 94–107; Flavio Raviola, "La Tradizione letteraria sulla fondazione di Neapolis," in *Hesperìa 2: Studi sulla grecità del occidente,* ed. Lorenzo Braccesi (Rome: Erma di Bretschneider, 1991), 19–40; and Nazarena Valenza Mele, "Napoli 1," *BTCGI* 12 (1993): 165–239. In 433, Diotimos helped conduct an Athenian fleet to Corcyra: Thuc. 1.45.2 with *ML* no. 61 = *IG* I³ 364 = *O&R* no. 148, line 9. See Silvio Cataldi, "La Spedizione di Diotimo in Italia e *I Sikeloi,*" *RFIC* 117 (1989): 129–80. At some point, Diotimos went to Susa on an embassy: Strabo 1.3.1. It is telling that "the Campanians" would later send cavalry to support an Athenian expedition in Sicily: consider Diod. 13.44.1–2 in light of Martin W. Frederiksen, "Campanian Cavalry: A Question of Origins," *Dial. di Arch.* 2:1 (1968): 3–31.

7. Cities in Italy and Sicily founded by Chalcidians of Euboea: Thuc. 6.3.1–3, 4.5; Strabo 5.4.4–7; Scymn. 251; Livy 8.22.5–6, 23.11; Vell. Pat. 1.4.1; Lutatius Daphnis ap. Serv. Dan. on Verg. *G.* 4.563; and *Sibyllinische Blätter* 11.53–56 (Diels). With regard to Neapolis, its environs, and the circumstances, especially those involving Syracusa, that pertained to it and the other Chalcidian foundations in and after the 470s, see Frederiksen, *Campania,* 54–157. Importance of ethnicity more generally: John Alty, "Dorians and Ionians," *JHS* 102 (1982): 1–14. Thucydides especially sensitive to its significance: Maria Fragoulaki, *Kinship in Thucydides: Intercommunal Ties and Historical Narrative* (Oxford: Oxford University Press, 2013).

8. The third wall: Andoc. 3.7, Aeschin. 2.174, Pl. *Grg.* 455d–e (with the scholia), Plut. *Per.* 13.7–8, *IG* I³ 440.127 with Meiggs, *AE,* 187–88; Lewis, *TYP,* 138–39; Podlecki, *PHC,* 99–100; and David H. Conwell, *Connecting a City to the Sea: The History of the Athenian Long Walls* (Leiden: Brill, 2008), 65–78. Note also Cratinus iv, F326 (PCG).

9. One city, one vote; its consequences; and the resentment it inspired: Thuc. 3.10.5 with Rahe, *SFAW,* Chapter 3, note 14, in context. Assertion of duty to prevent allies from fighting one another: Thuc. 6.76.3 with Ste. Croix, *OPW,* 120–21.

10. Samos: *IACP* no. 864. Samian *peraía* on the continent: Strabo 14.1.20 with Graham Shipley, *A History of Samos, 800–188 BC* (Oxford: Clarendon Press, 1987), 31–37. Longevity of territorial dispute: Plut. *Mor.* 296a = Arist. F576 (Rose) = F593 (Gigon). On a likely consequence of the territorial dispute in 440, see Diod. 15.49.1 with Simon Hornblower, "Thucydides, the Panionian Festival, and the Ephesia (III 104)," *Historia* 31:2 (2nd Quarter 1982): 241–45 (at 245).

11. Priene: *IACP* no. 861. Subjection to the Mermnads: Hdt. 1.15, 26–27. Subjection to Persia: 1.141–43, 154–56, 161. Twelve ships at Lade: 6.8.1. Contribution of *phóros* documented on seven occasions from 454/3 to 441/0: *ATL* I 388. See II 8–20 = *IG* I³ 259–70 = Paarmann, *A&P,* II 14–41 (with III 3–49). Missing from the list for 440/39: *ATL,* I 388. See II 21 = *IG* I³ 272 = Paarmann, *A&P,* 42–44 (with III 52–53).

12. For the details, the secondary literature, and the ancient sources, see Shipley, *A History of Samos,* 1–112. In this connection, note Günter Dunst, "Archaische Inschriften und Dokumente der Pentekontaetie aus Samos," *MDAI(A)* 87 (1972): 99–163 (at 149–55).

13. For the details, the secondary literature, and the ancient sources, see Vanessa B. Gorman, *Miletos, the Ornament of Ionia: A History of the City to 400 B.C. E.* (Ann Arbor: University of Michigan Press, 2001), 31–163, 215–36, 243–58, and *IACP* no. 854. Samian betrayal at Lade: Hdt. 6.14.2–3. Cities in Ionia bereft of fortifications in 427 (and no doubt earlier): Thuc. 3.33.2 with Plut. *Per.* 16.2. See Meiggs, *AE,* 149–51; Andrewes, *HCT,* V 35–36; and Hornblower, *CT,* I 414–15. The secondary literature concerning Miletus in this period needs to be adjusted in light of what now seems a virtual certainty: that *IG* I³ 21 pertains to 426/5 and not 450/49 and that the Milesians paid the *phóros* in 454/3: Rhodes, "After the Three-Bar 'Sigma' Controversy," 503 (in context), and Bjørn Paarmann, "The Revolt of Miletos in 454 and the Milesians in *IG* I³ 259.III.29," in *Athēnaiōn Episkopos,* 121–40.

14. Pericles at the helm: Plut. *Per.* 14.3–16.3 with Stadter, *CPP,* 183–99. Samian-Milesian conflict over Priene, Pericles' response, Samian revolt, Pissouthnes' conduct: Thuc. 1.115.2–5; Ar. *Vesp.* 281–85 (with the scholia); Diod. 12.27.1–3; and Plut. *Per.* 24.1, 25.1–4 with Stadter, *CPP,* 232–34, 242–46. Athens' unwillingness to tolerate wars within her league: Thuc. 6.76.3. Pissouthnes' father, grandfather, and great-grandfather: Hdt. 7.64.2. Debate concerning Artaxerxes' involvement: cf. Samuel K. Eddy, "The Cold War between Athens and Persia, c. 448–412 B.C.," *CPh* 68:4 (October 1973): 241–58 (at 250 with n. 51), with Lewis, *SP,* 55–60, and see Matt Waters, "Applied Royal Directive: Pissouthnes and Samos," in *Der Achämenidenhof/The Achamenid Court,* ed. Bruno Jacobs and Robert Rollinger (Wiesbaden: Harrassowitz Verlag, 2010), 817–28. Chronology: consider Thuc. 1.115.2 and Schol. Ar. *Vesp.* 283 in light of Charles W. Fornara and David M. Lewis, "On the Chronology of the Samian War," *JHS* 99 (1979): 7–19, and see Benjamin D. Meritt, "The Samian Revolt from Athens in 440–439 B.C.," *PAPhS* 128:2 (June 1984): 123–33 (at 128–31), who seems to me to be correct in insisting that we base our calculations on Thucydides' claim that the war between Samos and Miletus started six years (counting inclusively) after Athens and Sparta made peace. That the Byzantine rebellion postdates the spring of 440 follows from the fact that Byzantium paid *phóros* at that time: *ATL,* I 250. See II 20 = *IG* I³ 271 = Paarmann, *A&P,* II 39–41 (with III 49–52). Although valuable, the recent secondary literature on the Samian revolt— Kagan, *Outbreak,* 170–78 (with 386–87); Ronald P. Legon, "Samos in the Delian League," *Historia* 21:2 (2nd Quarter 1972): 145–58; Meiggs, *AE,* 188–94 (with 428); Trevor J. Quinn, *Athens and Samos, Lesbos, and Chios, 478–404 B.C.* (Manchester: Manchester University Press, 1981), 10–23; Shipley, *A History of Samos,* 113–22; Lewis, *TYP,* 143–45; and Podlecki, *PHC,* 118–28—needs adjustment with respect to Miletus in light of the recent revolution in epigraphy: note 13, above.

15. Megabyzus' revolt: Ctesias *FGrH* 688 F14.37–44. Note Ezra 7:7–8 and Nehemiah 2:1–8; cf. Kenneth G. Hoglund, *Achaemenid Imperial Administration in Syria-Palestine and the Mission of Ezra and Nehemiah* (Atlanta, GA: Scholars Press, 1992), 36–247 (esp. 86–247), with Christopher Ehrhardt, "Athens, Egypt, Phoenicia, c. 459–444 B.C.," *AJAH* 15:2 (1990): 177–96 (esp. 186–95), and see Briant, *CA,* 577–78, 973–74. Import of combining Greek hoplites with Persian cavalry: consider Xen. *An.* 2.5.23 in light of Lewis, *SP,* 79–80; note James Roy, "The Mercenaries of Cyrus," *Historia* 16:3 (July 1967): 287–323; and see Paul A. Rahe, "The Military Situation in Western Asia on the Eve of Cunaxa," *AJPh* 101:1 (Spring 1980): 79–96. Neo-Assyrian and Babylonian use of Greek mercenaries: Wolf-Dietrich Niemeier, "Archaic Greeks in the Orient: Textual and Archaeological Evidence," *BASO* 322 (2011): 11–32, and Nino Luraghi, "Traders, Pirates, Warriors: The Proto-History of Greek Mercenary Soldiers in the Eastern Mediterranean," *Phoenix* 60:1 (Spring–Summer 2006): 21–47. Egypt's Saite pharaohs and their use of Greek mercenaries: *ML* no. 7 and Hdt. 2.152–54, 161–69, 178–82, 3.1–7, 10–13 with Michel M. Austin, *Greece and Egypt in the Archaic Age, PCPhS* Suppl. 2 (1970): 15–22. Zopyrus at Athens: Hdt. 3.160, Ctesias *FGrH* 688 F14.45. With regard to Ctesias himself, see *Die Welt des Ktesias—Ctesias' World,* ed. Josef Wiesehöfer, Robert Rollinger, and Giovanni B. Lanfranchi (Wiesbaden: Harrassowitz Verlag, 2011).

16. Phoenician fleet expected, Byzantine rebellion, Athenians and allies quell both revolts: Thuc. 1.116–17 with Strabo 14.1.7, Androtion *FGrH* 324 F38, Diod. 12.27.4–28.4, Plut. *Per.* 25.4–28.3 (with Stadter, *CPP,* 246–60), Arist. F577 (Rose) = F594 (Gigon), *IG* I³ 48 = *ML* no. 56 = *O&R* no. 139. I cannot imagine that Pericles had designs on Cyprus at this time. Cf., however, Stesimbrotus *FGrH* 107 F8 and Cristina Corbetta, "La fallita Spedizione di Pericle a Cipro del 440/39," *RIL* 111 (1977): 155–66. Resort to siege engines: Ephorus *FGrH* 70 F194, Diod. 12.28.3–4. Sophocles' role: Ion of Chios F104 (Leurini) = *FGrH* 392 F6 with Leonard Woodbury, "Sophocles among the Generals," *Phoenix* 24:3 (Autumn 1970): 209–24. Cost of war: consider Isoc. 15.111 and Diod. 12.28.3–4, which need emendation, in light of Nep. *Timoth.* 1.2; note *IG* I³ 363 = *ML* no. 55 = *O&R* no. 138; and see Alec Blamire, "Athenian Finance, 454–404 B.C.," *Hesperia* 70:1 (January–March 2001), 99–126 (at 101–2), and G. Marginesu and Ath. A. Themos, "*Anélosan es tòn pròs Samíos pólemon:* A New Fragment of the Samian War Expenses (*IG* I³ 363 + 454)," in *Athēnaiōn Episkopos,* 171–84. For the secondary literature on the revolt and its suppression, see note 14, above. I have chosen a higher chronology than is favored by Meritt, "The Samian Revolt from Athens in 440–439 B.C.," 129, with an eye to the presence of the tragedian Sophocles (who

held office in 441/0) among the generals dispatched to reconquer Samos and to his absence from among the generals for the following year: see ibid. 127.

17. Tattooing of captives: Duris of Samos *FGrH* 76 F66, Ael. *VH* 2.9, Photius s.v. *Samíōn ho dêmos*, Suda *Samíōn ho dêmos*. Cf. Plut. *Per.* 26.4 and Photius s.v. *tà Samíōn hupoptúeis*, where some confusion is evident, and see Stadter, *CPP*, 249–51, with Christopher P. Jones, "Stigma: Tattooing and Branding in Graeco-Roman Antiquity," *JRS* 77 (1987): 139–55. Captured trierarchs and marines bound to planks and exposed: Duris of Samos *FGrH* 76 F67, read in light of Diod. 12.28.3, with Meiggs, *AE*, 191–92, and Stadter, *CPP*, 257–59. Cf. Peter Karavites, "Enduring Problems of the Samian Revolt," *RhM* 128:1 (1985): 40–56, who harbors grave doubts, with Pierre Ducrey, *Le Traitement des prisonniers de guerre dans la Grèce antique, des origines à la conquête romaine* (Paris: E. de Boccard, 1968), 208–15, and Lawrence A. Tritle, *A New History of the Peloponnesian War* (Malden, MA: Wiley-Blackwell, 2010), 14–15, who do not.

18. Pericles' boast: Ion of Chios F110 (Leurini) = *FGrH* 392 F16. On Ion, see Rahe, *SFAW*, Chapter 2, note 40. Funeral oration: Stesimbrotus *FGrH* 107 F9. Famous remark: Arist. *Rhet.* 1365a31–32. See Plut. *Per.* 28.4–8 with Stadter, *CPP*, 260–63.

19. Athenians imagined to have nearly lost command of the sea: Thuc. 8.76.4. Mytilenians contemplate rebellion in these years: 3.2.1, 13.1 with Hornblower, *CT*, I 382–83.

20. Spartans propose war at meeting of alliance: Thuc. 1.40.5–6, 41.2, 43.1 with Arnold Hugh Martin Jones, "Two Synods of the Delian and Peloponnesian Leagues," *PCPhS* 182, n.s. 2 (1952/3): 43–46. Cf. Antony Andrewes, "Thucydides on the Causes of the War," *CQ* n.s. 9:2 (November 1959): 223–39 (at 235–36); Nicholas G. L. Hammond, "The Origins and the Nature of the Athenian Alliance of 478/7 B.C.," *JHS* 87 (1967): 41–61 (at 51 n. 24); Kagan, *Outbreak*, 173–75, as well as Donald Kagan, *On the Origins of War and the Preservation of Peace* (New York: Doubleday, 1995), 77 n. 20; and Samons, *PCH*, 269 n. 29, with Ste. Croix, *OPW*, 200–203.

21. There is explicit reference to the Peloponnesians in the treaty worked out between Athens and Samos in 439, and this may have been an allusion to the Samians' appeal to Lacedaemon: *IG* I³ 48 = *ML* no. 56 = *O&R* no. 139, at line 7.

22. Corinthian hatred of Athens: Thuc. 1.103.4. I doubt very much that Corinth's decision in 440 was a sign that her relations with Athens were "good," as Hornblower, *CT*, I 83, claims.

23. Pericles and the Athenians think a renewal of war inevitable: consider Thuc. 1.44.2, which should be read alongside 33.2–3, in light of 40.2, and see Plut. *Per.* 8.7 with Thuc. 1.127.3, 140.2. Cf., however, 1.42.2.

24. Hagnon at Amphipolis: Thuc. 4.102.2–3, 5.11.1, which should be read in light of Diod. 12.32.1 and 3, Schol. Aeschin. 2.31, and Rahe, *SFAW*, Chapter 4, notes 27–28, in context. General at Samos: Thuc. 1.117. Old money: Cratinus F171 (PCG). Association with Pericles: Plut. *Per.* 32.3–4 with Stadter, *CPP*, 300–303. Cf. George E. Pesely, "Hagnon," *Athenaeum* n.s. 67:1–2 (1989): 191–209, who is unduly skeptical. Note Gomme, *HCT*, III 573–74, 578, 656; Kagan, *Outbreak*, 186–89; Meiggs, *AE*, 195–96; Lewis, *TYP*, 145; Hornblower, *CT*, II 319–31, 337; and Matthew A. Sears, *Athens, Thrace, and the Shaping of Athenian Leadership* (New York: Cambridge University Press, 2013), 77–79.

25. Amphipolis' geopolitical importance, Strymon region a source of timber and revenue for Athens: Thuc. 4.108.1, Livy 45.30.3 with Rahe, *SFAW*, Chapter 1, note 44. See also Zisis Bonias, "L'Importance de la plaine du Strymon comme voie de contacts culturels et commerciaux entre Grecs et Thraces," in *Grecs et indigènes de la Catalogue à la Mer Noire*, ed. Henri Tréziny (Paris: Errance, 2010), 235–39, and consider the case made by Zosia Halina Archibald, *Ancient Economies of the Northern Aegean: Fifth to First Centuries BC* (Oxford: Oxford University Press, 2013), that there was a symbiotic relationship between the Thracian interior and the towns on the Aegean coast.

26. Location of Amphipolis, walls, and bridge: note Thuc. 4.102.3, 103.4–5 and Eur. *Rhes.* 349 with *IACP* no. 553. Consider what can be gleaned from the summary excavation reports written by Dimitrios Lazaridis, "La Cité grecque d'Amphipolis et son système de défense," *CRAI* 121:1 (1977): 194–214; "Les Fortifications d'Amphipolis," in *La Fortification dans l'histoire du monde grec*, ed. Pierre Leriche and Henri Tréziny (Paris: Editions du Centre national de la recher-

che scientifique, 1986), 31–38; and *Amphipolis,* ed. Kalliopi and Thaleia Lazaridi, 2nd edition (Athens: Archaeological Receipts Fund, 2003), and by Chaido Koukouli-Chrysanthaki, "Excavating Classical Amphipolis," in *Excavating Classical Culture: Recent Archaeological Discoveries in Greece,* ed. Maria Stamatopoulou and Marina Yeroulanou (Oxford: BAR International Series, 2002), 57–73, and "Amphipolis," in *Brill's Companion to Ancient Macedon: Studies in the Archaeology and History of Macedon, 650 BC to 300 AD,* ed. Robin Lane Fox (Leiden: Brill, 2011), 409–36 (esp. 412–16). Then, see W. Kendrick Pritchett, "Amphipolis Restudied," in *SAGT,* III 298–346 (esp. 302, figure 13, and 308–16), whose sketch of the circuit as, he suspects, it existed in Hagnon's day may—for reasons pointed out by Hornblower, *CT,* II 326–27—be more accurate than the much grander circuit that Lazaridis thought likely at this time. Cf. Nicholas Jones, "The Topography and Strategy of the Battle of Amphipolis in 422 B.C.," *CSCA* 10 (1977): 71–104, whose view of the topography is predicated on the supposition that there was a bridge near the southwestern corner of Lazaridis' circuit. For this supposition, to date, no supporting evidence has been found. On the bridge that has been found, see also Rahe, *SFAW,* Chapter 4, note 27. I explored this site on 29 June 2017.

27. Euboean Chalcis as colonizer of the Chalcidice (as the term was more narrowly used in antiquity to refer to Sithonia and the area directly north of it): Diod. 12.68.5–6, read in light of Strabo 7 F11, 10.1.8 and Polyb. 9.28.2 with Pernille Flensted-Jensen, "The Chalkidic Peninsula and Its Regions," in *Further Studies in the Ancient Greek Polis,* ed. Pernille Flensted-Jensen (Stuttgart: Franz Steiner Verlag, 2000), 121–31 (at 125–31). Note Arist. *Pol.* 1274b23–25 and F98 (Rose), and see Donald W. Bradeen, "The Chalcidians in Thrace," *AJPh* 73:4 (1952): 356–80; Gomme, *HCT,* III 734–35; Denis Knoepfler, "The Calendar of Olynthus and the Origin of the Chalcidians in Thrace," in *Greek Colonists and Native Populations,* ed. Jean-Paul Descœudres (Oxford: Clarendon Press, 1990), 99–115, and "Le Calendrier des Chalcidiens de Thrace: Essai de mise au point sur la liste et l'ordre des mois eubéens," *Journal des Savants* 1:1 (1989): 23–59; and Julia Vokotopoulou, "Cities and Sanctuaries of the Archaic Period in Chalkidike," *ABSA* 91 (1996): 319–28. For the larger context, see Michalis Tiverios, "Greek Colonisation of the Northern Aegean," in *Greek Colonisation: An Account of Greek Colonies and Other Settlements Overseas,* ed. Gocha R. Tsetskhladze (Leiden: Brill, 2006–8), II 1–154 (esp. 1–51); Robin Lane Fox, *Traveling Heroes: Greeks and Their Myths in the Epic Age of Homer* (London: Allen Lane, 2008), esp. 53–72; and Bettina Tsigarida, "Chalcidice," in *Brill's Companion to Ancient Macedon,* 137–58 (esp. 137–52). The colonizing role attributed to Euboean Chalcis in antiquity has on occasion been called into in dispute—most recently in John K. Papadopoulos, "Phantom Euboians: A Decade On," in *Euboeans and Athens: Proceedings of a Colloquium in Memory of Malcolm B. Wallace,* ed. David W. Rupp and Jonathan E. Tomlinson (Athens: Canadian Institute in Greece, 2011), 113–33. Amphipolitan colonists drawn from nearby: Diod. 12.32.3, where *phrouríon* should be emended as *poléōn.* Argilians numerous among the settlers: Thuc. 4.103.3–4. Athenians notably few in number: 4.106.1. Dialect of Amphipolis Euboean Ionic: *Greek Historical Inscriptions, 404–323 BC,* ed. Peter J. Rhodes and Robin Osborne (Oxford: Oxford University Press, 2003), no. 49. On the manpower question, the argument advanced by Ste. Croix, *OPW,* 381, would have been even stronger had he taken into account the losses Athens incurred in Egypt in 454: see Samons, *PCH,* 107–8, 127–28.

28. Delphi and the hero Rhesus: Polyaen. *Strat.* 6.53, which should be read in light of Hom. *Il.* 10.426–45, 469–501; Marsyas of Philippi *FGrH* 136 F7; and Euripides' *Rhesus* with Irad Malkin, *Religion and Colonization in Ancient Greece* (Leiden: Brill, 1987), 81–84, and Philippe Bourgeaud, "Rhésos et Arganthoné," in *Orphisme et Orphée,* ed. Philippe Borgeaud (Geneva: Librairie Droz, 1991), 51–59. Edonians driven out: Thuc. 4.102.3. Fortifications thrown up in short order: Polyaen. *Strat.* 6.53.

29. Pericles (and Lamachus) in the Euxine and at Sinope (*IACP* no. 729): Plut. *Per.* 20.1–2 and *IG* I³ 1180, which supplies the date, with Stadter, *CPP,* 216–19. Lamachus' relative youth: Ar. *Ach.* 601. Amisos (*IACP* no. 712): Plut. *Luc.* 19.7, Theopompus of Chios *FGrH* 115 F389, Strabo 12.3.14, App. *B. Mithr.* 83 with Head, *Hist. Num.²* 496, where we learn that, in the fourth century, the city was called Peiraeus and that its coins featured an owl on the reverse. Astacus (*IACP* no. 737): Strabo 12.4.2, Memnon of Heraclea *FHG* III 536 (from Nymphis), and Diod. 12.34.5 (where

I accept the emendation of Niese). Spartocus' ascent: Diod. 12.31.1. Evidence for Athenian alliance with his son Satyrus I, who succeeded him in about 433/2: *Greek Historical Inscriptions, 404–323 BC* no. 64.20–24. *Phóros* reassessment in 425: *ATL,* II 40–43 (A9) = *ML* no. 69 = *IG* I³ 71 = *O&R* no. 153 = Paarmann, *A&P,* II 79–82 (with III 137–59). Lamachus in Euxine in 424: Thuc. 4.75.1–2, Diod. 12.72.4. Cf. *ATL,* III 114–17, with Gomme, *HCT,* I 367–68; Meiggs, *AE,* 197–99; Kagan, *Outbreak,* 180–81 with 387–89; and Lewis, *TYP,* 145–46, and consider the speculation advanced by Gocha R. Tsetskhladze, "The Pontic *Poleis* and the Achaemenid Empire: Some Thoughts on Their Experiences," in *Forme sovrapoleiche e interpoleiche di organizzazione nel mondo greco antico,* ed. Mario Lombardo and Flavia Frisone (Galatina: Congedo Editore, 2008), 438–45.

30. Corinthian colonies along the trade route: Alexander John Graham, *Colony and Mother City in Ancient Greece* (Manchester: University Press, 1964), 118–53, who is especially attentive to what can be inferred from the coinage issued. I visited Corcyra with an eye to assessing its strategic situation on 11–17 March 2019.

31. Corinthian argument in 441 at meeting of Spartan alliance: Thuc. 1.40.5–6, 41.2, 43.1.

32. Milesian *sumpoliteía:* Graham, *Colony and Mother City in Ancient Greece,* 98–117, and Gorman, *Miletos, the Ornament of Ionia,* 145–51.

33. Annual dispatch of *epidēmiourgoí* from Corinth to Potidaea: Thuc. 1.56.2 with Lilian H. Jeffery, "Demiourgoi in the Archaic Period," *Arch. Class.* 25–26 (1973–74): 319–30. Exceedingly close relations with other colonies: Thuc. 1.38.3. The coinage of these colonies tells a complex tale: Graham, *Colony and Mother City in Ancient Greece,* 118–53.

34. Long history of conflict between Corinth and Corcyra: Hdt. 3.48–54, Thuc. 1.13.2–4. Power and wealth of Corcyra, bitter Corinthian resentment in 430s: 1.25.3–4, 37–38. There was more to the Corinthians' resentment than mere pique. As both the Corcyraeans and the Corinthians made clear in their speeches at Athens, Corcyra was an almost necessary stop on the route to the west: cf. Kagan, *Outbreak,* 218–21, who underestimates the geopolitical importance of Corcyra, with Thuc. 1.36.2, 37.3–4, 44.3, 6.30.1, 43, 7.33.3–4; Xen. *Hell.* 6.2.4, 9; and Strabo 7.7.5, and see Pierre Lévêque, *Pyrrhos* (Paris: E. de Boccard, 1957), 125 n. 5; Franz K. Kiechle, "Korkyra und der Handelsweg durch das Adriatische Meer im 5. Jh. v. Chr.," *Historia* 28:2 (2nd Quarter 1979): 173–91; Wilson, *AC,* 106–12; and Morton, *RPEAGS,* 51–52, 143–228 (esp. 171–72), whose arguments need to be qualified with an eye to the role played by Epidamnus: Chapter 2, note 10, below. On her wealth as a source of Corcyra's power, see Kallet-Marx, *MENP,* 71–78. For an overview, see *IACP* no. 123.

35. Corinth's aggressiveness is clear: Salmon, *WC,* 270–97. In the absence of an understanding of what Athens' dominance of the Corinthian Gulf meant for Corinth in the late 450s, this aggressiveness will seem utterly irrational: ibid. 257–305.

36. Continuing Athenian ties to Naupactus: Thuc. 2.9.4, 69.1, 80, 83–84, 90–92; Diod. 12.48.1. Athenian control over Molycreium and Chalcis: Thuc. 1.108.5. At some point, Chalcis slipped from their grasp. But in 429 they recovered it: note Polyaen. *Strat.* 3.4.1, and see Thuc. 2.83.3, 84.4, 3.102.2.

37. In 429, when Phormio reached Naupactus, Chalcis was no longer under Athenian control: Polyaen. *Strat.* 3.4.1. Themistocles arbitrates dispute over Leucas (*IACP* no. 126): Rahe, *SFAW,* Chapter 1, note 7. Indemnity awarded Corcyra, colony declared shared responsibility: Theophrastus ap. *POxy.* 1012, F9.23–24 and Plut. *Them.* 24.1, confirmed by Thuc. 1.136.1. By 435, Leucas was fully in the Corinthian fold: 1.26.1, 27.2, 30.2–3, 46.1 with Graham, *Colony and Mother City in Ancient Greece,* 128–29. Anactorium a joint endeavor: Thuc. 1.55.1. Cf. Strabo 10.2.8 and *IACP* no. 114 with Gomme, *HCT,* I 195–96; and consider the implications of Thuc. 4.49.1. Origins of Apollonia disputed in the sources: cf. Thuc. 1.26.2 and Stephanus of Byzantium s.v. *Apollōnía, Gulákeia,* who treat her as a Corinthian foundation, with Paus. 5.22.4, who seems to suppose her a Corcyraean colony, as is strongly suggested by her early coinage (Graham, *Colony and Mother City in Ancient Greece,* 130–31); and see Scymn. 439–40 and Strabo 7.5.8, who report that the Corcyraeans shared in its foundation, with Gomme, *HCT,* I 160–61; *IACP* no. 77; and Pierre Cabanes, "Greek Colonisation in the Adriatic," in *Greek Colonisation,* II 155–85 (at 165–73). Apollonia nonetheless fully aligned with Corinth in 435: Thuc. 1.26.2 with Hornblower, *CT,* I 71.

38. Phormio at Samos: Thuc. 1.117.2. Expedition with thirty triremes, negotiation of an alliance with the Acarnanians: consider 2.9.4 in light of 2.68. Pericles laid the groundwork for this connection in 454: Rahe, *SFAW*, Chapter 5, note 53, in context. Phormio's thirty triremes defeat a force of fifty in circumstances unspecified: Polyaen. *Strat.* 3.4.2. For a different view of the likely circumstances than the one offered here, see John R. Hale, "Phormio Crosses the T," *MHQ* 8:4 (Summer 1996): 38–41. The date of Phormio's expedition is disputed. Some think that it actually preceded Pericles' expedition against Oeniadae; some situate it in the late 450s or early 440s; others put it after the Thirty Years' Peace. See Henry Theodore Wade-Gery, "Thucydides the Son of Melesias: A Study of Periklean Policy," *JHS* 52:2 (1932): 205–27 (at 216), reprinted in Wade-Gery, *EGH*, 239–70 (at 253–54); Gomme, *HCT*, II 202, 416–17; Nicholas G. L. Hammond, *Epirus: The Geography, The Ancient Remains, The History and Topography of Epirus and Adjacent Areas* (Oxford: Clarendon Press, 1967), 496–97; Meiggs, *AE*, 204 n. 1; Ste. Croix, *OPW*, 85–88, 330; Salmon, *WC*, 422–23; Peter Krentz and Christopher Sullivan, "The Date of Phormion's First Expedition to Akarnania," *Historia* 36:2 (2nd Quarter 1987): 241–43; Hornblower, *CT*, I 351–54 (with 66–67); Klaus Freitag, "Der Akarnanische Bund im 5. Jh. v. Chr.," in *Akarnanien: Eine Landschaft im antiken Griechenland*, ed. Percy Berktold, Jürgen Schmid, and Christian Wacker (Würzburg: Ergon Verlag, 1996), 75–86 (at 82–83); Podlecki, *PHC*, 138; Lazenby, *PW*, 17; and Ugo Fantasia, "Formione in Acarnania (Thuc. II 68, 7–8) e le origini della guerra del Peloponneso," *IncidAntico* 4 (2006): 59–98. I am inclined to think that Thucydides' failure to describe it as an old alliance is a sign that it was tolerably recent and that, as a formal alliance, it belongs in the late 440s, before the Samian revolt, or in the early 430s, after that rebellion was crushed. Had Phormio's expedition taken place as late as 433/2, there would presumably be some indication in the accounts of the Athenian treasurers, which for that year we possess: Ste. Croix, *OPW*, 330. That, in the pertinent years, the Athenians had their eye on the route to Italy and Sicily we can infer from the foundation of Thurii, from the treaties negotiated with Rhegium and Leontini, and from Thuc. 1.44.3, which should be read with Lewis, *AW*, 375. Note also Thuc. 3.86.4. For Athens' subsequent involvement in Acarnania, see Freitag, "Der Akarnanische Bund im 5. Jh. v. Chr.," 83–86.

Chapter 2. Pericles' Calculated Risk

Epigraph: Friedrich Nietzsche, "Was Ich den Alten Verdanke" 2, *Götzen-Dämmerung*, in Nietzsche, *Werke in Drei Bänden* (Munich: Carl Hanser Verlag, 1966), II 939–1033 (at 1028–29).

1. Thucydides on his reporting of events: 1.22.2–3.

2. Example illustrating Thucydides' capacity for error: cf. the list of generals provided at Thuc. 1.51.4 with the list provided in *ML* 61 = *IG* I³ 364 = *O&R* no. 148, lines 19–21, and see Gomme, *HCT*, I 188–90; Stadter, *CPP*, 269; and Hornblower, *CT*, I 95–96.

3. Thucydides on his reporting of the speeches delivered: 1.22.1 with Gomme, *HCT*, I 140–48, and Hornblower, *CT*, 59–60, who cite selectively from the vast secondary literature on this passage, and with Debnar, *SSL*, passim (esp. 14–23, 221–34), whose discussion is especially apt. In translating *diamnēmoneûsai*, I have kept in mind the possibility that Thucydides may have composed for himself and secured from others written memoranda summarizing the more memorable of the speeches they had heard: Mark Munn, *The School of History: Athens in the Age of Socrates* (Berkeley: University of California Press, 2000), 292–307. What George Cawkwell, "Thucydides' Judgment of Periclean Strategy," *YClS* 24 (1975): 53–70 (at 65–68), reprinted in Cawkwell, *CC*, 134–50 (at 146–48), says about the speeches in Thucydides' first book—that there is nothing in them that was "unthinkable in 432/1" could be extended to all of the speeches in Thucydides' work. No figure is reported to have said anything that was unthinkable at the time he putatively said it. Cf. Lendon, *SoW*, 417–25 (esp. 420–22), for a cogent—if, I think, ultimately unpersuasive—argument in favor of the view that the speeches were "of the author's free composition."

4. Cf. Thucydides' eulogy of Themistocles (1.138.3) with his statement of his own aim (1.22.4); note Dion. Hal. *Thuc.* 7–8; and see Paul A. Rahe, "Thucydides as Educator," in *The Past as Prologue: The Importance of History to the Military Profession*, ed. Williamson Murray and Richard Hart Sinnreich (Cambridge: Cambridge University Press, 2006), 95–110.

5. Theophr. F696 (Fortenbaugh).

6. Thomas Hobbes, "To the Readers," in Thucydides, *The Peloponnesian War: The Complete Hobbes Translation,* ed. David Grene (Chicago: University of Chicago Press, 1989), xxi–xxii.

7. Thomas Hobbes, "Of the Life and History of Thucydides," in Thucydides, *The Peloponnesian War: The Complete Hobbes Translation,* 577.

8. See Jean-Jacques Rousseau, *Émile, ou de l'éducation* IV, in *Oeuvres complètes de Jean-Jacques Rousseau,* ed. Bernard Gagnebin and Marcel Raymond (Paris: Bibliothèque de la Pleiade, 1959–95), IV 529.

9. See Nietzsche, "Was Ich den Alten Verdanke" 2, *Götzen-Dämmerung,* 939–1033 (at 1028–29).

10. Setting, wealth, population, and power of Epidamnus: Thuc. 1.24.1 and Strabo 7.5.8 with Gomme, *HCT,* I 158–59; *IACP* no. 79; and Pierre Cabanes, "Greek Colonisation in the Adriatic," in *Greek Colonisation: An Account of Greek Colonies and Other Settlements Overseas,* ed. Gocha R. Tsetskhladze (Leiden: Brill, 2006–8), II 165–73. Chief jumping-off point for Italy: Strabo 6.3.8 with Nicholas G. L. Hammond, *Epirus: The Geography, The Ancient Remains, The History and Topography of Epirus and Adjacent Areas* (Oxford: Clarendon Press, 1967), 469–70, and Hornblower, *CT,* I 68. Cf. Morton, *RPEAGS,* 162–77, who neglects the considerations raised by Hammond, with ibid. 81–85, where he attends closely to such considerations. Also cf. Kagan, *Outbreak,* 205, 211–12.

11. Corcyraean isolationism: Hdt. 7.168. Grounds for original Epidamnian appeal, Corcyraeans spurn: Thuc. 1.24.2–7 with Gomme, *HCT,* I 159, and Hornblower, *CT,* I 68–69. Note App. B. *Civ.* 2.39, Strabo 6.2.4. Reasons for thinking Corcyra democratic in 436: consider Thuc. 3.70 in light of Kagan, *Outbreak,* 208–9. Epidamnians seek Delphic sanction for appeal to Corinth, Corinthians seize opportunity: Thuc. 1.24.2, 25.1–3, 26.1 with Gomme, *HCT,* I 159–61; Robert C. T. Parker, "Greek States and Greek Oracles," in *Crux,* 298–326; and Hornblower, *CT,* I 68–71. For careful analyses, see Kagan, *Outbreak,* 205–21, and Wilson, *AC,* 25–27.

12. Volunteers sent to settle Epidamnus, Corinthian wariness of Corcyra: Thuc. 1.26.1–2. Corcyraean alliance with oligarchs and Illyrians, Epidamnus besieged: 1.26.3–4. Corinthians and allies organize relief force: 1.27. See Gomme, *HCT,* I 160–62; Wilson, *AC,* 27, 29–30; and Hornblower, *CT,* I 71–72.

13. Corcyraeans engage Sicyon and Sparta in appeal for arbitration: Thuc. 1.28.1–2. Warn that they may be forced to seek help elsewhere: 1.28.3. Further Corcyraean attempts at compromise: 1.28.4–5. See Gomme, *HCT,* I 162–63; Kagan, *Outbreak,* 224–26; Ste. Croix, *OPW,* 68–71; Salmon, *WC,* 284–85; Wilson, *AC,* 28–29; and Hornblower, *CT,* I 72–73.

14. Corcyraean failure to show up, as promised, to help fend off Xerxes' invasion: Hdt. 7. 168 with Rahe, *PC,* Chapters 6–7.

15. Corcyraean victory over Corinth at Leukimne, seizure of Epidamnus: Thuc. 1.29–30. Ethnic divisions produce stasis in Thurii and a turn against Athens: Diod. 12.35, where the dating cannot be supposed precise. Corinth prepares armada to reverse decision at Leukimne: Thuc. 1.31.1. Note Gomme, *HCT,* I 163–66; Kagan, *Outbreak,* 226–28; Wilson, *AC,* 31–40; and Hornblower, *CT,* I 73–74.

16. Corcyraean appeal to Athens, Corinthian objections, defensive alliance formed: Thuc. 1.31.2–45.1, Plut. *Per.* 29.1. Note Gomme, *HCT,* I 166–77, and Hornblower, *CT,* I 75–88. For the geopolitical calculations underpinning these developments, cf. Kagan, *Outbreak,* 228–42, and Wilson, *AC,* 106–12, 119–38, with Philip A. Stadter, "The Motives for Athens' Alliance with Corcyra (Thuc. 1.44)," *GRBS* 24:2 (1983): 131–36. Regarding the *epimachía* as such, see Ste. Croix, *OPW,* 328.

17. Lacedaemonius sent with ten triremes: Thuc. 1.45, Plut. *Per.* 29.1–2, and *ML* no. 61 = *IG* I³ 364 = *O&R* no. 148. For a detailed analysis, see Kagan, *Outbreak,* 243–45. Under pressure Pericles agrees to send twenty more: Thuc. 1.50.5–51.5, Plut. *Per.* 29.3, and *ML* no. 61 = *IG* I³ 364 = *O&R* no. 148. Commanders of the second expedition critics of Pericles friendly to Sparta: Podlecki, *PHC,* 138. See Nicholas G. L. Hammond, "Naval Operations in the South Channel of Corcyra, 435–433 B.C.," *JHS* 65 (1945): 26–37, reprinted as "Naval Operations off Corcyra," in Hammond,

Studies in Greek History: A Companion Volume to a History of Greece to 322 B.C. (Oxford: Clarendon Press, 1973), 447–70; Gomme, *HCT,* I 177–78, 187–90; Stadter, *CPP,* 264–69; and Hornblower, *CT,* I 88–90, 94–96.

18. Number of Corinthian ships at Leukimne: Thuc. 1.29.1 read in light of 1.27.2. Corinthian losses at Leukimne: 1.29.4–5. Battle of Sybota: 1.47–54. For the date, see *ML* no. 61 = *IG* I³ 364 = *O&R* no. 148. Note Gomme, *HCT,* I 182–95; Wilson, *AC,* 35–37, 41–64; and Hornblower, *CT,* I 91–97, and see Kagan, *Outbreak,* 245–50; Ronald P. Legon, "The Megarian Decree and the Balance of Greek Naval Power," *CPh* 68:3 (July 1973): 161–71 (at 161–63); and Lendon, *SoW,* 94–97.

19. Potidaea: *IACP* no. 598. In the Persian Wars: Rahe, *PC,* Chapter 8. Absent from the so-called tribute lists for 454–46, present thereafter, *phóros* paid in the spring of 432: *ATL,* I 386–87. See II 8–27 = *IG* I³ 259–280 = Paarmann, *A&P,* II 14–60 (with III 3–98), with Nicholas G. L. Hammond, Guy T. Griffith, and Frank W. Walbank, *A History of Macedonia* (Oxford: Clarendon Press, 1972–88), II 116, and Lewis, *TYP,* 138. It is, of course, conceivable that in the period stretching from 454 to 446, the Potidaeans contributed ships instead: see *ATL,* III 267–68. But there is no evidence that they ever did so, and the pertinent years do coincide with years in which Athens and Corinth were at odds. The Corinthian colonies Chalcis on the north shore of the Gulf of Patras and Molycreium a little north of the Corinthian Gulf to the west of Naupactus may also have been subject to Athens at this time: Thuc. 1.108.5, which should be read in light of 2.83.2–3, 84.4, 3.102.2.

20. Artabazus settles Chalcidians at Olynthus (*IACP* no. 588) under the command of Kritoboulos of Torone: Hdt. 8.127. Athenian instructions; Corinthian oaths; Spartan promises; quarrel with Perdiccas; revolt of the Bottiaeans, Chalcidians, and Potidaeans; Chalcidians to Olynthus; reinforcement from Corinth; initiation of siege at Potidaea: Thuc. 1.56–66 (where, I believe, Thucydides' use of *tà télē* at 1.58.1 should be read in light of its employment at 4.15.1), 71.4, 5.30.1–4; Diod. 12.34, 37.1; Pl. *Symp.* 219e–221a, *Chrm.* 153a–c; and *IG* I³ 48 and 1179 with Wesley E. Thompson, "The Chronology of 432/1," *Hermes* 96:2 (1968): 216–32 who cogently defends the chronological indications provided in the manuscripts of Thucydides. See also Gomme, *HCT,* I 199–225; Kagan, *Outbreak,* 273–85; Ste. Croix, *OPW,* 66–67, 79–85, 319–22; Salmon, *WC,* 292–96; Hornblower, *CT,* I 97–108; Lewis, *AW,* 375–76; and Lendon, *SoW,* 97–100, as well as Pernille Flensted-Jensen, "The Bottiaians and Their *Poleis,*" in *Studies in the Ancient Greek Polis,* ed. Mogens Herman Hansen and Kurt Raaflaub (Stuttgart: Franz SteinerVerlag, 1995), 103–32, which shows how little we know about the Bottiaeans; Michael Zahrnt, *Olynth und die Chalkidier: Untersuchungen zur Staatenbildung auf der Chalkidischen Halbinsel im 5. and 4. Jahrhundert V. Chr.* (Munich: Beck, 1971), 4–79; and Selene Psoma, *Olynthe et les Chalcidiens de Thrace: Études de numismatique et d'histoire* (Stuttgart: Franz Steiner, 2001), 189–221. It is possible that the Athenians acted provocatively by raising the *phóros* for Potidaea dramatically from six to fifteen talents in 439/8 or 435/4; it had certainly been jacked up to that level by 433/2: *ATL,* II 15–27 = *IG* I³ 266–79 = Paarmann, *A&P,* II 29–58 (with III 32–92) with Ste. Croix, *OPW,* 329; Meiggs, *AE,* 528–29; and Kallet-Marx, *MENP,* 79 n. 28. On Alexander's quarrel with the Athenians, see Rahe, *SFAW,* Chapter 3. On his son Perdiccas, see Hammond, Griffith, and Walbank, *A History of Macedonia,* II 103–4, 115–23. Note also J. W. Cole, "Perdiccas and Athens," *Phoenix* 28:1 (Spring 1974): 55–72; James T. Chambers, "Perdiccas, Thucydides, and the Greek City States," *Ancient Macedonia* 4 (1986): 139–45 (esp. 139–43); and Ernst Badian, "Thucydides and the Archē of Philip," in Badian, *FPP,* 171–85 (esp. 172–79). Perdiccas was still on the throne in 414: Thuc. 7.9. But by 410, his son Archelaos had succeeded him: Diod. 13.49.1. On Aristeus, see Henry D. Westlake, "Aristeus the Son of Adeimantus," *CQ* 41:1/2 (January–April 1947): 25–30, reprinted in Westlake, *Essays,* 74–83. As I discovered when I visited Olynthus on 27 June 2017, the layout of the settlement on the northern hill is now perfectly visible, thanks to the American excavators and the Greek authorities who more recently saw to its restoration.

21. Megarian Decrees: Thuc. 1.67.4; Ar. *Ach.* 515–39, *Pax* 605–10; Diod. 12.39.4; Plut. *Per.* 29.4–30.2. For an elaborate, ingenious, and ultimately unpersuasive piece of special pleading aimed at getting around the evidence strongly suggesting that, in passing the Megarian Decree, the Athenians voted to adopt what was, in effect, an empire-wide embargo on Megarian trade, cf. Ste.

Croix, *OPW*, 225–89—supported by Salmon, *WC*, 424–26, and, on the crucial issue, by Alf French, "The Megarian Decree," *Historia* 25:2 (2nd Quarter1976): 245–49 (at 245–47); Elie Bar-Hen, "Le Décret mégarien," *SCI* 4 (1978): 10–27 (at 20–24); and Brian R. MacDonald, "The Megarian Decree," *Historia* 32:4 (4th Quarter 1983): 385–410 (at 385–98). For a corrective, see Philippe Gauthier, "Les Ports de l'empire et l'*agora* athénienne: À propos du 'décret Mégarien,'" *Historia* 24:3 (3rd Quarter 1975): 498–503, along with Charles W. Fornara, "Plutarch and the Megarian Decree," *YClS* 24 (1975): 213–28 (at 222–27); Moses I. Finley, "The Fifth-Century Athenian Empire: A Balance Sheet," in *Imperialism in the Ancient World,* ed. Peter D. A. Garnsey and C. R. Whittaker (Cambridge: Cambridge University Press, 1978), 103–26 (at 120–21), reprinted as "The Athenian Empire: A Balance Sheet," in Finley, *Economy and Society in Ancient Greece,* ed. Brent D. Shaw and Richard P. Saller (London: Chatto & Windus, 1981), 41–61 (at 56–57); Lewis, *AW*, 376–77; Cawkwell, *TPW*, 32–33; and Podlecki, *PHC*, 141–43. Note Robert J. Bonner, "The Megarian Decrees," *CPh* 16:3 (July 1921): 238–45. For Athens' capacity to impose an embargo, see *IG* I³ 174–75.

22. The date can be inferred from a comparison of the speech in which the Corinthians sought to dissuade the Athenians from making an alliance with Corcyra (Thuc. 1.36.4–43.4), where there is no reference to any such decree and there surely would have been vehement objections had the embargo already been imposed, with Thucydides' summary of the arguments presented at Sparta after the battle of Sybota by the Megarians (1.67.4), in which the decree is not only mentioned but stressed. Note also the chronological implications of Diod. 12.39.4. On the meaning of *próteron* in Thuc. 1.42.2, cf. Gomme, *HCT*, I 175–76; Kagan, *Outbreak,* 256: Meiggs, *AE,* 430; and Ste. Croix, *OPW*, 230, with Christopher J. Tuplin, "Thucydides i.42.2 and the Megarian Decree," *CQ* n.s. 29:2 (1979): 301–7, who shows that it need not imply that a past condition is no longer in effect. For otherwise sensible overviews, see Kagan, *Outbreak,* 254–72; Meiggs, *AE,* 202–3, 430–31; and Cawkwell, *TPW*, 26–28. On the date, cf., however, Peter A. Brunt, "The Megarian Decree," *AJPh* 72:3 (1951): 269–82, reprinted with a postscript in Brunt, *SGHT*, 1–16—supported by Bar-Hen, "Le Décret mégarien," 17–19; Stadter, *CPP*, 275; and Hornblower, *CT*, I 86, who underestimates, in my opinion, the bitterness of the animosity the Corinthians continued to harbor for Athens in the period after 446. Had the Megarian Decrees been passed ca. 439, as these scholars suppose, had they been passed long before the Athenians agreed to an *epimachía* with the Corcyraeans, the embassy the Corinthians sent to Athens in 434/3 would surely have voiced much more than a generalized "suspicion." Cf. Lewis, *AW*, 371 n. 4. This having been said, Brunt asks all the right questions with regard to Thucydides' treatment of the Megarian Decrees. The answer, I believe, is that the historian is setting a puzzle for his readers and is inviting them to ponder whether Pericles is not up to something.

23. Occasion for Megarian Decree: Thuc. 1.139.2 with Gomme, *HCT*, I 447–50. Cf. Ar. *Ach.* 515–39, Ephorus *FGrH* 70 F196, Diod. 12.38.1–41.1, and Plut. *Per.* 30.1–2, which should be read with Stadter, *CPP*, 272–77, who is right in disparaging the contemporary claims, reported in these sources, that Pericles started the war to distract attention from his political troubles at home. Deeper motive: Kagan, *Outbreak,* 254–67. Megara only city on the Saronic Gulf to have supported Corinth at Sybota as well as Leukimne: cf. Thuc. 1.27.2 with 1.46.

24. Corinth on Athenians and Spartans: Thuc. 1.67.5–71.7 (esp. 70) with Clifford Orwin, *The Humanity of Thucydides* (Princeton, NJ: Princeton University Press, 1994), 41–43; Debnar, *SSL,* 30–47; and Seth N. Jaffe, *Thucydides on the Outbreak of War: Character and Contest* (Oxford: Oxford University Press, 2017), 62–76. Complaints of Megarians and Aeginetans, Corinthians appeal to Sparta, threaten search for help elsewhere: Thuc. 1.71.4–7. Argos likely alternative ally for Corinth: Schol. Thuc. 1.71.4–7. Opinions differ: Gomme, *HCT*, I 232–33; Kagan, *Outbreak,* 291–94; Ste. Croix, *OPW*, 206; Salmon, *WC*, 300; Hornblower, *CT*, I 116–17; and Lewis, *AW*, 378. It is telling that—with regard to Aegina, Megara, and Potidaea—no one mentions, as providing any sort of guarantee to these three *póleis,* the oath that the allies at Plataea in 479 took when they swore to defend the freedom and autonomy of the Plataeans: see Chapter 3, note 18, below.

25. Pericles supposed a convert to the policy prescriptions of Cimon: Kagan, *Outbreak,* 106–374. Cf. Samons, *PCH*, 135–53, who, in supposing Pericles a resolute disciple of Themistocles, is, I believe, closer to the truth. What follows is an argument I sketched quite briefly in Rahe, "Thu-

cydides as Educator," 107–8, and at greater length in Paul A. Rahe, "The Peace of Nicias," in *The Making of Peace,* ed. Williamson Murray and James Lacey (Cambridge: Cambridge University Press, 2009), 31–69 (at 33–59), and in "The Primacy of Greece: Athens and Sparta," in *Great Strategic Rivalries: From the Classical World to the Cold War,* ed. James Lacey (Oxford: Oxford University Press, 2016), 52–78 (at 62–76). For a similar analysis, see Karl Walling, "Thucydides on Policy, Strategy, and War Termination," *Naval War College Review* 66:4 (Autumn 2013): 47–85 (esp. 48–68).

26. Terms of Thirty Years' Peace: Rahe, *SFAW,* Epilogue (with note 1, where I cite the evidence and discuss the secondary literature). No provision guaranteeing to all freedom of the seas and access to Aegean ports: Thuc. 1.144.2. The evidence cited by Cawkwell, *TPW,* 31–34, to the effect that later agreements sometimes guaranteed freedom of the seas and access to ports is not germane to the question whether the Thirty Years' Peace included such a provision. Its inclusion in these later pacts could, in fact, be an attempt to avoid the difficulties that arose as a consequence of its absence from the agreement reached in 446. Athenian appeal for arbitration: Thuc. 1.78.4.

27. Megarian Decrees, Spartan overture, and Pericles' adamant refusal to consider repeal: Thuc. 1.67.4, 139.1–2, 140.2–5, 144.2, 145. Import: cf. Kagan, *Outbreak,* 254–72, 278–81, 321–24, 347–49, 369–72, with Rahe, "The Peace of Nicias," 31–69. As will become clear, the fact that in a speech at Athens Pericles treats the decrees as a trifle does not mean that he (or Thucydides) thought them such. Cf., however, Rood, *Thucydides,* 214–15.

28. Pericles a Themistoclean prior to 446: Rahe, *SFAW,* Chapters 2, 4–6.

29. Thucydides' praise for Pericles: 2.65.5–7.

30. Themistocles, Pericles, and Thucydides in agreement: Ste. Croix, *OPW,* 173–80, and Charles W. Fornara and Loren J. Samons II, *Athens from Cleisthenes to Pericles* (Berkeley: University of California Press, 1991), 118–19, 125–34, 140–46. Cf., however, Ste. Croix, *OPW,* 317, where we are told that "Pericles . . . was anxious to maintain the Thirty Years Peace indefinitely."

31. No other war until Sparta defeated: Thuc. 1.144.1. Tyrant *pólis:* 2.63.2. Everlasting memorials: 2.41.4. Universal dominion over the sea: 2.62. Memory of Athenian power: 2.64.3–6. Cf. Edmund F. Bloedow, "The Implications of a Major Contradiction in Pericles' Career," *Hermes* 128:3 (2000): 295–309, who wrongly thinks Thuc. 1.144.1 and 2.65.7 incompatible with 2.62.

32. Periclean expansionism: Meiggs, *AE,* 203–4; Lewis, *TYP,* 127–29, 141–43, 145–46; and Cawkwell, *TPW,* 23–25.

33. Corcyraean claims concerning proximity of war: Thuc. 1.33.3. Cf. the Corinthians at 1.42.2. Corcyraeans concerning Athenian expectations: 1.36.1. Thucydides' confirmation: 1.44.2. Pericles claims Spartans conspiring: 1.140.2. See also Plut. *Per.* 8.7. On the consequences, note Dion. Hal. *Thuc.* 10–12, and see Fornara and Samons, *Athens from Cleisthenes to Pericles,* 140–46.

34. If, in supposing that Thucydides recognized—and shared—Pericles' analysis, I go further than Peter J. Rhodes, "Thucydides on the Causes of the Peloponnesian War," *Hermes* 115:2 (2nd Quarter 1987): 154–65, thinks justified, it is because I attribute the historian's reticence in this particular to a deliberate pedagogical strategy aimed at inducing his readers to think through the crucial questions themselves.

35. Megarian contribution of three thousand hoplites: Hdt. 9.28.6. Athenian hoplites at Marathon: Rahe, *PC,* Chapter 4. Size of the Megarid: Ronald P. Legon, *Megara: The Political History of a Greek City-State to 336 B.C.* (Ithaca, NY: Cornell University Press, 1981), 21–25. Size of Attica: *IACP* no. 361. It says much about the fragility of commercial polities that, in the fourth century, Megara was expected to field less than half the contingent she had sent to Plataea: note Xen. *Hell.* 5.2.11–22; then, consider Diod. 15.31–32 in light of Legon, *Megara,* 268–71, and see Isoc. 8.118. To get around the contrast, one would have to follow MacDonald, "The Megarian Decree," 391–93, in supposing that the Megarian figure for 479 represented a total mobilization of the city's hoplites, and one would have to presume as well that the Athenian figure for 490 did not.

36. Metropolis cut off from colonies: French, "The Megarian Decree," 248–49, and MacDonald, "The Megarian Decree," 398–410. Note Bar-Hen, "Le Décret mégarien," 17–20.

37. Megarian deprivation: consider the testimony of Aristophanes (*Ach.* 495–556, 729–64, *Pax* 246–49, 605–14), who tellingly stresses the damage done by the obstacles to trade and not that

effected by ravaging, in light of what we can infer concerning the dependence of Greek cities on overseas commerce from Thuc. 1.120.2; then, consider Legon, *Megara*, 200–227, in light of what he has to tell us concerning the economy of Megara in ibid. 21–199 (esp. 21–25, 70–90, 120–41, 150–56, 165–68, 174–79), 278–85; and see Lewis, *AW*, 376–77. Cf., however, Legon, "The Megarian Decree and the Balance of Greek Naval Power," 163–71, and Legon, *Megara*, 219–21, who presumes that the Peloponnesus was dependent on imported timber, with Russell Meiggs, *Trees and Timber in the Ancient Mediterranean World* (Oxford: Clarendon Press, 1982), 116–53 (esp. 129–30 with 492 n. 50), who shows that this was not the case.

38. One could also argue on other grounds that the offer of arbitration was nothing more than a diplomatic ploy: Lawrence A. Tritle, *A New History of the Peloponnesian War* (Malden, MA: Wiley-Blackwell, 2010), 29–35. There was no plausible impartial arbitrator.

39. Compulsion due to fear inspired by growth in Athenian power: Thuc. 1.23.5–6, 33.2, 88, 118.2–3. Cf. Badian, *Outbreak*, reprinted with added material in Badian, *FPP*, 125–62, who argues in an essay as ingenious as it is perverse that Thucydides was a purveyor of "disinformation," no less dishonest than the reporters of the *Washington Post*, who aimed, "in his account of the origin and outbreak of the War, to show that it was started by Sparta in a spirit of ruthless *Realpolitik*," with Raphael Sealey, "The Causes of the Peloponnesian War," *CPh* 70:2 (April 1975): 89–109, who demonstrates that Thucydides held Pericles and Athens responsible for the outbreak of the war at this time, and see Lewis, *AW*, 371–73. Encroachment on Spartan alliance: Thuc. 1.118.2. Cf. Ste. Croix, *OPW*, 206–7, who cannot bring himself to take seriously the centrality of this passage, and Lendon, *SoW*, 86–105, who pays no heed to the fragility of the Spartan alliance. As the narrative in the preceding chapters suggests, Cawkwell (*TPW*, 23–25) is mistaken when he claims that, in speaking of the Spartans' fears, Thucydides had in mind only the period stretching from 446 to 432. Were that the case, the Athenian historian would not have detailed the growth of Athenian power in the years stretching from 478 to 446; he would not have ignored the foundation of Thurii, Diotimos' intervention at Neapolis, the forging of the alliances with Rhegium and Leontini, and Pericles' voyage to the Black Sea; and he would have given prominent place to the foundation of Amphipolis in his account of the Pentekontaetia: see Gomme, *HCT*, I 365–70. The fears of the Lacedaemonians waxed and they waned throughout the Pentekontaetia, as I have tried to demonstrate. That, however, Cawkwell is right in supposing that they grew once more in the years following the crushing of the Samian revolt one need not doubt: see Meiggs, *AE*, 203–4.

40. Leotychidas and Xanthippus: Hdt. 8.131, 9.90–106, 114. *Xenía* linking Archidamus with Pericles: Thuc. 2.13.1, Plut. *Per.* 33.3. Debate between Archidamus and Sthenelaidas, vote for war: Thuc. 1.79–88 with Gomme, *HCT*, I 246–56; Hornblower, *CT*, I 124–33; and Debnar, *SSL*, 59–76. Archidamus' appeal for resort to arbitration: Thuc. 1.85.2. In emphasizing Archidamus' reputation, as opposed to the qualities he actually possessed, Thucydides is clearly raising doubts. For a view opposed to my own, cf. Edmund F. Bloedow, "The Speeches of Archidamus and Sthenelaidas at Sparta," *Historia* 30:2 (2nd Quarter 1981): 129–43. Money the sinews of naval power, Peloponnesian deficiency: Kallet-Marx, *MENP,* 21–96.

41. That Pericles' strategy, though cautious and deliberate, was, in fact, aimed at Sparta's defeat is but rarely appreciated. For an exception to the rule, see Henry Theodore Wade-Gery, "Thucydides," in *OCD*⁴ 1472–75 (at 1474–75), which should be read in light of Henry Theodore Wade-Gery, "Thucydides the Son of Melesias: A Study of Periklean Policy," *JHS* 52:2 (1932): 205–27 (at 215–17), reprinted in Wade-Gery, *EGH*, 239–70 (at 252–55). I disagree with Wade-Gery only in supposing that Thucydides was more discerning than he was, for pedagogical reasons, willing to let on. Had Ste. Croix been willing to acknowledge the provocative character of the Megarian Decrees, the genuine damage that they did to Megara, and the significance for Sparta's allies of the precedent, he would been forced to rethink the character of Pericles' strategy and abandon his rejection of Wade-Gery's claim: cf. *OPW*, 208–10. In this connection, note the secondary literature cited in Chapter 3, notes 31, 33, and 36, below. Absence of proper Spartan strategy: Brunt, *SPSAW*, 255–80, reprinted in Brunt, *SGHT*, 84–111; and Kagan, *AW*, 18–24. Cf., however, Thomas Kelly, "Thucydides and Spartan Strategy in the Archidamian War," *AHR* 87:1 (February 1982): 25–54, reprinted in *The Armies of Classical Greece*, ed. Everett L. Wheeler (Aldershot: Ash-

gate, 2007), 393–422, and see Cawkwell, *TPW*, 40–43; and Ian S. Moxon, "Thucydides' Account of Spartan Strategy and Foreign Policy in the Archidamian War," *RSA* 8 (1978): 7–26.

42. Divine sanction sought from Delphi: Thuc. 1.118.3, 123.1–2, 2.54.4 with Kagan, *Outbreak*, 310–11, 314; Parker, "Greek States and Greek Oracles," 298–326; Hornblower, *CT*, I 195–96; and Debnar, *SSL*, 86–87 (with n. 29). Aim of embassies: Thuc. 1.126.1 with Kagan, *Outbreak*, 317.

43. First embassy: Thuc. 1.126.2–135.1, 139.1, and Plut. *Per.* 33.1–2. Cf. Gomme, *HCT*, I 447, who doubts that religious fear could influence the Athenians, with Kagan, *Outbreak*, 317–21; Robert R. Parker, *Miasma: Pollution and Purification in Early Greek Religion* (Oxford: Clarendon Press, 1983), 16–17, 183–84, 204, 206; Stadter, *CPP*, 306–8; and Hornblower, *CT*, I 202–3. Note Lendon, *SoW*, 102–3, with the attendant notes, who lays exclusive emphasis on the Spartans' assertion of rank, and John L. Marr, "What Did the Athenians Demand in 432 B.C.?" *Phoenix* 52:1/2 (Spring–Summer 1998): 120–24, who suggests, plausibly, that Athens' tart reply was aimed at Archidamus among others.

44. Demands issued by second and third embassies: Thuc. 1.139.1, 3 with Gomme, *HCT*, I 447, 450–51, and Kagan, *Outbreak*, 321, 324–25.

45. Athens dubbed a tyrant *pólis*: Thuc. 1.122.3, 124.3. Cf. 2.63.2, 3.37.2 with Christopher J. Tuplin, "Imperial Tyranny: Some Reflections on a Classical Greek Metaphor," in *Crux*, 348–75 (esp. 352–57). Lacedaemon known for opposition to tyranny: Rahe, *SR*, Chapter 4 (at notes 53–54). Freedom of the Greeks: Thuc. 1.124.3 with 1.140.3, 2.8.4–5, 72.1, 3.13.1–14.2, 32.2, 59.4, 4.85.1, 5, 86.1, 88.1, 108.2. Thought indistinguishable from collapse of Athens' hegemony: 4.85.1–2. See Hornblower, *CT*, I 246–47. To suppose that for the Spartans this was a war fought solely or even principally for the purpose of asserting rank, one would have to discount the particular demands made by Sparta at this time and reject altogether the authenticity of the arguments that Thucydides attributes to the Lacedaemonian leaders and their Corinthian allies on the eve of the war. Although rank was surely a consideration, there was much more at stake. Cf., however, Lendon, *SoW*, passim.

46. Archidamus still active in quest for peace: Plut. *Per.* 29.7. Second embassy makes it clear repeal of Megarian Decrees would suffice: Thuc. 1.139.1–2, Diod. 12.39.4–5, Plut. *Per.* 29.7–8.

47. Proposal concerning Megarian decrees a serious attempt to head off war: Kagan, *Outbreak*, 321–24. Cf. Elie Bar-Hen, "Le Parti de la paix à Sparte à la veille de la guerre du Péloponnèse," *AncSoc* 8 (1977): 21–31, and Salmon, *WC*, 302–3, who think this implausible, with Samons, *PCH*, 137–39, 148–53, who believes that the Spartans were exceedingly eager to avoid war. Turning inscriptions to the wall would suffice: Plut. *Per.* 30.1 with Stadter, *CPP*, 272–74—report confirmed by Ar. *Ach.* 537, as read by Lewis, *SP*, 49 n. 157.

48. The attempt made by the Spartans and Sicyonians to patch up the quarrel between Corinth and Corcyra and the misgivings they evidenced at the time concerning the former's aggressiveness in the west explain why, when the Corinthians later pressed the Spartans and then the members of their alliance for war, they laid far more stress on their grievance regarding Potidaea than on that regarding Corcyra: cf. Thuc. 1.24–55 (esp. 55.2) with 1.55–66 (esp. 66), and see 1.66–86 (esp. 71.4 and 85.2), 120–24, as well as Sealey, "The Causes of the Peloponnesian War," 93–97.

49. Evidence for lingering suspicion: Thuc. 7.18.2–3.

50. Pericles' speech: Thuc. 1.139.3–145.1 (emphasis added). Cf. George Cawkwell, "Thucydides' Judgment of Periclean Strategy," *YClS* 24 (1975): 53–70, reprinted in Cawkwell, *CC*, 134–50; Cawkwell, *TPW*, 43; and Anders Holm Rasmussen, "Thucydides on Pericles (Thuc. 2.65)," *C&M* 46 (1995): 25–46 (at 40), who, in translating *periésesthai*, emphasize surviving to the exclusion of prevailing, with Lazenby, *PW*, 32, who recognizes that Pericles is being "deliberately evasive." Note the locution at Thuc. 6.11.5, and see Ste. Croix, *OPW*, 208.

51. Pericles opposes a return to Egypt: Plut. *Per.* 20.3–4. Pericles' speech in 431: Thuc. 1.139.3–145.1 (and the scholia) with Gomme, *HCT*, I 453–54; Kagan, *Outbreak*, 325–32; and Hornblower, *CT*, I 226–28. Those who suppose Pericles' counteroffer (Thuc. 1.144.2) anything other than an insulting rhetorical flourish fail to give proper weight to the preconditions for Spartan security, on the one hand, and to Megara's need for access to the markets to her east, on the

other. Sparta's practice of *xenēlasía* was in no way like the Megarian Decrees. It imposed no real hardship on anyone: cf. Elias J. Bickerman, "*Autonomia:* Sur un passage de Thucydide (I, 144, 2)," *RIDA* ser. 2, 5 (1958): 313–44 (at 318–24), and Ste. Croix, *OPW,* 289.

52. Construction suspended, scattered funds consolidated on the acropolis: *IG* I³ 52A with Alec Blamire, "Athenian Finance, 454–404 B.C.," *Hesperia* 70:1 (January–March 2001), 99–126 (at 103–5). The date is uncertain: cf. Lisa Kallet-Marx, "The Kallias Decree, Thucydides, and the Outbreak of the Peloponnesian War," *CQ* n.s. 39:1 (1989): 94–113, who argues that the decrees were passed in 430/29, with Cawkwell, *TPW,* 29–30, 107–10, who argues cogently that this was done late in 433, and with Samons, *EO,* 107–63, who suggests that this was done in 432 in response to the clash between Athens and Corinth occasioned by the battle of Sybota. On the decrees more generally, see Loren J. Samons II, "The 'Kallias Decrees' (*IG* i³ 52) and the Inventories of Athena's Treasure in the Parthenon," *CQ* 46:1 (1996): 91–102.

53. Flocks to Euboea, valuables carted to Athens, countryside evacuated by majority: Thuc. 2.14–16. Cf. Peter Acton, *Poiesis: Manufacturing in Classical Athens* (Oxford: Oxford University Press, 2014), who underestimates the agrarian character of Athens at this time, with the material cited in Chapter 3, note 3, below.

Chapter 3. A Tug of War

Epigraph: Sun Tzū, *On the Art of War: The Oldest Military Treatise in the World,* trans. Lionel Giles (London: Luzac & Co., 1910), 3.17.1.

1. Theban surprise attack on Plataea: Thuc. 2.2–6. See also Hdt. 7.233.2, Dem. 59.98–101, and Diod. 12.41.2–42.2, and note Kagan, *AW,* 43–48. For Athens, strategically insignificant: Kagan, *AW,* 174, and Victor Davis Hanson, *A War Like No Other: How the Athenians and Spartans Fought the Peloponnesian War* (New York: Random House, 2005), 163–75.

2. Hellenic expectations: Thuc. 4.85.2, 5.14.3, 6.11.5, 16.2, 7.28.3. Cf. 3.13.3–5 and see Brunt, *SPSAW,* 255–80 (at 264–65), reprinted in Brunt, *SGHT,* 84–111 (at 94–96); Ste. Croix, *OPW,* 206–8; and Kagan, *AW,* 19–21, 23–24, 40–42. Note Thuc. 1.109.1–2.

3. Greek *pólis* profoundly agrarian: Rahe, *RAM,* I.ii–iv, and Victor Davis Hanson, *The Other Greeks: The Family Farm and the Agrarian Roots of Western Civilization* (New York: The Free Press, 1995). *Contado* the *città:* Niccolò Machiavelli, *Discorsi sopra la prima deca di Tito Livio* 1.40, in Machiavelli, *Tutte le opere,* ed. Mario Martelli (Florence: Sansoni, 1971), 125. Contrast with medieval commune: see Max Weber, *Economy and Society* (Berkeley: University of California Press, 1978), II 1349–54, 1359–63. See also Sally C. Humphreys, "Economy and Society in Classical Athens," and "Homo Politicus and Homo Economicus," in Humphreys, *Anthropology and the Greeks* (London: Routledge and Kegan Paul, 1978), 136–74; and Yvon Garlan, *Guerre et économie en Grèce ancienne* (Paris: La Découverte, 1989).

4. Themistocles on the Peiraeus: Thuc. 1.93.3–7. Preeminent foresight: 1.138.3.

5. Pericles on Athens as a virtual island: Thuc. 1.143.5. Logical consequence of Themistocles' vision: Peter Krentz, "The Strategic Culture of Periclean Athens," in *Polis and Polemos: Essays on Politics, War, and History in Ancient Greece in Honor of Donald Kagan,* ed. Charles D. Hamilton and Peter Krentz (Claremont, CA: Regina Books, 1997), 55–72 (esp. 61–65), and Peter Acton, *Poiesis: Manufacturing in Classical Athens* (Oxford: Oxford University Press, 2014).

6. Archidamus on land unravaged: Thuc. 1.82.3–4 with Kagan, *AW,* 50.

7. Archidamus' fears: Thuc. 1.80–82 (esp. 82.5). Army sixty thousand in number: Plut. *Per.* 33.5, *Mor.* 784e, and note Androtion *FGrH* 324 F39. Cf. Gomme, *HCT,* II 13, who has his doubts, and Kagan, *AW,* 19 n. 9, and Stadter, *CPP,* 310, who think the number impossibly large, with George Cawkwell, "Thucydides' Judgment of Periclean Strategy," *YClS* 24 (1975): 53–70 (at 55 n. 6), reprinted in Cawkwell, *CC,* 134–50 (at 135–36 n. 6), who suggests the inclusion of light-armed troops.

8. Archidamus musters and exhorts his army: Thuc. 2.10–11. In Thucydides, where a speaker gives one oration, arguing one position, and another later, arguing the opposite position,

one should, in trying to understand what is going on, ponder what each occasion required. See 1.22.1. That Thucydides is artful one need not doubt, but there is no reason to dismiss either of Archidamus' two speeches as inaccurate: cf. Virginia J. Hunter, *Thucydides: The Artful Reporter* (Toronto: Hakkert, 1973), 11–21, with Cawkwell, "Thucydides' Judgment of Periclean Strategy," 65–68, reprinted in Cawkwell, *CC*, 146–48. And there is no reason to suppose such a speaker inconsistent or to think that he had changed his mind.

9. Archidamus loiters at the Isthmus of Corinth, dispatches herald: Thuc. 2.12. Time spent at Oenoe, the Thriasian plain, and Acharnae: 2.18–21 with Kagan, *AW*, 48–53, and Lazenby, *PW*, 33–35. On Acharnae and the Acharnians, see Danielle L. Kellogg, *Marathon Fighters and Men of Maple: Ancient Acharnai* (Oxford: Oxford University Press, 2013). As Kellogg points out, most scholars think Thucydides' text needs emendation—either by reducing the number of hoplites attributed to Acharnae or by substituting *polîtaı* [citizens] for *hoplîtaı* in the pertinent passage. Note, however, Wesley E. Thompson, "Three Thousand Acharnian Hoplites," *Historia* 13:4 (October 1964): 400–413. As Aristophanes' play *The Acharnians* suggests, there was something special about this deme. Archidamus' conduct seems to me to be perfectly consistent with the speech he delivered at Sparta, arguing against an immediate recourse to war. Cf., however, Lewis, *AW*, 378.

10. Athenian reaction to Peloponnesians at Acharnae: Thuc. 2.21.1–23.1, Plut. *Per.* 33.3–8 with Kagan, *AW*, 53–56. There is no need to suppose that, in preventing an assembly meeting, Pericles exercised special powers, as Edmund F. Bloedow, "Pericles' Powers in the Counter-Strategy of 431," *Historia* 36:1 (1st Quarter 1987): 9–27, suggests. The Athenian's prestige was, I suspect, more than sufficient. On Archidamus, cf. Westlake, *Individuals*, 122–35, with Ian S. Moxon, "Thucydides' Account of Spartan Strategy and Foreign Policy in the Archidamian War," *RSA* 8 (1978): 7–26, and Edmund F. Bloedow, "Archidamus the 'Intelligent' Spartan," *Klio* 65:1 (1983): 27–49, who regard him as a master strategist and not merely as a superb tactician as do I.

11. Peloponnesian withdrawal in 431: Thuc. 2.23.1, 3. Cleon fiercely attacks Pericles' policy: Hermippus F47 K-A ap. Plut. *Per.* 33.8 with Gomme, *HCT*, II 75–76, and Kagan, *AW*, 53–54, 131 n. 32. For a defense of Cleon, see Lafargue, *Cléon*, 41–44.

12. Archidamus promotes *stásıs* at Athens: Thuc. 2.20.4–5 with Edmund M. Burke, "The Habit of Subsidization in Classical Athens: Toward a Thetic Ideology," *C&M* 56 (2005): 5–47 (esp. 5–21).

13. Second invasion of Attica: Thuc. 2.47.2, 55, 57.2, 59.1. Note Diod. 12.45.1–3.

14. Invasions and ravaging in 428 and 427: Thuc. 3.1, 26. No invasion in 429: 2.71.1.

15. Attica: size of territory: *IACP* no. 361. Number of acres farmed and olive trees tended, limits to effectiveness of ravaging: Thuc. 7.27.4 and *Hell. Oxy.* 20.4–5 (Chambers) with Victor Davis Hanson, *Warfare and Agriculture in Classical Greece*, revised edition (Berkeley: University of California Press, 1998). Cf. James A. Thorne, "Warfare and Agriculture: The Economic Impact of Devastation in Ancient Greece," *GRBS* 42:3 (2001): 225–53, who rightly emphasizes the vulnerability of cereal crops stored in granaries but overestimates the degree to which ripened grain, as yet unharvested, is combustible; and see Hanson, *A War Like No Other*, 35–64. Note also Lin Foxhall, "Farming and Fighting in Ancient Greece," in *War and Society in the Greek World*, ed. John Rich and Graham Shipley (London: Routledge, 1993), 134–45.

16. Expedition against Pharsalus: Thuc. 1.111.1. Led by Myronides: Diod. 11.83.3–4. The role played by this experience in teaching the Athenians the usefulness of cavalry has not always been appreciated: cf. Iain G. Spence, "Cavalry, Democracy and Military Thinking in Classical Athens," in *War, Democracy and Culture in Classical Athens*, ed. David M. Pritchard (Cambridge: Cambridge University Press, 2010), 111–38, whose account of the strategic rethinking responsible for the creation of Athens' cavalry corps is otherwise exemplary, with J. Hugh Hunter, "Pericles' Cavalry Strategy," *QUCC* n.s. 81:3 (2005): 101–8 (esp. 104–5).

17. Cavalry corps: Thuc. 2.13.8, Arist. *Ath. Pol.* 24.3 with Rhodes, *CAAP*, 303–4. Role assigned: Thuc. 2.22.2–3 (with Paus. 1.29.5–6), 3.1.2, 7.27.3–5; *Hell. Oxy.* 19.4 (Chambers). Boeotian cavalry essential to Peloponnesian operations: Thuc. 2.9.3, 4.95.2. Archidamus initiates siege of Plataea: 2.71–78, Dem. 59.101–2. See Josiah Ober, "Thucydides, Pericles, and the Strategy of Defense," in *The Craft of the Ancient Historian: Essays in Honor of Chester G. Starr*, ed. John W. Eadie

and Josiah Ober (Lanham, MD: University Press of America, 1985), 171–88, reprinted in Ober, *The Athenian Revolution: Essays on Ancient Greek History and Political Theory* (Princeton, NJ: Princeton University Press, 1996), 72–85; then, consider Xen. *Eq. mag.* 4.13–20, 7.5–15 in light of Iain G. Spence, "Perikles and the Defense of Attika during the Peloponnesian War," *JHS* 110 (1990): 91–109, and see Hunter, "Pericles' Cavalry Strategy," 101–8. See also Glenn R. Bugh, *The Horsemen of Athens* (Princeton, NJ: Princeton University Press, 1988), 81–85; Iain G. Spence, *The Cavalry of Classical Greece: A Social and Military History with Particular Reference to Athens* (Oxford: Clarendon Press, 1993), 121–33; and Leslie J. Worley, *Hippeis: The Cavalry of Ancient Greece* (Boulder, CO: Westview Press, 1994), 83–122. Had Archidamus managed to persuade the Plataeans to abandon their alliance with Athens, as he tried to do at the time of his arrival in their territory, he would no doubt have led the troops of the Peloponnesian League directly into Attica. Cf. Lendon, *SoW*, 147–50, who plays down the Lacedaemonian need to placate the Thebans and suggests on their part a game of one-upmanship with Athens. The Spartans' ruthless and unscrupulous treatment of the Plataeans in the wake of their surrender on terms in 427 does not inspire confidence that, had the Plataeans accepted their offer in 429 and chosen "to remain at rest" throughout the remainder of the war, the Lacedaemonians would have protected them from Theban aggression: see preface to Part II, note 12, below. As Thucydides (3.68.4) makes clear, the Spartans were exceedingly eager to please the Thebans.

18. Archidamus' negotiations with the Plataeans: Thuc. 2.71–74 with Debnar, *SSL*, 96–101. Cf. Ernst Badian, "Plataea between Athens and Sparta: In Search of Lost History," in *Boiotika: Vorträge vom 5. Internationalen Böotien-Kolloquium zu Ehren von Professor Dr. Siegfried Lauffer,* ed. Hartmut Beister and John Buckler (Munich: Editio Maris, 1989), 95–111 (esp. 95–102), reprinted in Badian, *FPP,* 109–23 (at 109–16); and Hornblower, *CT,* I 357–60, who misinterpret Thuc. 2.72.1 as proof that the same guarantee was extended by Pausanias on this occasion to all of those who fought at Plataea (including, notably, Aegina, Megara, and Potidaea) and that it was reinforced by an oath taken by all, with Rood, *Thucydides,* 217 n. 52, and Christopher B. R. Pelling, "Rhetoric and History II: Plataea (431–27 BC)," in Pelling, *Literary Texts and the Greek Historian* (London: Routledge, 2000), 61–81 (at 72–74), who show that the charges lodged by Archidamus are moral, not quasi-legal: the Plataeans, he claims, are abusing the formal, solemn guarantee of their autonomy to help the Athenians deprive others of that same autonomy.

19. Circumvallation of Plataea: Thuc. 2.75–77. Not complete until late September: 2.78.1–2 with Gomme, *HCT,* II 211–12 (with III 706–10); Kagan, *AW,* 102–5; Paul B. Kern, *Ancient Siege Warfare* (Bloomington: Indiana University Press, 1999), 103–9; and Lazenby, *PW,* 42–43. See also Dem. 59.101–2.

20. Attempt in 428 at a second invasion of Attica founders: Thuc. 3.15.1–16.2 with Gomme, *HCT,* II 270–72. Pericles' predictions: Thuc. 1.141.3–7. Archidamus' fears: 1.82.5.

21. Embassies with an eye to circumnavigation: Thuc. 2.7.3 with Hornblower, *CT,* I 244–45. Garrisons, special fund, triremes in reserve: Thuc. 2.24. Note 8.15.1, and see Kagan, *AW,* 57–58. *Hellespontophúlakes* and grain imports: *ML* no. 65 = *IG* I³ 61= *O&R* no. 150, lines 32–56 with Alexander Rubel, "*Hellespontophylakes*—Zöllner am Bosporos? Überlegungen zur Fiskalpolitik des attischen Seebundes (*IG* I³ 61)," *Klio* 83:1 (2001): 39–51, who suspects that from the 470s these officials were also collecting taxes. There would be no need for such magistrates if, as some suppose, the grain trade from the Black Sea at this time was strategically insignificant: cf., for example, Stanley M. Burstein, "*IG* I³ 61 and the Black Sea Grain Trade," in *Text and Tradition: Studies in Greek History and Historiography in Honor of Mortimer Chambers,* ed. Ronald Mellor and Lawrence A. Tritle (Claremont, CA: Regina Books, 1999), 93–104. For the strategic importance of Byzantium, see Polyb. 4.38.2–44.11 (esp. 4.38.2–11, 44.1–11). Blockade of Nisaea from Salamis: Thuc. 2.93.4 with Wallace E. McLeod, "Boudoron, an Athenian Fort on Salamis," *Hesperia* 29:3 (July–September 1960): 316–23 (with Plate 72). Note Thuc. 3.51.3–4.

22. Expeditionary force dispatched around the Peloponnesus: Thuc. 2.23.2–3 with Gomme, *HCT,* II 79–81. Raids Argolic Acte: Diod. 12.43.1 and Steph. Byz. *s.v. Áktē,* who may be repeating something that has since dropped out of the Thucydides manuscripts: Hornblower, *CT,* I 281.

Raids other coastal sites including Mothone (*IACP* no. 319), and Pheia (*IACP,* 492): Thuc. 2.25 with Gomme, *HCT,* II 82–85, and note also Diod. 12.43.2–5, Plut. *Per.* 34.1–4, Just. *Epit.* 3.7.5–6. See Kagan, *AW,* 58–59, and Lazenby, *PW,* 36–37. For a brief appreciation of Brasidas' feat, see Hutchinson, *Attrition,* 65–66. The fact that this expedition and those of a similar size subsequent to it were sent out before the harvest was completed calls into question the sharp distinction that Vincent J. Rosivach, "Manning the Athenian Fleet, 433–426 B.C.," *AJAH* 10:1 (1985): 41–66, draws between "summer sailors"—the farmers who, he thinks, manned the large expeditions sent out during the prime sailing season between late May and mid-September—and the semi-professional rowers who manned the smaller expeditions sent out for longer periods.

23. Sollium (*IACP* no. 137), Astacus (*IACP* no. 116), and Cephallenia: Thuc. 2.30. Cephallenian contribution at Leukimne: 1.27.2. Absence from Sybota: 1.46.1. Athenian embassy: 2.7.3. See Kagan, *AW,* 59–62.

24. Fleet dispatched to Locrian coast: Thuc. 2.26. Fort on Atalante: 2.32. Two triremes posted there: 3.89.3. See Diod. 12.44.1 and Kagan, *AW,* 62.

25. Pus from the eye of the Peiraeus: Arist. *Rh.* 1411a15. Expulsion of Aeginetans, resettlement at Thyrea, introduction of Athenians: Thuc. 2.27, Diod. 12.44.2–3, Plut. *Per.* 34.2. Cf. Hdt. 6.91 and Cic. *Off.* 3.11.46. Military motive: cf. Kagan, *AW,* 62–63, with Thomas J. Figueira, "Aigina and the Naval Strategy of the Late Fifth and Early Fourth Centuries," *RhM* n.f. 133:1 (1990): 15–51 (at 16–27), reprinted in Figueria, *Excursions in Epichoric History: Aeginetan Essays* (Lanham, MD: Rowman & Littlefield, 1993), 325–61 (at 326–35). Eclipse: Thuc. 2.28.

26. Annual invasions of the Megarid: Thuc. 2.31. Until 424, twice a year: 4.66–69 with Kagan, *AW,* 63–64, and Lazenby, *PW,* 38. Occasioned by murder of a herald, proposed by close associate of Pericles: Plut. *Per.* 30.2–4, *Mor.* 812d; Paus. 1.36.3, 40.3; Schol. Ar. *Ach.* 527; Schol. Ar. *Pax* 246, 609 with Kenneth J. Dover, "Anthemocritus and the Megarians," *AJPh* 87:2 (April 1966): 203–9; George L. Cawkwell, "Anthemocritus and the Megarians and the Decree of Charinus," *REG* 82:391 (July 1969): 327–35; and Podlecki, *PHC,* 140–42. Cf., however, Charles W. Fornara, "Plutarch and the Megarian Decree," *YClS* 24 (1975): 213–28 (at 213–22), who places the death of the herald Anthemocritus before the decision to exclude the Megarians from Athens' agora and the harbors of her empire. I find it impossible to believe—as Philip A. Stadter, "Plutarch, Charinus, and the Megarian Decree," *GRBS* 25:4 (1984): 351–72, and *CPP,* 274–83, drawing out the implications of Fornara's argument, does—that there was only one decree passed regarding the Megarian question, that it was proposed by Pericles' agent Charinus, that the Athenians began systematically ravaging the Megarid before the outbreak of the war, and that this was not itself considered an act of war. See Diod. 12.44.3.

27. Expedition against Epidaurus, cities of Argolic Acte, and Prasiae: Thuc. 2.56–57, Ar. *Pax* 242–43, Plut. *Per.* 35.1–3. Relative size of the expedition: Thuc. 6.31.2. Seizure of Epidaurus a threat to Corinth; possibly, a lure for Argos: Thuc. 5.53. Cf. Kagan, *AW,* 30–36, 71–78; A. James Holladay, "Athenian Strategy in the Archidamian War," *Historia* 27:3 (3rd Quarter 1978): 399–427 (at 400–402), reprinted in Holladay, *AFC,* 61–84 (at 62–63); Hornblower, *CT,* I 328–29; Lazenby, *PW,* 39; and Lendon, *SoW,* 138–41, who underestimate the strategic significance of what Pericles tried to do at Epidaurus, with Lewis, *AW,* 397–98. I doubt whether the attack on Epidaurus was occasioned by the onset of the plague and Athenian interest in the cult of Asclepius. The disease had not yet on any scale wreaked havoc: cf., however, Jon D. Mikalson, "Religion and the Plague at Athens, 431–423 BC," in *Studies Presented to Sterling Dow on His Eightieth Birthday,* ed. Alan L. Boegehold (Durham, NC: Duke University Press, 1984), 217–25 (at 220). Prasiae: *IACP* no. 342.

28. Abortive expedition to Potidaea: Thuc. 2.58, Diod. 12.46.2–5 with Kagan, *AW,* 78–80, and Lazenby, *PW,* 40. *Mēchanaí* as scaling ladders and battering rams: W. Kendrick Pritchett, "Akarnanian Walls and Scaling Ladders," in *SAGT,* VIII 115–43 (at 124–41). Negotiated surrender, colonization: Thuc. 2.70, Diod. 12.46.6–7 with Kagan *AW,* 97–99, and Lazenby, *PW,* 41. Bottiaeans and Chalcidians from Olynthus defeat Athens at Spartolus (*IACP* no. 612): Thuc. 2.79, Is. 5.42 with Kagan, *AW,* 106, and Lazenby, *PW,* 43–44.

29. Phormio at Potidaea: Thuc. 1.64–65, 2.29, 58.2 with Isoc. 16.29; Pl. *Symp.* 219e–221a,

Chrm. 153a–c. Dispatched to Naupactus: Thuc. 2.69, Diod. 12.47.1 with Lazenby, *PW,* 40–41. Seizure of Chalcis: Polyaen. *Strat.* 3.4.1, Frontin. *Str.* 3.11.1. Cf. Kagan, *AW,* 96–97, who thinks the blockade a departure from Periclean policy.

30. Diodorus' claim regarding Athenian expeditions: 12.42.6–8, 45.3.

31. Pericles' strategy purely defensive: Donald W. Knight, "Thucydides and the War Strategy of Perikles," *Mnemosyne* 4th ser. 23:2 (1970): 150–61; Ste. Croix, *OPW,* 208–10; Kagan, *AW,* 24–123; Cawkwell, "Thucydides' Judgment of Periclean Strategy," 53–70, reprinted in Cawkwell, *CC,* 134–50; Cawkwell, *TPW,* 43, 50–55; and Holladay, "Athenian Strategy in the Archidamian War," 399–427, reprinted in Holladay, *AFC,* 61–84.

32. Thucydides' expectations: 1.1–19, 5.26. Periclean *pronoía:* 2.65.6.

33. Periclean strategy and Thucydides' endorsement: 1.144.1, 2.65.6–11 (esp. 7) as interpreted by Arnold W. Gomme, "Four Passages in Thucydides," *JHS* 71 (1951): 70–80 (esp. 70–72, 74–80), reprinted in Gomme, *More Essays in Greek History and Literature* (Oxford: Basil Blackwell, 1962), 92–111 (esp. 93–97, 101–11). Strategy vs. Sparta offensive, unrelated risky ventures to be avoided: Henry D. Westlake, "Seaborne Raids in Periclean Strategy," *CQ* 39:3/4 (July–October 1945): 75–84, reprinted in Westlake, *Essays,* 84–100; Raphael Sealey, "Athens and the Archidamian War," *Proceedings of the African Classical Associations* 1 (August 1958): 61–87 (at 78–81), reprinted in Sealey, *Essays in Greek Politics* (New York: Manyland Books, 1967), 75–110 (at 94–99); B. X. de Wet, "The So-Called Defensive Strategy of Pericles," *Acta Classica* 12 (1969): 103–19; Terence E. Wick, "Megara, Athens, and the West in the Archidamian War: A Study in Thucydides," *Historia* 28:1 (1st Quarter 1979): 1–14; Lewis, *AW,* 381–88, 397–98; and Charlotte Schubert and Dewid Laspe, "Perikles' defensiver Kriegsplan: Eine thukydideische Erfindung?" *Historia* 58:4 (2009): 373–94 (esp. 386–89), who recognize some, but not all, of the ways in which Pericles' strategy was offensive. Of these, however, only Lewis attends to the manner in which Corinth was vulnerable. Although, in the article cited, Westlake denied that Thucydides knew what Pericles was up to, he later came to the opposite conclusion—Henry D. Westlake, "Athenian Aims in Sicily, 427–424 B.C.: A Study in Athenian Motivation," *Historia* 9:4 (October 1960): 385–402 (at 390 n. 24), reprinted in Westlake, *Essays,* 101–22 (at 108 n. 24)—perhaps under the influence of the essay by Gomme cited above and of Gomme, *HCT,* I 462, II 190–92, which treat the campaigns undertaken by Athens and Athenian policy more generally during and soon after the Archidamian War—apart from the Athenians' rejection of the peace offer of 425 and their involvement in Acarnania and at Mantineia—as I do below.

34. The seriousness of Athens' efforts in this regard belies Alf French's contention, "The Megarian Decree," *Historia* 25:2 (2nd Quarter 1976): 245–49 (at 246), that seizing the Megarid would be of no strategic value to the Athenians. Cf. Cawkwell, *TPW,* 33.

35. For the details, see Rahe, *SFAW,* Chapters 4–5.

36. Brunt, *SPSAW,* 255–80 (at 255–59), reprinted in Brunt, *SGHT,* 84–111 (at 84–89), rightly emphasized the fragility of Lacedaemon's league and the dangers that would attend a loss of prestige on her part. Ste. Croix, *OPW,* 208–9, correctly recognized that the war had rendered disintegration of the Spartan alliance a serious possibility and that this development might have enabled Athens to a achieve a decisive victory. Holladay, "Athenian Strategy in the Archidamian War," 427, reprinted in Holladay, *AFC,* 84, rightly believed that a peace agreement at any time between Athens and Sparta would have broken up "the solidarity" of the latter's league, as it did in 421. No one, however, has contemplated the possibility, suggested here, that a dissolution of the Peloponnesian League was Pericles' aim when he intervened in the Corinthian-Corcyraean conflict, then sponsored the Megarian Decrees, compelled the Lacedaemonians to choose between defending their alliance and abiding by the Thirty Years' Peace, and finally sought to force them to agree to a humiliating peace unacceptable to Corinth and Megara, if not to Lacedaemon's other allies as well. Cf. Lazenby, *PW,* 32, who fails to see what an opportunity this would present if the Argives and the Athenians were to join in exploiting it.

37. Corinthians focus on war at sea: Thuc. 1.120–24 with Kagan, *AW,* 21–23, and Lewis, *AW,* 389–90. Lacedaemon requests ships from her allies in Italy and Sicily: Thuc. 2.7.2 with Hornblower, *CT,* I 243–44. Note Diod. 12.41.1, where she is said to have requested two hundred tri-

remes from these powers, with Gomme, *HCT*, II 6–7, and see Cawkwell, "Thucydides' Judgment of Periclean Strategy," 54–61, reprinted in Cawkwell, *CC*, 135–41, and Thomas Kelly, "Thucydides and Spartan Strategy in the Archidamian War," *AHR* 87:1 (February 1982): 25–54, reprinted in *The Armies of Classical Greece*, ed. Everett L. Wheeler (Aldershot: Ashgate, 2007), 393–422.

38. Course of battle at Sybota: Thuc. 1.46–54, Diod. 12.33. Trireme contingents and losses: Thuc. 1.46.1, 47.1, 54.2 with Gomme, *HCT*, I 190–94, and Thomas Kelly, "Peloponnesian Naval Strength and Sparta's Plan for Waging War against Athens in 431 B.C.," *Alter Orient und Altes Testament* 203 (1970): 245–55. Land battle at sea: Thuc. 1.49.1–3 with Kagan, *Outbreak*, 245–50; *AT*, 62–69; Hornblower, *CT*, I 91–92; and Hutchinson, *Attrition*, 1–8.

39. Corinthians in Acarnania and on Cephallenia: Thuc. 2.33. Peloponnesians against Zacynthus: 2.66. Cf. Kagan, *AW*, 93–94, who thinks, as I do not, that this marks a change in Spartan strategy, with Kelly, "Thucydides and Spartan Strategy in the Archidamian War," 25–54.

40. Cnemus and the Ambraciot attempt to conquer Acarnania with Zacynthus, Cephallenia, and Naupactus to follow: Thuc. 2.80.1 with Kagan, *AW*, 107–8; Lewis, *AW*, 398–400; and Lazenby, *PW*, 44. Ambracia: *IACP* no. 113.

41. See Lionel Casson, "The Feeding of the Trireme Crews and an Entry in *IG* ii² 1631," *TAPhA* 125 (1995): 261–69, and André Wegener Sleewswyk and Fik Meijer, "The Water Supply of the *Argo* and Other Oared Ships," *Mariner's Mirror* 84:2 (May 1998): 131–38.

42. See Morton, *RPEAGS*, and James Beresford, *The Ancient Sailing Season* (Leiden: Brill, 2013), 107–212.

43. Tolmides' voyage: Rahe, *SFAW*, Chapter 5. Zacynthus, Cephallenia, Acarnania, and Corcyra deemed essential for carrying war around Peloponnesus: Thuc. 2.7.3. Ambraciots claim that without the first three places circumnavigation would be difficult for the Athenians: 2.80.1.

44. Brasidas in 431/30 ephor: Xen. *Hell.* 2.3.9–10 with Hornblower, *CT*, I 239. Attached to Cnemus as *xúmboulos:* Thuc. 2.85.1.

45. Failure of attack on Stratus (*IACP* no. 138): Thuc. 2.80.2–82.1, Diod. 12.47.4–5 with Kagan, *AW*, 108, and Lazenby, *PW*, 44–45. Ships from Leucas: Thuc. 2.84.5. See Gomme, *HCT*, II 214–16, who thinks that the last paragraph indicates that Cnemus returned to Leucas—which is not, I think, the point.

46. Phormio vs. the Peloponnesian fleet: Thuc. 2.83–84, Diod. 12.48.1 with Gomme, *HCT*, II 216–20; Kagan, *AW*, 108–11; *AT*, 69–72; John R. Hale, "General Phormio's Art of War: A Greek Commentary on a Chinese Classic," in *Polis and Polemos*, 85–103; Lazenby, *PW*, 45–46; and Hutchinson, *Attrition*, 8–14. Cf. Virginia J. Hunter, *Thucydides: The Artful Reporter* (Toronto: Hakkert, 1973), 43–60, who charges that Thucydides persistently confuses result with deliberate purpose, with Morton, *RPEAGS*, 51–53, 90–97 (esp. n. 37), who shows that the tale Thucydides tells concerning Phormio's anticipation of the wind apt to blow from the Corinthian Gulf at dawn is entirely plausible.

47. Discontent with Cnemus, dispatch of advisors: Thuc. 2.85.1–2 with Kagan, *AW*, 111, and Lazenby, *PW*, 46. Defects of Cnemus as a commander: Westlake, *Individuals*, 136–42.

48. Brasidas and the Peloponnesian preparations for a second battle: Thuc. 2.85.3. Phormio's request, Cretan distraction: 2.85.4–6. Cf. W. Robert Connor, "Nikias the Cretan? (Thucydides 2.85.4–6)," *AJAH* 1 (1976): 61–64, and Gabriel Herman, "Nikias, Epimenides and the Question of Omissions in Thucydides," *CQ* n.s. 39:1 (1989): 83–93, with Hornblower, *CT*, I 365–66. Cydonia and Aegina: Hdt. 3.44.1, 59.1–3; Strabo 8.6.16 with Thomas J. Figueira, "Four Notes on Aeginetans in Exile," *Athenaeum* 66 (1988): 523–51 (at 538–42), reprinted in Figueria, *Excursions in Epichoric History*, 293–324 (at 310–15), and *IACP* no. 968.

49. Thucydides son of Olorus an adult at the beginning of the war, starts his history right away: Thuc. 1.1.1, 5.26.5. General in 424/3 in Thrace: 4.104.4–106.4. Gold mines and connections in environs of Amphipolis: 4.105.1, Marcellin. *Vit. Thuc.* 19 with Matthew A. Sears, *Athens, Thrace, and the Shaping of Athenian Leadership* (New York: Cambridge University Press, 2013), 87–89. The life of Thucydides said to have been written by a certain Marcellinus is a somewhat haphazard compilation from earlier writings: Judith Maitland, "'Marcellinus' Life of Thucydides: Criticism and Criteria in the Biographical Tradition," *CQ* n.s. 46:2 (1996): 538–58. Residence in exile near

Amphipolis: Plut. *Cim.* 4.2–3; Marcellin. *Vit. Thuc.* 25, 46–47. In 422, Brasidas dies: Thuc. 5.10–11. Much of Thucydides' exile spent among the Peloponnesians: 5.26.5. Likely sojourn in Corinth: Ronald S. Stroud, "Thucydides and Corinth," *Chiron* 24 (1994): 267–304. Kinsman of Cimon: note Paus. 1.23.9, and see Plut. *Cim.* 4.2–3; Marcellin. *Vit. Thuc.* 2–4, 14–17, 32 with Rahe, *SFAW,* Chapter 3, note 18. Cimon grandson of Thracian king Olorus: Hdt. 6.39.2.

   50. Peloponnesians, Phormio address their men: Thuc. 2.86.6–89.11. Note Ar. *Eq.* 550–62.

   51. Phormio's second victory: Thuc. 2.90–92, Diod. 12.48.2–3 with Gomme, *HCT,* II 228–37; Kagan, *AW,* 113–15; Lewis, *AW,* 400–401; *AT,* 73–78; Lazenby, *PW,* 46–47; and Hutchinson, *Attrition,* 14–19. Polyaenus' claim (*Strat.* 3.4.3) that Phormio was the commander of the trireme which circled the merchantman and sank the Leucadian galley is certainly attractive. But the story may be too good to be true. See, however, John R. Hale, *Lords of the Sea: The Epic Story of the Athenian Navy and the Birth of Democracy* (New York: Viking Penguin, 2009), 161–69, who supplies a lively and imaginative reconstruction of the battle.

   52. Phormio in Acarnania: Thuc. 2.102.1–2.

   53. Phormio's homecoming: Thuc. 2.103. Commemorative dedications at Delphi: Paus. 10.11.6. Public burial: 1.29.3. Statue on the Acropolis: 1.23.9–10.

   54. Circumnavigation scheduled: Thuc. 3.3.2. Cf. Lazenby, *PW,* 48, who takes Thucydides' silence as an indication that Athens no longer maintained a squadron at Naupactus. Had there not been an ongoing blockade directed at Corinth, it would be hard to explain why a city capable of deploying ninety triremes at the battle of Sybota should not be expected to supply more than fifteen such galleys in 413: see Chapter 6, note 36, below.

   55. Peloponnesian raid on Salamis: Thuc. 2.93–94 (and the scholia), Diod. 12.49 with Gomme, *HCT,* II 237–41; Westlake, *Individuals,* 140–42; Kagan, *AW,* 116–17; Hornblower, *CT,* I 370–71; Lazenby, *PW,* 47–48; Hutchinson, *Attrition,* 66–68; and Lendon, *SoW,* 164–68. I see no reason to doubt that timidity and caution on the part of the Spartan leadership deflected the expedition from the Peiraeus. Cf., however, Caroline. L. Falkner, "Thucydides and the Peloponnesian Raid on Piraeus in 429 BC," *AHB* 6:4 (1992): 147–55; Ernst Badian, "The Road to Acanthus," in *Text and Tradition,* 3–35 (at 3–5); and Lendon, *SoW,* 163–64, with T. Rutherford Harley, "'A Greater than Leonidas,'" *G&R* 11:32 (February 1942): 68–83 (esp. 70–71).

   56. Preparations for Mytilenian revolt, Athens warned: Thuc. 3.2 and Diod. 12.55.1 with Kagan, *AW,* 132–36; Hornblower, *CT,* I 382–84; and Lazenby, *PW,* 49. Personal rivalries and resentments at Mytilene apparently played a role: Arist. *Pol.* 1304a4–10. For an overview of Athens' relations with the cities on Lesbos from 478 on, see Trevor J. Quinn, *Athens and Samos, Lesbos, and Chios, 478–404 B.C.* (Manchester: Manchester University Press, 1981), 24–38. For the relations between Mytilene (*IACP* no. 798), Methymna (*IACP* no. 797), and Tenedos, see Hugh J. Mason, "Mytilene and Methymna: Quarrels, Borders, and Topography," *EMC* 37, n.s. 12:2 (1993): 225–50.

   57. Athenian expedition, Mytilenian revolt, envoys to Sparta: Thuc. 3.3.1–4.5, Diod. 12.55.1–3 with Gomme, *HCT,* II 253–55; Kagan, *AW,* 136–38; Hornblower, *CT,* I 384–87; and Lazenby, *PW,* 50.

   58. Rebellion, request for aid, circumvallation: Thuc. 3.4.6–6.2, 8.1–15.1, 18.1–5; Diod. 12.55.2–5 with Gomme, *HCT,* II 259–70, 277–78; Kagan, *AW,* 138–43; Hornblower, *CT,* I 388–98, 403; and Lazenby, *PW,* 50–51. For a thorough examination of the pertinent military questions, see John B. Wilson, "Strategy and Tactics in the Mytilene Campaign," *Historia* 30:2 (2nd Quarter 1981): 144–63.

   59. Momentous opportunity asserted, second invasion and fleet requested: Thuc. 3.13.3–7. Slipways: 3.15.1 with the secondary literature cited in Rahe, *SFAW,* Chapter 1, n. 3; Robert M. Cook, "A Further Note on the Diolkos," in *Studies in Honour of T. B. L. Webster,* ed. John H. Betts, James T. Hooker, and John R. Green (Bristol: Bristol Classical Press, 1986–88), I 65–68; and Hornblower, *CT,* 398. Failure at the isthmus: Thuc. 3.15.2–16.2 with Gomme, *HCT,* II 270–72; Kagan, *AW,* 141–42; Hornblower, *CT,* I 398–400; and Lazenby, *PW,* 51. Circumnavigation of Peloponnesus led by Asopius son of Phormio: Thuc. 3.7.1–3 with Hornblower, *CT,* I 387–88.

   60. Appointment of Alcidas: Thuc. 3.16.3, 26.1; Diod. 12.55.6. Salaethus in Mytilene: Thuc. 3.25 with Gomme, *HCT,* II 287–88; Kagan, *AW,* 146, 151–54; Hornblower, *CT,* I 409; and Lazenby,

PW, 52–54. Cleomenes in Attica: Thuc. 3.26, Diod. 12.55.6 with Gomme, *HCT,* II 288–90, and Hornblower, *CT,* I 409. Alcidas dawdles, Mytilenians surrender: Thuc. 3.26.1, 27–29; Diod. 12.55.7 with Gomme, *HCT,* II 290–91; Kagan, *AW,* 147–48, 151–54; Hornblower, *CT,* I 409–11; and Lazenby, *PW,* 52–54. On the Athenian commander to whom they surrendered, see Henry D. Westlake, "Paches," *Phoenix* 29:2 (Summer 1975): 107–16, reprinted in Westlake, *Studies,* 50–59.

61. Alcidas in Ionia: Thuc. 3.29–31 with Gomme, *HCT,* II 291–93; Kagan, *AW,* 148–50; Hornblower, *CT,* I 410–13; and Lazenby, *PW,* 52–53. On the intervention of Teutaplius, see Donald Lateiner, "The Speech of Teutiaplius (Thuc. 3.30)," *GRBS* 16:2 (1975): 175–84.

62. Colophon: *IACP* no. 848. Persian mischief there: Thuc. 3.34 with *IG* I³ 37. Athenian general killed by Lycians: Thuc. 2.69. Another Athenian general defeated and killed by force of Carians and Samian exiles led by Pissouthnes' son Amorges: 3.19. Anaia: *IACP* no. 838. Zopyrus at Caunus: Ctesias *FrGH* 688 F14.45. All of this should be read with an eye to what we can learn concerning the so-called Xanthos Stele from Peter Thonemann, "Lycia, Athens, and Amorges," in *IAE,* 167–94. Note also Briant, *CA,* 975–76.

63. Alcidas dawdles in Ionia, then flees: Thuc. 3.32–33 with Gomme, *HCT,* II 294–95; Kagan, *AW,* 150–51; Hornblower, *CT,* I 413–15; and Lazenby, *PW,* 53–54. Alcidas' massacre of the captives suggests that he had not himself given much thought to the possibility that a rebellion might be raised in Ionia, as Lendon, *SoW,* 193–94, observes. The fact that he was sent to relieve the siege at Mytilene suggests, however, the opposite with regard to the authorities at Lacedaemon who had dispatched him on this voyage.

64. Brasidas made *xúmboulos:* Thuc. 3.69.1. Cf. Joseph Roisman, "Alkidas in Thucydides," *Historia* 36:4 (4th Quarter 1987): 385–421 (at 385–404), and Badian, "The Road to Acanthus," 5, who think Alcidas' conduct defensible, with Westlake, *Individuals,* 136, 142–47; Kagan, *AW,* 147–54; Lewis, *AW,* 402–4 (with 390–91); and Hutchinson, *Attrition,* 19–22, who do not.

65. Asopius' fate: Thuc. 3.7.1–5. Conflict at Corcyra: consider 3.69.2–81.4, 85 in light of 1.54.2–55.1, and see Gomme, *HCT,* II 358–72, 386; I. A. F. Bruce, "The Corcyraean Civil War of 427 B.C.," *Phoenix* 25:2 (Summer 1971): 108–17; Kagan, *AW,* 175–81; Wilson, *AC,* 87–106; Hornblower, *CT,* I 466–77, 489–91; *AT,* 78–79; and Lazenby, *PW,* 56–57. Alcidas's conduct: cf. Roisman, "Alkidas in Thucydides," 404–15; Badian, "The Road to Acanthus," 5–6; and Lazenby, *PW,* 57, who defend him, with Westlake, *Individuals,* 145–46, and Hutchinson, *Attrition,* 69–70, who do not.

66. For a summary view, see Salmon, *WC,* 306–16.

Part II. Fortune's Wheel

Epigraph: Winston S. Churchill, *My Early Life: A Roving Commission* (Glasgow: Fontana, 1959), 238.

1. Plague: Thuc. 2.47.2–54.5 (esp. 48.1) with note 3, below. I am indebted to my graduate student Clayton Hrinko for drawing my attention to the impact the plague is apt to have had on Persian calculations. Peloponnesian embassy to Persia: Thuc. 2.67 with Hdt. 7.137. One of many indicators of Spartan ambivalence vis-à-vis Persia: Thuc. 4.50.1–2 with Kagan, *AW,* 257–58, and Cawkwell, *TPW,* 45–49.

2. Thucydides' claim concerning Pericles' foreknowledge: 2.65.5–13.

3. What sort of thing the plague: Thuc. 2.48.3–49.8. Thucydidean autopsy and survey of diagnoses: Denys L. Page, "Thucydides' Description of the Great Plague at Athens," *CQ* n.s. 3:3/4 (July–October 1953): 97–119; Gomme, *HCT,* II 150–53; and Hornblower, *CT,* I 316–18. Case for smallpox: Robert Sallares, *The Ecology of the Ancient Greek World* (Ithaca, NY: Cornell University Press, 1991), 244–66. Smallpox or typhus: David M. Morens and Robert J. Littman, "Epidemiology of the Plague at Athens," *TAPhA* 122 (1992): 271–304. Measles: Page, "Thucydides' Description of the Great Plague at Athens," 111–19, and Bruce A. Cunha, "The Cause of the Plague of Athens: Plague, Typhoid, Typhus, Smallpox, or Measles?" *Infectious Disease Clinics of North America* 18 (2004): 29–43. Ebola: Powell Kasanjian, "Ebola in Antiquity," *Clinical Infectious Diseases* (11 June 2015): 1–6. Role played by natural selection: A. James Holladay and J. C. F. Poole: "Thucydides and

the Plague of Athens," *CQ* n.s. 29:2 (1979): 282–300, reprinted in Holladay, *AFC,* 127–45, along with various notes the two or Holladay wrote in response to the subsequent literature (ibid. 147–65). For an overview of the various interpretations given to the disease in antiquity and in more recent times, see Winfried Schmitz, "Göttliche Strafe oder medizinisches Geschehen—Deutungen und Diagnosen der 'Pest' in Athen (430–426 v. Chr.)," in *Pest: Die Geschichte eines Menschheitstraumas,* ed. Mischa Meier (Stuttgart: Klett-Cotta, 2005), 44–65.

4. Thucydides' description of the plague: 2.47.3–54.5 with Gomme, *HCT,* II 146–62, and Hornblower, *CT,* I 318–27. Diodorus on the putative environmental causes: 12.45.2, 58. Hoplite deaths at siege of Potidaea: Thuc. 2.58, Diod. 12.46.2–5. Implications to be drawn from fatality rate among hoplites and cavalrymen: cf. Thuc. 3.87.3 with 2.13.6–8, and see Barry S. Strauss, *Athens after the Peloponnesian War: Class, Faction, and Policy, 403–386 B.C.* (Ithaca, NY: Cornell University Press, 1987), 70–86; Mogens Herman Hansen, "Athenian Population Losses 431–403 B.C. and the Number of Athenian Citizens in 431 B.C.," in Hansen, *Three Studies in Athenian Demography* (Copenhagen: Det Kongelige Danske Videnskabernes Selskab, 1988), 14–28; and Lazenby, *PW,* 38.

5. Impact of the plague on mores and manners: Thuc. 2.50–53 with Clifford Orwin, "Stasis and Plague: Thucydides on the Dissolution of Society," *Journal of Politics* 50:4 (November 1988): 831–47, and *The Humanity of Thucydides* (Princeton, NJ: Princeton University Press, 1994), 172–92. Mass graves: Efie Baziotopoulou-Valvani and Ionna Tsirigoti-Drakotou, "Kerameikos Station," in *Athens: The City Beneath the City: Antiquities from the Athens Metropolitan Railway Excavations,* ed. Liama Parlama and Nicholas C. Stampolidis; trans. John Leatham, Colin Macdonald, and Christina Theohari (Athens: N. P. Goulandris Foundation, Museum of Cycladic Art, 2000), 265–74 (at 271–73).

6. In 430, Pericles sidelined, Athenians sue for peace: Thuc. 2.59.1–2, 65.3–4; Pl. *Grg.* 515e–516d; Diod. 12.45.4–5; Plut. *Per.* 34.5–35.5, *Mor.* 805c with Gomme, *HCT,* II 166–67, 184–89; Stadter, *CPP,* 316–25; Hornblower, *CT,* I 330–31, 341; and Podlecki, *PHC,* 150–52. Note Dion. Hal. *Thuc.* 14, and cf. Kagan, *AW,* 70–71, 80–84, 91–93. See also Plut. *Nic.* 6.3.

7. Pericles' characterization of the plague: Thuc. 2.61.3, 64.2. Athenian awareness of Apollo's warnings and of his partisanship: 2.17.1–2, 54.2–5 with Lisa Kallet, "Thucydides, Apollo, the Plague, and the War," *AJPh* 134:3 (Fall 2013): 355–82, and Alexander Rubel, *Fear and Loathing in Ancient Athens: Religion and Politics during the Peloponnesian War,* trans. Michael Vickers and Alina Piftor (New York: Routledge, 2014), 46–63. See also Paul A. Rahe, "Religion, Politics, and Piety," in *The Oxford Handbook of Thucydides,* ed. Ryan Balot and Sarah Forsdyke (Oxford: Oxford University Press, 2017), 427–41.

8. Fiscal expertise expected of aspiring politicians: Xen. *Mem.* 3.6.5–6 and Arist. *Rh.* 1359b8 with Lisa Kallet-Marx, "Money Talks: Rhetor, Demos, and the Resources of the Athenian Empire," in *Ritual, Finance, Politics: Athenian Democratic Accounts Presented to David M. Lewis,* ed. Robin Osborne and Simon Hornblower (Oxford: Clarendon Press, 1994), 217–51, and John K. Davies, "Athenian Fiscal Expertise and Its Influence," *MediterrAnt* 7:2 (2004): 491–512. Athenian reserves: Thuc. 2.13.3–5. Cf. Schol. Ar. *Plut.* 1193, and see Arnold W. Gomme, "Thucydides ii 13,3," *Historia* 2:1 (1953/54): 1–21, with Gomme, *HCT,* II 20–33; Hornblower, *CT,* I 253–55; and Kallet-Marx, *MENP,* 96–104. See also Diod. 12.40.1–3, Plut. *Per.* 31.3. Spartan morale: Kagan, *AW,* 84–85. It is, as Dionysius of Halicarnassus (*Thuc.* 14) observes, a great shame that Thucydides' allusion to the Athenian appeal for peace is so elusive. It would be instructive to know what the Athenians offered on this occasion and what the Lacedaemonians demanded.

9. Annual income from the empire: cf. Thuc. 2.13.3 with 1.96.2, and note Plut. *Arist.* 24.3–4; cf. Thuc. 7.57.4–5 with 1.117.3; note 4.108.1; consider 2.9.4–5 in light of Gomme, *HCT,* II 12; then see ibid. II 17–20; and Hornblower, *CT,* I 252–53. Other sources of income: Ar. *Vesp.* 657–60. No less than one thousand talents in total annual income from all sources: Xen. *An.* 7.1.27.

10. Cost of Potidaean campaign: Thuc. 2.70.2, Isoc. 15.113. Costs of pay to infantrymen and rowers: Thuc. 3.17.3–4. Cost of festivals, local defense, and the operation of the democracy: David M. Pritchard, *Public Spending and Democracy in Classical Athens* (Austin: University of Texas Press, 2015), 27–90. Epigraphical evidence for expenditures on the war at sea: *IG* I³ 369. Income, expenditures on the war, reassessment: Samons, *EO,* 171–211; Alec Blamire, "Athenian

Finance, 454–404 B.C.," *Hesperia* 70:1 (January–March 2001), 99–126 (at 106–12); and Pritchard, *Public Spending and Democracy in Classical Athens,* 91–99. To suppose that in 431 Athens' income and reserves were adequate for a long war—as Kallet-Marx, *MENP,* 96–170, does—one must avert one's gaze from the implications of Xen. *An.* 7.1.27 for the limited size of Athens' domestic income: see Samons, *EO,* 171–211. Capital levy: Thuc. 3.19.1. Note Ar. *Eq.* 923–25. Ordinary quadrennial reassessment of *phóros:* [Xen.] *Ath. Pol.* 3.5. Belated reassessment in 425/4 and its implications: cf. what was ordinarily collected each year before the war (cf. Thuc. 2.13.3 with 1.96.2, and see *ATL,* II 8–28 = *IG* I³ 259–80 = Paarmann, *A&P,* II 14–60 [with III 3–98] as interpreted by Kallet-Marx, *MENP,* 96–102, and Samons, *EO,* 25–164) with what was demanded in 425/4 (*ATL.* II 40–43 [A9] = *ML* no. 69 = *IG* I³ 71 = *O&R* no. 153 = Paarmann, *A&P,* II 79–82 [with III 137–59]); cf. Xen. *An.* 7.1.27 with Ar. *Vesp.* 660, Andoc. 3.8–9, Plut. *Arist.* 24.3–5; and see Meiggs, *AE,* 324–32; Lewis, *AW,* 420–21; Samons, *EO,* 171–211; and Blamire, "Athenian Finance, 454–404 B.C.," 106–12. Cf. Kallet-Marx, *MENP,* 164–70, who plays down Athens' fiscal difficulties and the significance of the reassessment. For a recent survey of taxation at Athens, see Peter Fawcett, "When I Squeeze You with *Eisphorai:* Taxes and Tax Policy in Classical Athens," *Hesperia* 83:1 (January–March 2016): 153–99. Note also Errietta M. A. Bissa, *Governmental Intervention in Foreign Trade in Archaic and Classical Greece* (Leiden: Brill, 2009), 49–65.

11. Plague delays Spartan acquiescence: Plut. *Per.* 34.3–4.

12. Peloponnesian conduct at Plataea dictated by calculations regarding the future terms of peace: cf. Thuc. 3.52.1–3 with 5.17.2, and see Gomme, *HCT,* II 336–37; Kagan, *AW,* 171–72; and Hornblower, *CT,* I 442–43. Subsequent trial of Plataeans a travesty: Thuc. 3.52.3–68.2, Paus. 3.9.3 with Gomme, *HCT,* II 337–57; Kagan, *AW,* 172–73; Hornblower, *CT,* I 443–63; Pelling, "Rhetoric and History II: Plataea (431–27 BC)," 61–81; Debnar, *SSL,* 125–46; and Lazenby, *PW,* 55–56. In Thuc. 5.31.5, I see a Spartan guarantee, issued at the beginning of the conflict, that her allies will not lose territory in the course of the war. I do not see in this passage evidence that, from the outset of the war, the Spartans were contemplating a settlement with Athens in which territory seized from the latter would be returned: cf., however, Lendon, *SoW,* 109–12 (with n. 5).

13. Recall of Pleistoanax: Thuc. 5.16.1–3 with Gomme, *HCT,* III 663–64; Robert C. R. Parker, "Greek States and Greek Oracles," in *Crux,* 298–326 (esp. 318–19, 324–25), and Hornblower, *CT,* II 464–67. Sacral kingship: Rahe, *SR,* Chapters 2–3.

14. Spartan peace offer: Ar. *Ach.* 652–54 (with 194–97). Return of the plague: Thuc. 3.87. On the likely date, cf. Kagan, *AW,* 82–83, 193–95, with Gomme, *HCT,* II 391, and see Lendon, *SoW,* 214–15. Cf. Lazenby, *PW,* 59, who is unwilling to rely on Aristophanes' testimony.

Chapter 4. A Loss of Strategic Focus

Epigraph: Plut. *Mor.* 347I–c.

1. Thucydides' judgment of Pericles and his successors: 2.65.5–13.

2. Funeral oration and eros: Thuc. 2.43.1–4 with Rahe, *SFAW,* Chapter 6. Mytilenian revolt and eros: Thuc. 3.45. Attempt to deter the Athenians by stressing the magnitude of an enterprise: 6.13.1. Attempt stirs up an eros for the expedition: 6.24–26. In this connection, see Paul A. Rahe, "Thucydides' Critique of *Realpolitik,*" *Security Studies* 5:2 (Winter 1995): 105–41, reprinted in *Roots of Realism: Philosophical and Historical Dimensions,* ed. Benjamin Frankel (London: Frank Cass, 1996), 105–41. Xenophon's Socrates: cf. the funeral oration of Pericles (Thuc. 2.35–46) with the strikingly different rhetorical posture that Socrates is said to have recommended to the man's like-named son (Xen. *Mem.* 3.5.7–21); note Socrates' pointed allusion to the damage done by the reform of the Areopagus at 3.5.19–21; and see 2.6.10–16 (with 3.6.2, 4.2.2), where he denounces Pericles and praises Themistocles. Cf. Wolfgang Will, *Thukydides und Perikles: Der Historiker und Sein Held* (Bonn: Habelt, 2003), and Robert D. Luginbill, *Author of Illusions: Thucydides' Rewriting of the History of the Peloponnesian War* (Newcastle: Cambridge Scholars, 2011), 61–261, whose depiction of Thucydides as an apologist for Pericles is based on a failure to recognize the criticism that the Athenian historian directs at his compatriot, with Edith Foster, *Thucydides, Pericles, and*

Periclean Imperialism (Cambridge: Cambridge University Press, 2010), who goes to the opposite extreme, neglects the juxtaposition with Themistocles, and depicts Thucydides as hostile to empire as such.

3. Invasions of the Megarid: Thuc. 2.31.3, 4.66.1. Seizure of Minoa, tightening of Nisaea blockade: 3.51, Plut. *Nic.* 6.4 with Kagan, *AW,* 170–71; Lazenby, *PW,* 55; and Geske, *Nicias,* 18–26. Continued presence at Naupactus: Thuc. 3.7.1–5, 69.2, 75–78, 91.1, 94–102, 105–14, 4.13.2 (where the triremes from Naupactus are tellingly called "ships on guard [*phrourídes*]").

4. Intervention in Sicily: Thuc. 3.86, Diod. 12.53–54. See also Pl. *Hipp. Mai.* 282b. Cf. Henry D. Westlake, "Athenian Aims in Sicily, 427–424 B.C.: A Study in Athenian Motivation," *Historia* 9:4 (October 1960): 385–402 (esp. 388–96), reprinted in Westlake, *Essays,* 101–22 (esp. 105–16), who underestimates Athens' capacity to interfere with merchantmen in the Corinthian Gulf, who incorrectly supposes that the establishment of a Syracusan hegemony in the west would increase the export of grain to the Peloponnesus, and who overestimates the prospect that the western Greeks would supply the Peloponnesians with ships; Kagan, *AW,* 181–88; and Lazenby, *PW,* 57–58, with Brunt, *SPSAW,* 255–80 (at 261–62), reprinted in Brunt, *SGHT,* 84–111 (at 91–92), and A. James Holladay, "Athenian Strategy in the Archidamian War," *Historia* 27:3 (3rd Quarter 1978): 399–427 (at 408–12), reprinted in Holladay, *AFC,* 61–84 (at 69–72). Cf. Lendon, *SoW,* 212–14, 222. Even when provoked, Sparta's Sicilian allies did next to nothing. In 412, after defeating the immense armada that Athens sent to Sicily in 416, Syracusa and her allies managed to send only twenty-two ships to support the Lacedaemonians: Thuc. 8.26.1.

5. Initial Athenian success in Sicily: Thuc. 3.88, 90, 99, 103, 115.1–2; Diod. 12.54.4–7. See also *FGrH* 577 F2—which should be read in light of Lionel Pearson, *The Greek Historians of the West: Timaeus and His Predecessors* (Atlanta, GA: Scholars Press, 1987), 26–28; A. Brian Bosworth, "Athens' First Intervention in Sicily: Thucydides and the Sicilian Tradition," *CQ* n.s. 42:1 (1992): 46–55; and Paus. 10.11.3–4, who is following Antiochus of Syracusa *FGrH* 555 F1. See Kagan, *AW,* 188–92; Germana Scuccimarra, "Note sulla prima spedizione ateniense in Sicilia (427–424 A.C.)," *RSA* 15 (1985): 23–52; Hornblower, *CT,* II 495–98; and Lazenby, *PW,* 58–59. For later developments, see Thuc. 3.115.4–5, 4.1, 24–25.

6. Vote to send forty more triremes to Sicily: Thuc. 3.115.3–6 with Kagan, *AW,* 192–93, and Lendon, *SoW,* 249–50. Possible financial contributions from Sicilian allies: *IG* I³ 291 with Carmine Ampolo, "I Contributi alla prima spedizione ateniese in Sicilia (427–404 A. C.)," *PP* 42 (1987): 5–11, who dates this inscription to the time of Athens' first—as opposed to her second, much larger—Sicilian expedition.

7. Sicilian powers forge a peace: Thuc. 4.58.1–65.2. Embassy from Catana, one Athenian general fined, two exiled: 4.65.3–4, read in light of Justin 4.4.1–2, with Westlake, "Athenian Aims in Sicily," 385–88, 399–402, reprinted in Westlake, *Essays,* 101–5, 116–22; Kagan, *AW,* 268–70; Silvio Cataldi, "I Processi agli strateghi ateniesi della prima spedizione in Sicilia e la politica cleoniana," in *Processi e politica nel mondo politico,* ed. Marta Sordi (Milan: Vita e pensiero, 1996), 37–63; and Lazenby, *PW,* 84.

8. Melos: Thuc. 3.91.1–3 and Diod. 12.65.1–3 with Lewis, *AW,* 409–10, and Michael G. Seaman, "The Athenian Expedition to Melos in 416 B.C.," *Historia* 46:4 (Fourth Quarter 1997): 385–418, who demonstrates that there is no evidence—*IG* V 1, 1 = *SEG* 39.370*, notwithstanding—that the Melians offered aid and comfort to the Lacedaemonians prior to 416. Note Kagan, *AW,* 197–200, and Holladay, "Athenian Strategy in the Archidamian War," 405, 407, reprinted in Holladay, *AFC,* 66, 68. Cf. Lendon, *SoW,* 219–22. Nicias successful: Thuc. 5.16.1.

9. Expedition to Tanagra: Thuc. 3.91.3–5 and Diod. 12.65.3–4 (where the relative chronology is confused).with Lewis, *AW,* 386–87, 409–10. Note Westlake, *Individuals,* 87–88; Kagan, *AW,* 200; Holladay, "Athenian Strategy in the Archidamian War," 407, reprinted in Holladay, *AFC,* 67–68; Lazenby, *PW,* 59–61; and Lendon, *SoW,* 222–26. Threat of siege and pledge to Plataeans: Thuc. 2.71–74. Escapees from Plataea: 3.20–24 with Lazenby, *PW,* 51–52. Citizenship conferred on survivors: Isoc. 12.93–94 and Dem. 59.103–6 with Kostas Kapparis, "The Athenian Decree for the Naturalisation of the Plataeans," *GRBS* 36:4 (Winter 1995): 359–78. Note, in this connection, Ar. *Ran.* 693–94, Lys. 23, Isoc. 14.61–62, Diod. 15.46.6, Hellanicus *FGrH* 4 F171. The decree of

naturalization passed in 427 may have been the fulfillment of a formal pledge issued at the beginning of the war or much, much earlier: Thuc. 3.55.3, 62.2 with Gomme, *HCT*, II 339–40; Hornblower, *CT*, I 449–50; and Christopher B. R. Pelling, "Rhetoric and History II: Plataea (431–27 BC)," in Pelling, *Literary Texts and the Greek Historian* (London: Routledge, 2000), 61–81 (at 61–67, 74–77). Cf. Ernst Badian, "Plataea between Athens and Sparta: In Search of Lost History," in *Boiotika: Vorträge vom 5. Internationalen Böotien-Kolloquium zu Ehren von Professor Dr. Siegfried Lauffer*, ed. Hartmut Beister and John Buckler (Munich: Editio Maris, 1989), 95–111 (esp. 102–11), reprinted in Badian, *FPP*, 109–23 (esp. 116–23), who is wrongly inclined to interpret Greek in light of Roman practices, treating what was de facto something like what the Romans called a *deditio in fidem* as a formal and legal act of submission. Without contradicting his predecessor, where Herodotus (6.108) speaks metaphorically of the Plataeans "handing themselves over" to the Athenians, Thucydides (3.68.5) speaks in formal terms of the two becoming "allies."

10. Demosthenes and Procles at Leucas: Thuc. 3.91.1, 94.1–2; Diod. 12.60.1 with Kagan, *AW*, 201. Cf. Lendon, *SoW*, 234, who overestimates what it would have cost Athens to wall off Leucas and leave the Acarnanians to maintain by land a siege.

11. Demosthenes' cockamamie scheme: Thuc. 3.94.3–95.1 with Lewis, *AW*, 386–87, 410. For a more positive view of Demosthenes' strategy than I think justified, cf. Kagan, *AW*, 201–9; Holladay, "Athenian Strategy in the Archidamian War," 412–14, reprinted in Holladay, *AFC*, 72–73; and Roisman, *Demosthenes*, 11–13, 23–27, with Brunt, *SPSAW*, 270, reprinted in Brunt, *SGHT*, 101. Cf., also, Lendon, *SoW*, 234–35 (with 478 n. 28), who finds it hard to believe that Demosthenes (or anyone else) would have contemplated so senseless a scheme. False notion that without the Boeotian cavalry there would be no invasions of Attica: Thuc. 4.95.2. Spartans capable of forming own cavalry units: 4.55.1–2.

12. Massacre in Aetolia: Thuc. 3.95.2–98.5, Diod. 12.60.1 with Kagan, *AW*, 203–5; Lazenby, *PW*, 61–62; Hutchinson, *Attrition*, 36–39; and Lendon, *SoW*, 234–36. For the topography, see W. Kendrick Pritchett, "Demosthenes' Campaign in Southern Aitolia in 426 B.C.," in *SAGT*, VII 47–82. Cleon brings charges against generals victorious at Potidaea: Thuc. 2.70.4 with Ar. *Eq.* 435–38 and Diod. 12.46.6–7.

13. Peloponnesian alliance with Aetolia against Naupactus: Thuc. 3.100.1, Diod. 12.60.2. Note *SEG* XXVI 461 and *ML* no. 67 = *O&R* no. 151, and see Gomme, *HCT*, II 408–9; Kagan, *AW*, 209; Ronald S. Stroud, "Thucydides and Corinth," *Chiron* 24 (1994): 267–304 (at 281–85); Hornblower, *CT*, I 514–15; and Hutchinson, *Attrition*, 39.

14. Heracleia Trachinia: Thuc. 3.92, Diod. 12.59.3–5 with Kagan, *AW*, 195–97, and Caroline Falkner, "Sparta's Colony at Herakleia Trachinia and Spartan Strategy in 426," *EMC* 43 n.s. 18:1 (1999): 45–58.

15. Expedition mounted against Naupactus, thwarted by Demosthenes and the Acarnanians: Thuc. 3.100.2–102.5; Diod. 12.60.2–3 with Gomme, *HCT*, II 409–10; Kagan, *AW*, 209–10; Hornblower, *CT*, I 515–16; Roisman, *Demosthenes*, 13–14, 27–32; Hutchinson, *Attrition*, 39–40; and Lendon, *SoW*, 236–39. Although there are those who think Thucydides biased against Demosthenes, I am persuaded that his dispassionate account of the man's conduct in 427 and the winter of 426 does full justice to the man's considerable virtues and to his shortcomings: cf. Eric Charles Woodcock, "Demosthenes, Son of Alcisthenes," *HSCP* 39 (1928): 93–108 (esp. 94–97); Max Treu, "Der Stratege Demosthenes," *Historia* 5:4 (November 1956): 420–47 (esp. 421–28); and Cawkwell, *TPW*, 50–55, 71–74, with Westlake, *Individuals*, 97–105, and see Roisman, *Demosthenes*, 11–32.

16. Eurylochos, Demosthenes, and the battle for Amphilochian Argos: Thuc. 3.102.5–7, 105–14; Polyaen. *Strat.* 3.1.2. For a fragmentary account, cf. Diod. 12.60.4–6. Dedications: *ML* no. 74 = *O&R* no. 164 and *SEG* XIX 392. See Gomme, *HCT*, II 411–13, 415–30; Kagan, *AW*, 210–17; Lewis, *AW*, 410–12; Hornblower, *CT*, I 516, 531–35; Lazenby, *PW*, 62–66; Hutchinson, *Attrition*, 40–45; Lendon, *SoW*, 239–45; and Lawrence A. Tritle, *A New History of the Peloponnesian War* (Malden, MA: Wiley-Blackwell, 2010), 77–81. Regarding the topography, cf. Nicholas G. L. Hammond, "The Campaigns in Amphilochia during the Archidamian War," *BSA* 37 (1936–37): 128–40, reprinted with additions as "Military Operations in Amphilochia," in Hammond, *Studies in Greek History: A Companion Volume to a History of Greece to 322 B.C.* (Oxford: Clarendon Press,

1973), 471–85, and *Epirus: The Geography, The Ancient Remains, The History and Topography of Epirus and Adjacent Areas* (Oxford: Clarendon Press, 1967), 238–48, with W. Kendrick Pritchett, "Demosthenes' Amphilochian Campaign in 426 B.C.," in *SAGT,* VIII 1–78.

17. Fall of Anactorium: consider Thuc. 4.49 in light of 1.55.1, 2.9.2. Note 1.46.1. Oeniadae forced to join the Athenian alliance: consider 4.77.2 in light of 1.111.3, 2.9.4, 82, 102.2, 3.114.2.

18. Stages in the collapse of Corinth's position along the trade route to the west: Salmon, *WC,* 306–18. Corinthian garrison at Leucas as well as at Ambracia: Thuc. 3.114.4, 4.42.3. Cf. Lewis, *AW,* 370–412, who does not, I think, properly appreciate what Athens had gained via the damage done Corinth.

19. Earthquakes stymie Peloponnesian invasion in 426: Thuc. 3.89.1. Invasion of 427 cut short: 4.2.1, 6.1; Diod. 12.59.1–2. Cf. Gomme, *HCT,* III 441, who wrongly supposes that the grain in question was Boeotian. These expeditions were sufficiently inefficient that it was well worth the time for the Athenians to plant their crops.

20. Pythodorus succeeds Laches: Thuc. 3.115.2, 5–6. Reinforcements for Sicily, task in Corcyra: 3.115.3–4, 4.2.2–3. Stronghold on Istone: 4.2.3, 46.1–2 with Kagan, *AW,* 219–20. Laches under fire: Ar. *Vesp.* 240–42, 836–995 with the scholia on 240 and 895. I explored the Istone massif and the coastal region nearby on 18 March 2019.

21. Demosthenes' Messenian scheme: Thuc. 4.2.4–3.3 with Gomme, *HCT,* III 438–39; Kagan, *AW,* 220–22; Cawkwell, *TWP,* 51–52; Lazenby, *PW,* 67–68; Hutchinson, *Attrition,* 53–54; and Lendon, *SoW,* 250–54. Concern with security: Robert B. Strassler, "The Opening of the Pylos Campaign," *JHS* 110 (1990): 110–12 (at 110–11). For the topography, which is not fully in accord with what appears in Thucydides' text, see W. Kendrick Pritchett, "Pylos and Sphakteria," in *SAGT,* I 6–29. Cf. John B. Wilson, *Pylos, 425 B.C.: A Historical and Topographical Study of Thucydides' Account of the Campaign* (Warminster: Aris & Phillips, 1979), whose account is compelling in certain particulars, with W. Kendrick Pritchett, "Thucydides and Pylos," in Pritchett, *Essays in Greek History* (Amsterdam: J. C. Gieben, 1994), 145–77, whose corrections I accept. In what follows, my aim is to show that, while Thucydides is certainly artful in describing this series of episodes, there is no reason to question his accuracy, judgment, and objectivity. Cf. Woodcock, "Demosthenes, Son of Alcisthenes," 97–104; Treu, "Der Stratege Demosthenes," 428–33, 439–47; and Westlake, *Individuals,* 106–11, who think otherwise, with Roisman, *Demosthenes,* 15–17, 33–41; then, cf. Virginia J. Hunter, *Thucydides: The Artful Reporter* (Toronto: Hakkert, 1973), 61–83, with Daniel Babut, "Interprétation historique et structure littéraire chez Thucydide: Remarques sur la composition du livre iv," *BAGB* 40:4 (1981): 417–39, and see Rood, *Thucydides,* 24–57 (esp. 24–46).

22. Generals unsympathetic, cite cost; appeal to taxiarchs and soldiers unsuccessful: Thuc. 4.3.3–4.1 with Kagan, *AW,* 222–23; Raymond Weil, "Stratèges, soldats, taxiarques (Thucydide, IV, 4, 1)," *RPh* 62:1 (June 1988): 129–33; Hornblower, *CT,* II 155–56; and Lazenby, *PW,* 67–69. Corinthians advocate fortifying positions in Attica: Thuc. 1.122.1. Pericles mentions option: 1.142.2–5. Cf. Treu, "Der Stratege Demosthenes," 439–47, and Ste. Croix, *OPW,* 209–10, who doubt the historicity of Thucydides' report regarding the pertinent passages in these two speeches, with George Cawkwell, "Thucydides' Judgment of Periclean Strategy," *YClS* 24 (1975): 53–70 (at 67), reprinted in Cawkwell, *CC,* 134–50 (at 147–48), and Henry D. Westlake, "The Progress of Epiteichismos," *CQ* n.s. 33:1 (1983): 12–24, reprinted in Westlake, *Studies,* 34–49, who show that, as a stratagem, the building of forts along these lines was nothing new. Atalante: Thuc. 2.32 with 3.89.3. Supposed a departure from Pericles' strategy: Treu, "Der Stratege Demosthenes," 439–47; Ste. Croix, *OPW,* 208–10; Kagan, *AW,* 27–28, 222; Holladay, "Athenian Strategy in the Archidamian War," 414–16, reprinted in Holladay, *AFC,* 73–75; and Cawkwell, *TPW,* 50–53 (with 43). Cf. Gomme, *HCT,* I 459, and Arnold W. Gomme, "Four Passages in Thucydides," *JHS* 71 (1951): 70–80 (esp. 70–72, 74–80), reprinted in Gomme, *More Essays in Greek History and Literature* (Oxford: Basil Blackwell, 1962), 91–111 (esp. 93–97, 101–11), as well as Henry D. Westlake, "Seaborne Raids in Periclean Strategy," *CQ* 39:3/4 (July–October 1945): 75–84 (at 78–79), reprinted in Westlake, *Essays,* 84–100 (at 89–91); Roisman, *Demosthenes,* 34; Lewis, *AW,* 380–86 (esp. 386); and Lafargue, *BP,* 120–24, who

recognize just how well this stratagem fit the offensive dimension of Pericles' strategy. Pertinent topography: Shepherd, *PS*, 32–49 (with the photographs on 50 and 52).

23. Risks and rewards: Holladay, "Athenian Strategy in the Archidamian War," 414–16, reprinted in Holladay, *AFC*, 73–75. Spartans fear helot desertions, Messenian revolt: Thuc. 4.41.2–3. With reason: 5.35.7, 56.2–3. Note 7.26.2.

24. Fortification of Pylos: Thuc. 4.4–5 with Kagan, *AW*, 222–23; John F. Lazenby, *The Spartan Army* (Warminster: Aris & Phillips, 1985), 113–14, and *PW*, 68–69; Hutchinson, *Attrition*, 54; Lendon, *SoW*, 252–54; Shepherd, *PS*, 35–42; and Lafargue, *BP*, 52–61. Cf. Diod. 12.61.1. As Lazenby points out, the lack of tools and the fact that provisions were in short supply (Thuc. 4.8.8) weigh against the hypothesis that Demosthenes had intended from the outset to employ the expeditionary force in fortifying a headland. Cf., however, Strassler, "The Opening of the Pylos Campaign," 113–25. I first visited Navarino Bay and Sphacteria while a student in the American School of Classical Studies' summer program in 1973, and I returned for a second look and for a close examination of Demosthenes' headland on 19 March 2019. I am living proof that a sedentary, out-of-shape, asthmatic septuagenarian with a lumbar problem can easily manage the slope at the point of access in the southeast.

25. Athenian commanders seek interception of Peloponnesian fleet: H. Awdry, "A New Historical Aspect of the Pylos and Sphacteria Incidents," *JHS* 20 (1900): 14–19, who nonetheless overstates the significance for Eurymedon and Sophocles of that fleet. It is not impossible that, upon hearing of the departure of the Athenian fleet from Athens, the Peloponnesians had withdrawn from Corcyra to Cyllene and that the Athenians tarried at Zacynthus because they had learned that the Peloponnesians were heading south, but there is no evidence to support this speculation. Cf., however, Strassler, "The Opening of the Pylos Campaign," 114–25.

26. The Spartans gather their forces at Coryphasium, occupy Navarino Bay, plan deployment of triremes at harbor entrances; the Athenians tarry at Zacynthus; Demosthenes prepares for assault and summons help, provisions short: Thuc. 4.5.1, 6.1–8.9 and Diod. 12.61.1–4 with Gomme, *HCT*, III 442; Kagan, *AW*, 223–27; Strassler, "The Opening of the Pylos Campaign," 121–23; Hornblower, *CT*, II 158–60; Lazenby, *The Spartan Army*, 114, and *PW*, 69–71; Hutchinson, *Attrition*, 54–56; and Lendon, *SoW*, 254. Thucydides' text, where he describes the length of the island and the width of the southern entrance to the bay, is in error and may be corrupt: note the emendation suggested with regard to the length of the island by William G. Clark, *Peloponnesus: Notes of Study and Travel* (London: J. W. Parker and Son, 1858), 220, and taken up by Wilson, *Pylos*, 52–53, and that suggested with regard to width of the southern entrance by Robert A. Bauslaugh, "Thucydides IV 8.6 and the South Channel at Pylos," *JHS* 99 (1979): 1–6, and Pritchett, "Thucydides and Pylos," 167–75. If these emendations are justified, the precision with which Thucydides discusses the topography and the events justifies the conviction of Pritchett, ibid. 174–75, that, at least part of the time, he must have been on the spot. If not, then, as Catherine Rubincam, "The Topography of Pylos and Sphakteria and Thucydides' Measurements of Distance," *JHS* 121 (2001): 77–90, suggests, he is using approximations supplied by his informants. The dispute matters not at all with regard to my reconstruction of events.

27. Demosthenes fends off assault: Thuc. 4.9.1–13.1, Diod. 12.61.3–62.7 with Gomme, *HCT*, III 444–45, 447–50; Kagan, *AW*, 227–29; Hornblower, *CT*, II 161–67; Lazenby, *The Spartan Army*, 116, and *PW*, 71–72; Hutchinson, *Attrition*, 56–57, 70–71; Lendon, *SoW*, 258–59; and Lafargue, *BP*, 61–70. Thucydides on Brasidas: Ernst Badian, "The Road to Acanthus," in *Text and Tradition: Studies in Greek History and Historiography in Honor of Mortimer Chambers*, ed. Ronald Mellor and Lawrence A. Tritle (Claremont, CA: Regina Books, 1999), 3–35 (at 6–8). Location of fortifications: note Wilson, *Pylos*, 54–61, and see Pritchett, "Thucydides and Pylos," 163–67. Cove: Strassler, "The Harbor at Pylos, 425 BC," 198–200. Cf. Michael Dyson, "Thucydides and the Sandbar at Pylos," *Antichthon* 36 (2002): 19–29, who doubts that, in 425, there was a sandbar linking Coryphasium in the extreme southeast to the mainland, and who suggests that the Spartans must have landed troops by ship from the harbor to attack the wall built immediately to the east of the cove. Five hundred yards of rocky shore in the west with few places suited to an amphibious landing:

Wilson, *Pylos,* 87–88, and Shepherd, *PS,* 40–41, 43–49, 52. *Mēchanaí* as scaling ladders and battering rams: Thuc. 4.13.1 as interpreted by Pritchett, "Thucydides and Pylos," 164 n. 30, citing W. Kendrick Pritchett, "Akarnanian Walls and Scaling Ladders," in *SAGT,* VIII 115–43 (at 124–41).

28. On first day, Spartan triremes block entrances to the harbor: Thuc. 4.8.5–9, 13.2–3; Diod. 12.61.3.

29. Speculation that the Spartans thought that the Athenians had gone away for good: John Wilson and Tim Beardsworth, "Pylos 425 B.C.: The Spartan Plan to Block the Entrances," *CQ* 20:1 (May 1970): 42–52 (at 50). Speculation that the Spartans were now eager to stage a battle within the harbor: Loren J. Samons II, "Thucydides' Sources and the Spartan Plan at Pylos," *Hesperia* 75:4 (October–December 2006): 525–40 (at 534–39); Lendon, *SoW,* 260–62; and Shepherd, *PS,* 50–53.

30. The dispute turns on the amount of space, to the left and the right, required by each ship if triremes in line abreast are not to run afoul of one another. Cf. Wilson and Beardsworth, "Pylos 425 B.C.," 42–52; Kagan, *AW,* 229; Robert B. Strassler, "The Harbor at Pylos, 425 BC," *JHS* 108 (1988): 193–203; Lazenby, *The Spartan Army,* 115–16, and *PW,* 71; Samons, "Thucydides' Sources and the Spartan Plan at Pylos," 525–40; Matthew A. Sears, "The Topography of the Pylos Campaign and Thucydides' Literary Themes," *Hesperia* 80:1 (January–March 2011): 157–68; and Shepherd, *PS,* 41–42, who err in supposing that the Peloponnesian fleet, arranged in line abreast, was too small to be able to block the southern entrance, with Lendon, *SoW,* 256–58, who, in an admirable display of nautical expertise, shows just how easily this could have been done even with a fleet, arranged in two or more lines abreast, considerably smaller than the fifty-eight or so triremes available to the Peloponnesians.

31. Athenian victory in Navarino Bay: Thuc. 4.13.3–14.4, Diod. 12.63.1 with Gomme, *HCT,* III 450–53; Wilson, *Pylos,* 89–91, 93; Roisman, *Demosthenes,* 36–37; Hornblower, *CT,* II 167–68; Lazenby, *The Spartan Army,* 116–18, and *PW,* 72–73; Hutchinson, *Attrition,* 57; and Lafargue, *BP,* 70–72.

Chapter 5. Lacedaemon at Bay

Epigraph: Julian Stafford Corbett, *Some Principles of Maritime Strategy* (London: Longman, Green & Co., 1911), 3

1. Truce negotiated, embassy dispatched to Athens: Thuc. 4.15–16, 7.71.7; Diod. 12.63.2 with Kagan, *AW,* 229–30; John B. Wilson, *Pylos, 425 B.C.: A Historical and Topographical Study of Thucydides' Account of the Campaign* (Warminster: Aris & Phillips, 1979), 91–93; Lazenby, *The Spartan Army,* 118–19; Hutchinson, *Attrition,* 57–58; and Shepherd, *PS,* 53–59.

2. Focus on Spartiates trapped: Thuc. 4.14.5, 15.2, 17.1, 19.1; Diod. 12.63.2. Note Thuc. 4.41.3, 108.7, 117.1, 5.15.1. Spartiates make up two-fifths of the garrison on Sphacteria: cf. 4.38.5 with 4.8.9. Prominence of those trapped: 5.15.1, 34.2.

3. Demographic implosion arising from the earthquake, the helot revolt, subsequent losses in battle, and possibly the plague, evidence for numbers in 418: Rahe, *SR,* Appendix 1 (with a full citation of the primary sources and the secondary literature in the notes, to which I would now add Timothy Doran, *Spartan Oliganthropia* [Leiden: Brill, 2018]). Focus of Spartan secretiveness: Thuc. 5.68.2.

4. Spartans come to blame themselves for starting the war: consider what the Spartans concede at Thuc. 4.20.2 in light of 7.18.2–3. See Henry D. Westlake, "The Naval Battle at Pylos and Its Consequences," *CQ* n.s. 24:2 (December 1974): 211–26, reprinted in Westlake, *Studies,* 60–77, who, in an exceptionally ingenious article, suggests that the naval defeat, which was hardly decisive, simply provided an occasion for those worried about the progress of the war to pursue a treaty of peace. Cf. Lendon, *SoW,* 263, where the significance of the Peloponnesians' surrender of their fleet is underestimated, with ibid. 267–68, where Lendon expresses a proper appreciation of what they might have been able to do had they retained that fleet, and cf. John Wilson and Tim Beardsworth, "Bad Weather and the Blockade at Pylos," *Phoenix* 24:2 (Summer 1970): 112–18 (esp. 116–18), who argue that it would have been exceedingly difficult, if not impossible, for the

Spartans on Sphacteria to effect an escape, with Hornblower, *CT*, II 168, who has his doubts. See also Lafargue, *BP*, 73–76.

5. Plato's cave: *Rep.* 7.514a–517d.

6. *Sophrosúnē* a consequence of being badly outnumbered by one's slaves: consider Thuc. 8.24.4 in light of 8.40.2.

7. Corinthian warning: Thuc. 1.70–71. Spartans harp on fortune and its aptness to change: 4.17.4–19.2. Offer peace, friendship, alliance, and shared hegemony, presume Athenians eager: 4.19.1–21.1. Cf. 2.8.4, and see Ar. *Pax* 1082 and Thuc. 5.8.11. See Kagan, *AW*, 231–34. Cf. Debnar, *SSL*, 147–64, who argues that the Lacedaemonians began at this time to speak in the manner of the Athenians.

8. Cleon's terms: Thuc. 4.21.2–3. Spartan envoys suggest the appointment of *xúnedroi*: 4.22.1. Fear of losing allies' trust: 4.22.3. Rejection of negotiations in private: 4.22.2. Decision to scuttle negotiations fiercely disputed in assembly by Nicias among others: Philochorus *FGrH* 328 F128 and Plut. *Nic.* 7.2 (which would make sense of Thuc. 5.16.1) with Alan L. Boegehold, "A Dissent at Athens, ca. 424–421 B.C.," *GRBS* 23:2 (1982): 147–56, citing Ar. *Eq.* 579–80; and Lewis, *AW*, 416. Cf. Gomme, *HCT*, III 458–60; Kagan, *AW*, 234–38; Ian Worthington, "Aristophanes' *Knights* and the Abortive Peace Proposals of 425 B.C.," *AC* 56 (1987): 56–67 (esp. 62–66); Lazenby, *PW*, 73–74; and Lafargue, *Cléon*, 52–56, and *BP*, 76–84, who entertain a far more favorable assessment of Cleon's maneuvers than I think justified, with Westlake, *Individuals*, 65–69; James Holladay, "Athenian Strategy in the Archidamian War," *Historia* 27:3 (3rd Quarter 1978): 399–427 (at 420–27), reprinted in Holladay, *AFC*, 61–84 (at 78–84); Cawkwell, *TPW*, 64–66; Lendon, *SoW*, 263–67; and Shepherd, *PS*, 59–61. Disposition of Nicias: Thuc. 5.16.1, 7.50.4, 77.1–4 with Diod. 13.12.6; Plut. *Nic.* 3, 23.

9. Athenian *pleonexía* intimated: Thuc. 4.22.1 with 17.4. Spartan withdrawal: Thuc. 4.22.3. Pointed usage of *metríōs* and its cognates: cf. 1.76.4–77.2, 2.65.5, and 3.46.4 with 4.22.3, and note the false claim at 5.111.4. Aristophanes makes the same point: *Eq.* 795–97, 965–66, 1086–87. Cf. Kagan, *AW*, 229–34, 258–59, who has a less ambitious estimation than I do of Pericles' ultimate aims; who believes that the peace on offer fell well short of what, he supposes, Pericles thought requisite—the Spartans' acceptance of the fact that Athens' defeat was beyond their capacity—and who thinks that the Athenians needed "a firmer guarantee than was offered," such as a surrender of Megara and Boeotia, with Holladay, "Athenian Strategy in the Archidamian War," 420–27, reprinted in Holladay, *AFC*, 78–84, who shares Kagan's modest estimation of Pericles' war aims and quite rightly wonders what more anyone could have supposed the Spartans could have offered. I do not think Boeotia anywhere near as useful to the Athenians as Megara; and, on my reading, the Spartans were willing to discuss—in private—a betrayal of Megara. Cf., also, Worthington, "Aristophanes' *Knights* and the Abortive Peace Proposals of 425 B.C.," 62–66, and Lafargue, *BP*, 76–84, who agree with Kagan on the need for firmer guarantees, with Cawkwell, *TPW*, 44, 64–66, and Lendon, *SoW*, 262–68, who have a better appreciation of what was on offer. One can reject Lendon's claim that, up to this point, what was at stake in the war was rank and only rank and nonetheless appreciate the practical, material significance that Lacedaemon's humiliation and loss of rank was likely to have. If prestige is a force-multiplier, its collapse is apt to lead to a precipitous decline in a polity's capacity to rally its allies and project power, as in due course we shall see.

10. Athenians retain Peloponnesian ships, stalemate in Navarino Bay, Athenians on verge of failure: Thuc. 4.23, 26.1–27.2 with Kagan, *AW*, 238–39, and Lazenby, *PW*, 74. Demosthenes' misgivings about a forced landing: Thuc. 4.29.3–30.1.

11. Cleon saddled with command: Thuc. 4.27.3–28.4. Conduct of Nicias mocked: Plut. *Nic.* 7.3–8.6. I do not think that there is anything egregious in Thucydides' assignment of motives to Cleon in this passage. The man had scotched the possibility of peace, and now that the Spartans had ceased to plead for a settlement and circumstances looked to an ever increasing degree unfavorable to the Athenians, he was like a fish wriggling on a hook. Cf. Westlake, *Individuals*, 69–73, 88; Kagan, *AW*, 239–44; Lewis, *AW*, 416–18; Hornblower, *CT*, II 185–88; Harriet I. Flower, "Thucydides and the Pylos Debate (4.27–29)," *Historia* 41:1 (1992): 40–57; Lazenby, *PW*, 74–75; and Lafargue, *Cléon*, 56–59, and *BP*, 84–88, with Cawkwell, *TPW*, 66–67, and Hutchinson, *Attrition*,

57–58. Flower, "Thucydides and the Pylos Debate," 41–46, and Cawkwell, *TPW,* 72–73, are, I think, right in drawing attention to Thucydides' reference to the *archḗ* at Pylos in 4.28.3. But, as the latter acknowledges, this need only mean that the *proboúleuma* being debated contemplated assigning Nicias the command at Pylos. Only if one is inclined to join Ernst Badian, as Flower is, in supposing Thucydides a purveyor of disinformation (Chapter 2, note 39, above), would one be prepared to suppose that, prior to the meeting described, the assembly had already voted to send a relief expedition to Pylos under Nicias' command. For an account friendlier to Nicias than I think justified, cf. Geske, *Nicias,* 26–45, 85–92, 165–67, with Ar. *Eq.* 356–58, who gets it right.

12. Cleon's self-righteous repudiation of the politics of friendship: Plut. *Mor.* 806f–807d with Victor Martin, "Aspects de la société athénienne," *BAGB* 39 (April 1933): 3–32 and 40 (July 1933): 7–43; Olivier Reverdin, "Remarques sur la vie politique d'Athènes au Ve siècle," *MH* 2:4 (1945): 201–12; and W. Robert Connor, *The New Politicians of Fifth-Century Athens* (Princeton, NJ: Princeton University Press, 1971). Note Ar. *Eq.* 731, 773–76, 790–91. Cleon and the Mytilenians: Thuc. 3.36–50 with James A. Andrews, "Cleon's Hidden Appeals (Thucydides 3.37–40)," *CQ* 50:1 (2000): 45–62. Note the punishment he later persuaded his compatriots to deal out to the Scionaeans: Thuc. 4.122.6, 5.18.8, 32.1, and cf. Arthur Geoffrey Woodhead, "Thucydides' Portrait of Cleon," *Mnemosyne* 4th ser., 13:4 (1960): 289–317 (at 298–300), who, in his influential defense of the demagogue, is prepared to countenance genocide on the grounds that "total war," though "a savage and bitter thing," must, "if it is to be fought at all, . . . be fought totally," and Lafargue, *Cléon,* 45–49, with Cawkwell, *TPW,* 63–64. Cleon's propensity to slander and prosecute magistrates, generals, and even wealthy private individuals as bribe takers, embezzlers, traitors, and conspirators: note Thuc. 5.16.1; consider Ar. *Eq.* 62–64, 257–63, 288, 300–302, 435–54, 471–87, 624–31, 710–11, 783–87, 824–29, 860–63, 875–80 in light of 164–67; and see *Vesp.* 342–45, 406–19, 463–76, 486–502 with Barbara Mitchell, "Kleon's Amphipolitan Campaign: Aims and Results," *Historia* 40:2 (1991): 170–92 (at 170–71, 186–88). Cf. Hornblower, *CT,* II 188, with Gomme, *HCT,* III 469–70, and see Andrewes, *HCT,* V 159–60. As Lewis, *AW,* 420–21, points out, when a man, who appears to have been Cleon's son-in-law, arranged later in 425 for a tripling of the *phóros* collected at the beginning of the war, he repeatedly resorted to threatening language, directed against magistrates chosen from among his fellow citizens, that was exceedingly violent and accusatory: see *ATL* II 40–43 (A9) = *ML* no. 69 = *IG* I³ 71 = *O&R* no. 153 = Paarmann, *A&P,* II 79–82 (with III 137–59) and Plut. *Arist.* 24.5. For a full-throated defense of Cleon's demagoguery, see Lafargue, *Cléon,* passim (esp. 19–35, 87–155).

13. Prosecutions of Miltiades, Themistocles, and Cimon: Rahe, *SFAW,* Chapters 3 and 4. Pronounced Athenian propensity after 432 for subjecting generals to trials for treason: Mogens Herman Hansen, *The Athenian Democracy in the Age of Demosthenes* (Oxford: Basil Blackwell, 1991), 215–18. Reaction of the self-styled *sṓphrones* in 425: Thuc. 4.28.5. Note Ar. *Eq.* 973–76. Cf. Hornblower, *CT,* II 188, with Gomme, *HCT,* III 469–70, and see Andrewes, *HCT,* V 159–60. On the role played by irony in Thucydides' description of Cleon's opponents as *sṓphrones,* see W. Robert Connor, *Thucydides* (Princeton, NJ: Princeton University Press, 1984), 115 (with n. 12).

14. Battle on Sphacteria: Thuc. 4.30.4–36.3 with W. Kendrick Pritchett, "Pylos and Sphakteria," in *SAGT,* I 6–29 (at 25–29); Kagan, *AW,* 244–47; Wilson, *Pylos,* 100–23; Lewis, *AW,* 418–19; Roisman, *Demosthenes,* 37–41; Lazenby, *The Spartan Army,* 119–23, and *PW,* 75–79; Hutchinson, *Attrition,* 58–60; Lendon, *SoW,* 268–74; and Shepherd, *PS,* 68–86. Cf. Cawkwell, *TPW,* 73–74; and Lafargue, *BP,* 89–106. Note Diod. 12.63.3–4. Komon: Paus. 4.26.2 with Pritchett, "Pylos and Sphakteria," 28–29.

15. Lacedaemonians on Sphacteria surrender, conveyed to Athens: Thuc. 4.37–39 and Diod. 12.63.3–4 with Hutchinson, *Attrition,* 60–62, and Lendon, *SoW,* 274–77. Cleon awarded front seat at the theater and free meals in the prytaneum: Ar. *Eq.* 281–83, 573–76, 702–4, 709, 763–66, 1404–5. For a shield dedicated on this occasion, see *IG* I³ 522 with Paus. 1.15.4. For the timetable, see Gomme, *HCT,* III 478, and Wilson, *Pylos,* 124–26. Demosthenes' cake: Ar. *Eq.* 54–57, 1200–1201 with 391–92, 743–44 and Roisman, *Demosthenes,* 75–76. Note also Ar. *Eq.* 777–79. If I do not follow Cawkwell, *TPW,* 70–74, and Lafargue, *BP,* 89–106, in positing a connection between Cleon and Demosthenes going back to the former's debate with Nicias regarding the relief expe-

dition, if not to the instructions given Eurymedon and Sophocles with regard to latter's employ-ment of their fleet, it is in part because of the testimony of Aristophanes.

16. Shock of Spartan surrender, verbal exchange with captive: Thuc. 4.40 (which should be read in light of Plut. *Mor.* 234e) with Kagan, *AW*, 248. Cf. Thuc. 4.34.1. On the *kaloì k'agathoí,* see Gomme, *HCT,* III 48–81; Ste. Croix, *OPW,* 371–76; and Hornblower, *CT,* II 195–96. Subsequent Spartan treatment of those who had surrendered on Sphacteria: Thuc. 5.34.2, Diod. 12.76.1, which should be read in light of Xen. *Lac. Pol.* 9.4–5 with Gomme, *HCT,* IV 36, and Kagan, *PNSE,* 47–48.

17. Thudippus and the *phóros:* preface to Part II, note 10, above. Cf. Félix Bourriot, "La Fa-mille et le milieu social de Cléon," *Historia* 31:4 (4th Quarter 1982): 404–35, with Lafargue, *Cléon,* 89–110 (esp. 98–100). Jury pay soon three obols a day: Ar. *Eq.* 51, 255, 904–5. Note 651–56, 797–809. Raised from two by Cleon after he became a general: Schol. Ar. *Vesp.* 88 and *Av.* 1541. See Arist. *Ath. Pol.* 27.2–4, 62.2 with Rhodes, *CAAP,* 338. Note Ar. *Eq.* 311–12, and see Lewis, *AW,* 420–21. Pay for members of the council: Thuc. 8.69.4; Arist. *Ath. Pol.* 24.3, 62.2 with Vincent J. Rosivach, "*IG* I³ 82 and the Date of the Introduction of Bouleutic *Misthos* in Athens," *ZPE* 175 (2010): 145–49. The introduction of these measures may have been a response to the economic distress inflicted by the war: Vincent Rosivach, "State Pay as War Relief in Peloponnesian-War Athens," *G&R* 58:2 (October 2011): 176–83.

18. Prisoners threatened, invasions of Attica cease, Coryphasium manned, helots desert, revolution feared, fruitless quest for peace: Thuc. 4.41, 5.15.2; Ar. *Eq.* 794–96, *Pax* 665–67; Diod. 12.63.3–5.

19. Raid on and ravaging of the Corinthiad, battle at Solygeia: Thuc. 4.42.1–45.1, Ar. *Eq.* 595–610, and Diod. 12.65.5–7 with Ronald S. Stroud, "Thucydides and the Battle of Solygeia," *CSCA* 4 (1971): 227–47, and "Thucydides and Corinth," *Chiron* 24 (1994): 267–304 (at 285–87). Note Westlake, *Individuals,* 89–90; Kagan, *AW,* 251–54; Salmon, *WC,* 318–20; and Hornblower, *CT,* II 197–98. Argive warning: Thuc. 4.42.3.

20. Methana (*IACP* no. 352), Hermione, Troezen, and Halieis: note Thuc. 4.45.2 and Diod. 12.65.7 with Kagan, *AW,* 254–55, and Lewis, *AW,* 419; then see *SEG* X 15, Thuc. 4.118.4, and *IG* I³ 75 and 88 with Hornblower, *CT,* II 203–4, whose dating of *SEG* X 15 needs correction in light of Peter J. Rhodes, "After the Three-Bar 'Sigma' Controversy: The History of Athenian Imperial-ism Reassessed," *CQ* n.s. 58:2 (December 2008): 500–506; Nikolaos Papazarkadas, "Epigraphy and the Athenian Empire: Re-Shuffling the Chronological Cards," in *IAE,* 67–88; and Lendon, *SoW,* 426–30.

21. Corcyra: Thuc. 4.46–48 with 4.2.3, 3.1, 5.2 and Polyaen. *Strat.* 6.20 with *IG* II² 403. An-actorium: Thuc. 4.49. See Kagan, *AW,* 255–56.

22. Conquest of Cythera and consequences: Thuc. 4.53–54; *IG* I³ 287, 369 = *ML* no. 72 = *O&R* no. 160, lines 20–22; Diod. 12.65.8–9 with George L. Huxley, "The History and Topography of Ancient Kythera," in *Kythera: Excavations and Studies Conducted by the University of Pennsyl-vania Museum and the British School at Athens,* ed. John N. Coldstream and George L. Huxley (Park Ridge, NJ: Noyes Press, 1973), 33–40, and *IACP* no. 336. See also Westlake, *Individuals,* 90–91; Kagan, *AW,* 261–63; Holladay, "Athenian Strategy in the Archidamian War," 407–8, re-printed in *AFC,* 68–69; Geske, *Nicias,* 106–11; and Lendon, *SoW,* 289–91, who underestimates Cythera's utility. Cythera garrisoned, raids on the Messenian and Laconian coasts, Spartans un-nerved: Thuc. 4.54.4–56.1 with Kagan, *AW,* 263–64; Lewis, *AW,* 423; and Lendon, *SoW,* 291–94, who emphasizes their symbolic import (which was considerable) almost to the exclusion of their strategic significance. For the island's strategic value, see Hdt. 7.235, Xen. *Hell.* 4.8.7–8. Scandea: Paus. 3.23.1, Strabo 8.5.1. There was apparently an Asine near Gytheion in the Gulf of Laconia: Strabo 8.5.2. If this is the place Thucydides had in mind, as some suppose, it is odd that he does not distinguish it from the Asine he had mentioned before: 4.13.1. Identity of Autocles: Davies, *APF* no. 2717. Freed helots: Thuc. 5.34.1 with Ronald F. Willetts, "The Neodamodeis," *CPh* 49:1 (January 1954): 27–32, and Masato Furuyama, "The Liberation of *Heilotai:* The Case of *Neodamo-deis,"* in *Forms of Control and Subordination in Antiquity,* ed. Toru Yuge and Masaoki Doi (Leiden: Brill, 1988), 364–68.

23. Epidauros Limera: Thuc. 4.56.2 with *IACP* no. 329. Thyrea: Thuc. 4.56.2–57.4, Diod. 12.65.9 with Thomas J. Figueira, "Four Notes on Aeginetans in Exile," *Athenaeum* 66 (1988): 523–51 (at 523–38), reprinted in Figueira, *Excursions in Epichoric History: Aiginetan Essays* (Lanham, MD: Rowman & Littlefield, 1993), 293–324 (at 293–310).

24. Megarian tribulations, factional strife, and plan to betray: Thuc. 4.66, Diod. 12.66.1, Paus. 1.40.4 with Kagan, *AW*, 270–73; Roisman, *Demosthenes*, 42; Hornblower, *CT*, II 229–34; and Lendon, *SoW*, 295–97.

25. Long Walls and Nisaea taken, Brasidas saves Megara, exiles from Pegae return, seize and tear down Long Walls: Thuc. 4.67–74, 109.1 and Diod. 12.66.2–67.1 with Westlake, *Individuals*, 111–15; Kagan, *AW*, 273–78; Lewis, *AW*, 423–25; Roisman, *Demosthenes*, 43–46; Rood, *Thucydides*, 63–69; Badian, "The Road to Acanthus," 8–10; Lazenby, *PW*, 86–87; Hutchinson, *Attrition*, 72–75; and Lendon, *SoW*, 297–300. See also Gomme, *HCT*, III 528–36, and Hornblower, *CT*, II 234–44. Cf. Holladay, "Athenian Strategy in the Archidamian War," 416–18, reprinted in Holladay, *AFC*, 75–77, who thought the entire venture foolhardy.

26. Cleon at Argos: Ar. *Eq.* 465. Word of Nicias' expedition comes to Corinth from Argos: Thuc. 4.42.3 with Hornblower, *CT*, II 200–201, who recognizes that there is a puzzle here.

27. The scheme of Demosthenes and Hippocrates: Thuc. 4.76–77 and Diod. 12.69.1–2 with Lendon, *SoW*, 300–303. Note also Roisman, *Demosthenes*, 18, 46–51, and Hornblower, *CT*, II 248–55. Cf. Kagan, *AW*, 278–81, 286–87, and Cawkwell, *TPW*, 50–51, who are friendlier to the venture than I think right, with Westlake, *Individuals*, 115–21, and Holladay, "Athenian Strategy in the Archidamian War," 418–19, reprinted in Holladay, *AFC*, 77–78. Siphae: Paus. 9.32.4.

28. Athenians rebuffed at Siphae, suffer severe losses after fortifying Delium: Thuc. 4.89.1–96.8, Diod. 12.69.2–70.4. Socrates, Laches, and Alcibiades: Pl. *Symp.* 220e–221b, *Lach.* 181b, *Ap.* 28e; Plut. *Alc.* 7.6. On the fate of one Orchomenian friendly to Athens, see *IG* I³ 73, which should be read in light of *IG* I³ 97. On the battle itself, see Gomme, *HCT*, III 558–68; Kagan, *AW*, 281–86; Hornblower, *CT*, II 286–308; Victor Davis Hanson, *Ripples of Battle: How Wars of the Past Still Determine How We Fight, How We Live, and How We Think* (New York: Doubleday, 2003), 171–243; Lazenby, *PW*, 87–90; Hutchinson, *Attrition*, 46–50; Lendon, *SoW*, 303–15; and Lawrence A. Tritle, *A New History of the Peloponnesian War* (Malden, MA: Wiley-Blackwell, 2010), 98–104. For the topography, see W. Kendrick Pritchett, "The Battle of Delion in 424 B.C.," in *SAGT*, II 24–36, and W. Kendrick Pritchett, "The Temple at Delion (424 B.C.)," in *SAGT*, III 295–97. On Pagondas' innovation with regard to the phalanx, see Pritchett, *GSW*, I 134–43; Victor Davis Hanson, "Epaminondas, the Battle of Leuktra (317 BC), and the 'Revolution' in Greek Battle Tactics," *CA* 7:2 (October 1988): 190–207; and Lewis, *AW*, 425. Cf. George L. Cawkwell, "Epaminondas and Thebes," *CQ* n.s. 22:2 (November 1972): 254–78 (at 260–62), reprinted in Cawkwell, *CC*, 299–333 (at 308–11), with John F. Lazenby, "The Killing Zone," in *Hoplites: The Classical Greek Battle Experience*, ed. Victor D. Hanson (London: Routledge, 1991), 87–109 (at 98–99). On hoplite battle in general, see Victor Davis Hanson, *The Western Way of War: Infantry Battle in Classical Greece*, 2nd edition (Berkeley: University of California Press, 2000); Pritchett, *GSW*, IV 1–93; and Rahe, *SR*, Chapter 3 (especially, notes 44–61 and their context, where I discuss in detail the objections recently made to the views espoused by Hanson and Pritchett). In pressing for battle against the wishes of the other Boetarchs, Pagondas appears to have been acting in a high-handed manner: Paus. 9.13.6.

29. Fall of Delium, total losses, rout at Sicyon: Thuc. 4.96.9–101.4 and Diod. 12.70.6 with Hornblower, *CT*, II 308–18; Lewis, *AW*, 425–26; Lazenby, *PW*, 90–91; and Lendon, *SoW*, 315–16. Pindar on Pagondas: F94b (Maehler). Memorial at Athens for those killed at the fort: Paus. 1.29.13. Thespian losses: *IG* VII 1888 and Thuc. 4.133.1 with Christoph W. Clairmont, *Patrios Nomos: Public Burial in Athens during the Fifth and Fourth Centuries* (Oxford: BAR, 1983), 232–34, and Pritchett, *GSW*, IV 132–33. Losses among the people of Tanagra: *IG* VII 585 with Clairmont, *Patrios Nomos*, 230–31, and Pritchett, *GSW*, IV 192–94. Booty and ransom money, panoplies displayed and stoa built at Thebes: Diod. 12.70.5.

30. Severity of losses: Lazenby, *PW*, 90. Chalcis and Eretria: Philochorus *FGrH* 328 F119, 130. Cf. Gomme, *HCT*, III 592 with Hornblower, *CT*, II 293. Some suspect that *IG* I³ 14 (*ML* no.

40 = *O&R* no. 121), 40 (*ML* no. 52 = *O&R* no. 131) and 41 record the settlement imposed on these Euboean cities at this time.

31. Athens unable to crush Chalcidian revolt: Thuc. 1.58.2, 2.79, 95–101; Diod. 12.50–51 with Kagan, *AW*, 106, 119–23.

32. Mustering for western Thrace: Thuc. 4.70.1–2, 74.1, 78.1.

Part III. A Peace to End All Peace

Epigraph: Sun Tzū, *On the Art of War: The Oldest Military Treatise in the World*, trans. Lionel Giles (London: Luzac & Co., 1910), 3.17.1.

1. Brasidas' helot warriors: Thuc. 4.80.2, 5, and Diod. 12.68.3–5 (where considerable confusion enters in) with Kagan, *AW*, 287–88.

2. Invitation and promise of support: Thuc. 4.79.2, 80.2, 83.5 with Kagan, *AW*, 288–89. Enthusiasm in cities under Athens' yoke: Thuc. 4.79.2. Increase in *phóros* assessed: preface to Part II, note 10, above. Impact of this reassessment on the cities in the Thraceward region in particular, see Meiggs, *AE*, 327. Brasidas' eagerness: Thuc. 4.81.1 with Hutchinson, *Attrition*, 71–72, 75–76. Lacedaemonian willingness: Thuc. 4.79.3–80.1.

3. Journey to Dium: Thuc. 4.78.1–79.1 and Diod. 12.67.1 with Kagan, *AW*, 289–90, and Ernst Badian, "The Road to Acanthus," in *Text and Tradition: Studies in Greek History and Historiography in Honor of Mortimer Chambers*, ed. Ronald Mellor and Lawrence A. Tritle (Claremont, CA: Regina Books, 1999), 3–35 (at 10–12).

4. Brasidas' initial moves in western Thrace: Thuc. 4.82–84 and Diod. 12.67.2 with Kagan, *AW*, 290–93; Badian, "The Road to Acanthus," 13–16; and Hutchinson, *Attrition*, 76. Acanthus (*IACP* no. 559) a colony of Andros: Michalis Tiverios, "Greek Colonisation of the Northern Aegean," in *Greek Colonisation: An Account of Greek Colonies and Other Settlements Overseas*, ed. Gocha R. Tsetskhladze (Leiden: Brill, 2006–8), II 1–154 (at 52–60).

5. Brasidas' speech at Acanthus: Thuc. 4.85–87 with Kagan, *AW*, 293; Badian, "The Road to Acanthus," 24–33; Debnar, *SSL*, 177–89; and Hutchinson, *Attrition*, 76. Cf. the argument that Archidamus made at Plataea: Thuc. 2.71–74 with Chapter 3, note 18, in context above.

6. Brasidas persuasive at Acanthus, Stagira, Argilos, Amphipolis, Myrcinus, Galepsos, Oisyme, Torone, and Scione: Thuc. 4.88, 102–16, 120.3 with Diod. 12.67.2; Hornblower, *CT*, II 86–89; and Debnar, *SSL*, 189–93. As Cawkwell, *TPW*, 98–99, points out, the emphasis that Brasidas placed on the oaths taken at Lacedaemon guaranteeing allied autonomy and the Acanthian demand that he take an oath himself are indicative of the fears that Lacedaemon's previous practice had inspired. Stagira: *IACP* no. 613. Stagira and Argilos colonies of Andros: Tiverios, "Greek Colonisation of the Northern Aegean," 52–54, 60–64.

7. Settlement and import of Amphipolis: Chapter 1, above. Argilos: *IACP* no. 554. Resources in Strymon basin: Rahe, *SFAW*, Chapter 1, note 44. Strymon bridge: Rahe, *SFAW*, Chapter 4, note 27. Eucles and Thucydides in the Thraceward region, Eucles *phúlax*: Thuc. 4.104.4. Dispositions at war's outset (including the *Hellespontophúlakes*): Chapter 3, note 21, above. Value of Thasos as a base, especially in winter: Dem. 4.32. It is a considerable stretch to assume that Thucydides' mention of "the Amphipolitans and the Athenians in the city" at 4.105.2 indicates the presence of a garrison: see Hornblower, *CT*, II 336–37. Cf., however, Peter J. Rhodes, "Commentary," in Thucydides, *History IV.1–V.24* (Warminster: Aris & Phillips, 1998), 289. Evidence for settlers from the Chalcidice reflecting Sithonia's colonization by Euboean Chalcis: Chapter 1, note 27, above.

8. Brasidas takes Amphipolis, Thucydides saves Eion: Thuc. 4.102.1–107.2, Diod. 12.68.1–3 with Gomme, *HCT*, III 573–80, 584–88, 734; Henry D. Westlake, "Thucydides and the Fall of Amphipolis," *Hermes* 90:3 (1962): 276–87, reprinted in Westlake, *Essays*, 123–37; Brunt, *SPSAW*, 255–80 (at 273–75), reprinted in Brunt, *SGHT*, 84–111 (at 105–7); Kagan, *AW*, 293–302, who is right to draw attention to the lack of infantry at Thucydides' disposal and to suggest that the only support that he might have been able to deliver in short order was psychological; John R. Ellis,

"Thucydides at Amphipolis," *Antichthon* 12 (1978): 28–35; Kallet-Marx, *MENP,* 172–76; Badian, "The Road to Acanthus," 16–24, who mistakes the deliberate reticence that so impressed Hobbes and Rousseau for strategic incomprehension; Lazenby, *PW,* 92–94; and Hutchinson, *Attrition,* 77–79. See also Hornblower, *CT,* II 329–38, and Rhodes, "Commentary," 286–92. Fire signals a communication device that Eucles may have employed: Thuc. 3.22.7–8, 80.2, 8.102.1; Polyb. 10.43–47. I am not of the opinion that Thucydides was culpably negligent—in my judgment, everything turned on Eucles' failure to secure the Strymon bridge and on the shortcoming singled out for emphasis by Brunt: the Athenians' failure to take the threat posed by Brasidas seriously and send a substantial hoplite force to western Thrace. Others, including Gomme; Westlake; Richard A. Bauman, "A Message for Amphipolis," *AClass* 11 (1968): 170–81; Kagan; and, most vehemently, Ellis and Badian think the historian—at least in some measure—at fault. Hutchinson, *Attrition,* 79, whose judgment of tactical competence is excellent, has nothing but praise for Thucydides. Thrace exceedingly cold in winter: Pl. *Symp.* 220a–b.

9. Alarmed Athenians dispatch garrisons: Thuc. 4.108.1–2, 5–6 with Hornblower, *CT,* II 340–42. Brasidas' options and intentions: Hutchinson, *Attrition,* 77–78. Fate of Thucydides: Thuc. 5.26.5. Cleon responsible: Marcellin. *Vit. Thuc.* 23–26 with Gomme, *HCT,* III 585.

10. Invitations to Brasidas: Thuc. 4.108.3–4. Myrcinus, Galepsos, Oisyme, Acte peninsula; triremes built; hoplite panoplies produced: 4.107.3, 109; Diod. 12.68.4–5.

11. History, economy, and significance of Torone: Alexander K. Cambitoglou and John K. Papadopoulos, "Historical and Topographical Introduction," in Cambitoglou, Papadopoulos, and Olwen Tudor Jones, *Torone I: The Excavations of 1975, 1976, and 1978* (Athens: Archaiologikē Hetaireia, 2001), Pt. 1, 37–88; Alan S. Henry, *Torone: The Literary, Documentary and Epigraphical Testimonia* (Athens: Archaiologikē Hetaireia, 2004); and *IACP* no. 620. The bay on the north side of Lekythos was deeper and much more capacious in the archaic and classical periods than it is today, see J. Lea Beness, Richard Dunn, Tom Hillard, Anthony Sprent, "The Coastal Topography of Ancient Torone," *MedArch* 22/23 (2009–10): 69–100. Mardonius' travails: Hdt. 6.43.1–45.2 with Rahe, *PC,* Chapter 3. Xerxes' canal: Hdt. 7.22–24, 37, 122 with Rahe, *PC,* Chapter 5. Still functioning: Thuc. 4.109.2. That these waters were still dangerous is evident from Diod. 13.41.1–3.

12. Brasidas takes Torone: Thuc. 4.110–16 and Diod. 12.68.6 with Alan S. Henry, "Thucydides and the Topography of Torone," *AEph* 132 (1993): 107–20 (esp. 107–17), whose observations I confirmed on a visit made to Torone and the Sithonia peninsula more generally on 27 June 2017. See also Benjamin D. Meritt, "Scione, Mende, and Torone," *AJA* 27:4 (October–November 1923): 447–60 (at 451–60); Gomme, *HCT,* III 580–83; Hornblower, *CT,* II 345–56; Lazenby, *PW,* 94–95; Hutchinson, *Attrition,* 80–82; and Lendon, *SoW,* 337–41. On postern gates and their function, see Frederick E. Winter, *Greek Fortifications* (London: Routledge and Kegan Paul, 1971), 234–51.

13. Scione (*IACP* no. 609) revolts: Thuc. 4.120–21 and Diod. 12.72.1 with Meritt, "Scione, Mende, and Torone," 450–51; Kagan, *AW,* 308; and Hutchinson, *Attrition,* 83. Potidaea the key to the control of Pallene: Xen. *Hell.* 5.2.15. I visited Potidaea, Mende, and Scione on 26 June 2017.

14. Aristonymos and Athenaios reach Torone: Thuc. 4.122.1–2. Pericleidas' visit to Athens in 465/4: Rahe, *SFAW,* Chapter 4 (at note 24).

Chapter 6. Mutual Exhaustion

Epigraph: Niccolò Machiavelli, *Dell'Arte della guerra,* in Machiavelli, *Tutte le opere,* ed. Mario Martelli (Florence: Sansoni Editore, 1971), 304.

1. The resolutely imperial outlook that, in the early years of the war, Thucydides' Athenians customarily voice with regard to their alliance (1.75, 76.2–3, 144.1, 2.36.2, 62.2–3, 63.1–2, 64.3, 5, 65.7, 11, 3.37.1–2, 39.2, 40.2–7, 45.6, 46.5–6, 47.5, 5.89, 91, 97, 99–101) is brutally evident in the terms of the Peace of Nicias negotiated in 422/1 (5.18.5–8) and in those of the Athenian-Argive alliance ratified in the summer of 420 (5.47.1–2), where Athens' league is formally recognized as an empire by Lacedaemon and Argos. It is also evident in the inscriptions recording decrees

passed in and not long after the 420s, though Polly Low, "Looking for the Language of Athenian Imperialism," *JHS* 125 (2005): 93–111, thinks otherwise: cf. *IG* I³ 19, 21, 27, 34 (*ML* no. 46 = *O&R* no. 154), 37 (*ML* no. 47), 39–40 (*ML* no. 52 = *O&R* no. 131), 41, 71 (*ML* no. 69 = *O&R* no. 153), 1453 (*ML* no. 45 = *O&R* no. 155), where the language and practices of empire are in evidence, with *ML* no. 40 = *IG* I³ 14 = *O&R* no. 121, which presupposes the existence of a genuine alliance, and with the inscription recording an Athenian decree passed with regard to Samos in 440/39 or 439/8 (*IG* I³ 48 [*ML* no. 56 = *O&R* no. 139]), which bespeaks a certain ambiguity. Whether *IG* I³ 39, 40 (*ML* no. 52 = *O&R* no. 131), and 41—all dealing with the aftermath of a revolt on the island of Euboea—pertain to 446 or to 423 is in dispute. Cf. Russell Meiggs, "The Growth of Athenian Imperialism," *JHS* 63 (1943): 21–34, "The Crisis of Athenian Imperialism," *HSCPh* 67 (1963): 1–36, and *AE*, 152–254, 425–27, 579–82, whose contention that the achievement of a peace of sorts with Persia ca. 449 marked the turning point would still be defensible if these three decrees could be dated to 446, with Harold B. Mattingly, "The Language of Athenian Imperialism," *Epigraphica* 36 (1974): 33–56, reprinted with necessary corrections in Mattingly, *The Athenian Empire Restored: Epigraphic and Historical Studies* (Ann Arbor: University of Michigan Press, 1996), 361–85, who thinks that they pertain to the Euboean rebellion mentioned by Philochorus as having occurred in 424/3 and that the shift in outlook took place later than Meiggs supposed, and see Peter J. Rhodes, "After the Three-Bar 'Sigma' Controversy: The History of Athenian Imperialism Reassessed," *CQ* n.s. 58:2 (December 2008): 500–506, and "What Remains of Periclean Imperialism," in *Athēnaiōn Episkopos: Studies in Honour of Harold B. Mattingly*, ed. Angelos P. Matthaiou and Robert K. Pitt (Athens: Ellēnikē Epigraphikē Etaireia, 2014), 39–49; and Nikolaos Papazarkadas, "Epigraphy and the Athenian Empire: Re-Shuffling the Chronological Cards," in *IAE*, 67–88. If, at the time of their rebellion in 428, the Mytilenians speak the language of alliance in their own regard rather than that of empire (Thuc. 3.10.2–13.1), it is because they supply ships and are independent allies and not, strictly speaking, Athens' subjects. Athenian awareness that empire unpopular: Thuc. 1.75.1, 4, 2.64.5. Note also 2.8.4–5, 4.108.3–6, 8.2. Cf. Geoffrey Ernest Maurice de Ste. Croix, "The Character of the Athenian Empire," *Historia* 3:1 (1954): 1–41, who envisaged Athens' empire as an instrument of the class struggle, with Donald W. Bradeen, "The Popularity of the Athenian Empire," *Historia* 9:3 (July 1960): 257–69; note the more modest claims Ste. Croix, *OPW*, 40, advanced eighteen years later; and consider the judicious treatment of this issue in Cawkwell, *TPW*, 92–106 (whose pointed mention of the Warsaw Pact deserves attention), and Lazenby, *PW*, 95. Damage to Athenian prestige: Thuc. 4.85.7, 108.2–5.

2. Brasidas *métrios*: Thuc. 4.81.2–3, 105.2, 108.2–3. Illustrated: 4.84–88. Leotychidas and Pausanias: Rahe, *SFAW*, preface to Part I and Chapter 1. Brasidas envied, prospects doubted, peace sought: Thuc. 4.108.6–7, 117.1–2, 5.12–13, 15 with Gomme, *HCT*, III 584; Brunt, *SPSAW*, 255–80 (at 275–77), reprinted in Brunt, *SGHT*, 84–111 (at 106–9); Kagan, *AW*, 302–3; and Hutchinson, *Attrition*, 77, 79–80, 82–83, 93–94. One-year truce: Thuc. 4.117–19. Cf. Lendon, *SoW*, 343–44, who toys with the idea that the Athenians were afraid of a general revolt.

3. Terms of truce and those who swore to uphold it: Thuc. 4.118–19 and Diod. 12.72.5 with Gomme, *HCT*, III 593–607, 701; Kagan, *AW*, 305–8 (esp. n. 11); Hornblower, *CT*, II 356–75; and Lendon, *SoW*, 344–46. If Atalante is not mentioned, it is perhaps because the Opuntian Locrians were not a party to the agreement. Subsequent battle between Tegea and Mantineia: Thuc. 4.134.1–2 with Lendon, *SoW*, 352–54.

4. Announcement of truce, dispute over Scione: Thuc. 4.122 and Diod. 12.72.6 with Kagan, *AW*, 309–10; Lazenby, *PW*, 96; and Lendon, *SoW*, 347–49. I do not share Kagan's conviction that it was inevitable that the Lacedaemonians discover that Brasidas had lied.

5. Subsidy cut: Thuc. 4.83.5–6. Mende revolts, Brasidas embraces, women and children evacuated, hoplites and peltasts sent: 4.123 and Diod. 12.72.7 with Gomme, *HCT*, III 612; Kagan, *AW*, 310; Hornblower, *CT*, II 388–90; and Lendon, *SoW*, 348–49. Wine of Mende: Alexander K. Cambitoglou and John K. Papadopoulos, "Historical and Topographical Introduction," in Cambitoglou, Papadopoulos, and Olwen Tudor Jones, *Torone I: The Excavations of 1975, 1976, and 1978* (Athens: Archaiologikē Hetaireia, 2001), Pt. 1, 37–88 (at 58–61). See also *IACP* no. 584. Abortive

Potidaea venture: Thuc. 4.135 with Gomme, *HCT*, III 626; Lendon, *SoW*, 354; and Hutchinson, *Attrition*, 88. Note Aen. Tact. 36.1.

6. Nicias and Nicostratus at Mende and Scione: Thuc. 4.129.2–131.2, 133.4; Diod. 12.72.8–10; and perhaps *IG* I³ 76 with Benjamin D. Meritt, "Scione, Mende, and Torone," *AJA* 27:4 (October–November 1923): 447–60 (at 447–51); Geske, *Nicias*, 132–41; and Hutchinson, *Attrition*, 86–88. Methone: *IACP* no. 541 and Richard Janko, "From Gabii and Gordion to Eretria and Methone: The Rise of the Greek Alphabet," *BICS* 58 (2015): 1–32. Nicostratus' Thracian connections: Matthew A. Sears, *Athens, Thrace, and the Shaping of Athenian Leadership* (New York: Cambridge University Press, 2013), 79–87. Cf. Westlake, *Individuals*, 157–58; Kagan, *AW*, 311–14; Hornblower, *CT*, II 402–7; and Hutchinson, *Attrition*, 87, who suppose Polydamidas a Spartiate with Lendon, *SoW*, 350–52 (with 501 n. 63). Note Eupolis F246 (PCG). On 26 June 2017, I visited the Mende, the beach on which Nicias first landed, and the environs of Scione.

7. Invasion of Lyncus: Thuc. 4.124.1–129.1 with Gomme, *HCT*, III 612–19; Hornblower, *CT*, II 390–402; Lazenby, *PW*, 97–98; Lendon, *SoW*, 349–50; and Hutchinson, *Attrition*, 84–85. Perdiccas turns on Brasidas: Thuc. 4.132.1–2 and perhaps also *IG* I³ 76 and 89 with Gomme, *HCT*, III 621–23; Kagan, *AW*, 314–15; James T. Chambers, "Perdiccas, Thucydides and the Greek City States," *Ancient Macedonia* 4 (1986): 139–45 (at 143–45); Lendon, *SoW*, 352; and Hutchinson, *Attrition*, 85–86. The dating of *IG* I³ 89 is in dispute: Hornblower, *CT*, II 407–8.

8. Evidence Ischagoras favors peace: Thuc. 5.21.1–3. Principles governing the composition of Spartan embassies: Arist. *Pol.* 1271a24–25, which I read more broadly than the immediate context requires. Commissioners to report back and young men to serve as *árchontes:* Thuc. 4.132.3 with Gomme, *HCT*, III 623–24, and Hornblower, *CT*, II 408–10. Cf. Kagan, *AW*, 315–16; Lendon, *SoW*, 352; and Hutchinson, *Attrition*, 86 who think the dispatch of these young men and their subsequent installation as *árchontes* in the cities an act unfriendly to Brasidas apt to be unwelcome in those cities, with Westlake, *Individuals*, 161 n. 1. Awareness that Lacedaemonian regime dependent on isolation, illegal for young men to go abroad and rationale: Rahe, *SR*, Chapter 1 (esp. notes 4 and 61 in context). Note Pl. *Leg.* 12.949e–953e and Arist. *Pol.* 1332b12–1333a16.

9. Outer circuit in the north at Amphipolis completed, palisade added to encompass the bridge: Thuc. 4.103.5, 5.10.6 with W. Kendrick Pritchett, "Amphipolis Restudied," in *SAGT*, III 298–346 (at 335–37), and Hornblower, *CT*, II 330, 447.

10. End of truce, renewal of war delayed: Thuc. 5.1 with Gomme, *HCT*, III 629–30; Hornblower, *CT*, II 421–22; and Lendon, *SoW*, 354–55, who speculates that the delay had something to do with Apollo.

11. Capture of Artaphernes, dispatch of Athenian embassy, news of Artaxerxes' demise: Thuc. 4.50.3. Death of Artaxerxes, assassination of Xerxes II, civil war in the Achaemenid realm, victory of Ochus: Ctesias *FGrH* 688 F15.47–51; Diod. 12.64.1, 71.1; and Paus. 6.5.7 with Leo Depuydt, *From Xerxes' Murder (465) to Arridaios' Execution (317): Updates to Achaemenid Chronology* (Oxford: BAR, 2008), 13–34. Treaty negotiated by Epilycus with Darius II: Andoc. 3.29, read with an eye to what Theopompus of Chios *FGrH* 115 F153–54 emphatically denies, and *ML* no. 70 (with the addendum added in the 1988 edition) = *IG* I³ 227 = *O&R* no. 157, which strongly suggests that Theopompus is in error and that these negotiations actually took place. Date ratified: note 13, below.

12. Persian ethnocentrism: Hdt. 1.134.2. Achaemenid emphasis on Persian identity: Rahe, *PC*, Chapter 1. Importance of the seven conspirators: Hdt. 3.84.2. It is telling that Darius II later appointed a Babylonian, where hitherto only Iranians had served, as satrap of Syria: Matthew Stolper, "Bēlšhunu the Satrap," in *Language, Literature, and History: Philological and Historical Studies Presented to Erica Reiner*, ed. Francesca Rochberg-Halton (New Haven, CT: Yale University Press, 1987), 389–402. Pissouthnes son of Xerxes' full brother Hystaspes, satrap at Sardis: Thuc. 1.115.3–5, 3.31.1, 34.2, read in light of Hdt. 7.64.2, with Lewis, *SP*, 55. Rebellions of Artyphius and Pissouthnes, dependence of both on Greek hoplites, Athenian Lycon commands Pissouthnes' mercenaries, Tissaphernes son of Hydarnes sent with two colleagues to quash, becomes satrap, marries Ochus' daughter: Ctesias *FGrH* 688 F15.51–55 with Briant, *CA*, 588–92, 973–74. Tissaphernes first mentioned as satrap of Sardis by Thucydides: 8.5.4–5. Timing of rebellion and Tissaphernes'

succession as satrap at Sardis inferred from Thucydides' report that Tissaphernes' hyparch Arsaces recruited exiled Delians from Pharnaces' satrapy for warfare in 422 or the first half of 421: 8.108.4–5, read in light of 5.1 and 32.1, with Andrewes, *HCT,* V 12–18, 356–57; Lewis, *SP,* 77–81; Hornblower, *CT,* II 423–24, III 764–71; and Briant, *CA,* 591. Cf., however, John O. Hyland, *Persian Interventions: The Achaemenid Empire, Athens and Sparta, 450–386 BCE* (Baltimore: Johns Hopkins University Press, 2018), 43–45.

13. Time required for journey from Ephesus to Susa: Hdt. 5.52–54, 8.98; Xen. *Cyr.* 8.6.17–18 with Henry P. Colburn, "Connectivity and Communication in the Achaemenid Empire," *JESHO* 56 (2013): 29–52. On the agreement reached at this time, see Henry Theodore Wade-Gery, "The Peace of Callias," in *Athenian Studies Presented to W. S. Ferguson, HSPh* Supplement I (1940), 121–56 (at 127–32), reprinted in Wade-Gery, *EGH,* 201–32 (at 207–11), and Lewis, *SP,* 76–79. Wade-Gery to the contrary notwithstanding, given the timing of Artaxerxes' death, it is clear that the treaty's ratification and promulgation at Athens cannot predate the summer of 422: Alec Blamire, "Epilycus' Negotiations with Persia," *Phoenix* 29:1 (Spring 1975): 21–26. It is, moreover, as Blamire argues, highly unlikely that the treaty was negotiated after the Peace of Nicias: cf., however, Antony E. Raubitschek, "The Treaties between Athens and Persia," *GRBS* 5:3 (1964): 151–59 (at 154–58), reprinted in Raubitschek, *The School of Hellas: Essays on Greek History, Archaeology, and Literature,* ed. Dirk Obbink and Paul A. Vander Waerdt (New York: Oxford University Press, 1991), 3–10 (at 5–9), and Wesley E. Thompson, "The Athenian Treaties with Haliai and Dareios the Bastard," *Klio* 53 (1971): 119–24.

14. Dispatch of Cleon: Thuc. 5.2.1, Diod. 12.73.2. Athenian hoplites reluctant to serve under Cleon: Thuc. 5.7.2. Cf. Kagan, *AW,* 317–18, who cannot bring himself to believe that Athenians could have given Cleon an independent command, with Cawkwell, *TPW,* 67.

15. Cleon at Torone: Thuc. 5.2.1–3.4 and Diod. 12.73.2–3 with Gomme, *HCT,* III 629–32; Kagan, *AW,* 319–21; Hornblower, *CT,* II 424–28; Lendon, *SoW,* 355–56; and Hutchinson, *Attrition,* 88–89.

16. Cleon tarries at Eion: Thuc. 5.6.1–2, Diod. 12.73.3 with Hutchinson, *Attrition,* 89. The suggestion—first advanced by Allen B. West and Benjamin D. Meritt, "Cleon's Amphipolitan Campaign and the Assessment List of 421," *AJA* 29:1 (January–March 1925): 59–69, restated with great vehemence by Arthur Geoffrey Woodhead, "Thucydides' Portrait of Cleon," *Mnemosyne* 4th ser., 13:4 (1960): 289–317 (esp. 297–98, 303–6), and subsequently embraced by many another scholar since—that at this time Cleon recovered a host of other cities for Athens and that, out of hostility to the man, Thucydides suppressed the fact is unfounded, as Arnold W. Gomme, "Thucydides and Kleon: The Second Battle of Amphipolis," *Ellenika* 13 (1954): 1–10 (at 4 n. 2), reprinted in Gomme, *More Essays in Greek History and Literature* (Oxford: Basil Blackwell, 1962), 112–21 (at 115. n. 2), and *HCT,* III 636, intimated; and W. Kendrick Pritchett, "The Woodheadean Interpretation of Kleon's Amphipolitan Campaign," *Mnemosyne* 4th ser., 26:4 (1973): 376–86, demonstrated in detail. Cf. Lafargue, *Cléon,* 73–75.

17. Outer circuit in the north now complete: note Thuc. 4.102.3–4 (where Hagnon's plan is described), cf. 4.103.4–106.4 (where only the *pólisma* appears to be fully fortified), with 5.8.4–10.1, 5–7, 11.1 (where the outer circuit in the north has clearly been completed); and see Pritchett, "Amphipolis Restudied," 298–346 (esp. 312–16, 335–41); Dimitrios Lazaridis, "Les Fortifications d'Amphipolis," in *La Fortification dans l'histoire du monde grec,* ed. Pierre Leriche and Henri Tréziny (Paris: Editions du Centre national de la recherche scientifique, 1986), 31–38 (esp. 36); and Hornblower, *CT,* II 325–27, 330, 447. Cleon's plan: Thuc. 5.7.3, 5 with Nicholas Jones, "The Topography and Strategy of the Battle of Amphipolis in 422 B.C.," *CSCA* 10 (1977): 71–104 (at 84–85). *Mēchanaí* as scaling ladders and battering rams: W. Kendrick Pritchett, "Akarnanian Walls and Scaling Ladders," in *SAGT,* VIII 115–43 (at 124–41).

18. Brasidas summons allies, situates himself on Cerdylium: Thuc. 5.6.3–5 with Gomme, *HCT,* III 636–37; Hornblower, *CT,* II 437; and Hutchinson, *Attrition,* 89.

19. Decision to conduct reconnaissance: Thuc. 5.7.1–2 with Hutchinson, *Attrition,* 89–90. Cf. Kagan, *AW,* 324, who dismisses Thucydides' testimony on the grounds that Cleon's "record of achievement" as a general was "amazing," and Lendon, *SoW,* 357–58, 502 n. 75, who echoes Kagan's

judgment, rejects Thucydides' testimony concerning Cleon's intentions, and suggests, instead, that he marched to Amphipolis to issue a challenge to Brasidas and to mock him if he failed to take it up.

20. Cleon's mood and expectations: Thuc. 5.7.3.

21. Brasidas returns to Amphipolis: Thuc. 5.8.1. That Clearidas was among Thucydides' informants seems highly likely—for the reasons spelled out in detail by Henry D. Westlake, "Thucydides, Brasidas, and Clearidas," *GRBS* 21:4 (1980): 333–39, reprinted in Westlake, *Studies*, 78–83. But I think it unlikely that he was the historian's main source for the thinking and conduct of Brasidas prior to the final Amphipolis campaign. There is much that Thucydides seems to know that he can only have learned from the man himself.

22. Vulnerability of army on the march: Veg. *Mil.* 3.6. Cleon climbs hill, Brasidas prepares surprise attack: Thuc. 5.7.3–10.1 with Pritchett, "Amphipolis Restudied," 298–346, who describes the topography in detail on the basis of the archaeological work done by Dimitrios Lazaridis. See also Hornblower, *CT,* II 438–45. For Lazaridis' field reports, see Chapter 1, note 26, above. Pritchett's account may need adjustment in one particular: there was an entrance to the city, unknown when he wrote, which might be the Thracian Gates, on the town's eastern wall alongside its acropolis: Chaido Koukouli-Chrysanthaki, "Excavating Classical Amphipolis," in *Excavating Classical Culture: Recent Archaeological Discoveries in Greece,* ed. Maria Stamatopoulou and Marina Yeroulanou (Oxford: BAR International Series, 2002), 57–73 (at 66). Brasidas' recent recruits and his efforts to equip them with the hoplite panoply: Diod. 12.68.5.

23. Cleon at the vantage point: Thuc. 5.7.4–5.

24. Battle of Amphipolis: Thuc. 5.10.2–10, 11.2–3 with Hornblower, *CT,* II 445–49; Lazenby, *PW,* 101–4; and Hutchinson, *Attrition,* 90–92. Cf. the boilerplate supplied by Diod. 12.74.1–2, where the Greek is frequently misread as containing an assertion that Cleon died heroically. Inscription: Paus. 1.29.11–13 with Gomme, *HCT,* III 659. The hoplite and his *aspís:* Rahe, *SR,* Chapter 3 (with the extensive secondary literature cited in notes 44–61). As scholars will notice, in my treatment of this part of Thucydides' narrative, I have adopted as my working hypothesis that it, like the other narrative passages in Thucydides, can in most, if not quite all, particulars be made to make sense without doing violence to the text. The alternative approach, adopted by the majority of scholars in recent decades, has been to suppose that the story has been skewed in nearly every respect to make Cleon look bad. Cf., for example, Woodhead, "Thucydides' Portrait of Cleon," 289–317; Barry Baldwin, "Cleon's Strategy at Amphipolis," *AClass* 11 (1968): 211–14; Virginia J. Hunter, *Thucydides: The Artful Reporter* (Toronto: Hakkert, 1973), 30–41; Kagan, *AW,* 321–30; Mitchell, "Kleon's Amphipolitan Campaign: Aims and Results," 172–73, 181–86; Lendon, *SoW,* 357–61 (with the attendant notes); and Lafargue, *Cléon,* 76–81—the last two of whom take this presumption as an invitation to do thoroughgoing rewrites of Thucydides' account. That the Athenian historian despised Cleon, that he went out of his way to highlight the defects he discerned in the man's character, and that, on at least one occasion, he attributes the man's conduct to a disreputable motive that may not have loomed that large in his calculations is clear: see Gomme, "Thucydides and Kleon: The Second Battle of Amphipolis," 1–10, reprinted in Gomme, *More Essays in Greek History and Literature,* 112–21, and Westlake, *Individuals,* 75–83. But that Thucydides was wrong to loathe Cleon and single him out for special attention and that he mischaracterized the man and systematically misrepresented his intentions and conduct as a statesman and general—this is by no means clear. For a more sober and judicious assessment of Thucydides' treatment of Cleon than can be found elsewhere (even in Gomme and Westlake), see Cawkwell, *TPW,* 56–74 (esp. 59–69).

25. Amphipolis honors Brasidas: Thuc. 5.10.11–11.1 and Arist. *NE* 1134b23. Note Diod. 12.74.3–4. Cf. Gomme, *HCT,* III 654–56, with Irad Malkin, *Religion and Colonization in Ancient Greece* (Leiden: Brill, 1987), 228–32, and see Hornblower, *CT,* II 449–56, and Debnar, *SSL,* 197–200. On the man and Thucydides' treatment of him, opinions vary: note Westlake, *Individuals,* 148–65; cf. Graham Wylie, "Brasidas—Great Commander or Whiz Kid?" *QUCC* n.s. 41:2 (1992): 75–95, with Jeannine Boëldieu-Trevet, "Brasidas: La Naissance de l'art du commandement," in *Esclavage, guerre, économie en Grèce ancienne: Hommage à Yvon Garland,* ed. Pierre Brulé and

Jacques Oulhen (Rennes: Presses Universitaires de Rennes, 1997), 147–58; and see Hutchinson, *Attrition*, 65–94. I think strategically sound Brasidas' overall view that, where there was something of genuine value at stake and the Spartiates were not themselves in substantial numbers at risk, his compatriots had everything to gain and next to nothing to lose from the audacity he customarily displayed. The Spartan Achilles: Pl. *Symp.* 221c with J. Gordon Howie, "The *Aristeia* of Brasidas: Thucydides' Presentation of Events at Pylos and Amphipolis," *Papers of the Langford Latin Seminar* 12 (2005): 207–84. Building, cist grave, larnax with bones of a man and a gold wreath: Chaido Koukouli-Chrysanthaki, "Excavating Classical Amphipolis," 60–61 (with figure 2), and "Amphipolis," in *Brill's Companion to Ancient Macedon: Studies in the Archaeology and History of Macedon, 650 BC to 300 AD*, ed. Robin Lane Fox (Leiden: Brill, 2011), 409–36 (at 415). The larnax and gold wreath can be found in the museum built on top of the find-spot.

26. Ramphias and his companions: Thuc. 5.12–13 (read in light of 3.93) and *IG* I³ 92 with Gomme, *HCT*, III 657; Irad Malkin, *Myth and Territory in the Spartan Mediterranean* (Cambridge: Cambridge University Press, 1994), 224–25; Hornblower, *CT*, II 457–58; and Lendon, *SoW*, 504 n. 85.

27. Spartan eagerness for peace: Thuc. 5.14.3–15.1 with Brunt, *SPSAW*, 277, reprinted in Brunt, *SGHT*, 108–9; Gomme, *HCT*, III, 658–59; Kagan, *AW*, 333–36; Lewis, *AW*, 430; Hornblower, *CT*, II 460–61; and Lendon, *SoW*, 363–65. Mantineian and Elean absence from Plataea in 479: Rahe, *PC*, Chapter 8 and Epilogue. Argive-Tegean axis in and after the 460s: Rahe, *SFAW*, Chapter 3 and Part II.

28. Freedom thought to require subjection of others: J. A. O. Larsen, "Freedom and its Obstacles in Ancient Greece," *CPh* 57:4 (October 1962): 230–34. To the material Larsen collected, one can add Pl. *Lys.* 207d–210d (esp. 210b). Athens and Thasos: Rahe, *SFAW*, Chapter 3. Troubles with Samos and Mytilene: Chapters 1 and 3, above.

29. Mantineian imperialism, Tegean and Spartan opposition: Thuc. 4.134.1–2, 5.33 with Gomme and Andrewes, *HCT*, IV 31–34; Thomas Heine Nielsen, "A Survey of Dependent *Poleis* in Classical Arkadia," in *More Studies in the Ancient Greek Polis*, ed. Mogens Herman Hansen and Kurt Raaflaub (Stuttgart: Franz Steiner Verlag, 1996), 63–105 (at 65–70, 79–84); Björn Forsén, "Population and Political Strength of Some Southeastern Arkadian *Poleis*," in *Further Studies in the Ancient Greek Polis*, ed. Pernille Flensted-Jensen (Stuttgart: Franz Steiner Verlag, 2000), 35–55 (at 51–54); and Hornblower, *CT*, III 78–79. Elean imperialism, Spartan opposition: Thuc. 5.31.1–5 with Gomme and Andrewes, *HCT*, IV 26–29; Caroline Falkner, "Sparta and Lepreon in the Archidamian War (Thuc. 5.31.2–5)," *Historia* 48:4 (4th Quarter 1999): 385–94; Thomas Heine Nielsen, "A Polis as Part of a Larger Identity Group: Glimpses from the History of Lepreon," *C&M* 56 (2005): 57–89 (esp. 58–74); and Hornblower, *CT*, III 71–74. For the background, see James Roy, "Hegemonial Structures in Late Archaic and Early Classical Elis and Sparta," in *Sparta: Comparative Approaches*, ed. Stephen Hodkinson (Swansea: Classical Press of Wales, 2009), 69–88, and Matt Kõiv, "Early History of Elis and Pisa: Invented or Evolving Traditions?" *Klio* 95:1 (2013): 315–68, whose judicious treatment of the legends concerning the origins of these communities and their early relations is a welcome corrective to the hyperskepticism that characterizes much of the current scholarship.

30. Athenians ready to treat: Thuc. 5.14.1–2, Ar. *Pax* 665–69. Cf. Diod. 12.74.5 with Gomme, *CT*, III 658; Lewis, *AW*, 430–32; and Hornblower, *CT*, II 459. Impact of Delium on Athenian morale: Xen. *Mem.* 3.5.4. State of Athenian finances: Gomme, *HCT*, III 687–89; Kagan, *AW*, 336–37; Kallet-Marx, *MENP*, 152–206; Samons, *EO*, 171–211; and Alec Blamire, "Athenian Finance, 454–404 B.C.," *Hesperia* 70:1 (January–March 2001), 99–126 (at 106–12). See also Lisa Kallet, "Epigraphic Geography: The Tribute Quota Fragments Assigned to 421/0–415/4," *Hesperia* 73:4 (October–December 2004): 465–96 (esp. 490–95), and note what is implied at Thuc. 6.12.1, 26.

31. Lacedaemon "ill-thought of in the extreme and regarded with contempt": Thuc. 5.28.2 with Gomme, *HCT*, IV 24, and Hornblower, *CT*, III 64. Peace of little advantage to Athens: Brunt, *SPSAW*, 277, reprinted in Brunt, *SGHT*, 109; Kagan, *AW*, 336–41; Lazenby, *PW*, 106; and Lendon, *SoW*, 365–67.

32. Proponents of war dead, proponents of peace active, personal motives: Thuc. 5.16.1–17.1 (read in light of Ar. *Pax* 261–86) with Westlake, *Individuals,* 93–96; Gomme, *HCT,* III, 659–64; Hornblower, *CT,* II 462–67; and Geske, *Nicias,* 141–61. Thucydides was not alone in bringing this charge against Cleon: Ar. *Eq.* 801–9. Cf. Kagan, *AW,* 331–33. Excessive piety of Nicias: Thuc. 7.50.4.

33. Ten negotiators from each city: Diod.12.75.4. Threat of fort: Thuc. 5.17.2. with Kagan, *AW,* 341–42; Henry D. Westlake, "The Progress of Epiteichismos," *CQ* n.s. 33:1 (1983): 12–24, reprinted in Westlake, *Studies,* 34–49; and Lendon, *SoW,* 365. Seventeen take the oath: Thuc. 5.19. The number of seventeen almost certainly reflects the inclusion of the two kings, who are listed first; the ephor eponymous, who is listed next, and his four colleagues; and the ten Spartan *xúnedroi:* see Antony Andrewes and David M. Lewis, "Note on the Peace of Nicias," *JHS* 77:2 (1957): 177–80, who also make a compelling case for the view that the Athenians elected one commissioner per tribe and that they appear in tribal order on Thucydides' list of the seventeen Athenians who swore. Five Spartan villages and Lacedaemonian propensity for appointing commissions of five: Rahe, *SR,* Chapter 4 (esp. n. 15).

34. Peace of Nicias, dating, and terms: Thuc. 5.17.2–20.3. Cf. Diod. 12.74.5–6, Plut. *Nic.* 9.3–9 with Gomme, *HCT,* III 664–87; Andrewes, *HCT,* IV 18–21; Kagan, *AW,* 342–45; Lewis, *AW,* 431–32; Ernst Baltrusch, *Symmachie und Spondai: Untersuchungen zum griechischen Völkerrecht der archaischen und klassischen Zeit (8–5 Jahrhunderts v. Chr.)* (Berlin: Walter de Gruyter, 1994), 169–85; Hornblower, *CT,* II 467–93; and Lendon, *SoW,* 362. On Panactum, see Thuc. 5.3.5.

35. Boeotians, Megarians, Corinthians Eleans vote against, refuse to abide by Peace of Nicias; Chalcidians and others in the Thraceward region balk: Thuc. 5.17.2, 22.1–2, 31.6, 35.3 and Ar. *Pax* 466, 481, 500–502 with Gomme, *HCT,* III 665, 690–91; Kagan, *PNSE,* 17–24; Salmon, *WC,* 320–23; Hornblower, *CT,* II 469, 478, 495–96, III 83, 60–61; and Lendon, *SoW,* 362–63. Note also Michael Zahrnt, *Olynth und die Chalkidier: Untersuchungen zur Staatenbildung auf der Chalkidischen Halbinsel im 5. and 4. Jahrhundert V. Chr.* (Munich: Beck, 1971), 66–79.

36. At Sybota, the Corinthians had deployed ninety triremes: Thuc.1.46.1. Eight years after the Athenian blockade had been lifted, when the Spartans hoped to deploy a navy of one hundred new galleys, they requisitioned from Corinth only fifteen triremes: 8.3.2. Even if we suppose, as we no doubt should, that the Corinthians maintained a flotilla in the Corinthian Gulf and that some of the ships that returned from Sicily were Corinthian vessels, the evidence suggests that, as a maritime power, Corinth was nothing like what she had once been. Note 7.17.4, 34, 8.13, and see Andrewes, *HCT,* V 10, and Hornblower, *CT,* III 757.

37. Alliance proposed in 425: Chapter 5, above. Motives for alliance in 421, terms and date: Thuc. 5.22.2–25.1, 5.39.3. Nicias the chief proponent: Plut. *Nic.* 10.2. Cf. Diod. 12.75.1 with Gomme, *HCT,* III 691–98; Andrewes, *HCT,* IV 17–23; Kagan, *PNSE,* 24–28; and Hornblower, *CT,* II 495–500, III 41–43. Cf. Philip S. Peek, "Spartan and Argive Motivation in Thucydides 5.22.2," *AJPh* 118:3 (Autumn 1997): 363–70, and Cinzia S. Bearzot, "Argo nel V secolo: Ambizioni egemoniche, crisi interne, condizionamenti esterni," in *Argo: Una Demcrazia diversa,* ed. Cinzia S. Bearzot and Franca Landucci Gattinoni (Milan: Vita e pensiero, 2006), 105–46 (at 124–26). The fact that the agreement to act in tandem in making war and negotiating alliances and peace pacts (Thuc. 5.39.3) is not expressly mentioned in the document that Thucydides quotes has given rise to considerable discussion: Gomme and Andrewes, *HCT,* IV 43–45, and Hornblower, *CT,* III 92–93. Delegates, though dismissed, tarry at Lacedaemon: cf. Thuc. 5.22.2 with 27.1; see Gomme, *HCT,* III 691, and Rood, *Thucydides,* 95 n. 55; and consider W. Robert Connor, *CPh* 79:3 (July 1984): 230–35 (at 233 n. 2). Cf. Andrewes, *HCT,* IV 22–23; Dover, *HCT,* V 428–31; and Hornblower, *CT,* II 495–96, III 58–60. Note also Ste. Croix, *OPW,* 97, who suggests that a clause similar to the one concerning a helot revolt was included in Lacedaemon's treaties with her allies.

38. Armistice attended by jealousy and suspicion: Thuc 5.26.1–3 with Paul A. Rahe, "The Peace of Nicias," in *The Making of Peace,* ed. Williamson Murray and James Lacey (Cambridge: Cambridge University Press, 2009), 31–69, and Karl Walling, "Thucydides on Policy, Strategy, and War Termination," *Naval War College Review* 66:4 (Autumn 2013): 47–85 (esp. 47–48, 77–78). For other assessments of the peace and alliance, see Kagan, *AW,* 345–49, and *PNSE,* 17–32; Rood, *Thucydides,* 78–80; Lazenby, *PW,* 106–8; and Lendon, *SoW,* 369–81.

Chapter 7. The Peloponnesus in Flux

Epigraph: Thomas Hobbes, *Leviathan* 1.13, in *The Clarendon Edition of the Works of Thomas Hobbes: Leviathan 2. The English and Latin Texts (i)*, ed. Noel Malcolm (Oxford: Clarendon Press, 2012), 192.

1. See *Great Strategic Rivalries: From the Classical World to the Cold War*, ed. James Lacey (Oxford: Oxford University Press, 2016).

2. Thucydides on Corinth's goal: 5.25.1 with Kagan, *PNSE*, 33–36, and Rood, *Thucydides*, 95–97. On Corinth's aim and expectations, opinions differ markedly. Cf. Henry D. Westlake, "Corinth and the Argive Coalition," *AJPh* 61:4 (1940): 413–21, who supposes that the Corinthians wanted Argos to take Sparta's place and renew the war with Athens, with Guy T. Griffith, "The Union of Corinth and Argos (392–386 BC)," *Historia* 1:2 (1950): 236–56 (at 236–38), who takes as indicative of her motives Corinth's claim that Lacedaemon was out to enslave her allies; note Donald Kagan, "Corinthian Diplomacy after the Peace of Nicias," *AJPh* 81:3 (July 1960): 291–310, and *PNSE*, 24, 33–38, who (rightly, in my opinion) believes that Corinth's aim was to force Lacedaemon back into the war with Athens but predicates his analysis of Corinthian conduct on divisions not known to have existed at Corinth; consider Robin Seager, "After the Peace of Nicias: Politics and Diplomacy, 421–416 B.C.," *CQ* 26:2 (1976): 249–69 (at 254), who supposes that Corinth's only motive was revenge; and see Salmon, *WC*, 320–29, who believes that hostility to Athens was Corinth's chief motive and who suggests that she flirted with getting Argos to take the lead against the Athenians but was more than ready to rejoin Lacedaemon if the latter could be induced to renew the war.

3. Thucydides' location while in exile: Chapter 3, note 49, in context, above. Extraneous events ignored: Hornblower, *CT*, III 55–57. Cf., for example, *IG* I³ 370 = *ML* no. 77 = *O&R* no. 170, at lines 2–10, on the campaign Euthydemos conducted in Thrace in 418.

4. Statesmen at sea: Henry D. Westlake, "Thucydides and the Uneasy Peace: A Study in Political Incompetence," *CQ* n.w. 21:2 (November 1971): 315–25, reprinted in Westlake, *Studies*, 84–96. Misperception the norm: Rood, *Thucydides*, 83–108. Thucydides' pedagogical focus: Paul A. Rahe, "Thucydides as Educator," in *The Past as Prologue: The Importance of History to the Military Profession*, ed. Williamson Murray and Richard Hart Sinnreich (Cambridge: Cambridge University Press, 2006), 95–110.

5. Argive with Peloponnesian delegation heading for Susa: Thuc. 2.67.1. Note Hdt. 7.137. Argive tips off Corinthians regarding Nicias' incursion: Thuc. 4.42.3. Oligarchic faction at Argos willing to do Sparta's bidding: 5.76.2–3. Cf. Lazenby, *PW*, 127–28, who is too quick to deny the significance of this information. Corinth and Argos long at odds: Rahe, *SFAW*, Chapter 4. See also Cinzia S. Bearzot, "Argo nel V secolo: Ambizioni egemoniche, crisi interne, condizionamenti esterni," in *Argo: Una Democrazia diversa*, ed. Cinzia S. Bearzot and Franca Landucci Gattinoni (Milan: Vita e pensiero, 2006), 105–46 (esp. 106–22), and Hornblower, *CT*, III 57. Likely political preference of the Argives approached: Thuc. 5.76.2–3 with Donald Kagan, "Argive Politics and Policy after the Peace of Nicias," *CPh* 57:4 (October 1962): 209–18, and Salmon, *WC*, 326–27. Role played by *xenía* in the ephors' dealings with these Argives: Plut. *Nic.* 10.7–8 with Lynette G. Mitchell, *Greeks Bearing Gifts: The Public Use of Private Relationships in the Greek World, 435–323 BC* (Cambridge: Cambridge University Press, 2002), 51–55. For the institution of *xenía* as such, see Gabriel Herman, *Ritualised Friendship and the Greek City* (Cambridge: Cambridge University Press, 1987). Thucydidean parsimony with Argive names deliberate: Simon Hornblower, "Thucydides and the Argives," in *Brill's Companion to Thucydides*, ed. Antonios Rengakos and Antonis Tsakmakis (Leiden: Brill, 2006), 615–28.

6. Corinthian agitation: Thuc. 5.25.1. Suspicion and contempt directed at Athens and Sparta alike: Diod. 12.75.1–5. Envoys stir up the Argives: Thuc. 5.27–28 with Andrewes, *HCT*, IV 17–23; Salmon, *WC*, 324; Kagan, *PNSE*, 37–40; Bearzot, "Argo nel V secolo," 126–31; and Hornblower, *CT*, III 58–62. Argive pretensions: Diod. 12.75.6.

7. Argos invites defensive alliance: Thuc. 5.27–28, 48.2. For the character of the Argive democracy, see the material collected in Rahe, *SFAW*, Chapter 3, note 31. Regarding the city's

prosperity, see also Ar. *Pax* 475–78 and Diod. 12.75.6 with Bearzot, "Argo nel V secolo," 121–22, and Catherine Morgan, "Debating Patronage: The Cases of Argos and Corinth," in *Pindar's Poetry, Patrons, and Festivals: From Archaic Greece to the Roman Empire*, ed. Simon Hornblower and Catherine Morgan (Oxford: Oxford University Press, 2007), 213–63 (at 249–63).

8. Argives establish elite hoplite force: Diod. 12.75.7, confirmed by Thuc. 5.67.2. Possible precedent: Hdt. 6.92.2, Thuc. 1.107.5. Political consequences: 5.76.2–3, 81.2, 82.2; Diod. 12.79.4–80.3; Plut. *Alc.* 15.3; Paus. 2.20.2; Arist. *Pol.* 1304a25 with Kagan, "Argive Politics and Policy after the Peace of Nicias," 209–18, and Hans van Wees, "Tyrants, Oligarchs, and Citizen Militias," in *Army and Power in the Ancient World*, ed. Angelos Chaniotis and Pierre Ducrey (Stuttgart: Franz Steiner Verlag, 2002), 61–82 (esp. 78). Cf. Gomme and Andrewes, *HCT*, IV 105–6, 149–51, where considerable ambivalence is evidenced; and Hornblower, *CT*, III 177–79, who is loath to suppose Thucydides' account incomplete and to give Ephorus his due.

9. Mantineia accepts Argive invitation: Thuc. 5.29.1 with Andrewes, *HCT*, IV 24–25; Hornblower, *CT*, III 65–67; and James Capreedy, "Losing Confidence in Sparta: The Creation of the Mantinean Symmachy," *GRBS* 54:3 (2014): 352–78. Strategic location of Mantineian empire: Thuc. 5.33 with Gomme and Andrewes, *HCT*, IV 31–34, and Hornblower, *CT*, III 78–79. Sciritis: *IACP*, 577.

10. Uproar in the Peloponnesus, treaty a source of suspicion, Corinthians identified as instigators: Thuc. 5.29.2–30.1 and Diod. 12.75.1–5 with Gomme and Andrewes, *HCT*, IV 25, and Hornblower, *CT*, III 67–68.

11. Spartan complaints, charge oaths about to be violated and injustice already done: Thuc. 5.30.1 with Hornblower, *CT*, III 68–69. On the agreement to accept majority rule, cf. Andrewes, *HCT*, IV 25–26, and Ste. Croix, *OPW*, 101–23 (esp. 101–2, 104, 110–11, 115–16, 118–20), who suppose this a feature of the Peloponnesian League, with Jon E. Lendon, "Thucydides and the 'Constitution' of the Peloponnesian League," *GRBS* 35:2 (1994): 159–77 (esp. 160–67), who suspects, as do I, that it was an agreement made on the eve of this particular war with an eye to promoting solidarity among highly disparate allies.

12. Canny Corinthian response to Spartan complaints: Thuc. 5.30.2–4 with Andrewes, *HCT*, IV 26; Kagan, *PNSE*, 40–42; and Hornblower, *CT*, III 69–71. Agreement that none of Lacedaemon's allies would lose any of their possessions and pertinence to Corinth's grievance regarding Sollium and Anactorium: Thuc. 5.31.5 with Lendon, "Thucydides and the 'Constitution' of the Peloponnesian League," 160–67.

13. Elean empire early on, Minyan cities seized and sacked in Herodotus' time: Rahe, *SFAW*, Chapter 3, note 42, in context, and James Roy, "Hegemonial Structures in Late Archaic and Early Classical Elis and Sparta," in *Sparta: Comparative Approaches*, ed. Stephen Hodkinson (Swansea: Classical Press of Wales, 2009), 69–88. Lepreum within the region which came to be called Triphylia: *IACP* no. 306 with Thomas Heine Nielsen, "*Triphylia*: An Experiment in Ethnic Construction and Political Organisation," in *Yet More Studies in the Ancient Greek Polis*, ed. Thomas Heine Nielsen (Stuttgart: Franz Steiner Verlag, 1997), 129–62, and "A Polis as Part of a Larger Identity Group: Glimpses from the History of Lepreon," *C&M* 56 (2005): 57–89 (esp. 58–74), who is far more confident that this region was not called Triphylia in the fifth century than an absence of positive evidence warrants in a case where the communities in the region are almost never mentioned and the region as such is never identified. Note Strabo 8.3.3, 30, 33, and see Kõiv, "Early History of Elis and Pisa." Triphylia treated in the 420s by Elis as part of Eleia: Thuc. 5.34.1, Ar. *Av.* 150. Lepreate Olympic victors proclaimed as Eleans: Paus. 5.5.3 with *IvO* 155. Lepreate hoplites at Plataea: Hdt. 9.28.4, *ML* no. 27.11.

14. Evidence Lepreum a dependency of Elis: Ar. *Av.* 149–50; Thuc. 5.31.2; Xen. *Hell.* 3.2.22–31; Strabo 8.3.30, 33; and Paus. 3.8.3, 5.5.3 with Antony Andrewes, "Argive *Perioikoi*," in *"Owls to Athens": Essays on Classical Subjects Presented to Sir Kenneth Dover*, ed. E. M. Craik (Oxford: Clarendon Press, 1990), 171–78 (at 172); James Roy, "The *Perioikoi* of Elis," in *The Polis as an Urban Centre and as a Political Community*, ed. Mogens Herman Hansen (Stuttgart: Franz Steiner Verlag, 1997), 282–320 (esp. 283–86, 289–99); and Nielsen, "*Triphylia*," 139–41. Epeioi a comparable case: Xen. *Hell.* 3.2.30–31.

15. Lepreum's quarrel with Elis, Spartan interference, Elis defects to Corinth and Argos, citing prewar agreement: Thuc. 5.31.1–5 with Gomme and Andrewes, *HCT*, IV 26–29; Caroline Falkner, "Sparta and Lepreon in the Archidamian War (Thuc. 5.31.2–5)," *Historia* 48:4 (4th Quarter 1999): 385–94; Hornblower, *CT*, III 71–74; and James Capreedy, "A League within a League: The Preservation of the Elean Symmachy," *CW* 101:4 (Summer 2008): 485–503 (esp. 494–99). Lepreum on border with Messenia, strategic significance: Thuc. 5.34.1 with Annalisa Paradiso and James Roy, "Lepreon and Phyrkos in 421–420," *Klio* 90:1 (2008): 27–35 (esp. 31–33).

16. Corinthians and Chalcidians ally with Argos, Tegea refuses option: Thuc. 5.31.6, 32.3–4 with Hornblower, *CT*, III 77. Cleandridas at Tegea: Rahe, *SFAW*, Chapter 6, note 12. Proud community: Maria Prezler, "Myth and History at Tegea—Local Tradition and Community Identity," in *Defining Ancient Arkadia*, ed. Thomas Heine Nielsen and James Roy (Copenhagen: Det Kongelige Danske Videnskabernes Selskab, 1999), 89–129.

17. Corinthians lose heart and become fearful: Thuc. 5.32.4 with Hornblower, *CT*, III 78. Boeotian, Megarian reluctance: Thuc. 5.31.6. Corinthian approach to Boeotians: 5.32.5–7. See Seager, "After the Peace," 254–55; Salmon, *WC*, 327–29; and Kagan, *PNSE*, 43–45. There is some disagreement regarding the procedures by means of which the ten-day truce was renewed: note Thuc. 5.26.2, and cf. Andrewes, *HCT*, IV 11, with Michael Arnush, "Ten-Day Armistices in Thucydides," *GRBS* 33:4 (1992): 329–53, and David Whitehead, "The Ten-Day Truce (Thucydides, 5.26.2, etc.)," in *Les Relations internationales*, ed. Edmond Frézouls and Anne Jacquemin (Paris: Diffusion de Boccard, 1995), 189–210, and see Hornblower, *CT*, III 47–48.

18. Pleistoanax liberates Parrhasia, razes fort at Cypsela: Thuc. 5.33.

19. Freed helots and *neodamódeis* settled at Lepreum: Thuc. 5.34.1 with Gomme and Andrewes, *HCT*, IV 34–36; Nielsen, "A Polis as Part of a Larger Identity Group," 67–74, 81; Paradiso and Roy, "Lepreon and Phyrkos in 421–420," 27–35; and Hornblower, *CT*, III 80–82. On the *neodamódeis*, who are first mentioned here, see Ronald F. Willetts, "The Neodamodeis," *CPh* 49:1 (January 1954): 27–32, and Masato Furuyama, "The Liberation of *Heilotai*: The Case of *Neodamodeis*," in *Forms of Control and Subordination in Antiquity*, ed. Toru Yuge and Masaoki Doi (Leiden: Brill, 1988), 364–68. The fact that they are said to have been brigaded with the Sciritae and *Brasídeioi* at Mantineia in the year 418 (Thuc. 5.67.1) but are not mentioned again when the role played in the battle by the Sciritae and *Brasídeioi* is discussed (5.68.3, 71.2, 72.3) suggests that their numbers were comparatively negligible. Belated, reluctant decision to treat those captured at Sphacteria as *homoíoi*: Thuc. 5.34.2, Diod. 12.76.1 with Gomme, *HCT*, IV 36, and Kagan, *PNSE*, 47–48.

20. Lots cast, Lacedaemon releases prisoners, mission of Ischagoras and his colleagues, cities refuse to honor terms, Clearidas drags his feet, Peloponnesians evacuate but Amphipolis not handed over: Thuc. 5.21, 34.1, 35.3–5 with Gomme, *HCT*, III 689–90; Henry D. Westlake, "Thucydides, Brasidas, and Clearidas," *GRBS* 21:4 (1980): 333–39 (esp. 337–39), reprinted in Westlake, *Studies*, 78–83 (esp. 80–82); and Hornblower, *CT*, II 493–94, III 82–84. Theophrastus on bribery by Nicias: Plut. *Nic.* 10.1.

21. Spartan prisoners sent home: Thuc. 5.24.2. Nicias' initiative: Plut. *Nic.* 10.8. See Kagan, *PNSE*, 26–32.

22. Spartan breach of peace, suspicion grows, helots withdrawn from Coryphasium: Thuc. 5.25.2, 35.2–7 with Kagan, *PNSE*, 19–20, 48–50.

23. Hyperbolus: Ar. *Pax* 680–81 with *Eq.* 1302–5, *Pax* 921, 1319 and Kagan, *PNSE*, 60–62. Alcibiades son of Cleinias: Davies, *APF* no. 600. Background, upbringing, military service, role as assessor, character, Spartan connection and name: Hdt. 8.17; Thuc. 5.43.2, 6.15–18, 89.2–4, 8.6.3; Pl. *Alc.* I 104a–c, 105a–e, 113b–114b, 121a–b, 123c, *Prt.* 309a–c, 316a, 320a, *Symp.* 215b–221b (with *Chrm.* 153a–c); Lys. 19.52; And. 4.11; Isoc. 5.58–61, 16.25–29; and Plut. *Alc.* 1–12 with Jean Hatzfeld, *Alcibiade: Étude sur l'histoire d'Athènes à la fin du Ve siècle*, 2nd edition (Paris: Presses Universitaires de France, 1951), 1–73; Gomme and Andrewes, *HCT*, IV 48–50; Kagan, *PNSE*, 62–65; Walter M. Ellis, *Alcibiades* (London: Routledge, 1989), 1–35; Hornblower, *CT*, III 99–102; and David Stuttard, *Nemesis: Alcibiades and the Fall of Athens* (Cambridge, MA: Harvard University Press, 2018), 10–97. Note also David Gribble, *Alcibiades and Athens: A Study in Literary Presentation* (Oxford: Clarendon Press, 1999).

24. Alcibiades' like-named grandfather resigns Spartan *proxenía*: Gomme and Andrewes, *HCT*, IV 50, and Rahe, *SFAW*, Chapter 4. Alcibiades' opposition to treaty and withdrawal from Coryphasium, opinion, motives: Thuc. 5.43.2–3, 45.2 and Plut. *Alc.* 14.1–5 with Hatzfeld, *Alcibiade*, 73–83; Kagan, *PNSE*, 60–62, 65; Hornblower, *CT*, III 102–3; and Stuttard, *Nemesis*, 97–101. Note also Thuc. 6.89.2–3.

25. Cleobulus and Xenares counsel the Boeotians and Corinthians: Thuc. 5.36 with Gomme and Andrewes, *HCT*, IV 38–41; Kagan, *PNSE*, 50–52; and Hornblower, *CT*, III 84–87. Cf. Kagan, *PNSE*, 52, who cannot see why the Boeotians would cooperate, with Seager, "After the Peace," 257, who sees the logic.

26. Corinthian oligarchy: Plut. *Dion* 53.2–4 with Salmon, *WC*, 231–39. Boeotian constitution: note Thuc. 4.91, 5.31.6, 37.4–38.4; Arist. *Pol.* 1278a25, 1321a26–29 (Thebes), Arist. ap. Pollux 10.165 (Orchomenos); Heracleid. F43 (Thespiae); and Paus. 9.13.6; then, see *Hell. Oxy.* 19.2–4 (Chambers) with I. A. F. Bruce, *An Historical Commentary on the Hellenica Oxyrhynchia* (Cambridge: Cambridge University Press, 1967), 102–9, 157–64, and Hornblower, *CT*, III 89–90.

27. Boeotians meet high-ranking Argives on the road, exact same proposal presented: Thuc. 5.37.2–3 (my emphasis). Cf. Gomme and Andrewes, *HCT*, IV 41; Seager, "After the Peace of Nicias," 257–58; and Kagan, *PNSE*, 52–53, who fail to reflect on what it was that caused these two Argives to intercept the Boeotians, with Thomas Kelly, "Cleobulus, Xenares, and Thucydides' Account of the Demolition of Panactum," *Historia* 21:2 (2nd Quarter 1972): 159–69 (at 159–62), who is surely right in suspecting that there was collusion between the ephors and these Argives. Cf., however, Rood, *Thucydides*, 99, and Hornblower, *CT*, III 87–88, who pay insufficient attention to the significance of the fact that the ephors know whom to tip off.

28. Preliminary proposal for alliance with Corinth and other cities, reticence required of Boetarchs, councils resist proposal, Argive alliance a nonstarter: Thuc. 5.37.4–38.4 with Gomme and Andrewes, *HCT*, IV 42–43, and Hornblower, *CT*, III 88–91. Cf. Kagan, "Corinthian Diplomacy after the Peace of Nicias," 302–6, and *PNSE*, 53–55, as well as Kelly, "Cleobulus, Xenares, and Thucydides' Account of the Demolition of Panactum," 162–63, who suppose the Corinthians opposed to a Spartan alliance with Argos and attribute to them an incapacity to appreciate the degree to which the Argive threat in the Peloponnesus was an obstacle to Lacedaemonian aggressiveness abroad.

29. Spartan request for prisoners and Panactum, separate alliance the price, Panactum razed, ancient agreement as pretext: Thuc. 5.39.2–3, 42.1 with Gomme and Andrewes, *HCT*, IV 43–45; Seager, "After the Peace of Nicias," 257–60; and Hornblower, *CT*, III 91–93, 98–99. Location of Panactum: Eugene Vanderpool, "Roads and Forts in Northwest Attica," *CSCA* 11 (1978): 227–45 (esp. 231–40). Significance: Mark H. Munn, "New Light on Panakton and the Attic-Boiotian Frontier," in *Boiotika: Vorträge vom 5. Internationalen Böotien-Kolloquium zu Ehren von Professor Dr. Siegfried Lauffer*, ed. Hartmut Beister and John Buckler (Munich: Editio Maris, 1989), 231–44.

30. Argives learn of Spartan-Boeotian alliance and of the demolition of Panactum before the Athenians and the Spartan authorities do: cf. Thuc. 5.40.1 with 5.42, and cf. Andrewes, *HCT*, IV 45, who thinks the discrepancy due to a slip on Thucydides' part, with Kelly, "Cleobulus, Xenares, and Thucydides' Account of the Demolition of Panactum," 159–69; Seager, "After the Peace of Nicias," 259–60 (with the notes); and Kagan, *PNSE*, 57–58, who rightly regard it as indicative of skullduggery and wrongly suppose Cleobulus and Xenares responsible. Cf. Rood, *Thucydides*, 101, who, in an effort to deny that disinformation was involved, posits close contact between the Argives and the Boeotians at a time when, Thucydides makes clear, the two were not in communication at all; and Hornblower, *CT*, III 93–94, who misunderstands Kelly's argument. Argives badly misinterpret meaning, panic and seek Spartan alliance: Thuc. 5.40.2–3 with Gomme and Andrewes, *HCT*, IV 46–47, and Hornblower, *CT*, III 94–96.

31. Terms of draft Spartan-Argive alliance: Thuc. 5.41 with Gomme and Andrewes, *HCT*, IV 47, and Hornblower, *CT*, III 96–97. Ancient duel: Hdt. 1.82.

32. Prisoners and Panactum restored to Athenians, Athenian bitterness over destruction of fort and Spartan-Boeotian alliance, Spartan envoys sent home: Thuc. 5.42 with Hornblower, *CT*, III 98–99. Cf. Gomme and Andrewes, *HCT*, IV 44–45, with Lazenby, *PW*, 277 n. 11.

33. Alcibiades intervenes at Argos, draws in: Thuc. 5.43.1–44.2, read in light of 6.61.3 with Herman, *Ritualised Friendship and the Greek City*, 148; Diod. 12.77.2. Cf. Gomme and Andrewes, *HCT*, IV 50, with Hornblower, *CT*, III 102–4, and see Hatzfeld, *Alcibiade*, 83–87; Kagan, *PNSE*, 65–66; and Stuttard, *Nemesis*, 101–4. Note Thuc. 6.89.2–3.

34. Philocharidas: Thuc. 4.119.2, 5.19, 21.1, 24. Endius Alcibiades' *xénos*: 8.6.3. Spartan practice of appointing to embassies men of differing views: Arist. *Pol.* 1271a24–25. Spartan embassy to head off Argive alliance, secure Coryphasium for Panactum, and make excuses for Boeotian alliance: Thuc. 5.44.3. Alcibiades' trick: 5.45; Plut. *Nic.* 10.4–6, *Alc.* 14.6–12 with Kagan, *PNSE*, 67–70; Ellis, *Alcibiades*, 37–40; Lazenby, *PW*, 109–10; and Hornblower, *CT*, III 104–7. Cf. Hatzfeld, *Alcibiade*, 87–93; Peter A. Brunt, "Thucydides and Alcibiades," *REG* 65:304 (1952): 59–96 (at 65–69), reprinted in Brunt, *SGHT*, 17–46 (at 22–24); Gomme and Andrewes, *HCT*, IV 50–53; and Stuttard, *Nemesis*, 104–7, who fail to recognize the necessity of courting Alcibiades and the significance of Plut. *Alc.* 14.6–12 (esp. 8–10) and therefore cannot see why the Spartan envoys should have been so cooperative; and Paolo A. Tuci, "*Hesychia* Spartana et *Neoteropoiia* Ateniese: Un Caso di manipolazione nelle trattative per le alleanze del 420 A.C.," *Aristonothos* 8 (2013): 71–104. Cf. Robert C. Kebric, "Implications of Alcibiades' Relationship with Endius," *Mnemosyne* 4th ser., 29:1 (1976): 72–78, and Herman, *Ritualised Friendship and the Greek City*, 146–50, who, for different reasons, think that Endius must have been party to Alcibiades' plot. It is, I believe, far more likely that he was indifferent to the machinations of his *xénos*—and perhaps even amused.

35. Thanks to earthquake, Nicias manages to get embassy sent to Lacedaemon; stymied by Xenares' associates: Thuc. 5.45.4–46.4 and Plut. *Nic.* 10.6–7 with Gomme and Andrewes, *HCT*, IV 53–54; Westlake, *Individuals*, 169–71; Kagan, *PNSE*, 70–71; and Hornblower, *CT*, III 107–9. Treaty itself: Thuc. 5.46.5–47.12, confirmed by *IG* I³ 83, which is virtually identical. See Gomme and Andrewes, *HCT*, IV 54–63; Kagan, *PNSE*, 71–74; Karl-Wilhelm Welwei, "Zur 'Herrschaftsterminologie' in der Quadrupleallianz von 420 v. Chr.," *ZPE* 111 (1996): 88–92; and Hornblower, *CT*, III 109–20. Cf. Michael Clark, "Thucydides in Olympia," in *Text and Tradition: Studies in Greek History and Historiography in Honor of Mortimer Chambers*, ed. Ronald Mellor and Lawrence A. Tritle (Claremont, CA: Regina Books, 1999), 115–34, with Hornblower, *CT*, III 109–12.

36. Corinth turns to Sparta: Thuc. 5.48.2–3 and Diod. 12.77.3 with Gomme and Andrewes, *HCT*, IV 63–64; Seager, "After the Peace of Nicias," 262–63 (esp. n. 101); Salmon, *WC*, 328–30; Rood, *Thucydides*, 95–97; and Hornblower, *CT*, III 120–22.

37. Peace and no peace: Thuc. 5.25–26, 48.1 with Hornblower, *CT*, III 41–53.

Chapter 8. An Opportunity Squandered

Epigraph: Niccolò Machiavelli, *Discorsi sopra la prima deca di Livio* II.10, in *Tutte le opere*, ed. Mario Martelli (Florence: Sansoni Editore, 1971), 159–60.

1. Four-power alliance aimed at destruction of Spartan power: Plut. *Alc.* 15.1–2 with Kagan, *PNSE*, 71–75, and Lazenby, *PW*, 110.

2. Lacedaemon fined, barred from the 420 Olympic games; Lichas whipped: Thuc. 5.49–50, Xen. *Hell.* 3.2.21–23, Diod. 14.17.4, Paus. 6.2.2 with Gomme and Andrewes, *HCT*, IV 64–67; Kagan, *PNSE*, 75–76; James Roy, "Thucydides 5.49.1–50.4: The Quarrel between Elis in 420 B.C., and Elis' Exploitation of Olympia," *Klio* 80:2 (1998): 360–68; Annalisa Paradiso and James Roy, "Lepreon and Phyrkos in 421–420," *Klio* 90:1 (2008): 27–35; and Hornblower, *CT*, III 122–35. There were, it seems, a great many occasions in which such fines were imposed: Sophie Minon, *Les Inscriptions éléennes dialectales (VIe–IIe siècle avant J.-C.)* (Geneva: Droz, 2007), nos. 3, 4, 6, 9–10, 14, 22, 30.3–6 with James Roy, "The Nature and Extent of Elean Power in the Western Peloponnese," in *Forme sovrapoleiche e interpoleiche di organizzazione nel mondo greco antico*, ed. Mario Lombardo and Flavia Frisone (Galatina: Congedo Editore, 2008), 293–302 (esp. 297–98). Lichas' status: Thuc. 5.22.2, 76.3. Note Hdt. 2.160. Eventual revenge: Jon E. Lendon, "Homeric Vengeance and the Outbreak of Greek Wars," in *War and Violence in Ancient Greece*, ed. Hans van Wees (London: Duckworth, 2000), 1–30, and James Roy, "The Spartan-Elean War of c. 400," *Athenaeum* 97 (2009): 69–86 (esp. 75–86).

3. Conference with Corinth: Thuc. 5.50.5. Fate of Heracleia Trachinia: 5.51.1–52.1, Diod. 12.77.4.

4. Alcibiades tours the Peloponnesus, Long Walls at Patras: Thuc. 5.52.2; Isoc. 16.15; Paus. 7.6.4; Plut. *Alc.* 15.6 with Gomme and Andrewes, *HCT,* IV 69–71; Kagan, *PNSE,* 78–82; Lazenby, *PW,* 111; Hornblower, *CT,* III 139; and Stuttard, *Nemesis,* 107–12. In this connection, see John K. Anderson, "A Topographical and Historical Study of Achaea," *ABSA* 49 (1954): 72–92 (esp. 83–86). Note also Catherine Morgan and Jonathan Hall, "Achaian *Poleis* and Achaian Colonisation," in *Introduction to an Inventory of Poleis,* ed. Mogens Herman Hansen (Copenhagen: Det Kongelige Danske Videnskabernes Selskab, 1996), 164–232. Traces of the Long Walls at Patras have been found: *IACP* no. 239.

5. Cult and Argive hegemony: Rahe, *SFAW,* Chapter 3, note 28, in context. Argive insistence on victim owed Apollo Pythaeus by Epidaurus: Thuc. 5.53 and Diod. 12.78.1–2 with Gomme and Andrewes, *HCT,* IV 71–72, 136, and Hornblower, *CT,* III 140–42. Cowing Corinth, ease in sending aid to Argos: Thuc. 5.53 with Gomme and Andrewes, *HCT,* IV 72–73; Robin Seager, "After the Peace of Nicias: Politics and Diplomacy, 421–416 B.C.," *CQ* 26:2 (1976): 249–69 (at 263); Kagan, *PNSE,* 82–84; Walter M. Ellis, *Alcibiades* (London: Routledge, 1989), 42; Lazenby, *PW,* 111; and Hornblower, *CT,* III 142–43.

6. Agis to Leuctron, allies summoned for post-Carneios campaign: Thuc. 5.54.1–2 with Harald Popp, *Die Einwirkung von Vorzeichen, Opfern und Festen auf die Kriegführung der Griechen im 5 und 4 Jahrhundert v. Chr.* (Erlangen: Merkel, 1959), 92–103; Gomme and Andrewes, *HCT,* IV 73–74; and Kagan, *PNSE,* 84–86. Location of Leuctron: Rahe, *SR,* Chapter 4, note 28. On the *diabatéria* and the examination of the entrails, note Popp, *Die Einwirkung von Vorzeichen, Opfern und Festen auf die Kriegführung der Griechen,* 42–46; Walter Burkert, *Homo Necans,* trans. Peter Bing (Berkeley: University of California Press, 1983), 40 (with n. 22); and M. D. Goodman and A. James Holladay, "Religious Scruples in Ancient Warfare," *CQ* n.s. 36:1 (1986): 151–71 (at 153–60), reprinted in Holladay, *AFC,* 185–207 (at 186–95); then, cf. Pritchett, *GSW,* III 68–71, with Hornblower, *CT,* III 143–44, and see Michael A. Flower, *The Seer in Ancient Greece* (Berkeley: University of California Press, 2008). On the Carneia, see Nicolas Richer, *La Religion des Spartiates: Croyances et cultes dans l'Antiquité* (Paris: Les Belles Lettres, 2012), 383–456 (esp. 413–19, 447–54), 547–49. Agis' propensity for marching out and coming back: Thuc. 3.89.1, 5.54.1–2, 55.3; Xen. *Hell.* 3.2.24. Cf. Lazenby, *PW,* 111–12, who fails to highlight the role accorded the king and his seer in such circumstances.

7. Argives plunder Epidauria, manipulate calendar; Epidaurus' allies hold back: Thuc. 5.54.3–4 with Gomme and Andrewes, *HCT,* IV 75; Kagan, *PNSE,* 86; Ellis, *Alcibiades,* 42; Lazenby, *PW,* 112; and Hornblower, *CT,* III 144–45. Cf. Diod. 12.78.2 where it is Troezen that is ravaged.

8. Peace conference, Epidauria ravaged, abortive Spartan march to Caryae, Alcibiades arrives with a thousand Athenians: Thuc. 5.55 with Gomme and Andrewes, *HCT,* IV 75–77; Seager, "After the Peace of Nicias," 263–65; Kagan, *PNSE,* 86–88; Ellis, *Alcibiades,* 42–43; and Hornblower, *CT,* III 145–47. Identity of Euphamidas: Thuc. 2.33.1, 4.119.2.

9. Winter skirmishing: Thuc. 5.56 with Gomme and Andrewes, *HCT,* IV 77–78; Kagan, *PNSE,* 88–90; and Hornblower, *CT,* III 147–49.

10. List of generals: Charles W. Fornara, *The Athenian Board of Generals from 510 to 404* (Wiesbaden: Franz Steiner, 1971), 62–63, who errs only in including Alcibiades, whose exclusion from office is expressly indicated at Diod. 12.79.1 and is implicit in what Thucydides says and does not say about his status at 5.61.1–2. Cf., also, Gomme, *HCT,* IV 88, and Robert Develin, *Athenian Officials, 684–321 BC* (Cambridge: Cambridge University Press, 1989), 144, who, with Fornara, reject Diodorus' evidence and resist the inference from Thucydides on the basis of a restoration of Alcibiades' name in *IG* I³ 370 = *ML* no. 77 = *O&R* no. 170 at lines 17 and 21 that is possible but by no means necessary; Andrewes, *HCT,* IV 88, who is equivocal; and Hornblower, *CT,* III 161, who follows Andrewes' lead, with Hatzfeld, *Alcibiade,* 103 (including n. 1); Kagan, *PNSE,* 90–91; Ellis, *Alcibiades,* 43–44 (with n. 38); Lazenby, *PW,* 113; and Stuttard, *Nemesis,* 112–13. Depth of Spartan concern, various possible reasons for timing of march: Thuc. 5.57.1 with Hatzfeld, *Alcibiade,* 103; Gomme and Andrewes, *HCT,* IV 78–79; Seager, "After the Peace of Nicias," 265–66; Kagan, *PNSE,*

89–92; Ellis, *Alcibiades*, 43; Lazenby, *PW*, 113; and Hornblower, *CT*, III 149–50. I do not share Lazenby's bizarre view that elections in antiquity never turned on public policy, and I think Hatzfeld, Andrewes (*HCT*, IV 79 n. 1), Kagan, and Ellis correct in suspecting that the Spartan leaders might suppose, as Andrewes puts it in the course of gently correcting Gomme (*HCT*, IV 78–79), that there would be "less chance of retaliation" when the likes of Alcibiades were less influential in Athens.

11. Geopolitical significance of Phlius vis-à-vis Sicyon and Pellene: Yannis A. Lolos, *Land of Sikyon: Archaeology and History of a Greek City-State* (Princeton, NJ: American School of Classical Studies, 2011), 124–28, 148, 167–72. Lacedaemon's allies: Thuc 5.57, 58.4 with Gomme and Andrewes, *HCT*, IV 79–80; Kagan, *PNSE*, 91; Lazenby, *PW*, 113–14; and Hornblower, *CT*, III 150–51. Where no information is provided, I base my estimate of the size of the pertinent contingents on the number of hoplites these cities dispatched to Plataea: Hdt. 9.28–30. In the case of Megara, which suffered severe losses during the Archidamian War, and Epidaurus, which had to retain soldiers at home for the city's defense against Argive raiders, I have used a reduced estimate. On Pellene in Achaea, see Morgan and Hall, "Achaian *Poleis* and Achaian Colonisation," 169–71, and *IACP* no. 240. Helots at Plataea: Hdt. 9.10.1, Plut. *Arist.* 10.8. For the use of light-armed troops in conjunction with cavalry, see Thuc. 4.93.3; Xen. *Eq. mag.* 5.13, *Hell.* 7.5.24; Caesar *BG* 1.48.5. Number of Spartiates and *períoikoi*: cf. Thuc. 5.68 with 4.8.9, 38.5; and see Rahe, *SR*, Appendix 1 (with notes 19–29 and their context), where I indicate why, in contrast with most scholars (who are incredulous), I think that we should trust the results of Thucydides' careful investigation (which is, after all, the only evidence we have). I assume that, although the Lacedaemonians sent five-sixths of the available hoplites to Mantineia in a time of emergency, they dispatched the normal complement of two-thirds on this occasion. Tegeates and other Arcadians: Lazenby, *PW*, 113. Phlius threatened by Argos, loyal to Lacedaemon: Xen. *Hell.* 7.2 with *IACP* no. 355 and David Fearn, "Mapping Phleious: Politics and Myth-Making in Bacchylides 9," *CQ* n.s. 53:2 (November 2003): 347–67. Given the revolts that they had had to cope with in the past and their recent fears, I cannot imagine that the Spartans would ever have armed ordinary helots as hoplites. When abroad with them, the Spartans were always on their guard: Xen. *Lac. Pol.* 12.2. Cf., however, Peter Hunt, *Slaves, Warfare and Ideology in the Greek Historians* (Cambridge: Cambridge University Press, 1998), 56–62, who thinks that they employed and deployed them as hoplites at Plataea, on this occasion, and at Mantineia.

12. Splendor of Hellenic army, autopsy: Thuc. 5.60.3 with Gomme and Andrewes, *HCT*, IV 85–86; Ronald S. Stroud, "Thucydides and Corinth," *Chiron* 24 (1994): 267–304 (esp. 289–92); and Hornblower, *CT*, III 157–58.

13. Number of Elean hoplites: Thuc. 5.58.1, Diod. 12.78.4. Just under three thousand Mantineian hoplites: 12.78.4. Subject allies included: Thuc. 5.58.1. Note also 5.65–74, 75.5; Lys. 34.7, and see Rahe, *SFAW*, Chapter 4, note 7. Argives field ca. seven thousand hoplites a quarter of a century later at Nemea: Xen. *Hell.* 4.2.17. Lose six thousand earlier at battle of Sepeia: Rahe, *SFAW*, Chapter 3, note 29. See Gomme and Andrewes, *HCT*, IV 80–81; Kagan, *PNSE*, 92; Lazenby, *PW*, 114; and Hornblower, *CT*, III 151.

14. Expedition budget passed in 419/8: Inferred from *IG* I³ 370 = *ML* no. 77 = *O&R* no. 170, which shows that no funds were budgeted for this expedition in 418/7 when it took place. Late arrival of the Athenians, numbers small: Thuc. 5.59.3, 61.1. Cf. Andrewes, *HCT*, IV 83, 86–87, 147, and Seager, "After the Peace of Nicias," 263–66, who say little or nothing about the numbers and explain away the late arrival, and Hornblower, *CT*, III 159–61, and Stuttard, *Nemesis*, 113–14, who discuss neither, with Hatzfeld, *Alcibiade*, 103–4; Gomme, *HCT*, IV 147; and Kagan, *PNSE*, 92–93.

15. Themistocles as forerunner: Rahe, *SFAW*, Chapters 2–3. Prospect of victory on the cheap: Thuc. 6.16.6. Cf. Gomme, *HCT*, IV 128; Dover, *HCT*, IV 248; Edmund F. Bloedow, "On 'Nurturing Lions in the State': Alcibiades' Entry on the Political Stage in Athens," *Klio* 73:1 (1991): 49–65; and Hornblower, *CT*, III 347–48, who fail to appreciate what Alcibiades very nearly pulled off, with Plut. *Alc.* 15.1–2, and see Hatzfeld, *Alcibiade*, 83–106; Malcolm F. McGregor, "The Genius of Alcibiades," *Phoenix* 19:1 (Spring 1965): 27–46 (at 28–31); Kagan, *PNSE*, 71–74, 133, 142–43; Ellis, *Alcibiades*, 40–41; and Lazenby, *PW*, 110.

16. Eupolis on opposition to expedition: F99.30–34 (PCG). For an emphatic denial that politics could have played any role in delaying the expedition's departure, cf. Lazenby, *PW,* 116 (with n. 34), who was aware of this fragment but failed to take it into account. For a brief discussion, see Hornblower, *CT,* III 159. Gomme (*HCT,* IV 128) thought the failure to send a sufficient number of troops a function of the struggle between Nicias and Alcibiades. Andrewes (*HCT,* IV 129) thought that overconfidence might be the cause and doubted that the elections conferred a victory on those opposed to Alcibiades' policy: Antony Andrewes, "The Peace of Nicias and the Sicilian Expedition," *CAH* V² 433–63 (at 440–41).

17. Interception of the Lacedaemonians and Tegeans at Methudrion in Maenalia, not far from Orchomenos: Thuc. 5.58.2 with Gomme and Andrewes, *HCT,* IV 81; Kagan, *PNSE,* 93; Lazenby, *PW,* 114; and Hornblower, *CT,* III 151–52. For the location of Methudrion, her connection with Orchomenos, and the road which led there from the Megalopolitan plain, see Paus. 8.27.4, 35.5–10, 36.1, and Polyb. 4.10.10 with William Loring, "Some Ancient Routes in the Peloponnese," *JHS* 15 (1895): 25–89 (at 76–77), and *IACP* no. 283.

18. Argive coalition heads up Nemea road, Agis outflanks and surrounds them by dividing army into three contingents—two of which take other routes into the Argive plain: Thuc. 5.58.3–59.4 (where at 5.58.3, with the oldest and best manuscripts, I read *órthrion* ["at first light"] rather than *órthion* ["steep"]). On these events, see Gomme and Andrewes, *HCT,* IV 81–82; Kagan, *PNSE,* 96–98; Lazenby, *PW,* 115; Hutchinson, *Attrition,* 100–104; and Hornblower, *CT,* III 152–54. Trestus pass suited to carts: Paus. 2.15.2.

19. Parley, truce, Agis blamed, army at Nemea: Thuc. 5.59.5–60.4 and Diod. 12.78.3–6 with Gomme and Andrewes, *HCT,* IV 84–85; Kagan, *PNSE,* 99; Lazenby, *PW,* 115; Hutchinson, *Attrition,* 103–5; and Hornblower, *CT,* III 155–57. Two ephors accompany expeditions: Xen. *Lac. Pol.* 13.5 with Hdt. 9.76.3 and Xen. *Hell.* 2.4.36. Cf. Lazenby, *PW,* 261 n. 16, 278 n. 32, who doubts Xenophon's general claim about the presence of the ephors and who draws attention to Thuc. 6.88.10 where the ephors are juxtaposed with "those in authority." Cf., however, on this passage, Dover, *HCT,* IV 361, and Hornblower, *CT,* III 510–11. The Greek phrase *hoi en télei* is used, variously, to refer to those in authority who have jurisdiction over the particular matter under consideration. In the passage cited by Lazenby, it almost certainly means "the little assembly" with the ephors, who have first met separately and are therefore mentioned as having reached a preliminary judgment, subsequently presiding over a meeting of the *gerousía* where the matter was discussed at greater length. Had Agis been faced with a military, as opposed to a political question, the pertinent authorities would have been the polemarchs: Xen. *Lac. Pol.* 13.1.

20. Cf. Lazenby, *PW,* 115–17, echoed on the crucial point by Hornblower, *CT,* III 155, who contends that everything that took place, including Agis' acceptance of the proposal of the two Argives, is explicable on military grounds, with Hatzfeld, *Alcibiade,* 104–5, and Donald Kagan, "Argive Politics and Policy after the Peace of Nicias," *CPh* 57:4 (October 1962): 209–18, and *PNSE,* 93–101, whose argument that political calculations were involved cannot be so easily dismissed (although Kagan may take things too far in suggesting that the negligence on display at Methudrion and the foolhardiness in evidence when the coalition army marched up the Nemea were due to treason); consider Herman, *Ritualised Friendship and the Greek City,* 142–46, 156–61, in light of the book's argument as a whole, and see Gomme and Andrewes, *HCT,* IV 86, who both point to a conflict at Argos between pro-Spartan and pro-Athenian groups.

21. Rage vented against Thrasylus: Thuc. 5.60.5–6 and Diod. 12.78.5. Charadrus: Paus. 2.25.2. See Gomme and Andrewes, *HCT,* IV 86; Kagan, *PNSE,* 101; Hutchinson, *Attrition,* 105; and Hornblower, *CT,* III 158–59. On the stark contrast between the Spartans and the Argives as depicted here, see Simon Hornblower, "Sticks, Stones, and Spartans: The Sociology of Spartan Violence," in *War and Violence in Ancient Greece,* ed. Hans van Wees (London: Duckworth, 2000), 57–82, reprinted in Simon Hornblower, *Thucydidean Themes* (Oxford: Oxford University Press, 2011), 250–74.

22. Athenian arrival; authorities ask departure, resist allowing presentation before the assembly: Thuc. 5.61.1 with Hatzfeld, *Alcibiade,* 104–5; Gomme and Andrewes, *HCT,* IV 86–87;

Kagan, *PNSE*, 102–5; Hutchinson, *Attrition*, 105–6; and Hornblower, *CT*, III 159–61. Note also Diod. 12.79.1.

23. Alcibiades in the Argive assembly, march on Orchomenos: Thuc. 5.61.2–5 and Diod. 12.79.1–2 with Hatzfeld, *Alcibiade*, 105; Kagan, *PNSE*, 104–5; Lazenby, *PW*, 117–18; Hutchinson, *Attrition*, 106; Hornblower, *CT*, III 161–62; and Stuttard, *Nemesis*, 112–15.

24. Anger directed at Agis, advisors imposed: Thuc. 5.63 (where I accept the emendation suggested by Haase) and Diod. 12.78.6 with Gomme and Andrewes, *HCT*, IV 89–91; Kagan, *PNSE*, 105–6, 108–9; Lazenby, *PW*, 118; Hutchinson, *Attrition*, 106; and Hornblower, *CT*, III 166–68. Case of Leotychidas and the razing of his house: Rahe, *SFAW*, Chapter 1, note 57.

25. Tegea selected for assault, Eleans withdraw in a rage: Thuc. 5.62 with Gomme and Andrewes, *HCT*, IV 88–89; Kagan, *PNSE*, 110–11; Lazenby, *PW*, 118; Hutchinson, *Attrition*, 106; and Hornblower, *CT*, III 163. Note also Diod. 12.79.3. Cf. Stuttard, *Nemesis*, 115–16, who suspects that Alcibiades accompanied the army.

26. Spartan response to emergency at Tegea: Thuc. 5.64 and Diod. 12.79.3 with Gomme and Andrewes, *HCT*, IV 91–96; Kagan, *PNSE*, 107–11; John F. Lazenby, *The Spartan Army* (Warminster: Aris & Phillips, 1985), 125–26, and *PW*, 118–19; Hutchinson, *Attrition*, 106–7; and Hornblower, *CT*, III 168–69. Location of Oresthasion: Rahe, *SR*, Chapter 4, note 29. Perfect spot for a rendezvous with those coming from Messenia: Rahe, *PC*, Chapter 8 (at note 41). On the valley shared by Tegea and Mantineia, the location of the Heracleum, and the positioning of Agis' army, see W. Kendrick Pritchett, "The Battles of Mantineia (418, 262, and 297 B.C.)," in *SAGT*, II 37–72 (esp. 46–49), whose account supersedes all previous discussions of the topography.

27. Day One at Mantineia: Thuc. 5.65. Propensity for flooding a problem in Arcadia: James Roy, "The Economies of Arkadia," in *Defining Ancient Arkadia*, ed. Thomas Heine Nielsen and James Roy (Copenhagen: Det Kongelige Danske Videnskabernes Selskab, 1999), 320–81 (at 324 with nn. 19–20). On the maneuvers, cf. W. J. Woodhouse, "The Campaign and Battle of Mantinea in 418 B.C.," *ABSA* 22 (1916–18): 51–84, and *King Agis of Sparta and His Campaign in Arcadia in 418 B.C.* (Oxford: Clarendon Press, 1933), who supposed Thucydides biased against Agis and badly confused, with Arnold W. Gomme, "Thucydides and the Battle of Mantineia," in *Essays in Greek History and Literature* (Oxford: Basil Blackwell, 1937), 132–55, who defends the Athenian historian's discernment and integrity, and see Pritchett, "The Battles of Mantineia," 41–44, 49, 62, and Kagan, *PNSE*, 111–15, 119. Note also Gomme and Andrewes, *HCT*, IV 96–99; Lazenby, *The Spartan Army*, 126, and *PW*, 119–20; Hutchinson, *Attrition*, 107; and Hornblower, *CT*, III 170–73. Given that Thucydides may not have been told more than he reports, that what we have is an incompletely polished draft, and his propensity for reticence, I do not share Lazenby's supposition that his failure to identify the senior Spartiate as a *xúmboulos* rules out the possibility that he was just that.

28. Eleans and Athenians in transit: Thuc. 5.75.5. Cf. Kagan, *PNSE*, 114, 118, who speculates on the supposition that the Argive commanders and Agis were aware of the reinforcements on the way.

29. Coalition phalanx forms up, shocks Spartans: Thuc. 5.66.1–2, read in light of Paus. 8.11.1, with Gomme and Andrewes, *HCT*, IV 99–103 (esp. 101); Kagan, *PNSE*, 119–23; and Hutchinson, *Attrition*, 107–8. Cf. Lazenby, *The Spartan Army*, 126–28, and *PW*, 120–21; and Hornblower, *CT*, III 170, 173–74, who, with regard to the unmentioned obstruction, prefer special pleading to trying to make sense of what Thucydides actually says. I first visited the site in the summer of 1973 while a student in the summer session of the American School of Classical Studies at Athens; I returned on 18 March 2019; and I can vouch for the fact that an army marching to the Heracleum from the south would not have been able to see an army deployed immediately to the north of either of the two ridges until the two armies were quite close.

30. Spartan *kósmos* and chain of command, display of discipline: Thuc. 5.66.2–4 with Gomme and Andrewes, *HCT*, IV 102–3; Lazenby, *The Spartan Army*, 128; and Hornblower, *CT*, III 174.

31. Makeup, order of battle, and size of the two armies: Thuc. 5.67–68, 71.2 with Hatzfeld, *Alcibiade*, 105–6; Gomme and Andrewes, *HCT*, IV 103–17; Kagan, *PNSE*, 123–24; Lazenby, *The*

Spartan Army, 128–29, and *PW*, 121–23; Hutchinson, *Attrition*, 108–12; and Hornblower, *CT*, III 174–82, who supposes—wrongly, I think—that, when the Lacedaemonians settled at Lepreum the freed helots who had accompanied Brasidas to Thrace, they somehow kept together the mercenaries in Brasidas' little army who had been evacuated at the same time and that the latter were included among the *Brasídeioi* mentioned here by Thucydides. Force left in the Argolid to guard the territory: Thuc. 5.75.4. Arcadians of Maenalia: Thomas Heine Nielsen, "Arkadia: City-Ethnics and Tribalism," in *Introduction to an Inventory of Poleis*, 117–63 (at 132–38). For another approach to estimating the number of hoplites that Tegea could field which dovetails fairly well with my own estimate, see James Roy, "Tegeans at the Battle near the River Nemea in 394 B.C.," *PP* 26 (1971): 439–41 For another view, cf. Björn Forsén, "Population and Political Strength of Some Southeastern Arkadian *Poleis*," in *Further Studies in the Ancient Greek Polis*, ed. Pernille Flensted-Jensen (Stuttgart: Franz Steiner Verlag, 2000), 35–55. The size of the Lacedaemonian contingent is a matter of dispute. Many distinguished scholars have argued that the number Thucydides provides is impossibly low and contend that it should be doubled—including Henry Theodore Wade-Gery, Arnold Toynbee, Antony Andrewes, George Forrest, John Lazenby, Geoffrey Hutchinson, and Simon Hornblower. Like Arnold W. Gomme; George L. Cawkwell, "The Decline of Sparta," *CQ* 33:2 (1983): 385–400 (at 385–90), reprinted in Cawkwell, *CC*, 275–98 (at 276–83); and Henk W. Singor, "The Spartan Army at Mantinea and Its Organization in the Fifth Century BC," in *After the Past: Essays in Honour of H. W. Pleket*, ed. Willem Jongman and Marc Kleijweg (Leiden: Brill, 2002), 235–84, however, I think that rejecting Thucydides' testimony on a matter where he claims precise knowledge is to saw off the limb on which we are trying to sit: see Rahe, *SR*, Appendix 1 (especially, notes 20–21, where much of the pertinent secondary literature is cited). Here I would only add that, on Thucydides' calculation, the size of the ordinary *lóchos* would have been about six hundred hoplites—which is the number he gives for the *lóchos* of the Sciritae before the *Brasídeioi* and the *neodamódeis* were thrown in with them. In my view, the confusion about the numbers arises because scholars overestimate the size of the army fielded by the Argives. I do not think that the Spartan army just appeared larger, as Cawkwell suggests. According to Thucydides (5.71.2), it really was larger. Nor do I think that army entirely made up of Spartiates, as Singor suggests.

   32. Exhortations and songs: Thuc. 5.69 with the scholia. Cf. Gomme and Andrewes, *HCT*, IV 117–18, where Andrewes expresses doubts that by *nómoi* here songs, not customs, are being referenced, with Hornblower, *CT*, III 183–85, and see Lazenby, *The Spartan Army*, 129–30, and *PW*, 123. Lacedaemonian pipes and rhythmic marching: Thuc. 5.70 with Gomme and Andrewes, *HCT*, IV 118–19; Lazenby, *PW*, 123; Hutchinson, *Attrition*, 112; and Hornblower, *CT*, III 185–87. Piping a hereditary profession: Hdt. 6.60. Later without a doubt, lambdas emblazoned on shields: Xen. *Hell.* 4.4.10.

   33. Hoplite line drifts right: Thuc. 5.71.1 with Hornblower, *CT*, III 187.

   34. Agis' orders ignored, Lacedaemonians routed on the left: Thuc. 5.71.1–72.3 with Gomme and Andrewes, *HCT*, IV 119–21; Kagan, *PNSE*, 124–30; Lazenby, *The Spartan Army*, 129–33, and *PW*, 123–25; Hutchinson, *Attrition*, 112–14; and Hornblower, *CT*, III 187–89.

   35. Easy Lacedaemonian victory in the center; Athenians on the left flank encircled, protected by cavalry: Thuc. 5.72.4–73.1 with Gomme and Andrewes, *HCT*, IV 121–24; Kagan, *PNSE*, 129–31; Lazenby, *The Spartan Army*, 133–34, and *PW*, 125–26; Hutchinson, *Attrition*, 114–15; and Hornblower, *CT*, III 189–90.

   36. Fate of the Mantineians and the elite Argive unit: Thuc. 5.73.2–4 and Diod. 12.79.4–7. Cf. Gomme, "Thucydides and the Battle of Mantineia," 150–51; Gomme and Andrewes, *HCT*, IV 124–25; Lazenby, *The Spartan Army*, 133–34, and *PW*, 125; and Hornblower, *CT*, III 177–79, who are too quick in rejecting Diodorus' testimony, with Kagan, *PNSE*, 131–32, who is, I believe, right in embracing it. The argument that the silence of Thucydides on a question rules out our relying for additional information on another source would have a great deal more weight were Thucydides not so often silent. This is especially true with regard to political intrigue and domestic political strife—about which the Athenian historian is notoriously reticent. Diodorus' mention of Pharax here indicates that Ephorus was not simply elaborating on what Thucydides said, as some

of the scholars cited above suppose. For the man's subsequent career, see Xen. *Hell.* 3.2.12, Diod. 14.79, Paus. 6.3.15. Note also Theopompus of Chios *FGrH* 115 F192.

37. Aftermath and losses: Thuc. 5.74, 75.2. Fate of Aristocles and Hipponoidas: 5.72.1.

Epilogue. The End of the Athenian Challenge

Epigraph: Winston S. Churchill, *Marlborough: His Life and Times* (London: Harrap, 1947), II 381.

1. Thucydides on the battle of Mantineia: 5.74.1, 75.3 with Gomme and Andrewes, *HCT,* IV 125–26, 128; Kagan, *PNSE,* 133–34; Lazenby, *PW,* 126–28; and Hornblower, *CT,* III 191, 193–94.

2. Renewal of coalition war with Epidaurus: Thuc. 5.75.3–5, read in light of *IG* I³ 370 = *ML* no. 77 = *O&R* no. 170, lines 11–15, with Gomme and Andrewes, *HCT,* IV 128–30; Kagan, *PNSE,* 134; Lazenby, *PW,* 236; Hornblower, *CT,* III 194; and Stuttard, *Nemesis,* 116–17.

3. Spartans impose settlement in the Peloponnesus, role of the Argive one thousand: Thuc. 5.76.1–82.1, Aen. Tact. 17.2–4, Arist. *Pol.* 1304a25–27, Diod. 12.80.1–3, Plut. *Alc.* 15.3 with Gomme and Andrewes, *HCT,* IV 130–50; Ephraim David, "The Oligarchic Revolution in Argos, 417 BC," *AC* 55 (1986): 113–24; Kagan, *PNSE,* 134–37; Lazenby, *PW,* 126–28; and Hornblower, *CT,* III 177–79, 194–209. Mantineia: see also Xen. *Hell.* 5.2.2 with Gomme and Andrewes, *HCT,* IV 148, and Hornblower, *CT,* III 207. Arrangement with Elis: note Simon Hornblower, "Thucydides, Xenophon, and Lichas: Were the Spartans Excluded from the Olympic Games from 420 to 400 B.C.," *Phoenix* 54:3/4 (Autumn–Winter 2000): 212–25, and James Roy, "The Spartan-Elean War of c. 400," *Athenaeum* 97 (2009): 69–86 (at 70–74); then, see Andrewes, *HCT,* IV 148–49, and Lazenby, *PW,* 127.

4. Democratic counterrevolution at Argos: Thuc. 5.82.2–83.3, 84.1; Arist. *Pol.* 1304a25–27; Diod. 12.80.3, 81; Paus. 2.20.1–2; Plut. *Alc.* 15.3–5; and *IG* I³ 86 with Gomme and Andrewes, *HCT,* IV 106, 150–53, 155–56; Andrewes, *HCT,* V 261–64; Kagan, *PNSE,* 138–42; Lazenby, *PW,* 128–29; Hornblower, *CT,* III 209–14, 225–26; and Stuttard, *Nemesis,* 117–19.

5. Churchill, *Marlborough,* II 381.

Author's Note and Acknowledgments

This book is intended as the third volume in a series dedicated to the study of Sparta and her conduct of diplomacy and war from the late archaic period down to the second battle of Mantineia. Like the series' prelude, *The Spartan Regime: Its Character, Its Origins,* and its immediate predecessors in the series proper, *The Grand Strategy of Classical Sparta: The Persian Challenge* and *Sparta's First Attic War: The Grand Strategy of Classical Sparta, 478–446 B.C.,* it has been a long time in gestation, and I have incurred many debts along the way. I was first introduced to ancient history by Donald Kagan when I was a freshman at Cornell University in the spring of 1968. The following year, I took a seminar he taught on the ancient Greek city and another seminar on Plato's *Republic* taught by Allan Bloom. After graduating from Yale University in 1971, I read *Litterae Humaniores* at Wadham College, Oxford, on a Rhodes Scholarship. It was there that my ancient history tutor W. G. G. Forrest first piqued my interest in Lacedaemon.

I returned to Yale University in 1974 for graduate study. There, three years later, I completed a dissertation under the direction of Donald Kagan entitled *Lysander and the Spartan Settlement, 407–403 B.C.* In the aftermath, I profited from the comments and suggestions of Antony Andrewes, who was one of my readers, and my interest in Achaemenid Persia, which was already considerable, was increased when David M. Lewis sent me the page proofs of his as yet unpublished *Sparta and Persia.* It was my intention at that time to turn my thesis into a book focused on Sparta, Athens, and Persia, and I carved out of it an article on the selection of ephors at Sparta and penned another in which I discussed the makeup of the Achaemenid Persian army at the time of Cunaxa, the tactics the Persians customarily employed, and the relative strength of Greek hoplites faced with such a challenge. But the book I had in mind I did not write.

Instead, with encouragement from Bernard Knox during the year in which I was a Junior Fellow at the Center for Hellenic Studies, I got sidetracked. I wrote one 1,200-page work entitled *Republics Ancient and Modern: Classical Republicanism and the American Revolution;* then, three shorter monographs—one on Machiavelli and English republicanism, another on the political philosophy of Montesquieu, and a third on modern republicanism in the thought of Montesquieu, Rousseau, and Tocqueville. In the intervening years, I ordinarily taught a lecture course on ancient Greek history in the fall and a seminar on some aspect of that subject in the spring, and I frequently gave thought to Lacedaemon, to questions of diplomacy and war, and to the work I had once done with George Forrest and Don Kagan. This book, like its companions, is a belated acknowledgment of what I owe them both.

I have also profited from the labors of John S. Morrison, John F. Coates, N. Boris Rankov, Alec Tilley, and the others in Britain, in Greece, and elsewhere who, in the 1980s and 1990s, contributed to designing, building, launching, and to rowing and sailing in sea trials a reconstructed trireme that they named the *Olympias*. If we now have a better sense of trireme warfare than scholars did in the past, it is because of the labors and ingenuity of the practitioners of what has come to be called "experimental archaeology" who devised this project and lent a hand.

I would also like to record my debt to the late Patrick Leigh Fermor. Long ago, when Peter Green learned that I was interested in the manner in which the rugged terrain in certain parts of Messenia might have facilitated banditry and resistance on the part of Lacedaemon's helots, he suggested that I contact Paddy, who had learned a thing or two about this sort of resistance while serving on Crete during the Second World War. In the summer of 1983, I followed up on this recommendation. Our meeting over a somewhat liquid lunch at Paddy's home in Kardamyli paved the way for a series of visits, often lasting a week or more, that took place at irregular intervals over the twenty-three years following that memorable repast. On nearly every occasion, our conversations returned to ancient Sparta; and in 1992, when *Republics Ancient and Modern* appeared, Paddy wrote a generous appraisal of it for the *Spectator*.

Part of this volume was produced while I was a W. Glenn Campbell and Rita Ricardo-Campbell National Fellow at the Hoover Institution on the campus of Stanford University, where I received added assistance from the Earhart Foundation, These were invaluable opportunities, and I am grateful for the support I received.

The remainder of this book was written in years in which I was teaching history at Hillsdale College. I am grateful to the Charles O. Lee and Louise K. Lee Foundation, which supported the chair I held and still hold at the college; to the trustees of the college and to its president, Larry Arnn; and to my colleagues and students there, who were always supportive. I owe a special debt to Clifford Humphrey, Caleb Vogel, and Carmel Kookogey, who helped me check the notes; and to Dan Knoch, the director of the Hillsdale College library; to Maurine McCourry, who arranged for the purchase of books; and to Pam Ryan, who handled interlibrary loan. Librarians are the unsung heroes of the academic world, and no one knows better than I how much we scholars owe them.

The fact that I was able to finish this book and its predecessor I owe to Dr. Marston Linehan, Dr. Peter Pinto, Dr. Piyush Kumar Agarwal, and the staff at the Clinical Center of the National Institutes of Health in Bethesda, Maryland—where in the summer of 2012 I was treated for prostate cancer and for complications attendant on surgery and in and after 2016 I was treated for bladder cancer. Had Dr. Pinto not devised a new method for diagnosing prostate cancer, had he not done my surgery with great precision, and had he and his colleagues not found a way to eliminate the lymphocele that bedeviled me in the aftermath, and had Dr. Agarwal not scraped out the cancer growing in my bladder, I would not now be in a position to write these words.

Throughout the period in which this book was written, my four children were patient, and they and my wife kept me sane. From time to time, they brought me back to the contemporary world from classical antiquity, where, at least in my imagination, I may sometimes have seemed more at home than in the here and now.

Index